THIS ITEM HAS BEEN
DISCARDED BY THE
UNIVERSITY
OF PUGET SOUND
COLLINS MEMORIAL LIBRARY

Goals in a Global Community

OTHER PERGAMON TITLES OF INTEREST

Bicknell & McQuiston — *Design for Need: The Social Contribution of Design*

Epstein & Jackson — *The Feasibility of Fertility Planning*

Georgescu-Roegen — *Energy and Economic Myths*

Menon — *Global Dialogue*

Schaff — *History and Truth*

Schlegel et al. — *Towards a Redefinition of Development*

GOALS IN A GLOBAL COMMUNITY
The Original Background Papers for
Goals for Mankind
A Report to the Club of Rome

Edited by

Ervin Laszlo

and

Judah Bierman

VOL. I – Studies on the Conceptual Foundations

PERGAMON PRESS
NEW YORK / TORONTO / OXFORD / SYDNEY / FRANKFURT / PARIS

Pergamon Press Offices:

U.S.A.	Pergamon Press Inc., Maxwell House, Fairview Park, Elmsford, New York 10523, U.S.A.
U.K.	Pergamon Press Ltd., Headington Hill Hall, Oxford OX3, OBW, England
CANADA	Pergamon of Canada, Ltd., 207 Queen's Quay West, Toronto 1, Canada
AUSTRALIA	Pergamon Press (Aust) Pty. Ltd., 19a Boundary Street, Rushcutters Bay, N.S.W. 2011, Australia
FRANCE	Pergamon Press SARL, 24 rue des Ecoles, 75240 Paris, Cedex 05, France
WEST GERMANY	Pergamon Press GmbH, 6242 Kronberg/Taunus, Frankfurt-am-Main, West Germany

Copyright © 1977   The Research Foundation of the State University of New York

Library of Congress Catalog Card No. 77-79971

All Rights Reserved. No part of this publication may be reproduced, stored in a retrieval system or transmitted in any form or by any means: electronic, electrostatic, magnetic tape, mechanical, photocopying, recording or otherwise, without permission in writing from the publishers.

ISBN 0-08-022221-8

Printed in the United States of America

CONTENTS

Preface	Ervin Laszlo, Judah Bierman	
Long Term Trends and the Evolution of Complexity	Ilya Prigogine, Peter M. Allen, Robert Herman	1
The Historical Evolution of Mankind's Inner and Outer Dimensions	Alastair M. Taylor	65
Current Prospects of Sustainable Economic Growth	Thomas E. Jones	117
Motivation and Goals for Global Society	K. B. Madsen	181
Personality Traits and Problems of Global Planners	R. Felix Geyer	207
Assessing the Solar Transition	Robert H. Murray, Paul A. LaViolette	221
Whither the Club of Rome?		279
The Club of Rome of the Future vs The Future of the Club of Rome	Ervin Laszlo	281
Public Feedback for the Club of Rome	Michelle Carlson	287
Science and Myth: Two Proposals to the Club of Rome	Ann Corrigan	297
Value Orientation in Social Analysis	Larry McCord	309
Toward a Global Spirit	Daniel Schwartz	315
The Readiness is All	Judah Bierman	323
Bibliography		327
Index		331

PREFACE

The two volumes of Goals In A Global Community contain the original background papers from which Ervin Laszlo created Goals For Mankind, a report to the Club of Rome. The first volume presents six basic studies on the conceptual background of the idea of a global community. The second volume will present some thirty international values and goals studies representing beliefs and desires of peoples in all parts of the global community. Like Goals For Mankind, these two volumes continue the work of the Club of Rome as represented in the prior reports and their supporting studies. Like Limits to Growth, the first popular report, Goals For Mankind was a general, non-technical summary of the "basic research" relevant to the theme of the report. And like the earlier collected papers of Toward Global Equilibrium, these two volumes of Goals In A Global Community provide the technical studies undergirding the general report. Both reports reflect the continuing concerns of the Club of Rome for the dilemmas that seem to frame mankind's future. But there are differences between the first and fourth reports which reflect both the changing state of the art and the evolving role of the Club of Rome.

Goals For Mankind was a first step in a new direction. It moves the discussion out of the shadow of the computer to where the mind and heart-made ought can contend with the machine-made must. For it begins the description of the human predicament in terms of the diverse images of possibility that drive our differing national and social behaviors. It begins the asking of the question, "Can humanity create a global community with these apparently conflicting, and yet so fundamentally similar, goals?" Goals For Mankind answers with a conditional yes, conditional but positive. It is not content with the observation that the only alternative to global community is no globe and no human communities at all. It suggests that the dilemmas of national separateness and class struggles are not so absolute as we have assumed. And it announces the time for action. Thus, it asserts that the "politics of the future" is not like politics in the past, an art of the merely possible. The future demands rather an "art of the necessary," where necessary includes a large value component.

The second volume of Goals In A Global Community, to be issued as The International Values and Goals Studies, contains some thirty values and goals statements organized into three major groups. The statements represent assessments by knowledgeable individuals of the current goals and values of people and groups in their areas, the advanced industrialized nations, the communist world and the third world. They offer an obvious basis for discussions of global community on a new level. In the present volume, partly by way of introduction, we offer some studies of the conceptual foundations underlying the idea of global community. In addition, we include a series of brief seminar papers which grew out of a review of the goals statements against the background of the three prior reports to the Club of Rome. The specific focus of the seminar papers should be clear from the collection title, the question posed to the participants, "Whither the Club of Rome?"

The papers in this volume assay the needs, the difficulties and the possibilities of moving the discussion, and related actions, beyond total emphasis on the race between the world's physical resources and its human survival needs, in which technologies provide an unpredictable variable and the computer technicians serve as midwives with tunnel vision. These essays offer scientific and historical justifications for entering goals and values as factors in the calculus of concern. They are loosely linked by the common theme of the possibility of a global community, a new world system.

The first report, by Prigogine, Allen and Herman, from the cutting edge of investigations of non-equilibrium systems, suggests that our own socioeconomic systems may be more effectively understood in light of such dissipative systems and that our visions of the world we must create need not be limited to the images of classical mechanics and entropy theory, of essentially closed systems. The second essay, by Alastair Taylor, suggests that the tale of history, properly read, will force us to recognize we have already entered a new stage of civilization -- new societal needs, new forms, new possibilities. Both offer legitimation for the search for global community.

These two are followed by three other primary studies, based essentially in the social sciences. Thomas E. Jones suggests the considerations necessary to make sustainable economic growth a global possibility, with all that implies for the satisfaction of human wants. K. B. Madsen, analyzing changes in motivations and searching for motivations for change on a psychological model suggests why "social motives are the strongest driving forces behind change of goals for global community." Finally, R. Felix Geyer explores the problems of global planners caught "in a balancing act between involvement attitudes and planning attitudes." The merest reading will convince that these essays are not wish fantasies. Each warns of the difficulties even as, in fact sometimes more than, it trumpets the possibilities. But all proclaim, beyond the survival need, the positive, if conditional, <u>yes</u>. The final paper in the main section serves as an example of how a central problem of global survival, energy, can be approached if we go beyond the dilemma and doom scenario of closed systems. In assessing the possibilities of a transition to solar energy, LaViolette and Murray offer a system-rigorous analysis part of whose theoretical foundations take us back to Prigogine's research.

The seminar papers are different in kind. They do not so much justify or assess the work of the Club of Rome as urge it to new directions. Professor Laszlo sets the theme in his suggestion that the Club take on the new role of active information catalyst. Ann Corrigan and Michelle Carlson each make specific suggestions for activities related to the problems of eliciting and disseminating the goals information necessary for decisions. Larry McCord and Daniel Schwartz support the plea for more attention to values as data for planning. They all respond to the question of "whither" with demands for the inclusion of more value orientation in the thinking of the Club and more propaganda activity, in the best sense, on its agenda. Professor Bierman appends a brief note from the vantage of his own interest in the literature of utopia. The seminar shared the common conclusion: The Club of Rome must continue to risk advocacy and it must recognize that human values are a fact of human existence on this globe, the largest figure in the people's <u>futurum</u>, and therefore the crucial question mark in mankind's future.

Judah Bierman

Ervin Laszlo

Portland, Oregon
February 1977

ACKNOWLEDGMENTS

Ervin Laszlo, Project Director of the Goals for Mankind Report to the Club of Rome would hereby like to gratefully acknowledge the invaluable services and facilities put at his disposal by the United Nations Institute for Training and Research (UNITAR) through the courtesy and cooperation of Dr. Davidson Nicol, Executive Director, and Mr. Philippe DeSeynes, head of the Project on the Future.

Credit for graphics and index - Ruth Miller and Jack Miller; for typing - Sharon Swanson.

I am also indebted to Ruth Miller for general editorial assistance.

J. B.

LIST OF CONTRIBUTORS

Peter M. ALLEN - Senior Research Fellow, Université Libre de Bruxelles

>Service de Chimie Physique II
>Code Postal n° 231
>Campus Plaine U.L.B.
>Boulevard du Triomphe
>1050 Bruxelles, Belgium

Judah BIERMAN - Professor of English and General Studies, Portland State University

>Department of English
>Portland State University
>P.O. Box 751
>Portland, Oregon 97207

Michelle CARLSON - Futures Seminar

>Systems Science Ph.D Program
>Portland State University
>P.O. Box 751
>Portland, Oregon 97207

Ann CORRIGAN - Futures Seminar

>Systems Science Ph.D Program
>Portland State University
>P.O. Box 751
>Portland, Oregon 97207

Felix GEYER - Head, Methodology Section, Netherlands Joint Social Research Centre, Amsterdam

>Stichting Interuniversitair Instituut voor
>Sociaal-wetenschappelijk onderzoek
>o.z. achterburgwal 128
>Amsterdam, The Netherlands 75083

Robert HERMAN - Head of the Traffic Science Department of General Motors Research Laboratories

>Research Laboratories
>General Motors Corporation
>General Motors Technical Center
>Warren, Michigan 48090

Thomas E. JONES - Adjunct Assoc. Prof., Graduate School of Management, Polytechnic Institute of New York

>61 Horatio Street, Apt. 1F
>New York, N.Y. 10014

Ervin LASZLO - Professor of Philosophy, Director, Goals for a Global Society Project, State University of New York, Geneseo

> Unitar
> 801 United Nations Plaza
> New York, N.Y. 10017

Paul A. LAVIOLETTE - Systems Science Ph.D Program, Portland State University. General systems theorist, solar energy research

> Systems Science Program
> Portland State University
> P.O. Box 751
> Portland, Oregon 97207

K. B. MADSEN - Professor of General Psychology, Royal Danish School of Educational Studies, Copenhagen

> Kaerdale Alle 14
> 2610 Rodovre
> Copenhagen, Denmark

Larry McCORD - Futures Seminar

> Systems Science Ph.D Program
> Portland State University
> P.O. Box 751
> Portland, Oregon 97207

Robert H. MURRAY - Vice-President, Systems Research and Analysis, Prometheus College Center for Energy Research, Analysis and Planning, Tacoma, Washington; energy consultant

> 2735 N.E. 28th St.
> Portland, Oregon, U.S.A.

Ilya PRIGOGINE - Head, Department of Chimie-Physique, Universite de Bruxelles; Director of the Center for Statistical Mechanics and thermodynamics, University of Texas at Austin

> Service du Chimie-Physique
> code postal n° 231
> Campus Plaine U.L.B.
> Boulevard du Triomphe
> 1050 Bruxelles, Belgique

Daniel SCHWARTZ - Futures Seminar

> Systems Science Ph.D Program
> Portland State University
> P.O. Box 751
> Portland, Oregon 97207

Alastair M. TAYLOR - Professor of Political Studies and Geography, Queen's University, Kingston, Ontario Canada

    Cartwright's Point
    Kingston, Ontario
    K7K 5E2 Canada

EDITOR'S NOTE

One's view of the future, as full of promise or of threat, is likely to reflect one's focus on the creative or destructive aspects of perceived changes. But if one focusses not merely on the changes but on the accelerating pace of change, of history, one is likely to ask, as R.N. Adams asks, whether the evolution of human society is the manifestation of some underlying natural law, and if so what the basis of such law could be (Adams, 1975). In recent years, the study of open, non-equilibrium systems has provided one focus of such inquiry. Some interesting and unexpected properties of such systems have come to light in the work of the Brussels school of thermodynamics. Prigogine, Allen and Herman present below an extended survey of some of the most striking results of work in this field especially as it relates to the evolution of complex systems. The following brief statement by the authors provides a summary for the reader who wishes to understand the basic features of the work without going into the technical details.*

---

*Readers interested in a more detailed analysis should consult G. Nicolis and I. Prigogine, <u>Self-Organization Phenomena in Non-Equilibrium Systems</u> Wiley-Interscience.

LONG TERM TRENDS AND THE EVOLUTION OF COMPLEXITY

Ilya Prigogine, Peter M. Allen and Robert Herman

The Copernican revolution led to the first major breakthrough in our understanding of nature, and the subsequent Newtonian formulation of mechanics exerted an extraordinary influence on all branches of knowledge and understanding, but attempts to formulate social evolution in terms of classical dynamics served only to show that no useful relationship existed between them. There is no preferred direction to time in the classical equations of motion (or in quantum mechanics, its modern generalization); neither is there the progressive complexification and diversification that characterizes living systems. Moreover, even inside physics itself, it soon appeared that classical dynamics was not a sufficiently wide conceptual framework to contain the essential aspects of the observation of nature. It proved necessary to introduce a distinction between "reversible" and "irreversible" transformations or "processes." An example of the former is wave propagation (neglecting friction), and of the latter, heat conduction.

This distinction gave rise to the science of thermodynamics which has two fundamental laws. The first says that energy may be transformed, for example from a chemical form to a mechanical one, as in an internal combustion engine, but that it is neither created nor destroyed, remaining constant in time. The second law, however, introduces a direction to time by saying that an isolated system (one for which neither energy nor matter may enter or leave) will evolve through irreversible processes to the state of maximum entropy. Boltzmann has shown that the physical meaning of entropy is closely related to "molecular disorder." The second law then takes on its familiar form saying that the entropy of the universe can only increase and the ultimate fate of the universe is "thermal death"--total disorder. This type of evolution is clearly not the basis for the natural laws governing the evolution of living systems-an entirely different evolution. Instead of a progressive growth of complexity, the second law of thermodynamics predicts a destruction of improbable molecular configurations and a tendency to establish uniformity.

A very basic point we have to take into account is that living systems are never isolated from their environment. All living systems must exchange energy and matter with their environment. Whether it be an amoeba, a human individual or a city, death will follow isolation once reserves have been exhausted. The basis for any natural law describing the evolution of social systems must be the physical laws governing open systems, i.e., systems embedded in their environment with which they exchange matter and energy.

An important element in the behavior of systems in far from equilibrium conditions is the presence of "feedback" interactions between the elements composing the system (molecules in chemistry, cells in an organism, neurons in the brain and individuals in society). If such interactions exist, then it is found that for a certain critical flow of energy or matter in and out of the system a new type of structure or organization may appear spontaneously. The structures resulting in these circumstances are entirely different from an "equilibrium" structure such as a crystal. A crystal, once formed, needs no further contact with the environment in order to persist. It can be stored indefinitely without expending energy.

The situation is quite different for nonequilibrium structures in open systems. A town isolated from the surrounding area will immediately start to decay. In other words, these structures are maintained only by the constant dissipation of energy, and it is for this reason that Prigogine (1967) called them "dissipative structures" in contrast to "equilibrium structures" such as crystals.

Dissipative structures are the manifestation of self-organization. This self-organization may take multiple forms. For example, in chemical systems it may consist of either rhythmic changes of composition (chemical clocks) or in concentration pattern formation. These processes involve the coherent motion of billions of molecules and are clearly inconsistent with the idea of "molecular disorder." The possibility that such a phenomenon of self-organization would be a basis for our understanding of the evolution of biological and social systems is heightened when we realize that all living systems do seem to possess these "non-linear" feedback interactions between their elements. The complicated catalytic action of enzymes and nucleotides, the chemical interactions of insect societies and the complex relationships between goal seeking members of a society are just three examples.

As is discussed more fully below, the evolution of dissipative structures has been studied in physical and chemical systems and reveals two complementary aspects. In one phase the system behaves deterministically according to the average values of the variables involved, while in the other a fluctuation is amplified until it changes the entire structure, whereupon the former phase recommences in different circumstances. The exact nature of the fluctuation is inherently unpredictable from a knowledge of the average values, and so the evolution of a dissipative structure is a self-determining sequence according to the scheme:

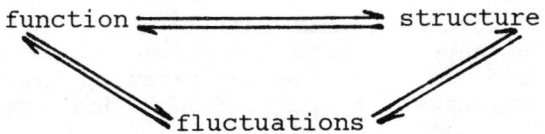

In ecosystems, "functions" correspond to the terms entering the equations of population dynamics expressing birth and death, competition, predation and parasitism. The "structure" resulting is the solution of these equations describing then the trophic organization of the ecosystem at a given time. If we identify "fluctuations" with the appearance of genetic mutants, then our description is of biological evolution, embracing both Darwinian and Lamarckian ideas, since it is not necessary to specify exactly the mechanism of "mutation." In fact the "fluctuations" can equally well correspond to a behavioral change, and if imitative mechanisms are present in the ecosystem, fluctuations of this type can be amplified. Indeed, this latter type of evolution would seem to correspond to the socio-cultural and technological evolution experienced by man.

The study of the evolution of ecosystems in these terms is only beginning, but already certain long term trends can be discerned in the simple cases studied so far. For example, an ecosystem containing a single trophic level of species in competition for resources evolves in such a way that hitherto untapped resources are exploited, and each resource is exploited with increasing effectiveness. Specialization will occur and will be the more marked if the system is rich in each resource. Physical diversity within the ecosystem is related to the resource richness.

In ecosystems containing two trophic levels (predator/prey; herbivore/plant; consumer/producer), it can be shown that providing the predator and the prey both evolve at the same rate, the benefits of the mutual evolution accrue to the consumer (predator, herbivore). An interesting indication that emerges from even very simple models is that if the "consumer" evolves more quickly than the "producer," then the whole ecosystem is endangered and ecological disaster can result.

The mode of evolution characterizing man is that of innovation, e.g., changes in technology, that can be imitated by his fellows, and this "Lamarckian" type of evolution is indeed more rapid than the genetic evolution of the species on which he preys. If man's inventiveness is directed towards simply improving the effectiveness of hunting-gathering techniques then he will eventually endanger the ecosystem of which he is part. Agriculture can be seen as a way of restoring the balance. Man's innovative powers are used to accelerate the "evolution" of his prey.

If we turn now to long-range trends in social systems, the first question we may ask is what features there are in common between the functioning of a society and that of a dissipative structure. Firstly, societies have complex non-linear interactions between their elements derived from the cooperation and conflicts involved in the attempts of individuals and groups to attain "goals." Secondly, they are subject to local "behavioral fluctuations," meaning that sometimes new behavior can appear, such as an invention, a modification of group organization, or a new goal or belief, and this can either be suppressed by the social environment or will grow and spread until the society itself is modified. Here again we find the dual aspects of change and determinism, and the theory briefly described here and discussed in more detail below should therefore serve as a background for discussion of the evolution of social systems. One of the main problems which characterize social systems is that of defining the variables in terms of which value judgements are made, variables such as "quality of life," for example. These questions require elucidation before such a mechanism can be applied widely to social systems.

We may summarize this brief discussion by saying that this mechanism for understanding long term trends in complex self-organizing systems does not "reduce" the possibilities of "change." Change can always occur and, in this theory, in new dimensions of freedom. However, understanding the evolutionary mechanisms of complex systems will permit qualified predictions to be made and in so doing lessen the risks inherent in following certain paths. As Whitehead said "It is the job of the future to be dangerous," but one should add that it is ours to try to anticipate it.

THE EVOLUTION OF COMPLEXITY AND THE LAWS OF NATURE

In a working paper "Mankind in Transition: The Evolution of Global Society," E. Laszlo asks, "Is our age of rapid and often unforeseen change an aberration in the evolutionary history of our species, an unprecedented event, or can we discern the general thrust of the change by putting it into a historical context?" Analyzing the patterns in the evolution of complexity, Laszlo notes that "There is a growing indication that biological and sociocultural evolution are aspects of the same fundamental process of evolution in nature." It is precisely this indication that we analyze in the present essay. Let us start with a few introductory remarks.

Our era is witnessing great advances in knowledge in the natural sciences. The dimensions of the physical world that we can explore at present have increased to truly fantastic proportions. On the microscopic scale elementary particle physics reveals processes involving physical dimensions of the order of 10^{-15} cm and times of the order of 10^{-22} sec. On the other hand, cosmology leads us to times of the order of 10^{10} years (the age of the universe) and therefore to distances of the order of 10^{28} cm (the distance to the event horizon, i.e., the furthest distance from which physical signals can be received). Even more important perhaps than this increase in dimensions is the resulting change in the character of the behavior of the physical world which has been discovered recently.

At the beginning of this century, physics seemed to be on the verge of reducing the basic structure of matter to a few stable "elementary particles" such as electrons and protons. At the present time we are far from such a simple description. Whatever the future of theoretical physics may be, "elementary" particles appear to be of such great complexity that the old adage "the simplicity of the microscopic" no longer holds.

The change in our point of view is equally valid in astrophysics. Whereas the great originators of western astronomy stressed the regularity and eternal character of celestial motions, we now see that such a qualification applies, at best, only to very limited aspects such as planetary motion. Instead of finding stability and harmony, wherever we look we discover evolutionary processes leading to diversification and increasing complexity. This shift in our vision of the physical world leads us to investigate branches of theoretical physics and of mathematics which are likely to be of interest in this new context.

Classical mechanics has been immensely successful in dealing with problems concerning trajectories such as, for example, the planetary orbits within our solar system. The scope of classical mechanics has been greatly enlarged by the formulation of quantum mechanics and relativity theory. Nevertheless, there remains a gap between considerations of dynamics (even when quantum or relativistic effects are included) and the problems of evolution, diversification and innovation that interest us here.

Basically, classical dynamics "reduces" the physical world to trajectories ("world-lines") such as are shown in Fig. 1 in the case of a "one-dimensional" universe.

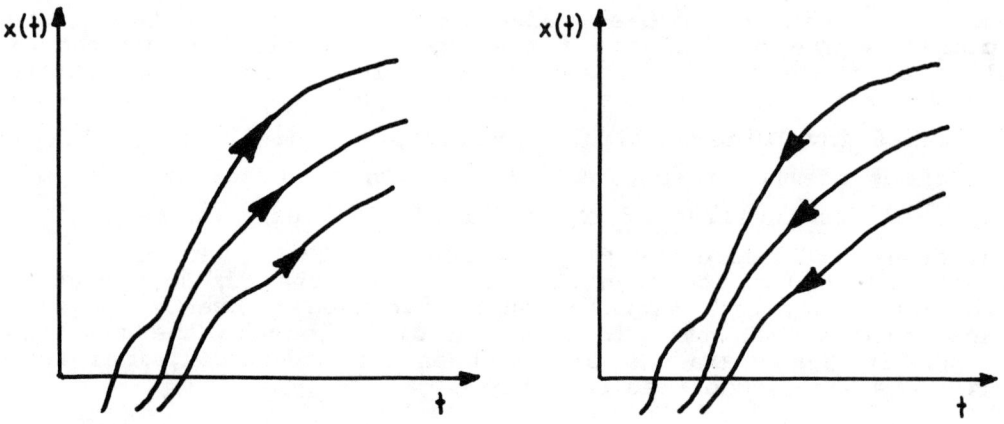

Fig. 1 - World lines.

The position x(t) of a test particle as a function of time is represented by each trajectory. The important feature here is that dynamics makes no distinction between the future and the past. Both the motion (a) "forward" in time and (b) "backward" in time are possible. However, we cannot describe processes involving evolution in any nontrivial way without introducing the concept of direction of time.

Obviously new tools are necessary. Over the past few years great progress has been made in this direction. Nonequilibrium thermodynamics provides us with important clues about where to probe for the formation of new structures. Recent developments in fluctuation theory (Malek-Mansour and Nicolas, 1975) provide information concerning how self-organization in nonequilibrium systems may arise and lead to a new type of order. We have described this type of order as "order through fluctuations" (Prigogine, et al, 1972) to contrast it with order in equilibrium systems. Similarly, such branches of mathematics as stability theory (Minorski, 1962) and the theory of bifurcations (Sattinger, 1973) have lately received increasing attention. It is the aim of this essay to present an introductory survey of the recent development of these new concepts and tools which appear appropriate to describe phenomena such as evolution, increasing complexity and diversification.

There is, however, one important aspect which we shall not discuss here. That is the relation between irreversibility and the laws of classical or quantum mechanics. Important advances have also been made (Prigogine, et al, 1973) in those subject areas. However, the highly technical character of the subject precludes us from a discussion of this problem. Suffice it to mention that irreversibility is by no means in contradiction with the laws of dynamics but, on the contrary, follows from these laws whenever a sufficient degree of "complexity" is reached (Prigogine, et al) (In classical dynamics this degree of complexity is already attained in the three body problem!). Even though limited in this way, we hope that our presentation will assist the reader in viewing problems of biological and sociocultural evolution in a proper context.

In order to avoid misunderstandings, let us stress that our presentation does not imply any attempt to "reduce" sociocultural evolution to the laws of physics. Far from that, the analysis of even the simplest examples of self-organization shows an unexpected wealth of aspects, and any simple "automatic" extrapolation to situations involving human sociology is, of course, out of the question. Nevertheless, it is important to point out that life, with its associated biological and sociocultural evolutionary aspects, no longer appears as an exception to the laws of nature, successful only because of the intervention of an army of Maxwell demons struggling with the laws of nature. Rather these aspects of life appear to be in conformity with these laws when the important features of "nonequilibrium" and "nonlinearity" are properly taken into account (Prigogine, 1972).

BOLTZMANN'S ORDER PRINCIPLE

It is remarkable to note that the idea of evolution was formulated in the nineteenth century almost simultaneously in physics (Carnot, 1824; Clausius, 1857; Thomson), in biology (Darwin, 1868), and in sociology (Spencer, 1904); but, the interpretation of this idea was quite different in the various fields. As we shall see presently, in physics evolution and irreversibility were associated with the "forgetting of initial conditions" and the dissolution of structures, while in biology and sociology they were linked from the start to increasing complexity.

In physics a basic distinction must be made between "reversible" and "irreversible" processes. A simple example of an irreversible process is heat conduction. For example, a metallic bar which is initially hot at one end and cold at the other will, if isolated, gradually attain a uniform distribution through heat transfer (see Fig. 2).

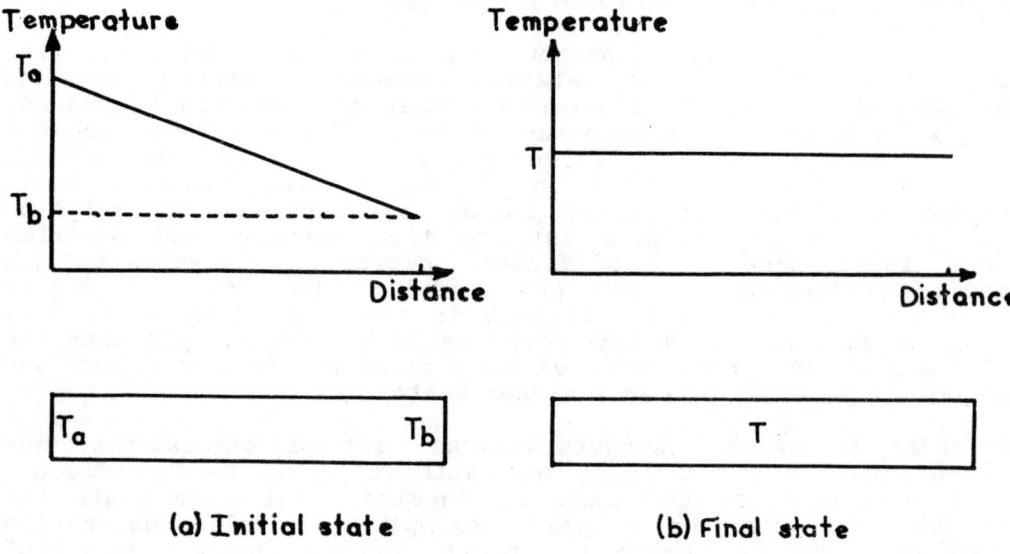

Fig. 2 - Heat conduction in a bar.

This type of behavior is described by the "second law of thermodynamics." However, before formulating this law it is useful to classify various systems in the following way: firstly, there are "isolated" systems which can exchange neither matter nor energy with the outside world (see Fig. 3);

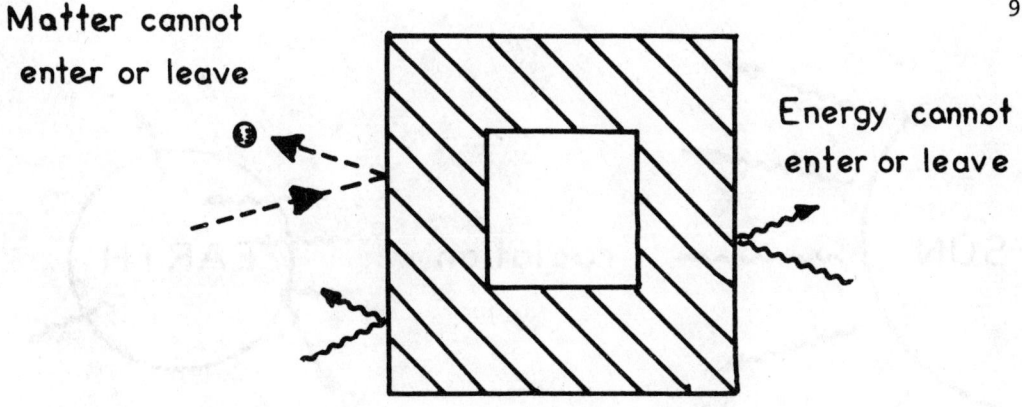

Fig. 3 - An isolated system.

secondly, there are closed systems which can exchange energy (but not matter) with the outside world (see Fig. 4).

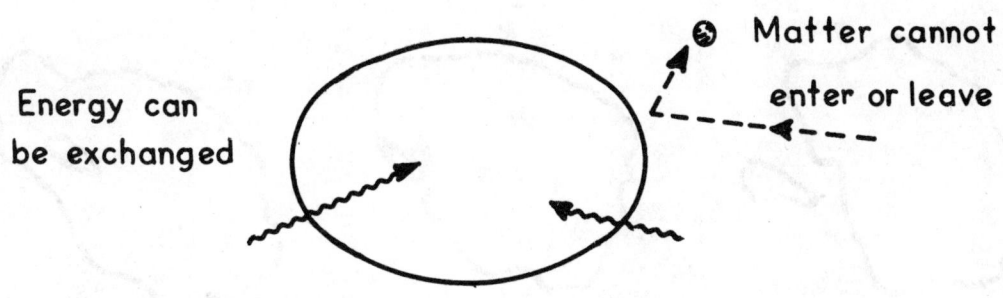

Fig. 4 - A closed system.

The earth affords an example of a closed system if we neglect meteoritic falls and cosmic dust. The earth receives solar and stellar radiation and itself radiates into the cold regions of interstellar radiation (see Fig. 5).

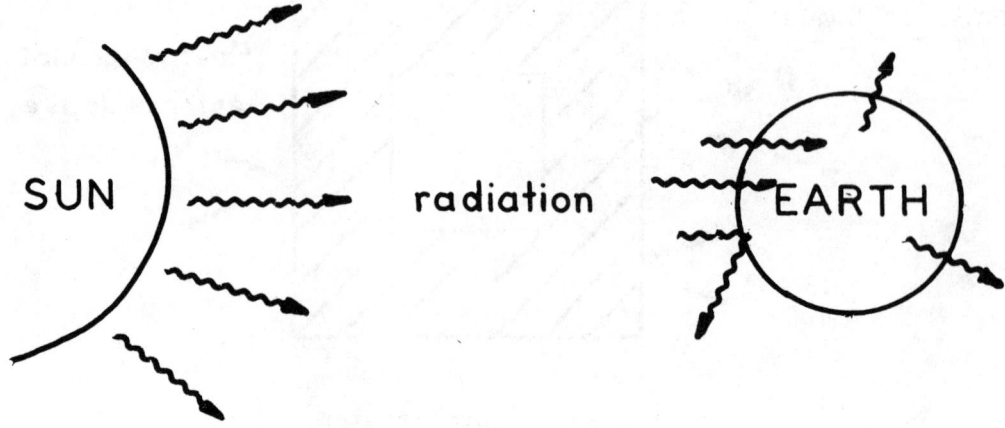

Fig. 5 - The earth is approximately a closed system.

The third type of system is one which is free to exchange both matter and energy with the external world - an "open" system (see Fig. 6).

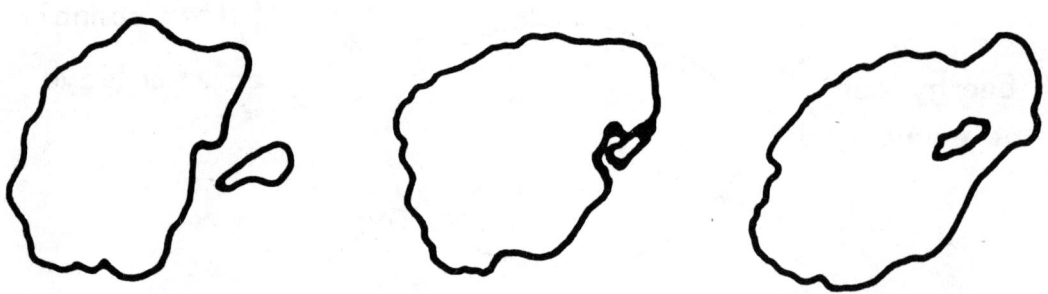

Fig. 6 - An amoeba engulfing its food is an example of an open system.

Another example of an open system is a town. It is clearly a center of the flow of food, fuel, building materials, etc., and it sends out finished products and wastes (see Fig. 7).

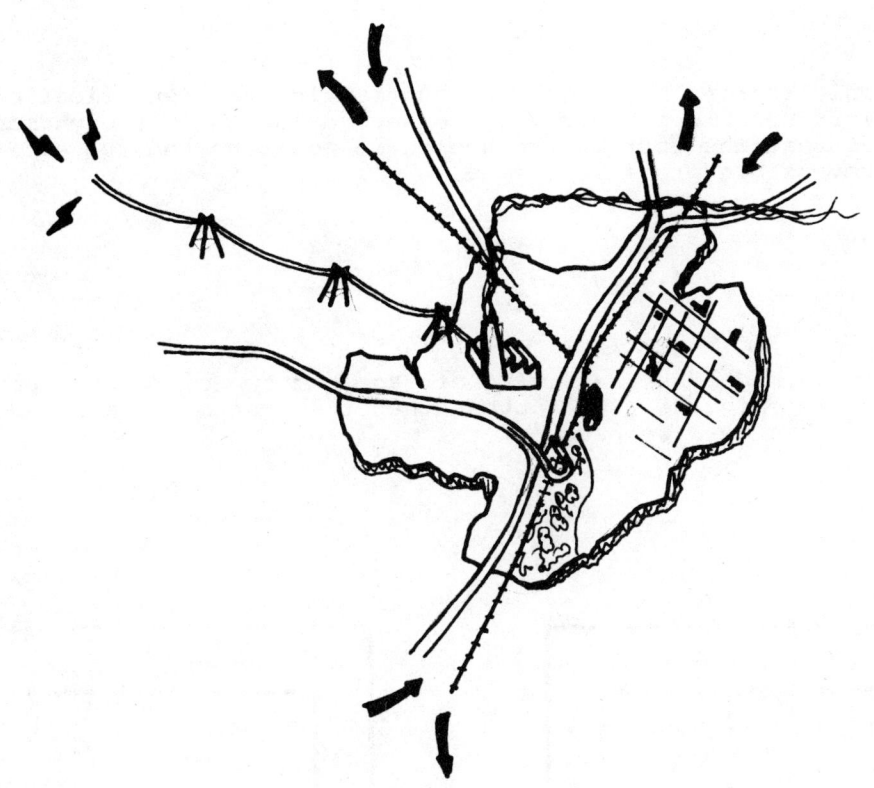

Fig. 7 - A town - an open system.

Thermodynamics deals with the general principles governing the evolution of macroscopic systems formed by a large number of molecules. The first law of thermodynamics expresses the conservation of energy: any change of energy must result from energy transfers across boundaries. The second law, however, deals with the distinction between reversible and irreversible processes. This distinction introduces a preferential direction of time. To express this distinction quantitatively, one can introduce a new function, namely, "entropy." Entropy, unlike energy, is not conserved. The usual symbol for entropy is S. Its change in the small time interval dt is written as dS. It is made up of two terms: the first, $d_e S$ is the transfer of entropy across the boundaries of the system, and the second $d_i S$, is the entropy produced within the system. We have, therefore, the relation

$$dS = d_e S + d_i S \quad . \tag{1}$$

The basic feature of entropy production is its identification with irreversible processes. The second law of thermodynamics assumes that the entropy production is positive and due entirely to irreversible processes, i.e.,

$$d_i S \geq 0 \ . \tag{2}$$

An example might be the mixing of gases at two different temperatures (see Fig. 8). We suppose that the system is isolated so that in this case we have

$$S_2 - S_1 = \Delta S = \int d_i S > 0 \ . \tag{3}$$

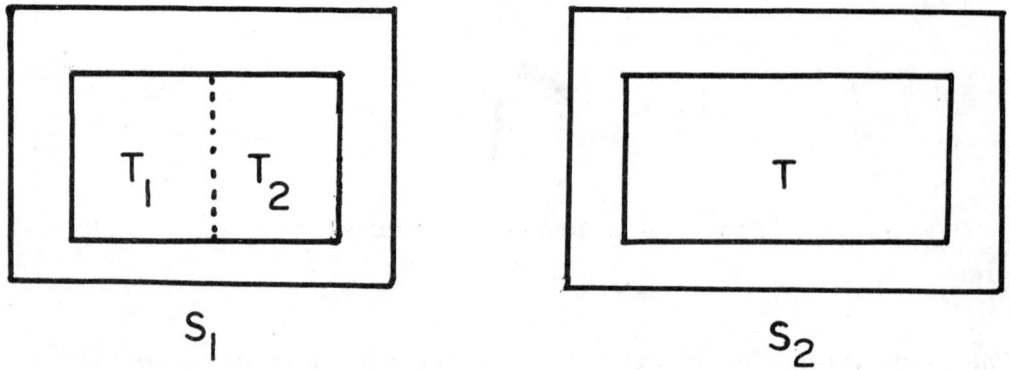

Fig. 8 - An irreversible process.

The entropy flow $d_e S$ is zero and in this example the second law reduces to the usual classical statement that the entropy increases in an isolated system.

When $d_i S = 0$, only reversible processes can be taking place. An example of such a process is that of waves of small amplitude spreading on the surface of a pond after a stone has been dropped. Neglecting small frictional effects, we can say the waves do not increase the entropy.

Entropy occupies a unique position. We have already seen that energy is conserved. Other quantities which are not conserved can either be created or destroyed, increased or diminished, in the course of evolution. The entropy production, on the contrary, can only be positive or zero. The second law therefore provides us with a universal law of macroscopic evolution, since the quantity of entropy appertaining to the system and its environment can only increase in the course of time.

Now let us ask what such an increase in entropy may mean in terms of the molecules involved. In order to provide an answer, we must explore the microscopic meaning of entropy. We return to the consideration of a gas or a liquid and inquire what entropy may mean in such a physical system. It was Boltzmann (1872) who first pointed out that entropy was a measure of molecular disorder and, therefore, that the law of entropy increase was simply a law of increasing disorganization. Let us take a simple example: consider a container divided into two identical parts by a permeable partition (see Fig. 9).

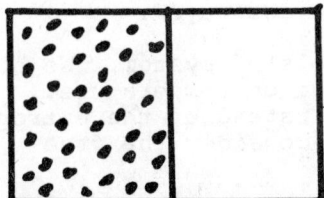 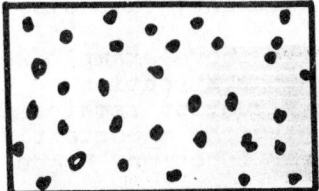

Fig. 9 - Distribution of molecules between two compartments.

The number of ways, P, in which N molecules can be divided into two groups N_1 and N_2 is given by the simple combinatorial formula

$$P = \frac{N!}{N_1! \, N_2!} \qquad (4)$$

[where $N! = N(N-1)(N-2)\ldots 3\cdot 2\cdot 1$].

The quantity P is called the "number of complexions."

Starting from any initial values of N_1 and N_2 we find after a sufficiently long time that an equilibrium situation is reached where, except for small fluctuations, there is equipartition of the molecules between the two compartments ($N_1 \simeq N_2 \simeq N/2$).

It is easily seen that this situation corresponds to the maximum value of P, and that in the course of evolution P has increased. This type of consideration led Boltzmann to identify the number of complexions, P, with the entropy through the relation

$$S = k \log P \; , \qquad (5)$$

where k is Boltzmann's universal constant. This relation indicates clearly that an entropy increase expresses growing molecular disorder as reflected in the increasing number of complexions. In such an evolution, the initial conditions are "forgotten." If in the initial state one of the compartments is favored by having a larger number of particles than the other compartment, this disymmetry will always be destroyed.

In the above example we have treated an isolated system. We now turn our attention to closed systems at a given temperature. The situation remains similar except that instead of the entropy S being the important function we must now consider the free energy function, F, defined by

$$F = E - TS \; , \qquad (6)$$

where E is the energy of the system and T is the temperature in degrees Kelvin. The evolution of the system is now determined by the decrease of the free energy. At equilibrium the free energy reaches a minimum value. The structure of Equation (6) reflects a competition between the energy E and the entropy S. At low temperatures the second term is negligible, and the minimum value of F imposes structures corresponding to minimum energy and generally to low entropy. At increasing temperatures, however, the system shifts to structures of higher and higher entropy.

Experience confirms these considerations since at low temperatures we find the solid state characterized by an ordered structure of low entropy while at higher temperatures we find the high entropy gaseous state. The formation of certain types of ordered structures in physics is a consequence of the laws of thermodynamics applied to a closed system at equilibrium.

Boltzmann also stated the laws which govern the distribution of molecules among the energy levels of a system at equilibrium. Boltzmann's formula for the probability, P_r, of the occupation of a given energy level is

$$P_r \propto e^{-E_i/kT}, \qquad (7)$$

where K is again Boltzmann's constant, T the temperature, and E_i the energy of the chosen level. Suppose we consider a simplified system with only three energy levels. Then Boltzmann's formula, Equation (7), tells us the probability of finding a molecule in each of the three states at equilibrium. At very low temperatures T - 0 the only significant probability is that corresponding to the lowest energy level and we come to the scheme of Fig. 10 where virtually all the molecules are in the lowest energy state E1, since

$$e^{-E_1/kT} \gg e^{-E_2/kT}, \; e^{-E_3/kT}, \qquad (8)$$

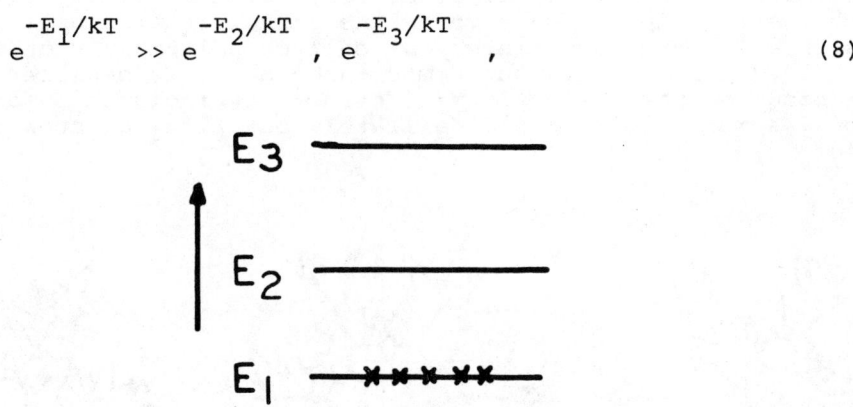

Fig. 10 - Low temperature distribution.

At high temperatures, however, the three probabilities become roughly equal

$$e^{-E_1/kT} \simeq e^{-E_2/kT} \simeq e^{-E_3/kT}, \qquad (9)$$

and, therefore, the three states are approximately equally populated (see Fig. 11).

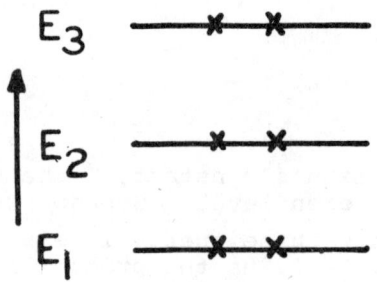

Fig. 11 - High temperature distribution.

Boltzmann's probability distribution, Equation (7), provides us with the principle that governs the structure of equilibrium states. It may appropriately be called "Boltzmann's order principle." It is of paramount importance as it is capable of describing an enormous variety of structures including, for example, some as complex and delicately beautiful as snow crystals (Fig. 12).

Fig. 12 - Typical ice crystals, describable by "Boltzmann's Order Principle."

Boltzmann's order principle states that systems, in the course of time, tend toward the most probable state, as given by the number of corresponding complexions. This leads to an increase of the entropy, S, for isolated systems or a decrease of the free energy, F, in closed systems.

It is very interesting to note that the formulation of the second law, as presented in Equations (1) and (2), applies both to nonequilibrium and equilibrium situations. In spite of this, most of classical thermodynamics as developed in the nineteenth century was limited to equilibrium situations. There may have been various reasons for this. First, practically all of the most striking results of classical thermodynamics correspond to equilibrium situations. Well known examples are the Gibbs Phase Rule and the Law of Mass Action which have become integral parts of every introductory text in physical chemistry. However, other, often implicit considerations, also played an important role. Nonequilibrium was considered as a perturbation temporarily preventing the appearance of structure identified with the order at equilibrium. To grow a beautiful crystal we require near equilibrium conditions and to obtain a good yield from a thermal engine we need to minimize irreversible processes such as friction and heat losses.

However, even in classical physics there are many phenomena where nonequilibrium may lead to order. When we apply a thermal gradient to a mixture of two different gases, we observe an enrichment of one of the components at the hot wall while the other concentrates at the cold wall. This phenomenon, already observed in the nineteenth century, is called thermal diffusion. In the steady state the entropy is generally lower than it would be in a uniform mixture. This shows that nonequilibrium may be a source of order. It is this observation which was the starting point of the outlook originated by the Brussels school (Glansdorff and Prigogine, 1971). Obviously, the role of irreversible processes becomes much more marked when we turn to biological or social phenomena.

Even in the simplest cells, the metabolic function involves several thousand coupled chemical reactions and, in consequence, requires a delicate mechanism for their coordination and regulation. In other words we need an extremely sophisticated <u>functional</u> organization. Furthermore, the metabolic reactions require specific catalysts, the enzymes, which are large molecules possessing a spatial organization, and the organism must be capable of synthesizing these substances. A catalyst is a substance that accelerates a certain chemical reaction but is not itself used up in the reaction. Each enzyme or catalyst performs one specific task, and if we look at the manner in which the cell performs a complex sequence of operations, we find that it is organized on exactly the same lines as a modern "assembly line" (see Fig. 13).

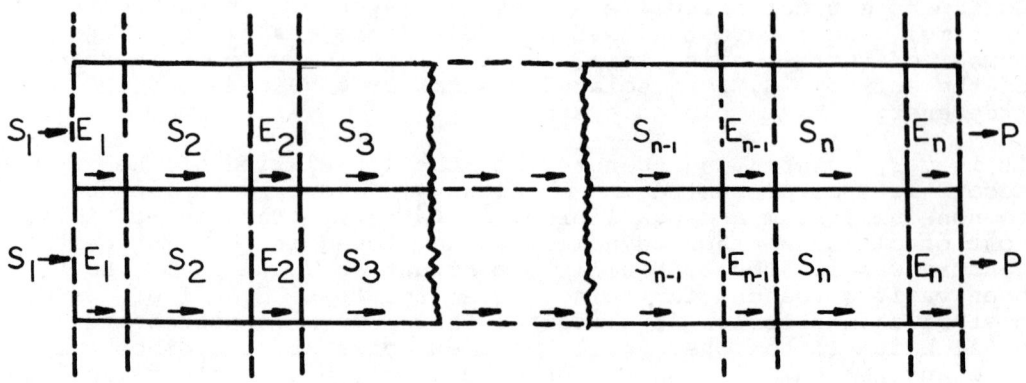

Fig. 13 - Mozaic model of multienzyme reaction. Substrate S_1 is changed by successive modifications to the product P by the action of "captive" enzymes.

The overall chemical modification that must be carried out is broken down into successive elementary steps, each of which is catalyzed by a specific enzyme. The initial compound is channeled from left to right in the diagram, and at each membrane an "imprisoned" enzyme performs a given operation on the substance, then sends it on to the next stage (Smeach and Gold, 1976). Such an organization is quite obviously not the result of an evolution toward molecular disorder! Biological order is both architectural and functional, and furthermore, at the cellular and supercellular level, it manifests itself by a series of structures and coupled functions of growing complexity and hierarchical character. This is contrary to the concept of evolution as described in the thermodynamics of isolated and closed systems. Do we then have to conclude, as did Callois, that "Clausius and Darwin cannot both be right," or should we introduce, with Spencer (1904), some new principle of nature such as the "instability of the homogeneous," or "a differentiating force, creator of organization."

As long as such difficulties remain, "living" processes are in some sense pushed "outside nature" and physical laws. One is consequently tempted to ascribe an accidental character to living organisms, and to imagine the origin of life as being the result of some highly improbable event such as the "spontaneous" formation of D.N.A.

Indeed, in classical dynamics a sharp distinction is made between "events and regularities." The laws of dynamics deal with regularities between events but not with the events themselves. The events are the initial conditions about which classical dynamics can make no statement. At most, we could use Boltzmann's probabilistic interpretation of the second law of thermodynamics to ascribe a probability to each possible initial condition. Once this initial condition is known, physics prescribes an irreversible process which will lead the system to its most probable state.

Life considered as a result of "improbable" initial conditions is in this view compatible with the laws of physics (initial conditions are arbitrary!) but does not follow from the laws of physics (which do not prescribe the initial conditions). This is the outlook supported, for example, by Monod in his well known book <u>Chance And Necessity</u> (Monod, 1970). Moreover, the maintenance of life would appear in this view to correspond to an on-going struggle by an army of Maxwell demons against the laws of physics to maintain the highly improbable conditions which permit its existence.

<u>Our point of view is entirely different: that living processes, far from being in any way outside nature, on the contrary, follow from the laws of physics appropriate to specific nonlinear interactions and to conditions far from equilibrium. These specific features may then permit the flow of energy and matter to build and maintain functional and structural order.</u>

There is a striking difference between the chemical composition of even the simplest cell and its environment. Remember that the average molecular weight of a protein is ~10^5 while that of water is 18! We are in a sense in the position of a visitor from another world who, on finding a suburban house, wishes to understand its origin. Of course the house is not in conflict with the laws of mechanics or else it would have fallen down. However, this is beside the point; what is of interest is the technology available to the house builders, the choice of materials, the needs of the occupants, their sense of aesthetics, etc. The house cannot be understood outside the culture in which it is embedded. Furthermore, the house is an open system and cannot be understood in isolation. The same is true for biomolecules such as proteins or nucleic acids. Their architecture conforms strictly to the laws of physical chemistry. Still, we have to understand the structure of the medium in which proteins form. In other words, our aim is to understand biological and social structure as phenomena which are both influenced by and can themselves act on their environment and as phenomena occurring spontaneously in open systems maintained far from equilibrium.

DISSIPATIVE STRUCTURES

The main conclusion that we can draw from the considerations of the first section is that biological and social organization involves a new type of structure, which has a different origin and requires a different explanation from that of equilibrium structures such as crystals. A common feature of social and biological structures is that they occur in open systems and that their organization depends vitally on the exchange of matter and energy with the surrounding medium. However, the requirement of an open system is not a sufficient condition to ensure the appearance of such structure. As we shall explain presently, this is possible only if the system is maintained "far from equilibrium" and if there exist certain types of "nonlinear" mechanisms operating between the various elements of the system.

An open system can exist in three different regimes. First, there is that of thermodynamic equilibrium, where flows and currents have eliminated temperature or concentration differences, entropy has risen to a new larger value, and uniformity is attained. For isolated systems, this is the state of maximum molecular disorder, maximum entropy, and the equilibrium state is governed by Boltzmann's order principle. The second possible regime is one that differs only slightly from that of equilibrium but where small temperature or concentration differences are maintained across the system so that it remains slightly out of equilibrium. If this perturbation from equilibrium is sufficiently small, then we may analyze the system by adding only a small correction to the equilibrium state - and this is therefore termed "a state of linear nonequilibrium." For such a state it is possible to show, however, that the system moves as close as possible to the state of maximum molecular disorder and that the appearance of any new structure or organization is not possible (Clansdorff and Prigogine, 1971).

However, the situation becomes quite different for the third possible regime, which is that resulting when the constraints are maintained at values which drive the system far from equilibrium. It is under these conditions that new structures and new types of organization can appear spontaneously, and these are termed "dissipative structures."

The other basic feature necessary for the appearance of dissipative structures is the existence of certain types of nonlinear interaction mechanisms which act between the elements of the system. For example, the hydrodynamical equations describing the behavior of fluid subjected to temperature gradients provide just such a nonlinearity. A most striking example of a dissipative structure is provided by a pan of liquid heated evenly from below. When the heating is gentle, the liquid is in the second regime of linear nonequilibrium, and heat passes through the liquid by conduction. However, as the heating is intensified, at a certain well-defined temperature gradient convection cells suddenly appear spontaneously. As can be seen in Fig. 14, the cells are very regular. This corresponds to a high degree of molecular organization when energy is transferred from thermal agitation to macroscopic convection currents.

Boltzmann's ordering principle would assign almost zero probability to such an occurrence and is plainly incapable of describing a phenomenon of this type. We may imagine that there

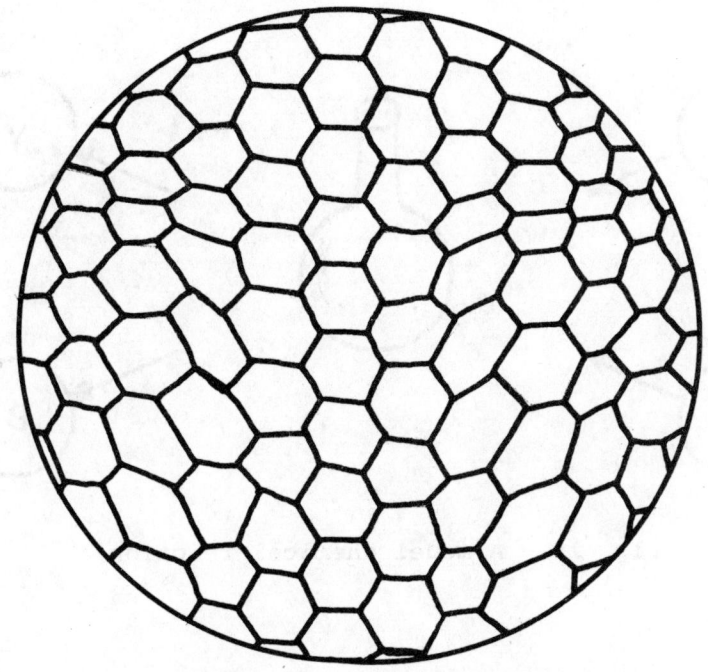

Fig. 14 - Pattern of convection cells, viewed from above in a liquid heated from below.

are always small convection currents appearing as fluctuations from the average state, but below a certain critical value of the temperature gradient these fluctuations are damped and disappear. On the contrary, above some critical value certain fluctuations are amplified and give rise to a macroscopic current. A new molecular order appears which corresponds basically to a giant fluctuation stabilized by exchanges of energy with the outside world. This is the order characterized by the occurrence of dissipative structures. Unlike equilibrium structures, dissipative structures may have a coherent behavior involving the cooperation of a large number of units.

If we turn now to chemical reactions we find an even richer spectrum of possible dissipative structures. Let us try to understand the reason for this. Consider a simple chemical reaction:

$$A + X \rightarrow B + Y . \tag{10}$$

This equation states that if a molecule A collides with a molecule X they can react and form molecules Y and B (see Fig. 15).

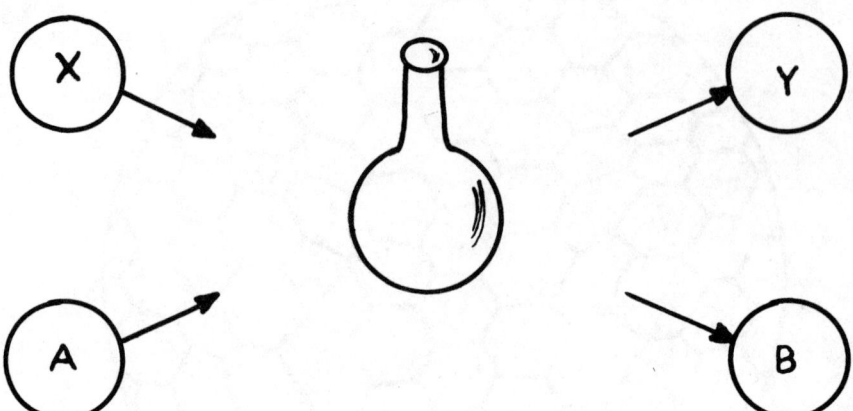

Fig. 15 - A model chemical reaction.

Chemical kinetics describes how the concentrations of the various components change as a result of chemical reactions. For example, if we have reaction (10) we find that X and A molecules disappear at the same rate as Y and B appear. This rate is proportional to the frequency with which collisions between X and A occur. If this frequency is assumed to be proportional to the concentrations of the species X and A, we then have:

$$\frac{dX}{dt} = \frac{dA}{dt} = - k \, X \, A = - \frac{dY}{dt} = - \frac{dB}{dt} \, , \qquad (11)$$

where X, Y, A and B refer to the concentrations of the various molecular species and k the chemical rate constant. Of course, we must realize that the inverse collision may also occur:

$$Y + B \rightarrow X + A \, , \qquad (12)$$

and if the chemical constant for the forward reaction is k^+ and for the inverse k^-, then we have:

$$\frac{dX}{dt} = \frac{dA}{dt} = - k^+ \, X \, A + k^- \, Y \, B = - \frac{dY}{dt} = - \frac{dB}{dt} \, . \qquad (13)$$

Now in a closed or isolated chemical system, where there is no matter flowing in or out of the system, Equation (13) can only lead to equilibrium values for X, Y, A and B related through

$$\frac{X_{eq} A_{eq}}{Y_{eq} B_{eq}} = \frac{k^-}{k^+}, \qquad (14)$$

where the overall rate of the forward reaction equals the rate of the inverse reaction. Equation (14) expresses the law of mass action mentioned earlier. However, such a system can be driven arbitrarily far from this state of chemical equilibrium by adjusting the rate at which one pumps in, for example, the molecules X or A and extracts Y or B. Chemical kinetics results from collisions between molecules. This then leads to many ways in which nonlinear kinetic equations may appear. In consequence a multiplicity of possible dissipative structures can develop. Consider, for example, the action of a catalyst. This may be a substance which accelerates a certain chemical reaction. An example is represented schematically in Fig. 16.

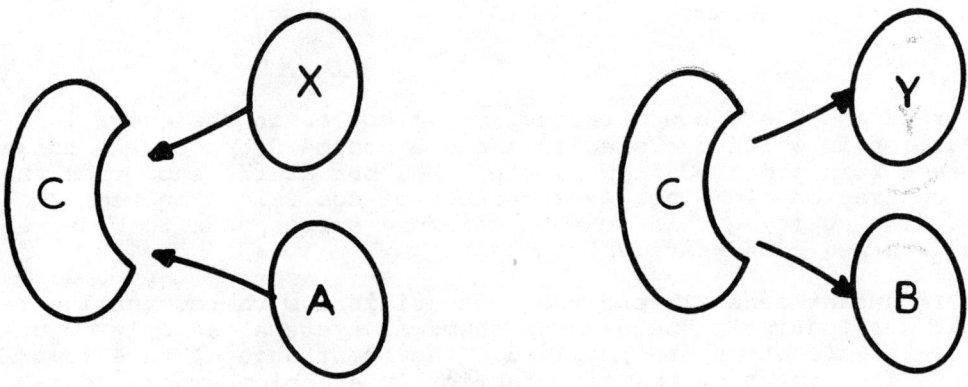

Fig. 16 - A model catalytic chemical reaction.

In some cases one speaks of "autocatalytic" reactions. This refers to situations where a molecule catalyzes the reaction in which it is produced. For example the reaction scheme

$$X + Y \to 2X \qquad (a)$$

corresponds to the production of 2X molecules starting from one molecule of X and one of Y. In this case the chemical rate equation is given by

$$\frac{dX}{dt} = k\,X\,Y \quad . \tag{b}$$

In this special case, when Y is held at a constant concentration, we obtain the well known equation describing the exponential growth of X.

When one substance, say X, produces another, Y, which itself produces X, we have what is termed "cross-catalysis." This is the case in the following kinetic scheme which has been extensively studied in recent years (Lefever, 1968a):

$$\begin{aligned} A &\rightleftharpoons X & (a) \\ B + X &\rightleftharpoons Y + D & (b) \\ 2X + Y &\rightleftharpoons 3X & (c) \\ X &\rightleftharpoons E & (d) \end{aligned} \tag{15}$$

where X and Y are now intermediate molecules in the overall reaction in which the species A and B become D and E. In this scheme Y is produced from X, step (b), but at the same time the concentration of X increases because of collisions between X and Y, step (c). This scheme therefore corresponds to what we have termed cross-catalysis.

An important general result of nonequilibrium thermodynamics is that dissipative structures in chemical systems can only occur if catalytic steps are involved. The importance of this remark comes from the fact that in practically all biochemical reactions, as well as in social phenomena, there are catalytic steps. We shall return to this point later. Let us first consider in detail the type of dissipative structures which may occur as a consequence of scheme (15). We consider the simple limiting situation in which we neglect the inverse reactions in (15). We obtain therefore:

$$A \to X \quad (a)$$
$$B + X \to Y + D \quad (b)$$
$$2X + Y \to 3X \quad (c) \quad \quad (15')$$
$$X \to E \quad (d)$$

An example of a dissipative structure corresponds to the appearance of spatial inhomogeneities. To study this situation, let us imagine that the reaction occurs in two boxes side by side and with the diffusion of X and Y occurring between them (Lefever, 1968b), as may be seen in Fig. 17.

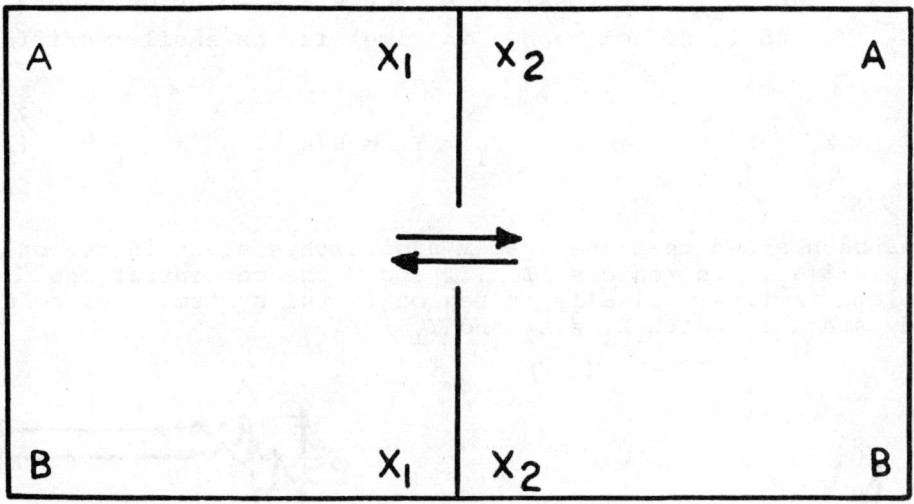

Fig. 17 - Two box model.

For box 1, we have the following kinetic equations:

$$\frac{dX_1}{dt} = A + X_1^2 Y_1 - (B + 1)X_1 + D_X(X_2 - X_1)$$

(16a)

$$\frac{dY_1}{dt} = B X_1 - X_1^2 Y_1 + D_Y(Y_2 - Y_1)$$

and for box 2:

$$\frac{dX_2}{dt} = A + X_2^2 Y_2 - (B + 1)X_2 + D_X(X_1 - X_2) \qquad (16b)$$

$$\frac{dY_2}{dt} = B X_2 - X_2^2 Y_2 + D_Y(Y_1 - Y_2),$$

where the term $D_X(X_2 - X_1)$ gives the quantity of X flowing into or out of box 1 resulting from the difference in concentration between X_1 and X_2. One possible steady state solution (where X_1, X_2, Y_1 and Y_2 do not change in time) is, as easily verified:

$$X_1 = X_2 = A \ ; \qquad Y_1 = Y_2 = B/A \ . \qquad (16c)$$

It has been shown that the system adopts this state in region I of Fig. 18(a). In regions II, III and V the concentrations oscillate in time. Finally in region IV the system moves to a steady state in which $X_1 \neq X_2$ and $Y_1 \neq Y_2$.

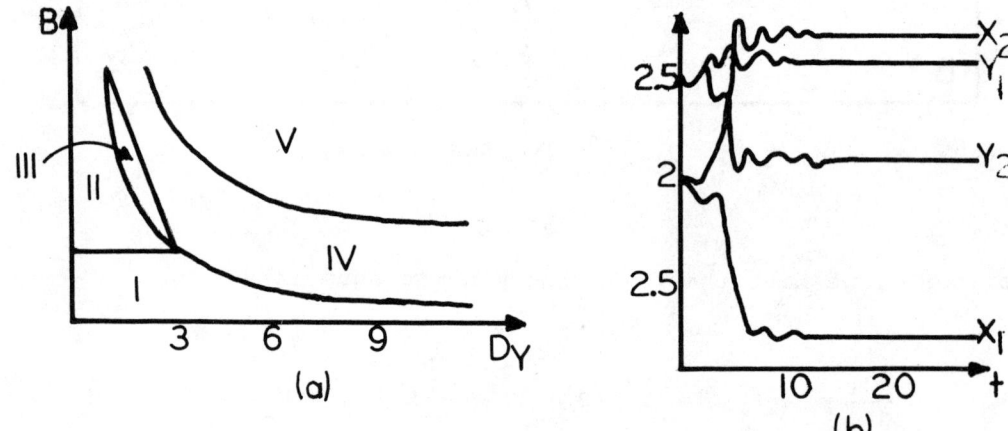

Fig. 18 - Behavior of the two box model.
    (a) Phase diagram.
    (b) Effect of perturbation corresponding to Region IV.

Let us analyze more closely the situation in this region (see Fig. 18(b)). We start with the homogenous state, $X_1 = X_2$; $Y_1 = Y_2$. Then, a perturbation in Y_2 causes the rate of production of X_2 to increase due to step (c) of Equation (15'). Under the conditions in region IV this tendency cannot be arrested by the "leveling" effect of the diffusion between the boxes 1 and 2. Rather, the system evolves toward a new state representing a condition of dynamic balance between the different rates of production in the two domains and the "equalizing" flows between the boxes. In this way the system reacts to small internal fluctuation in the values of X and Y by adopting a final inhomogeneous distribution which, as can be shown, is incapable of further modification by small fluctuations of X and Y. The time evolution of the various concentrations is shown graphically in Fig. 18(b). The small initial fluctuation in Y_2 leads to a progressive amplification.

In a real system, instead of having two separate boxes, spatial effects occur in three dimensions, and the concentrations vary continuously throughout the system, rather than having simply two different values. The mathematical treatment is more complicated, and we shall not discuss it here. Let us simply describe some of the different possible organizations and structures which can arise from equations (15) taking into account the effect of diffusion. We obtain in this way the following differential equations:

$$\frac{\partial X}{\partial t} = A + X^2 Y - (B + 1)X + D \frac{\partial^2 X}{\partial r^2}$$

$$\frac{\partial Y}{\partial t} = B X - X^2 Y + D \frac{\partial^2 Y}{\partial r^2} ,$$

(17)

where D is the diffusion coefficient. We have supposed here that the diffusion occurs along a single geometrical direction, r. These equations always admit the stationary solution:

$$X = A , \quad Y = B/A ,$$

(18)

corresponding to uniformity throughout the system. However, for a range of values of the quantities A, B and the diffusion coefficient D, this is not the stable solution adopted by the system.

Several cases are possible:

(1) If the diffusion coefficients are very large, then the system will remain homogeneous, but can change from the stationary steady state to a sustained oscillation of the concentrations X and Y (Lefever and Nicolas, 1972). This type of behavior is known as that of a "limit cycle" and is illustrated in Fig. 19.

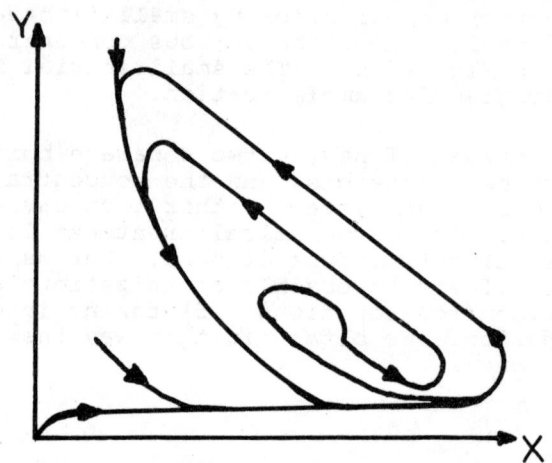

Fig. 19 - Stable, steady oscillations of the intermediates X and Y.

Whatever the initial state, the system tends to a single unique well-defined periodic solution imposed by the constraints. In this case we obtain what might be appropriately termed a chemical clock.

(2) If the diffusion is not sufficiently high, homogeneity may not be maintained by the system which then acquires a spatio-temporal organization corresponding to the propagation of concentration waves or stationary chemical waves (HerschKowitz-Kaufman and Nicolis, 1972), as in Fig. 20.

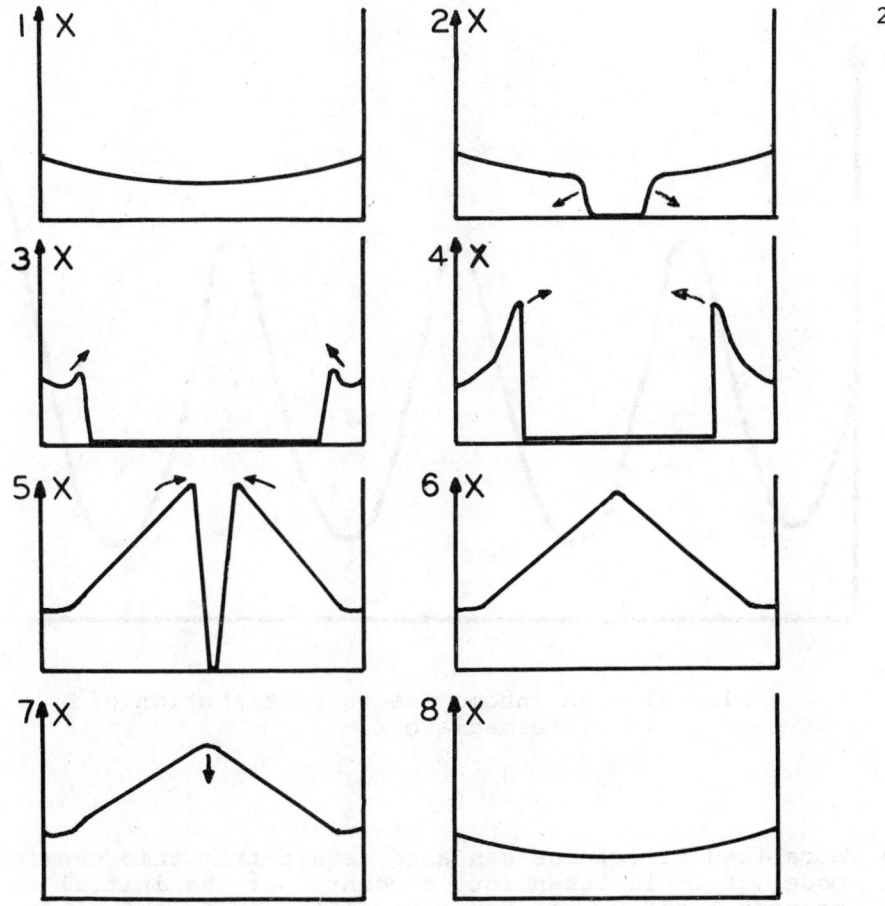

Fig. 20 - Repeated propagation of concentration waves as shown by the sequence of events 1-8.

(3) A third possibility is the appearance of a new stationary state in which X and Y are distributed inhomogeneously. Figure 21 shows an inhomogeneous distribution of X as a function of space.

A very interesting facet of this type of solution is the possibility of spontaneously generating polarity in a hitherto uniform system. This observation is of great importance to our understanding of morphogenesis, the appearance of form, for example, during the development of an embryo from an initially homogenous egg. When the uniform steady state becomes unstable, the "polarity" adopted by the system will depend on the perturbation that occurs within the system.

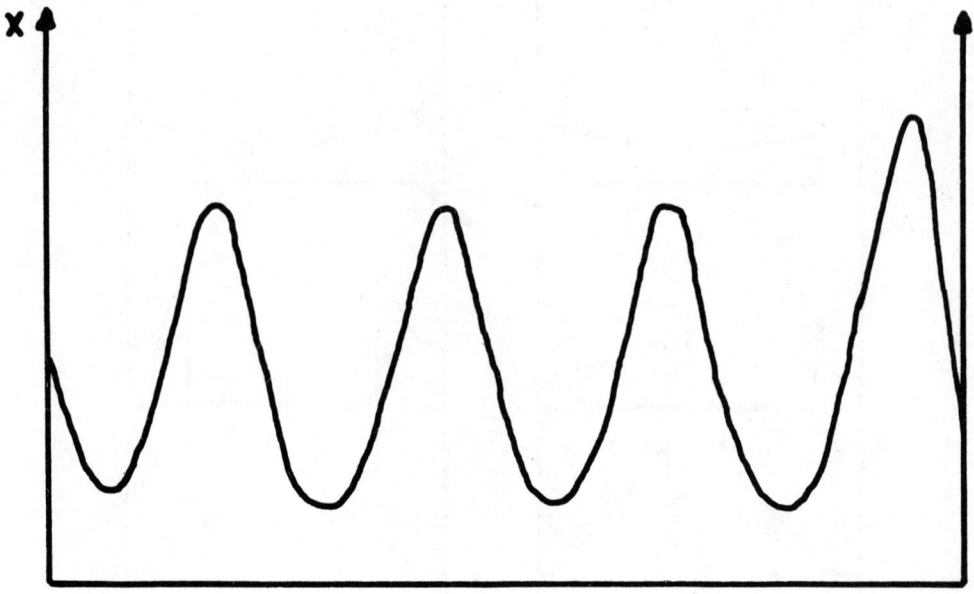

Fig. 21 - An inhomogeneous distribution of intermediate X.

(4) Localized structures can also result from this chemical model if it is taken into account that the initial substances A and B, see Equation (15'), must in fact diffuse through the system (Lefever, 1968a). The spatial distribution of these substances inside the system becomes non-uniform even if their values at the boundaries are maintained constant in time and uniform over the boundaries.

Figure 22 shows the type of stationary dissipative structure that can be obtained under these conditions beyond a critical point of instability. The spatial organization is in this case limited to a small region outside of which the distribution corresponds to the so-called "thermodynamic" solution (i.e., that which is valid for small linear perturbations from the equilibrium state).

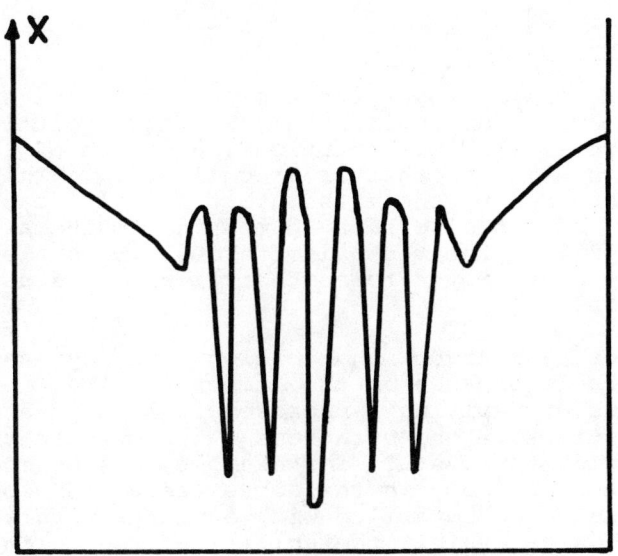

Fig. 22 - A dissipative structure possessing its own characteristic length scale.

Thus, dissipative structures can appear as a "totality" with dimensions imposed by their own underlying mechanism. Conversely, the dimensions of the system plan an essential role in the formation of dissipative structures. A sufficiently small system will always be dominated by the boundary conditions--the conditions imposed at the walls of the vessel. In order for the "nonlinearities" to be able to lead to a choice between various possible solutions, it is necessary to go beyond some critical spatial dimensions. Only then can the system acquire a degree of autonomy with respect to the outside world. The simple examples we have discussed do not by any means exhaust the great variety of behavior of dissipative structures. It should be noted that the examples have all referred to one-dimensional situations. Obviously, the wealth of structure increases greatly when two- or three-dimensional situations are considered.

In all cases dissipative structures are characterized by coherent behavior on a supermolecular level. This coherent behavior may manifest itself in the appearance of a time periodicity, as in a chemical clock, or in characteristic lengths, as in the situation of Fig. 22. In both cases the characteristic time (or length) is large with respect to molecular times (or size). It may typically correspond to a fraction of a second or to a millimeter, while characteristic molecular times and sizes would be 10^{-13} sec and 10^{-7} cms.

The study of this chemical model, and of others, has enabled the mathematics describing the behavior of dissipative structures to be developed and their properties explored. As the system is driven further away from equilibrium, a single solution can branch into several possible solutions, and each of these, in turn, may branch still further from equilibrium. This type of behavior is described by the mathematics of "bifurcations" or "catastrophes" and has also been termed the "mathematics of chaos" (Thom, 1972). The mechanism through which a system leaves one branch and moves to another will be discussed in the next section.

It has sometimes been argued that biology and physics would remain unreconcilable because of the "impossibility" on the basis of physical laws of deriving a macroscopic structure with its own characteristic size and with some autonomy with respect to the outside world. A crystal, for example, has neither characteristic size nor autonomy in the above sense. Biology, on the contrary, seems to be filled with entities with well-defined dimensions and which exhibit the ability of choice in their behavior. Our simple chemical model appears to provide us with a primitive version of such biological features.

Examples of dissipative structures are at present well known in both chemistry and physics. The so-called Belusov-Zhabotinski reaction (Zhabotinski, 1964) exhibits all the features we have described. Many other such oscillating reactions acting like chemical clocks have now been investigated. In physics the production of intense coherent light beams, as in lasers, provides us with another spectacular example of a dissipative structure (Haken, 1974). We shall, however, not go into any analysis of such self organization in physics and chemistry as we are particularly interested in this discussion in biological and social implications.

Let us consider, therefore, the link between the simple models we have mentioned on the one hand and biological structures and functions on the other. In other words, let us examine in what manner dissipative structures may be involved in living systems.

If we examine the fundamental reactions which take place in the living cell we find elaborate control mechanisms which ensure that the various vital chemical reactions take place at the correct rate and at the right moment. For instance, one type of control ensures that no excessive production of the energy-rich molecules such as ATP (Adenine Triphosphate) will occur. This occurs through a control of the rate at which a particular protein (enzyme) acts in the catalysation of some specific reaction. One of the best studied biochemical chains from this point of view is glycolysis, a process of great importance for the energetics of living cells. Experiments show that the concentrations of the chemicals participating in the reaction exhibit sustained time oscillations, with perfectly reproducible periods and amplitudes (Gerisch and Hess, 1974). A mathematical model, based on data concerning the reactions steps, can be constructed and the above experimental results can be identified

with oscillations of the limit cycle type which arise when the
stationary uniform state can no longer be sustained. In other
words glycolysis is a temporal dissipative structure (Goldbeter,
1975).

A second type of control mechanism in living cells affects the
rate of synthesis of various protein molecules within a cell.
Jacob and Monod have proposed several ingenious models for
this: either the products of the metabolic action of the enzymes act on the genetic material to inhibit the synthesis, or
the initial metabolites added to the medium have the effect of
switching on the action of part of the genetic material (Jacob
and Monod, 1961). Again, mathematical models may be constructed
for this process which show that the activated and inactivated
regimes correspond to two different branches of solutions and,
as we shall explain later, they are separated by an instability.

A number of other vital biological processes rely on the ability
of certain cell membranes to switch abruptly from a state of
low ionic permeability to an excited state of high permeability.
The former is a polarized state arising from the maintenance of
different ionic charge densities on the two sides. In the excited state, depolarization occurs almost instantly. This can
again be interpreted as an abrupt change of the solution of the
kinetic equations from one branch to another as a result of the
system being driven far from equilibrium by the charge density
(Blumental, et al, 1970).

An important remark in considering the role of dissipative
structures in the biological and social sciences is that the
equations governing growth, decay and interaction of biological
populations and social systems are very closely analogous to
those of chemical kinetics. The equations for the growth and
decay of an ecosystem containing a population of a predator
species Y and its prey X may serve to illustrate this point.
The classical model we shall now present is that associated
with the names of Volterra and Lotka (Lotka, 1956). The prey
population is supposed to multiply at a steady rate per individual in the absence of the predator as expressed mathematically by

$$\frac{dX}{dt} = k\,X \quad . \tag{19}$$

This equation corresponds to the autocatalytic reaction $A + X \rightarrow 2X$ considered before. We may visualize A as the food supply of
the prey X. However, we also have to take into account the
effect that the prey population X is diminished by the number of
prey captured by the predator per unit time. This is supposedly
proportional to the density of predator multiplied by that of the
prey and is similar to the probability of reaction $X + Y \rightarrow 2Y$.

As a result of the two processes we obtain for the prey the following equation:

$$\frac{dX}{dt} = kX - SXY \ . \tag{20}$$

The predator, on the other hand, has an individual death rate D per unit time, but his population increases because of the capture of prey. Again taking into account the above two processes we obtain

$$\frac{dY}{dt} = -DY + S'XY \ . \tag{21}$$

The strong resemblance to chemical systems prompts us to ask whether dissipative structures occur at this level of description of biological populations, causing self-organization similar to that which we have seen in chemical reactions.

The answer is affirmative and several examples have now been analyzed. Certain unicellular organisms exist in two forms of organization, either as isolated individuals or as aggregates in which a primitive form of cell differentiation is observed. The best studied group exhibiting this behavior are the slime molds belonging to the genus amoeba. Their aggregation is controlled by cyclic AMP (Adenosine Monophosphate) that is secreted by the cells. The initiation of the aggregation can be understood as occurring when the chemical attraction of the cyclic AMP overcomes the random diffusive motion of the amoeba (Keller and Segal, 1970). The uniformity of the spatial distribution of the amoeba becomes unstable at this point, and the amoeba move closer together and form an aggregate centered on some point where the first fluctuation of density happened to occur. This phenomenon, whereby a chemical released in the system attracts or repels a population of cells or organisms, is called chemotaxis.

Moving further up the biological scale of complexity, we come to the social insects. Among insects social organization attains a maximum complexity with the hymenoptera and the termites, and the survival of the individual is practically impossible outside the group. The regulation of castes, nest construction, formation of paths, and transport of material or of prey are different aspects of the organization reigning in the colony. Recently two of these aspects have been studied using the mathematical techniques developed above. For example, take path formation in the case of soldier ants. One may observe the collective movement of several thousand individuals and a macroscopic structure of pathways which has characteristics specific to each species (Wilson, 1971) as illustrated in Fig. 23.

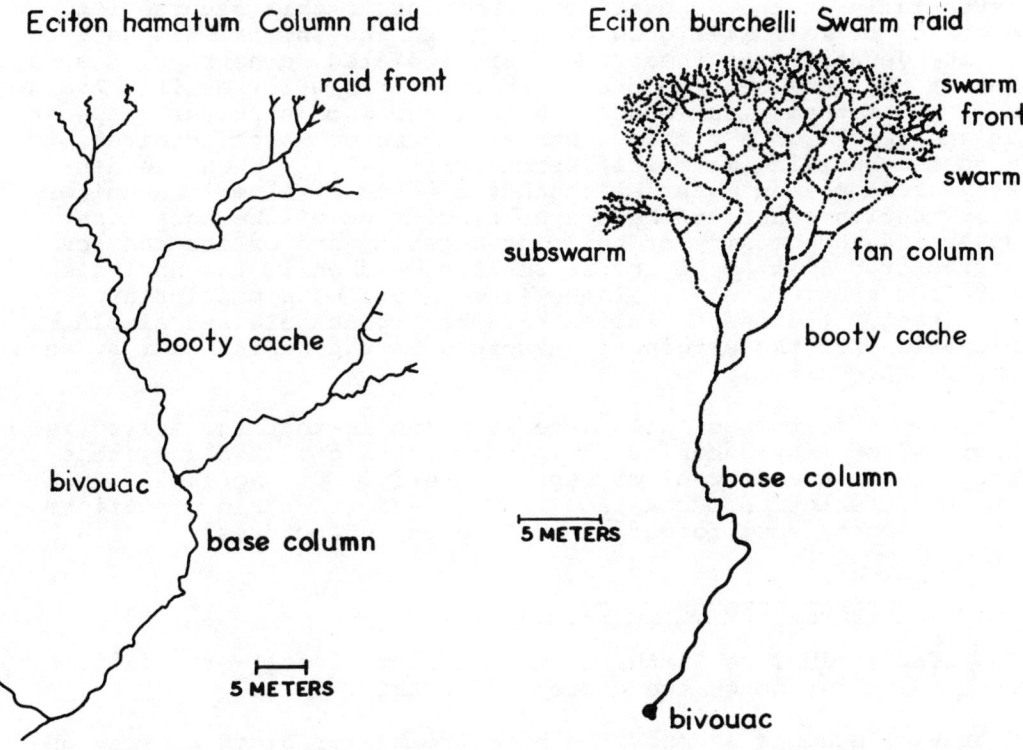

Fig. 23 - Two characteristic patterns of paths made by different species of ant (from E. O. Wilson).

Again, we find a "catalytic" element present which is the production by individuals of "pheromones" which are chemical attractors. A simple mathematical model shows that above a certain density of ants the solution corresponding to their uniform distribution in space becomes unstable and the colony will adopt an inhomogeneous angle-dependent stationary state whose branching structure depends on the particular properties of the individuals, and hence will be species specific (Deneubourg, communication).

A similar analysis can be made of the problems pertaining to the construction of a termite's nest. This occurs in two phases (Grassé, 1959). Firstly, there is an uncoordinated phase characterized by a random deposition of building material. However, when by chance one of these deposits becomes sufficiently large the second phase commences. The termites deposit material preferentially on the deposit corresponding to this fluctuation. A pillar or wall will grow depending on the initial disposition of the deposit. If these units are isolated, construction stops. But if they are near to one another an arch will result. Again, a simple mathematical model can show how such structures appear as the result of a simple chemical attractor which termites mix with the building material (Deneubourg, 1976). When the density of deposited material reaches a certain value, the uniform distribution ceases to be a stable solution of the equations governing the density of building material and of the chemical attractor. Spatial structure results, and while the analysis is far from predicting any of the fine detail of a particular termite nest, it does present an extremely plausible and simple explanation for the origin of structure in the nests built by such insect communities.

The common feature of all these examples is that the system is composed of many subunits in interaction and that the systems are open to the flow of matter and energy. The nonlinearities in the interaction mechanisms result, under certain conditions, in the spontaneous formation of coherent structures.

ORDER THROUGH FLUCTUATIONS

In order to analyze further the mechanism of self-organization, we have to introduce the concept of stability.

A trivial example is provided by a triangular block resting on a table. If we put a flat side down as the base, we have a stable state because if we rock the triangle slightly it returns to that original state. If, on the other hand, we attempt to balance the block on a point of the triangle, then although this is theoretically a possible equilibrium state, the tiniest perturbation will cause the triangle to leave the initial state and move to a stable one, namely, resting on a flat side (see Fig. 24).

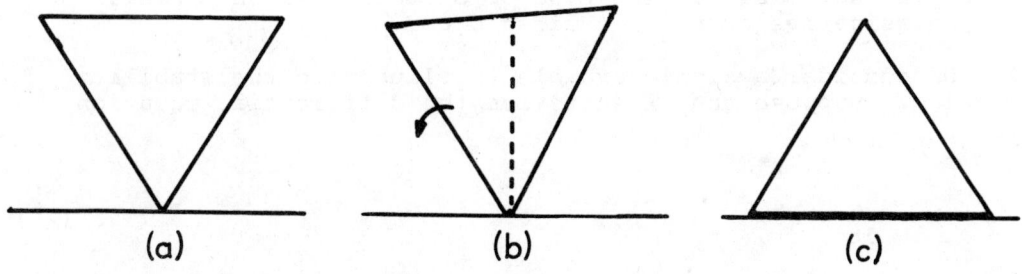

Fig. 24 - Block initially in unstable stationary state (a), moves to a stable state (c).

Now, in the systems we have discussed previously, which are made up of a multitude of subunits, any given state will always undergo small, local perturbations due to the random movement of these subunits. Thus, the stability of a given state is constantly being explored, and the persistence of any state therefore presupposes its stability. This molecular mechanism for probing instability is the occurrence of fluctuations.

In chemical systems near equilibrium, for example, the source of fluctuations of concentrations is molecular motion. As has been discussed, however, near equilibrium the system always moves to the state of minimum free energy, and this fact guarantees the stability of the state. Any small fluctuation will be counteracted by a response of the system which will bring it back to the state of minimum free energy.

Let us analyze the effect of small perturbations with respect to some given reference state. As the result of the assumption of small perturbations, the equations of change may be linearized. Such linear equations admit solutions of an exponential form

$$e^{\omega t}, \tag{22}$$

where ω is a "frequency" which may be complex, i.e., $\omega = \omega_1 + i \omega_2$. If we have m interacting units, we obtain m values of ω which are the roots of an m-th order equation (the so-called "secular" equation). Stability results if the real parts of the m roots are all negative or vanishing. The exponential solution which results from the perturbation (22) will die out in time or at least not increase. On the contrary, if one of the roots has a positive real part, the perturbation $e^{\omega t}$ will be amplified. This is the type of situation which prevails when dissipative structures first occur.

Let us consider a simple example to illustrate the stability problem. Suppose that x satisfies the differential equation

$$\frac{dx}{dt} = ax - bx^2 , \qquad (23)$$

where a and b are real numbers. There are two stationary states:

$$x° = 0$$
$$x° = a/b . \qquad (24)$$

For small perturbations from one of these stationary states, we obtain an exponential solution of the form (22) with the frequency (ω) given by

$$\omega = a - 2b\,x° . \qquad (25)$$

From this relation we see that the stability of state $x° = 0$ depends on the sign of a. It is stable when a is positive and unstable for a negative. On the contrary, the state $x° = a/b$ leads to $\omega = -a$. Thus it is stable for $a > 0$ and unstable for $a < 0$. A dissipative structure could arise at the state where stability changes into instability. In our example this would be for $a = 0$.

We have already stressed the close relation between stability and fluctuations. A dissipative structure can, indeed, be considered a giant fluctuation stabilized by exchanges of matter and energy.

This mechanism should be contrasted with Boltzmann's principle which is valid for equilibrium, where it is the situation corresponding to the maximum number of molecular complexions which determines the macroscopic features. In dissipative structures, on the contrary, the macroscopic order which arises after an instability is determined by the fastest growing fluctuation. This new type of order may therefore be termed "order through fluctuation." Let us illustrate these conditions using our previous examples. In the case of scheme (15'), p. 25, corresponding to the two box model, we see in Fig. 18 how a small fluctuation leads the system to an entirely new state with different concentrations of species X and Y in the two boxes. It takes a large disturbance, however, to change this new state which is stable to small fluctuations. Therefore, this system registers small fluctuations that occurred in the past and presents certain features which resemble a primitive memory. Behavior of this type has indeed been observed with "real" chemical reactions by Thomas and his coworkers (Thomas, 1975).

In all the biological examples given above, from glycolytic oscillations to the construction of termite nests, the mechanism of self organization is "order through fluctuation" whereby the undifferentiated uniform state becomes unstable to small deviations from uniformity.

The evolution of such systems consists of two stages. There is first the regime existing between instabilities, which is deterministic in the sense that equations such as those of chemical kinetics or population dynamics determine what happens to the variables of the system. Stage two, however, is the behavior of the system near instability. This is a "stochastic" or "chance" phenomenon, because the evolution of the system is decided by which fluctuation occurs first and drives the system to a new stable state.

This behavior can be summaried through the following scheme:

```
                    (deterministic)
         Function ═══════════════> Space-time Structure
  (e.g., chemical mechanism)
            ↖                        ↙
                  (stochastic)
                  Fluctuations
```

To use the language of social sciences, function can be viewed as being the "microstructure" of the system while the large scale spatial or spatiotemporal organization corresponds to a "macrostructure." A fluctuation leads to a local modification of the microstructure which, if the regulation mechanisms prove inadequate will change the macrostructure. This in turn determines the "spectrum" of the future fluctuations that may occur. Thus, we find here a natural expression of the idea that societies function as a machine - referring to the deterministic periods between instabilities, and society as being dominated by "critical events" (e.g., "great men") - which occur at the points of instability. Far from opposing "chance" and "necessity," we see that both aspects are essential in the description of nonlinear systems far from equilibrium.

It is only during the past few years that a quantitative study of fluctuations arising in such systems has really started and the results have been very interesting and surprising. In order to understand these new aspects of fluctuation theory, let us again consider a simple chemical example such as,

$$A \rightleftarrows X \rightleftarrows F \quad . \tag{26}$$

In agreement with our previous schemes, the chemical equation for X is (see section 3 of this paper)

$$\frac{dX}{dt} = A + F - 2X \quad , \tag{27}$$

where all the chemical kinetic rate constants have been taken equal to unity.

Now it should be understood that such equations are only valid as <u>averages</u>. In each volume element, the number of collisions fluctuates as does the number of particles A and X. To include the effect of fluctuations we have to go beyond the chemical equations, e.g., Equation (27), and study the probability distribution of the number of particles of type X. We denote this distribution function by P(X). In this simple case it can be shown that the steady state distribution is represented by a Poisson distribution

$$P(X) = \frac{\langle X \rangle^X e^{-\langle X \rangle}}{X!} \quad , \tag{28}$$

where $\langle X \rangle$ is the average number of molecules X as obtained from the chemical equation (27) in the steady state,

$$\langle X \rangle = \frac{A + F}{2} \quad . \tag{29}$$

The Poisson distribution appears in many problems of physics, chemistry and operations research. It may be applied, for example, to the number of independent telephone calls occurring in a given time interval of time. Its properties are well known. For example, in a Poisson distribution the mean square deviation from the average

$$\langle \delta x^2 \rangle \equiv \langle (x - \langle x \rangle)^2 \rangle$$

can be shown to be equal to the average, namely,

$$\langle \delta x^2 \rangle = \langle x \rangle . \tag{30}$$

Let us stress a few important consequences of this result:

1. The mean square deviation does not introduce any new parameters since it is identical to the macroscopic average $\langle x \rangle$;

2. Fluctuations are small in large systems as the calculated mean square fluctuation is given by

$$\frac{\sqrt{\langle \delta x^2 \rangle}}{\langle x \rangle} = \frac{1}{\sqrt{\langle x \rangle}} . \tag{31}$$

For large systems we may neglect the right hand side. This is one of the aspects of the celebrated law of large numbers.

The Poisson distribution implies a universal law for fluctuations since it applies to both large and small fluctuations. If we introduce the concentration $x = X/V$, the left hand side of Equation (31) becomes proportional to $1/V$. The Poisson distribution is of central importance in chemical kinetics as it applies to all equilibrium or near equilibrium situations whatever the complexity of the chemical reaction scheme.

What happens now for nonequilibrium situations where dissipative structures may occur? We may expect that the features we have emphasized will no longer be verified. Instead of being determined by the macroscopic state, fluctuations may now drive the average to a new value whenever the steady state is unstable. In this sense the law of large numbers has to break down. Moreover, the size of the fluctuation, i.e., its coherence length, now becomes essential. The probability distribution is markedly different for small and for large fluctuations. The situation becomes quite similar to that in the classical theory of the nucleation of a liquid drop in a supersaturated vapor. Below a critical size (called the size of an "embryo") a droplet is unstable, while beyond this size it grows and changes the vapor into a liquid (see Fig. 25).

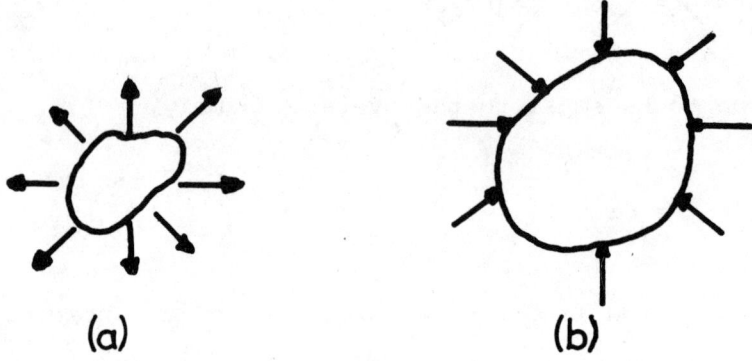

Fig. 25 - Nucleation of a liquid droplet in supersaturated vapor.
(a) droplet below the critical size
(b) droplet above the critical size

Such a nucleation effect appears also in the formation of any dissipative structure. Its appearance can be traced back to two antagonistic effects. Let us now consider a fluctuation in the volume element ΔV (see Fig. 26). The instability inside ΔV tends to amplify the fluctuation.

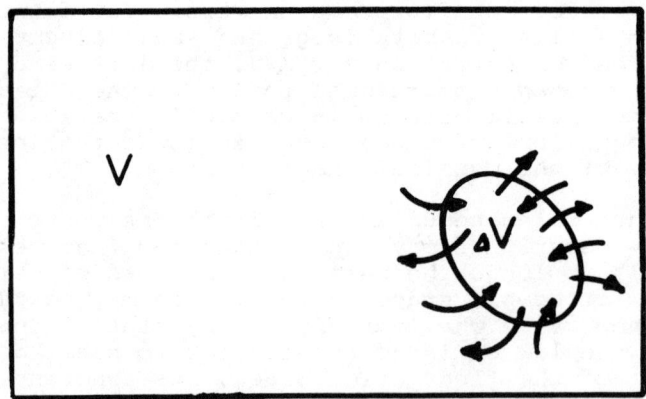

Fig 26 - The nucleation of a dissipative structure.

However, it is necessary also to consider the effect of the large outside environment in which fluctuations may be neglected. The outside world thus acts as a mean field which tends to damp the fluctuation through the interactions which occur on the boundaries of the fluctuating region. This is a very general result. In the case of small-size fluctuations, boundary effects will dominate and fluctuations will regress. On the contrary, for large-scale fluctuations, boundary effects become negligible. Between these limiting cases lies the actual size of nucleation. This is the reason why a general law of fluctuations independent of size, such as is given by a Poisson distribution, is no longer valid.

More details concerning this aspect of fluctuations can be found elsewhere (Nicolis, et al, 1974). We shall return to the importance of this result in the two last sections of this paper. Fluctuations and their growth or decay play an important role in the fascinating question of the existence of a limit to complexity. We return to this problem in Section 6 as well.

Let us now analyze more closely the types of fluctuations we may have to consider. This is a prerequisite for introducing the concept of structural stability which is basic to the evolution of ecosystems (studied in the next section).

The first type corresponds to fluctuations in composition as discussed in our examples of chemical systems. Similarly, depending on the problem considered, we may have fluctuations of temperature, pressure, densities, etc. Also, the parameters that we have supposed constant in our reaction schemes (i.e., the "given concentrations") may also fluctuate. In ecosystems containing biological populations, such fluctuations correspond to fluctuations of the environment. For example, we may consider fluctuations in the available resources, a problem of obvious importance in describing biological evolution.

A second important type of fluctuations is that relating to the "structural stability" of the system. As a simple illustration let us examine a simplified form of the Lotka-Volterra equations corresponding to the prey-predator competition:

$$\frac{dx}{dt} = by \; ; \qquad \frac{dy}{dt} = -bx \; . \tag{32}$$

In the (x,y) phase space, we have an infinite set of closed trajectories surrounding the origin (see Fig. 27).

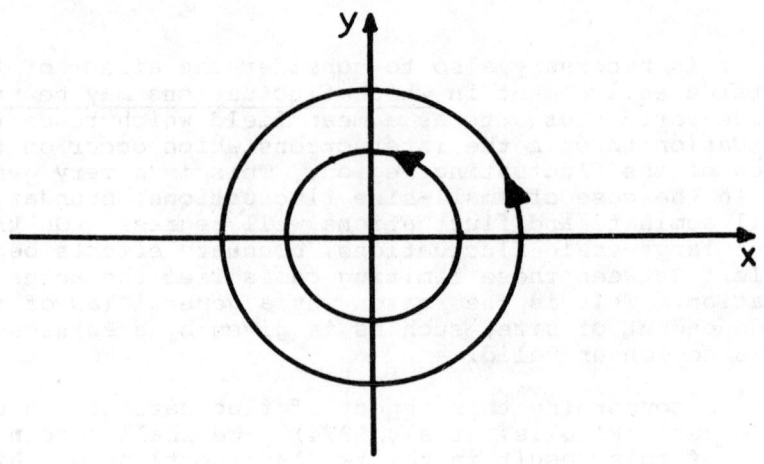

Fig. 27

(see main text)

Now compare the solution of equation (32) with those arising from the following equations:

$$\frac{dx}{dt} = by + ax \ ; \qquad \frac{dy}{dt} = -bx + ay \ . \qquad (33)$$

In this latter case, even for the smallest value of the parameter a, the point $x = 0$, $y = 0$ is asymptotically stable, being the end point toward which all trajectories in phase space converge as indicated in Fig. 28. By definition, equation (32) are termed "structurally unstable" with respect to "fluctuations" which alter slightly the mechanism of interaction between x and y and introduce terms, however small, or the type shown in equation (33).

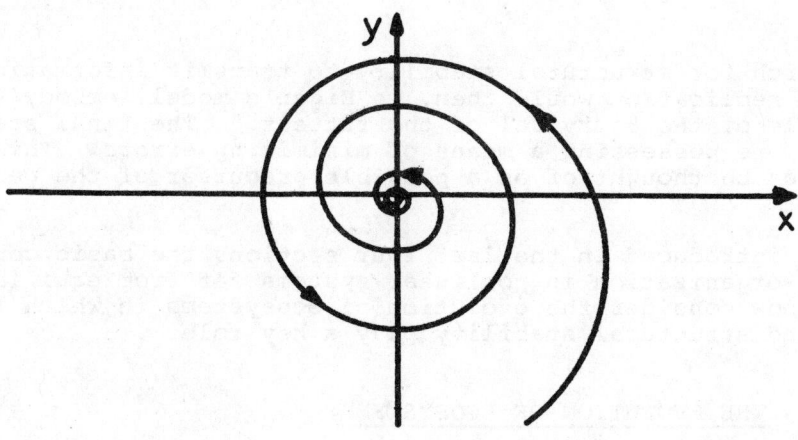

Fig. 28

(for interpretation, see main text)

This example may seem somewhat artificial, but consider a chemical scheme describing some polymerization process where polymers are constructed from molecules A and B which are pumped into the system. Suppose the polymer has the following molecular configuration:

ABABAB ...

Suppose the reactions producing this polymer are autocatalytic. Then, if an error occurs and a modified polymer appears such as

ABAABBABA ... ,

it may multiply in the system as a result of the modified autocatalytic mechanism. Eigen has presented a model containing these important features and has shown in simple cases that the system would evolve toward an optimum stability with respect to the occurrence of errors in the replication of polymers. His model is based on the idea of "cross-catalysis." Nucleotides produce proteins which in turn produce nucleotides (Eigen, 1971):

nucleotides ⇌ proteins .

The search for structural stability to transmit information for correct replication would then, in Eigen's model, embody the principle of the "survival of the fittest." The final state will be one possessing a means of minimizing errors. This property can be thought of as a possible precursor of the genetic code.

We have introduced in the last four sections the basic concepts of self-organization in nonlinear systems far from equilibrium. Let us now consider the evolution of ecosystems in which fluctuations and structural stability play a key role.

THE EVOLUTION OF ECOSYSTEMS

As we have remarked earlier, the equations describing the change of biological populations as a result of birth, death and interaction with other species are strikingly similar to the equations of chemical kinetics. The simplest equation representing the growth of species X, for example, is our "autocatalytic" equation (third section of this paper) corresponding to $A + X \rightarrow 2X$; A is the "food" which gives rise to X. This leads to equation (19) corresponding to exponential growth (see Fig. 29).

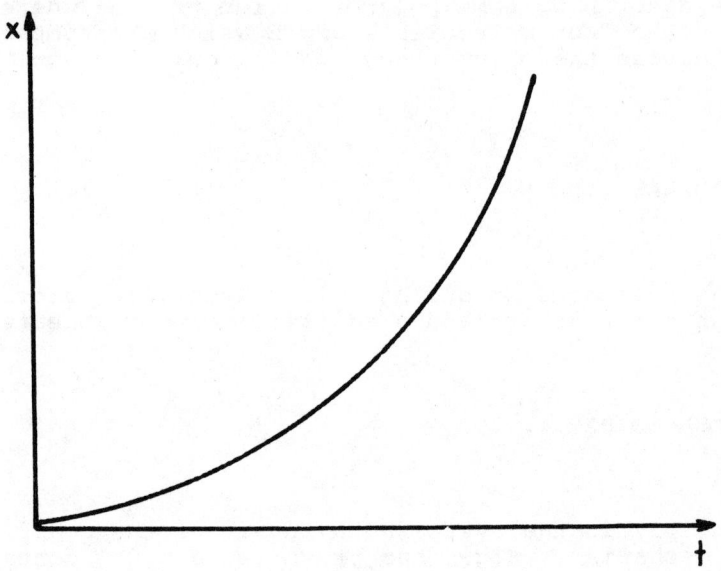

Fig. 29 - Exponential growth.

However, this equation supposes that the population could grow indefinitely, assuming that an infinite quantity of resources are available to permit this. In fact, in any actual ecosystem there is always a natural limit to growth, and we may link this to that of the first vital substance to become scarce in the system. The simplest growth law for the population x of a single species is then given by the so-called logistic equation:

$$\dot{x} = Kx(N - x) - dx ,* \tag{34}$$

where K and d are respectively the birth and death rate coefficients and N measures the saturation capacity of the medium. The quantity KN - d is often called the biotic potential (see Fig. 30).

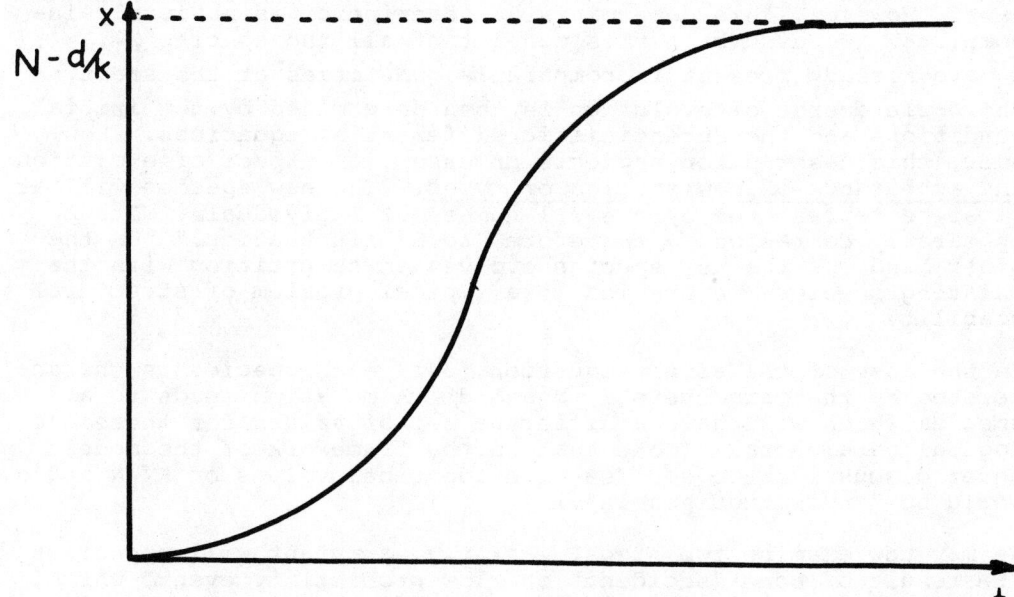

Fig. 30 - Limited growth.

Now, in order to model biological evolution we must take into account the following three factors: a) reproduction, b) selection, c) variation. The reproductive aspect is clearly represented, in an average sense, by our "autocatalytic" growth expression. Selection occurs because of the limit that has been placed on growth. For example, if we have three species i = k, 2 and 3 present initially, then

---

*The symbol $\dot{x}$ here and following replaces the standard form $\frac{dx}{dt}$ in order to avoid confusion with dx as the death rate.

$$\dot{x}_1 = K_1 x_1 (N - x_1 - x_2 - x_3) - d_1 x_1$$

$$\dot{x}_2 = K_2 x_2 (N - x_1 - x_2 - x_3) - d_2 x_2$$

$$\dot{x}_3 = K_3 x_3 (N - x_1 - x_2 - x_3) - d_3 x_3 \ . \tag{35}$$

Starting from any initial condition with various amounts of the species present, x_1, x_2 and x_3, the system will move to a state where the species with the largest value of K/d will be dominant. However, this deterministic description is obviously incomplete. We assume in this model that all the species x_1, x_2, x_3 are already present in comparable quantities at the start.

The whole course of evolution is then determined by the initial conditions and the deterministic differential equations. However, this description neglects an essential aspect of evolution: the appearance of new species or types. The new species will at first be represented by a small number of individuals. Its appearance corresponds, therefore, to a "fluctuation." On the other hand, as the new species evolves in competition with the existing species, we are led to a typical problem of structural stability.

In the case of the simple equation (34), each species is characterized by the parameters K, N and d. A mutation leads to a species which will have a different set of values for these ecological parameters. (Note that in the framework of the model under discussion two species with identical values of K, N and d would be "indistinguishable".)

We may now examine two steps. Firstly, a mutant will appear as the result of some "accident" or "low probability event" which, as we have mentioned, can be seen as a fluctuation in reproduction. Furthermore, chance continues to be all important while only a few such mutants exist since the time change of their numbers will obey stochastic dynamics: an individual either is born, lives or dies, he does not do a little of each! Here also the size of the fluctuation will play an important role.

The second stage starts, however, when and if a mutant manages to multiply sufficiently to constitute a "population" whose growth or decay can be described by an equation for the "average" behavior, which then adds to the macroscopic equations already existing. The question we now ask is: will the new population grow to some finite value or will it be rejected by the ecosystem? Again, we have the two aspects that we have discussed before – the arrival on the scene of "mutations" or "innovations" which are governed by chance, and the response of the system which is deterministic (Allen, 1975).

Let us examine in detail how the evolutionary process occurs in the most simple case of a single species in a system of limited resources. This situation is again described by

$$\dot{x}_1 = K_1 x_1 (N_1 - x_1) - d_1 x_1 . \tag{36}$$

The population moves toward the stable steady state, $x_1^o = N_1 - d_1/K_1$. This state represents a dynamic balance between the x_1 that are being born and those that are dying. However, suppose that by some "accident" one of the "x" born at a certain moment is different. Let us say an individual x_2 appears. After some time, perhaps there are a sufficient number of x_2 present to be able to describe their multiplication or decay by an equation such as:

$$\dot{x}_2 = K_2 x_2 (N_2 - x_2 - \beta x_1) - d_2 x_2 . \tag{37}$$

The species x_2 may have different values of the parameters K, N and d and in addition may exploit different food resources which can be expressed by introducing the factor β where $0 \leq \beta \leq 1$. If $\beta = 1$, the new species x_2 uses exactly the same resources as x_1, while for $\beta = 0$ they have no common resources. Partial overlap is expressed by β between zero and unity.

The new equations for the whole system are, instead of (36), the set:

$$\dot{x}_1 = K_1 x_1 (N_1 - x_1 - \beta x_2) - d_1 x_1 ,$$

$$\dot{x}_2 = K_2 x_2 (N_2 - x_2 - \beta x_1) - d_2 x_2 , \tag{38}$$

and the state existing at the moment that mutant appears is

$$x_1^o = N_1 - d_1/K_1 ; \quad x_2^o = 0 . \tag{39}$$

The response of the system to this small quantity of mutant is deterministic and can be calculated using exactly the same method as in Section 4 to establish the condition for a root of the secular equation to have a positive real part. This is then the condition for "growth," and for an evolutionary step to occur.

If,

$$N_2 - d_2/K_2 > \beta(N_1 - d_1/K_1) \ , \tag{40}$$

then the mutant will grow to some finite value and occupy a "niche" in the system. (A similar analysis can be made for a sexually reproducing diploid species resulting in similar trends.)

Several cases are possible. If the species x_2 is a mutant occupying exactly the same niche as x_1, then $\beta = 1$ and we find that x_2 grows if,

$$N_2 - d_2/k_2 > N_1 - d_1/K_1 \ , \tag{41}$$

and it completely replaces x_1. The total system moves to the stable steady state $x_1^\circ = 0$; $x_2^\circ = N_2 - d_2/K_2$. The species x_1 has become extinct. Successive mutations within the same niche will be rejected for values of "N - d/K" smaller than the pre-existing one and will replace that type if "N - d/K" is greater than the pre-existing one. We conclude that evolution will lead to the steadily growing exploitation of each niche and that the population carried by each band of resources will increase. Evolution than has the appearance exemplified in Fig. 31.

Another possible evolution is that the species x_2 may differ from x_1 in its choice of resources. In the case of the exploitation of an entirely different niche $\beta = 0$ and the condition for the growth of x_2 is given by

$$N_2 - d_2/K_2 > 0 \ . \tag{42}$$

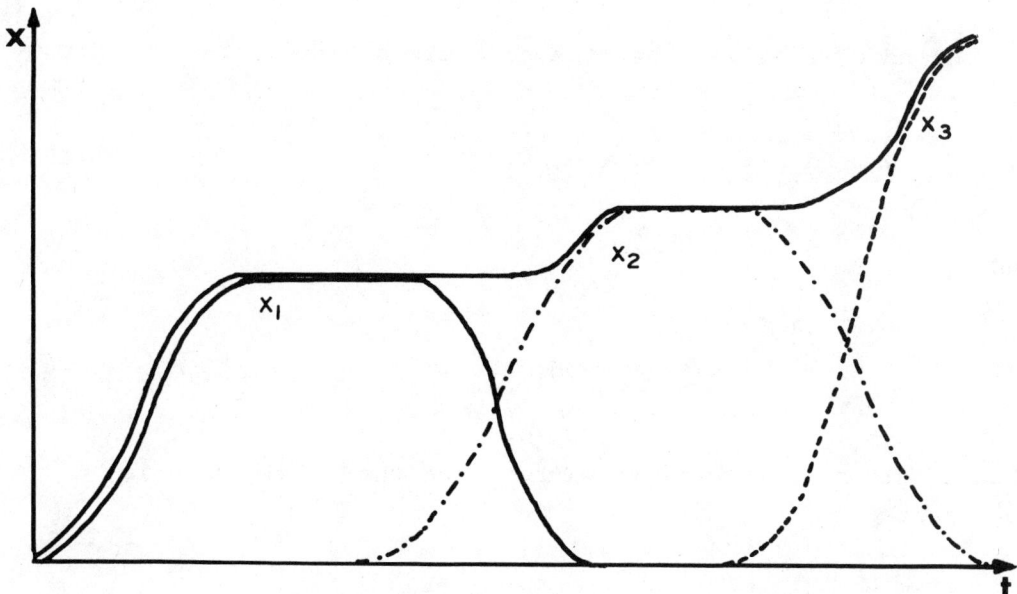

Fig. 31 - A niche occupied successively by species of increasing effectiveness.

Thus, if x_2 is viable in this niche it will grow to a steady population $x_2^° = N_2 - d_2/K_2$ and coexist with $x_1^° = N_1 - d_1/K_1$. We find again that evolution leads to a fuller exploitation of the medium. If we consider the intermediate case when there is an overlap of resources, we find two cases. If in addition to the condition

$$N_2 - d_2/K_2 > \beta(N_1 - d_1/K_1) , \tag{43}$$

we have

$$\beta(N_2 - d_2/K_2) > N_1 - d_1/K_1 , \tag{44}$$

then x_2 replaces x_1 and the final population is greater than the initial one $N_1 - d_1/K_1$.

The second case arises when the conditions are

$$N_2 - d_2/K_2 > \beta(N_1 - d_1/K_1) \quad , \tag{45}$$

and

$$\beta(N_2 - d_2/K_2) < N_1 - d_1/K_1 \quad , \tag{46}$$

Then x_2 grows, but coexists with x_1 and the final state is represented as

$$x_1^\circ = \left\{ N_1 - d_1/K_1 - \beta(N_2 - d_2/K_2) \right\} / (1 - \beta^2) \quad ,$$

$$x_2^\circ = \left\{ N_2 - d_2/K_2 - \beta(N_1 - d_1/K_1) \right\} / (1 - \beta^2) \quad , \tag{47}$$

with the total population given by

$$x_1^\circ + x_2^\circ = \left\{ N_1 - d_1/K_1 + N_2 - d_2/K_2 \right\} / (1 + \beta) > N_1 - d_1/K_1 \quad . \tag{48}$$

In summary, we find that if there is a certain "plasticity" of the "genetic" matter, there can only result a greater exploitation of the environment.

In this very simple system, evolution leads to the gradual filling of the available resource spectrum and to the increasing effectiveness of the exploitation of each resource. Of course, the above case has been chosen because it is especially simple. However, a mathematical criterion can be derived which is valid for the general case of n-interacting genotype populations which are perturbed by the arrival of small quantities of several mutant populations (Allen, 1976a). (Such a criterion is necessary when one considers genetic evolution since a single mutant allele may result in more than one mutant genotype.) Such considerations lead to an interpretation of the evolution of ecosystems in terms of a "dialogue" between fluctuations leading to innovations and the deterministic response of the interacting species already existing in the ecosystem. The basic aspect is the selective advantage which is introduced through the new values of the parameters (such as K, N, d) which enter into the equations describing the population dynamics. Note that the exact mechanism of fluctuations is left unspecified. Briefly speaking, Darwinism supposes an origin of fluctuations based on random genetic variation, which may certainly be appropriate for many aspects of biological evolution, while Lamarckism supposes a "learning" mechanism of the individuals trying to adapt to the environment. Socio-cultural evolution would seem to correspond more closely to this second type of interpretation.

However, the precise mechanism would play a central role if we would like to calculate the time scale of the evolution. The "Lamarckian" socio-cultural evolution has a time scale determined by the speed of "innovations" while the "Darwinian" evolution is obviously related to the fidelity and speed of replication of the genetic material.

It has often been stated that Darwin's "survival of the fittest" is a tautology. This is not true. However, the problem of the definition of the "fittest" can be obtained only through a suitable analysis of the type of population equations describing the ecosystem such as discussed above.

Let us now turn to a few additional examples. By refining our arguments, it is possible to determine whether a given environment will favor evolution toward species which exploit only a narrow band of the resource spectrum, i.e., "specialists," or favor species which exploit a wide range of resources, i.e., "generalists". In order to do this, it is necessary to describe the detailed dependence of the parameters K and N of a species on the various resources that are distributed throughout the system. Using arguments developed by Maynard-Smith (Maynard Smith, 1974) this dependence can be made explicit for the case where the resources consist of different types of particles scattered through the available space and replenished constantly. We shall not give the details of the calculation here but simply state the result. Systems rich in each resource (where each type of resource is thickly scattered) tend to favor the evolution of species exploiting only a narrow band of resource types - "specialists," whereas systems where each resource is thinly scattered evolve "generalist" species.

It is further possible to deduce how many species will be found occupying a fully evolved ecosystem with a given resource spectrum. The species packing is determined by the level of environmental fluctuation (May, 1973), and in particular by the amount and coherence of resource fluctuation. The greater the fluctuation the greater the niche separation must be for the long term coexistence of neighboring species. Knowing the niche width from our evolution theory, we can now say that ecosystems rich in resources and not suffering large fluctuations will have the greatest number of species. Environmental fluctuations will reduce this number. A system with sparsely scattered resources, if their densities do not fluctuate greatly, will be populated by "generalist" species with considerable niche overlap, while a poor system with fluctuating resources will be filled with a few "generalist" species (Allen, 1976b).

These results are born out in a very general sense by the change in the diversity of species from the pole to the equator. The solar energy spectrum lies in the same wavelength range everywhere, but what differs is the quantity of energy available at each wavelength. The diversity of flora and fauna increases markedly with decreasing latitude culminating in the extraordinary richness and diversity of the equatorial forests. In a detailed example of the distribution of finch species (Darwin's finches) on the Galapagos Islands, one finds results also in agreement with these predictions.

As we shall see, the question of the origin and regulation of the division of labor within insect colonies can be studied using these techniques. An important remark is that for evolutionary discussion, the "unit" which will be subject to selection is not the single ant or bee, but the collectivity - the colony. We find that the appearance of a division of labor, of "castes," within the insect society is the result of evolution of large colonies existing in a rich medium, where the relative numbers in each caste will be regulated by the action of chemical substances which repress or accelerate the formation of "soldiers," for example (Deneuberg and Allen).

The evolution of a predator-prey ecosystem, based on the equations of Lotka and Volterra, has also been studied. The prey evolves as we have described in our closed system and as is shown in Fig. 31 so as to exploit the available resources more efficiently. In addition, it evolves in such a way as to avoid capture and destruction by the predator. The predator, on the other hand, evolves so as to increase the frequency of capture of prey and to decrease its own death rate.

The resulting evolution of such a system is reminiscent of an "arms race" between predator and prey where successive improvements of the hunting techniques of the predator are countered by the improvements in the avoidance techniques of the prey. The second effect of evolution is a result of the increasing resource exploitation of the prey and the decreasing death rate of the predator. This situation can be described by the following equations:

$$\dot{x} = Kx(N - x) - sxy , \qquad x° = d/s$$

$$\dot{y} = - dy + sxy , \qquad y° = K/s(N - d/s) , \qquad (49)$$

and the ratio of predator to prey is given by

$$\frac{y°}{x°} = \frac{K}{d}(N - d/s) \quad .$$

The ratio of predator to prey increases slowly with evolution (see Fig. 32).

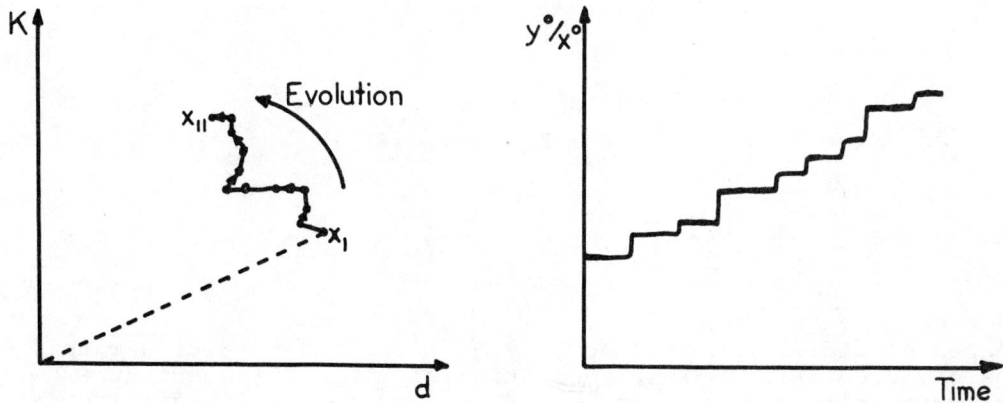

Fig. 32 - The effect of evolution on the predator-prey ecosystem of equations.

The evolutionary process favors the predator, because it 'uses' the prey to exploit the primary resources for it. Thus the evolution of the means by which the prey does this favors the predator just as the improvement of a tool favors the user.

We should like now to discuss a final example. In a previous example we studied the evolution due to changes in the parameters K, N and d which appear in equation (36). But, as we have said, different types of instabilities are possible. For example, let us study a system of equations such as

$$\dot{x}_i = K_i x_i (N - \sum_{i=1}^{n} \varepsilon_{ij} x_j) - d_i x_i \tag{50}$$

and suppose that x_i corresponds to the number of ants in a colony i, and in particular that ε_{ij} corresponds to the fraction of overlap of the territories exploited by colonies i and j. We assume, for the sake of simplicity, that $\varepsilon_{ij} = \varepsilon_{ji}$ and $\varepsilon_{ii} = 1$, $0 \le \varepsilon_{ij} \le 1$. Furthermore, if we suppose that initially all the ant colonies are of the same type and that the individual ants making up this type of colony are all identical, then we may study the evolution of the system resulting from the appearance of a new type of colony in which there exists a subdivision of the ants into soldiers Y and workers Z. The population dynamics would then be described by equations of the type:

$$\dot{x} = K\, x(N - x - Y - Z) - dx - \beta\, x\, Z \, , \tag{51a}$$

$$\dot{Y} = K'\, Y(N - x - Y - Z) - dY \, , \tag{51b}$$

$$\dot{Z} = K''\, Y(N - x - Y - Z) - dZ \, , \tag{51c}$$

where the undifferentiated colony of x is in competition with the differentiated colony consisting of Y,Z. The quantity $\beta x Z$ corresponds to the destruction of the undifferentiated colony x by the soldiers Z of the differentiated colony. Note also that in this model soldiers Z evolve from workers Y, see Equation (51c). The "fluctuation" we have to study corresponds to the appearance of polymorphism in the colony YZ. The stability of this fluctuation can be related both to the wealth of the environment exploited and to the mechanism by which the relative numbers of workers and soldiers are regulated in the differentiated colony (Deneuberg and Allen).

There is no limit to the type of fluctuations which may be considered, and no ecological equations can be structurally stable to all possible innovations. Because of this we have to expect a continuous diversification corresponding to this expansion into an area of "unused freedom" (Bateson, 1972). There is, therefore, no "end" to history; as some trends stop, other trends will start. As Starr and Rudman have observed in connection with technological evolution (Adams, 1975),

> An historical survey of the performance growth of specific technical options reveals two predominant characteristics. First, when the performance of a given type of device or system is plotted against time it follows a sigmoid curve

> .... The second... is that the overall growth of a specific technological field often exhibits in exponential pattern.

Comparing this remark with Fig. 31, we see that socio-cultural and biological evolution do indeed follow similar patterns. How far all this is from the closed universe of classical physics.

Since the advent of quantum mechanics, many attempts have been made to relate microscopic indeterminacy, i.e., the celebrated Heisenberg Uncertainty Principle, to macroscopic behavior. We now see that the situation is much simpler, for the macroscopic equations themselves contain the element of stochasticity which leads to "macroscopic indetermininacy." Problems such as self-organization in nonequilibrium systems require both aspects - the deterministic one where averages represent accurately the physical state of the system and the stochastic one which is important near bifurcation points and instabilities. It is the cooperation of these two features which leads to a faithful representation of some of the basic aspects of evolving systems.

REMARKS ON SOCIO-CULTURAL EVOLUTION

Arnold Toynbee has devoted his entire life to studying the forces which shape human history. It may, therefore, be appropriate to introduce this section with a quotation from his Study of History (Toynbee, 1946) in which he described his quest for a "positive factor" which would be responsible for the "differentiation of history." He writes

> In my search up to the present point, I have been experimenting with the play of soul-less forces--vis inertiae and race and environment--and I have been thinking in deterministic terms of cause and effect. Now that these maneuvers have ended, one after another, in my drawing blank, I am led to consider whether my successive failures may not point to some mistake in method. Perhaps I have fallen a victim to 'the apathetic fallacy' against which I sought to put myself on guard at the outset of my inquiry. Have I not erred in applying to historical thought, which is a study of living creatures, a scientific method of thought which has been devised for thinking about inanimate Nature? And have I not also erred further in treating the outcomes of encounters between persons as cases of the operation of cause-and-effect? The effect of a cause is inevitable, invariable and predictable. But the initiative that is taken by one or other of the live parties to an encounter is not a cause; it is a challenge. Its consequence is not an effect; it is a response. Challenge-and-response resembles cause-and-effect only in standing for a sequence of events. The character of the sequence is not the same. Unlike the effect of a cause, the response to a challenge is not predetermined, is not necessarily

uniform in all cases, and is therefore intrinsically unpredictable. I will now look at my problem with new eyes. I will see 'persons' where, so far, I have been seeing 'forces'. I will picture the relations between persons as being challenges to evoke responses, instead of causes that produce effects. I will follow Plato's lead: I will turn away from the formulae of science in order to hearken to the language of mythology."

The outcome of our discussion indicates that we no longer need to make the transition from "science" to "mythology." The mechanism of challenge and response may be incorporated into a scientific framework.

It is not our aim to present a detailed discussion of sociocultural evolution (such as is contained in Laszlo's text elsewhere in this volume). However, we wish to present a few simple remarks. We believe that the interplay between function ⇌ structure ⇌ fluctuation (see Section 4 of this paper) is basic to the understanding of social structures and of their evolution.

The very existence of complex systems, such as a tropical forest or a modern society, poses an interesting problem from the start. Is there a limit to complexity? The question has been discussed many times in the literature; an excellent presentation is given in a monograph by May (1973). The more elements that enter into interaction, the higher the degree of the secular equation determining the characteristic frequencies of the system (see Section 4) and the greater the chance, therefore, of having at least one positive root and hence instability.

Several authors have suggested that ecological evolution selects certain particular types of systems that are stable. It is nevertheless difficult to give a quantitative form to such a suggestion. Our approach leads to a different answer. A sufficiently complex system will generally be in a metastable state. The value of the threshold of metastability depends on the competition between growth and damping through "surface effects." Many complex systems are also systems in which the interactions with the surroundings (which in social problems correspond to such mechanisms as the flow of information) are also strong. Certainly, our present society is characterized both by a high degree of complexity and a rapid dissemination of information as compared to primitive societies. The question "Is there a limit to complexity?" may have a less clear cut answer than those that have been considered up to the present. According to our results, an important aspect of the answer would be that complexity is limited by stability which, in turn, is limited by the strength of the system-environment coupling. We cannot go into more detail here, but we see that the idea of "progress" or continuous increase of complexity is far from a simple one (Prigogine, et al, 1974).

Let us now turn to structural stability. Carneiro, following Herbert Spencer, has emphasized the difference between quantitative changes in culture and qualitative ones (Carniero, 1969). He distinguishes cultural development, in which new cultural traits are coming into being, from cultural growth. In our terminology, cultural development would correspond to instabilities in which stochastic effects play a basic role while cultural growth corresponds to "deterministic developments." Adams (1975) discusses in detail "vertical" and "horizontal" oscillations arising at points of cultural development.

As early as 1922, Lotka formulated his law of maximum energy flux. In thermodynamic terms, it corresponds to a law of increase of entropy production per individual. This law seems to agree with the laws of technological evolution. As Leroi-Gouran has written (Janne, 1963):

> In the technical domain the only features which will be transmitted are those which represent an improvement in the procedures. One may adopt a language which is less supple, a religion which is less developed, but one will never exchange a plough for a hoe.

The plough leads necessarily to an augmentation of the exploitation of natural resources and in consequence a greater energy consumption per individual. Lotka's law finds its natural interpretation in a succession of structural instabilities. Of course, there is no question of classifying societies according to a single criterion such as their energy or entropy production. This is merely one characteristic of the evolution, but a very important one because of its universality.

One should not forget that the difficulty of applying structural stability theory to human problems appears from the start. We have to determine the relevant variables. In some cases, such as problems concerning vehicular traffic flow, this is relatively simple. In other problems, however, one needs to introduce such elusive variables as "quality of life" which are much more difficult to handle in a quantitative manner.

In his recent essay *Energy And Structure*, R. Adams writes:

> ... man's particular relation to the environment is fundamentally similar to that of any other species, in that it is a continuing effort to exercise sufficient control to extract energy from the environment. Particularly typical of man, however, is his cultural mode of behavior which leads him to seek this security of control through constant redefinition of himself and his environment, permitting him to develop his society into an ever expanding system. The argument suggests that the constant expansion is inherent in man's energy using role within the thermodynamic system, that he is not doing anything particularly "unnatural" by virtue of his behavior! (Adams, 1975).

This is also our general conclusion. While sociocultural evolution has, of course, its own very specific characteristics, the recent advances of the natural and mathematical sciences point to the view that it is one of the many aspects of the evolution of our physical universe, in which nonlinear processes and nonequilibrium conditions play a significant role in self-organization.

ACKNOWLEDGMENTS

We wish to thank our colleagues at the Université Libre de Bruxelles; The Center for Statistical Mechanics, University of Texas at Austin; the General Motors Research Laboratories and the University of California, Berkeley; for many stimulating and valuable discussions. Among these at Brussels are Drs. A. Babloyantz, J.L. Deneubourg, P. Glansdorff, R. Lefever, G. Nicolis and Miss I. Stengers; at Austin Prof. R. Adams and Dr. J. Turner; at General Motors A.V. Butterworth and Dr. P.F. Chenea; and at Berkeley Prof. E. Jantsch.

REFERENCES

Adams, R.N., *Energy and Structure*, University of Texas Press, Austin and London, 1975.

Allen, P.M., *Bull. Math. Biol.* 37, 4,389 (1975).

Allen, P.M., To appear, (1976).

Allen, P.M., *Proc. Nat. Acad. Sci.* (U.S.A.) 73, 665 (1976).

Auchmuty, J.F.G. and G. Nicolis, *Bull. Math. Biol.* 37, 323 (1975).

Bateson, G. *Steps to an Ecology of Mind* Ballantine Books, New York, 1972.

Blumenthal, R., J.P. Changeux, R. Lefever, *J. of Membrane Biol.* 2, 351 (1970).

Boltzmann, L., *Weitere Studien uber das Warmegleich gewich unter Gasmoleculen*, Wien, Ber., 275, 1872.

Carneiro, R.L., *The Measurement of Cultural Development in the Ancient Near East and in Anglo-Saxon England*, Sec. 31, 8, 1013 1969.

Carnot, S. *Reflexions sur la Puissance Metries du Feu*, Bachelier, Paris 1824. Reprinted Dover, New York.

Clausius, R., *Ann. Phys.* 100, 353 (1857).

Darwin, C., *The Origin of Species*, John Murray, (1859). Republished Penguin Books, 1968.

Deneubourg, J.L. to appear, (1976).

Deneubourg, J.L., in *Order Through Fluctuation and the Social System*, Communication given by I. Prigogine at the College de France.

Deneubourg, J.L. and P.M. Allen, to appear.

Eigen, M., *Naturwissenschaften*, 58, 465 1975.

Gerisch, G. and B. Hess, *Proc. Nat. Acad. Sci.* U.S.A., 71, 2118 (1974).

Glansdorff, P. and I. Prigogine, *Structure, Stability and Fluctuations*, Wiley, Interscience, London, 1971.

Goldbeter, A., *Nature*, 253, 5492, 540 1975.

Grassé, P.O., *Insectes Sociaux* 6, 41 1959.

Haken, H., ed., Cooperative Effects, North Holland-Elsevier 1974.

Herschkowitz-Kaufman, M. and G. Nicolis, J. Chem. Phys. 56, 5, 1890 (1972).

Herschkowitz-Kaufman, M., Thèse de Doctorat, Université Libre de Bruxelles, 1973.

Jacob, F. and J. Monod, Cold Spring Harbor Symp. on Biol., (1961).

Keller, E.F. and L.A. Segal, J. Theor. Biol. 26, 399 (1970).

Lefever, R., Bull. Class. Sci., Acad. Roy. Belg. 54, 712 (1968a).

Lefever, R., J. Chem. Phys. 49, 11, 4977 (1968b).

Lefever, R. and J.L. Deneubourg, eds., Adv. in Chem. Phys. 29 (1975).

Lefever, R., and G. Nicolis, J. Theor. Biol. 30, 267 (1972).

Leroi-Gourhan, A., quoted from H. Janne, Le Systeme Social: Essai de Theorie Generale, Edit. Universite de Bruxelles, 315, 1964.

Lotka, A., Elements of Mathematical Biology, Dover, 1956.

Mahar, T.J. and B. Matkowski, SIAM, J. Appl. Math., in press.

Malek-Mansour, M. and G. Nicolis, J. Stat. Phys. B, 197 (1975a).

Malek-Mansour, M. and G. Nicolis, J. Stat. Phys. 13, 3 (1975b).

May, R.M., Model Ecosystems, Princeton University Press, Princeton 1964.

Maynard Smith, J., Models for Ecology, Cambridge University Press, Cambridge England, 1974.

Minorski, N., Non-Linear Oscillations, Van Nostrand, Princeton, 1962.

Monod, J., Le Hasard et la Necessite, Seuil, Paris, 1970.

Nicolis, G., M. Malek-Mansour, K. Kitihara and A. Van Nypelseer, Phys. Lett. 48A, 217 (1974).

Nicolis, G., and J.F.G. Auchmuty, Proc. Nat. Acad. Sci., U.S.A. 71, 2748 (1974).

Prigogine, I., Etude Thermodynamique des Phenomenes Irreversibles, Thèse 1945, Desoer, Liège, 1947.

Prigogine, I., Thermodynamique de la Vie, *Recherche* 3, 547 1972.

Prigogine, I., C. George, F. Henin and L. Rosenfled, *A Unified Formulation of Dynamics and Thermodynamics*, *Chemica Scripta*, 4 1973.

Prigogine, I., A. Grecos and C. George, *Proc. Nat. Acad. Sci.*, To be published.

Prigogine, I., G. Nicolis and A. Babloyantz, *Physics Today* 23, 11 & 12, 1972.

Prigogine, I., G. Nicolis, R. Herman and T. Lam, *Collective Phenomena*, 2 1974.

Prigogine, I., R. Lefever, J.S. Turner, and J.W. Turner, *Phys. Lett.* 317 (1975).

Sattinger, D., *Topics in Stability and Birfurcation Theory*, Springer-Verlag, Berlin 1973.

Smeach, S.C., and D.H.J. Gold, *J. Theor. Biol.* 51, 79 (1976).

Spencer, H., *Study of Sociology*, Paul Kegan, London, 1904.

Susman, M., *Growth and Development*, Prentice-Hall, New Jersey, 1964.

Thom, R., *Stabilité Structurelle et Morphogenèse*, Benjamin, Reading, Mass., 1972.

Thomas, D., *Adv. Chem. Phys.* 29, 113 (1975).

Toynbee, A., *A Study of History*, Revised and abridged by A. Toynbee and J. Caplan, Oxford University Press, 1972.

Wilson, E.O., *The Insect Societies*, Harvard University Press, Cambridge, Mass. 1971.

Zhabotinski, A.M. *Dokl. Akad. Nauk.* U.S.S.R. 157, 392 (1964).

THE HISTORICAL EVOLUTION OF MANKIND'S
   INNER AND OUTER DIMENSIONS

Alastair M. Taylor

OUTER CHANGES, INNER CHOICES

It is now generally accepted that the rate of change in contemporary societies is accelerating and, unless we learn to cope with it, may occasion some form of 'future shock'. But change from where to where? Can we find a perspective to throw light on the situation of mankind at present? Can we find a framework for thinking about the future?

The philosopher George Santayana has warned that "those who cannot remember the past are condemned to repeat it." Unhappily, we may not be able to repeat the past even should we forget our history, since our interventions in the natural processes of the biosphere could turn out to be irreversible: no return to the past would then be possible. Yet the past cannot be easily dismissed. History may not in fact repeat itself, but the processes underlying the long evolution of our species, and later of our societies, may find new exemplification in the events that we are witnessing at present and that await us in the future. If we do not want to set ourselves adrift on the seas of change, we should make use of our knowledge of the evolutionary processes that brought forth man and his technological societies as compass points by which to orient ourselves. The future may be open and unpredictable, but its options and probabilities need not be unknown. The dynamic of the processes which launch us on the road to the future can be understood and the opportunities they offer may be explored.

Here we present a broad historical framework for thinking about the future. We focus first on the changes brought about in the span of recorded history. Yet we recall that even recorded history is but a brief moment in the evolution of life on earth. If we telescope the age of our planet into a single year, making some five billion years equivalent to 12 months, we would find that the first eight months were probably devoid of life altogether. The next two months would be taken up with the simplest plant and animal forms. Not until the last week of December do any mammals appear - and only around 6 p.m. on December 31 would members of the genus <u>Homo</u>, our ancient predecessors, enter the global stage.* And how has mankind spent that brief allotment? By far the greatest length of time has been given over to making stone tools and surviving at the most primitive stage of subsistence - that of food-gathering and hunting. The revolutionary changeover from the nomadic seeker after food to the farmer who raised grain and domesticated animals would occur in the last ninety seconds before midnight on December 31st. And into the final minute must be crowded all of humanity's later accomplishments: the use of metal, the creation of civilizations, the mastery of the oceans, the harnessing of steam, then gas, electricity, and oil, and finally, in the last half-second, electronics, atomic energy, and space technology.

The metaphor of terrestrial evolution compressed into the span of one year underscores the remarkable acceleration of the rate of change in human affairs. Those changes are unprecedented both in their magnitude and in the problems which they are creating. Whereas some three million years were involved in producing the first billion people on earth, it now requires but approximately 15 years to produce another billion - every second of every day, the world's population increases by almost two more births than deaths, so that human numbers will be between five and six billions - or perhaps more - by the end of this century. This "population explosion" in contemporary times is paralleled by an exponential increase in the rate of travel, from the ten miles per hour average speed of horse and buggy at the end of the 19th century to six hundred miles per hour commercial jet speeds only seventy-five years later - and now supersonic speeds in turn. A further parallel to exponential rates of change is found in the area of communication. Here the spread of information has moved from the range of the human voice to the speed of mounted messengers in the span of most of recorded history, to explode from there to the simultaneous dissemination of many copies of documents in the 15th century (with the invention of movable type), to today's virtually instantaneous communication of information in image and sound through TV and radio waves that circle the globe at more than seven times per second.

Energy and raw material consumption has also risen exponentially. The United States alone has used up more resources since World War II than all the world's peoples in the whole of previous history. Spectacular growth rates in turn characterize Western Europe, the Soviet Union, and Japan.

Processes of exponential growth cannot continue indefinitely, unless all time, space, and physical constraints are removed. On earth, however, mankind lives on a finite planet where physical laws govern the range of possibilities. It is evident that there are 'outer limits' constraining the resources the

---

*In this calculation, 1 month equals about 417 million years; one hour equals just over 560 thousand years; one minute equals about 9341 years, and one second equals about 156 years.

earth can offer and the loads it can take.* As there are presently no practical possibilities for the colonization of other planets, we have to make do with our finite habitat. Never before has mankind approached so close to planetary limits; in this regard the contemporary situation is historically unprecedented. Even if in earlier times the physical environment produced seemingly absolute constraints, for example, in space, water, sunlight and other forms of energy, and human settlements had to limit their growth in the corresponding respects, there were always other places to settle, with more resources and often a more generous environment. Today, almost all habitable land areas are already settled, and the population, if it grows, cannot greely move to new areas. It must inevitably become denser in those areas it already inhabits. The greater part of the natural resources of the earth are taken into account in the calculation of contemporary rates of usage, and it is known that within the next century most of the presently required fossil fuels, minerals and ores will be all but exhausted. Even the amount of heat generated by modern technological societies is subject to physical constraints: beyond critical thresholds the climate becomes modified; beyond further thresholds the environing natural ecosystems become disturbed and many species risk extinction; and beyond still further thresholds the amount of heat the atmosphere of the earth can absorb and radiate into space is surpassed, temperatures mount, and the human species itself then faces extinction.

Physical constraints do not mean absolute limits: often they are relative to human wisdom and ingenuity. Whether the earth can feed and support five or fifty billion people depends on the technology and management of agriculture and the resources necessary for essential services. Whether 20 or 200 people can live per square kilometer, and whether they live at a level of major deprivation or in comfort, likewise depends on the use and management of the available resources. The water of the sea can serve as a source of energy in nuclear fusion technology; it can also serve as a source of drinking water through large-scale (likewise nuclear) desalination processes. The desert can be irrigated, the oceans harvested, alternative raw materials developed--the scope of human ingenuity opens wide new vistas.

Our planetary situation is not without constraints, yet these remain relative to our capabilities to manage our wants and demands within the scope of our technologies. To be effective with respect to the constraints of the planetary environment, and to distribute equitably the benefits which this environment can confer on human beings, we must adjust our wants and demands to the limits of possibility and to the requirements of justice and well-being.

The contemporary condition of humankind calls for a creative updating and enlargement of the goals, values, and beliefs which

---

*See Chapter 5 for details.

presently guide the behavior of individuals and societies. The
'outer dimension' of sociocultural existence changes rapidly but
still offers a wide spectrum of possibilities; the choice among
them will be made by the forces that emerge in the interplay of
the diverse factors of man's inner dimension.

Belief, values, and goals have seldom if ever played such a critical role in the determination of man's destiny as they do today. The inner dimension has always acted on the outer, and
maintained or further evolved its processes. However, only in
periods of social tranformation were values and goals crucial
elements in determining the future. At times when new ideas
spread rapidly, and established values and institutions lost
their hold over man's mind, the direction of change could be
quickly and decisively influenced by the substance of the ideas.

Such is the case today. Traditional values are questioned;
established institutions unsettled. There is a widespread feeling of lack of direction combined with a wide-ranging search for
ideas of relevance, new and old. And there is also a tremendous
superstructure of technology that is capable of implementing a
wider variety of futures than man has ever dreamed of heretofore.

The inner dimension of contemporary societies - the beliefs,
values, and goals of people in our diverse nations and cultures -
can decide the shape of things to come. It will effect a choice
among the possibilities offered to us in the welter of rapid
changes in the outer dimension of agricultural, industrial, economic, and ecologic processes.

Let us now place the relation of the inner to the outer dimension in historical context and get a clearer view of how past
societies have coped with the problems confronting them. We may
gain new insights into how our societies could master contemporary problems through creative innovations in the goals and
values of their own inner dimensions.

FROM TRIBAL BANDS TO MODERN NATION-STATES

In the course of history, humanity has come a long way, from
living in food-gathering bands to industrial national, and perhaps soon global, societies. Along this road we find the records of the transformations and development of the outer dimension of objective conditions and processes, as well as of the
inner dimension of subjective beliefs, values, and goals. The
two dimensions of social existence have constantly interacted.
The conditions and processes of societies invariably influence
the beliefs, values, and goals of their members, while the latter in turn affect the way societies manage their objective
conditions.

Any assessment of the contemporary situation of humankind must
therefore include both the outer and the inner dimensions. Beliefs, values, and aspirations which are unsuited to the conditions and processes of a society can misdirect the conduct of

human affairs and produce crises and even catastrophes. If not rectified, they can bring about the extinction of entire populations.

Our historical review is not intended as another 'grand theory' or interpretation of history, but as an illustration of the importance of meshing the two dimensions. A reexamination of sociocultural evolution in this perspective can throw new light on the problems we face today.

In the following sections, we offer brief analyses of five characteristic stages of human sociocultural evolution. These are not the only stages that one could distinguish, nor is the transition between them causal and deterministic. They illustrate, however, the ongoing mutual adaptation of processes and conditions with beliefs, values and goals in history, and hold important lessons for the present and the future. Although they admit of exceptions and ignore numerous detailed intermediary stages, the stages we distinguish form an evolutionary sequence and lead chronologically to the new age which we are entering at present. The stages are the following:

STAGE ONE: Earliest Food-Gathering Societies

STAGE TWO: Primitive Food-Purchasing Societies

STAGE THREE: Advanced Agricultural Societies

STAGE FOUR: Pre-Modern European Societies

STAGE FIVE: Modern Industrial Nation-States

STAGE ONE

Earliest Food-Gathering Societies: The Outer Dimension
Mankind existed at the historically first, food-gathering stage of social life and organization for some 99 percent of its more than three million years of existence. This comprises the Paleolithic age, where man was a hunter-fisherman equipped with a lithic (stone and flint) technology marked by structural simplicity, conservatism and endurance. This technology developed slowly in the direction of progressive specialization and miniaturization with the invention of microliths. But the capacity of our Paleolithic forebears to manage their environment was stringently curtailed by the toolmaking limitations inherent in flint and bone, the small amount of energy available, and by the fluctuations in food supplies available in a hunting-fishing economy.

Food-gathering societies were built into, and dependent upon, the natural ecosystems. These in turn formed local mosaics, with little physical interaction among those that lacked common boundaries. What people did in one environment had relatively little effect on what went on in another. Interactions were limited by the kinship system and by physical space, which was sparsely populated by small human groups.

People in food-gathering societies possessed the least effective technologies for the satisfaction of their needs and control of their environment. The traditional view that Paleolithic peoples had to struggle from dawn to dusk simply to survive must be modified. In favorable environments, men and women enjoyed considerable leisure time for recreation and enriching their lives esthetically. (This was the experience, for example, of a succession of Amerind habitations - stretching for some 8,000 years or more - recently studied in detail by archeologists in the lower Illinois River valley.) However, technological innovations occurred over an immense time-scale, within a societal organization that was basically simple, highly conservative, and resistant to change. Thus, sociocultural evolution was slow and undramatic in Paleolithic times, especially because of minimal contacts among different groups compared with those at later societal stages.

Hunting and foraging societies possessed relatively few available resources. Their dependence upon human muscles for energy was mitigated in time by the controlled use of fire. Yet they remained particularly vulnerable to environmental conditions over which they could exercise little or no control - including climatic changes (such as a sequence of four glaciations in the northern hemisphere and alterations in the rainfall patterns in the middle and lower latitudes), the vagaries of weather, and often a migrating and undependable food supply. These societies were largely nomadic yet had a well-defined sense of territoriality that delimited each group's space for hunting and foraging.

Given existing environmental and technological constraints, the resulting small size and low density of population required the organization of people into small <u>bands</u>, composed of from five to ten families, i.e., 20 to 50 individuals. Hunting-foraging band comprised independent nuclear family structures. These were of the simplest type, consisting of a co-habiting man and woman with their offspring. Its head was neither subject to the authority of his relatives nor economically dependent upon them. Various economic factors help account for the prevalence of the independent nuclear family. The limited food supply in a hunting economy discouraged supporting large numbers of persons, such as may be found in extended families (which included more than one nuclear or polygamous family). Nomadism required spatial movement on a broad scale, which militated against the larger extended family. It also limited the size and amount of the hunters' personal belongings.

<u>Earliest Food-Gathering Societies: The Inner Dimension</u>
Already in the simplest family structure and societal organization of food-gathering societies we find social ranking (as we do also among non-human primates). But whereas systems of social stratification in technologically sophisticated and politically complex societies are based upon groups, such as classes

and castes, in food-gathering societies status was associated with the individual. Social distinctions in a patrilineal band emphasized those of sex, generational status and age, and categories of kinship (whereby the father's relatives comprised one's "own" or intimate group, while the mother's relatives made up the "others" with whom more restrained and formal conduct was the rule).

In food-gathering societies this form of social ranking co-existed with basically egalitarian values and aspirations. A band had as its head a male relative who was regarded as first among equals. In such a relationship status conferred prestige rather than economic privilege or political power. What has been described as a "striking harmony" occurred between the kinship system and an egalitarian value system. The latter operated on the principle that all members of the group share its wealth because they are interrelated. In Paleolithic societies, all game killed belonged to the group and was shared among its members. However, the best portions would go by right to elders and medicine men.

Although members of a band lived in a basically egalitarian relationship, the individual was invariably subordinated to the collectivity into which he or she had been born. Each person remained subject to its social organization, its authority and patterns of behavior, its traditions and rites, and its relations with the seen world of sentient creatures and the unseen world of spirits and animistic forces. Private property was limited to privileges such as names, songs, dances, and membership in communal fellowships (sodalities), together with one's tools, weapons, and ornaments. The hunter's occupation, which required the acceptance of large risks with physical survival often in balance, generated self-reliance and initiative to a greater extent than was needed in societies which were food-producing and could store surpluses against contingencies. Such initiative did not extend into a self-assertiveness that divorced the individual from his obligations to the group, however, or denied the paramountcy of its claims and rights. It was the community that undertook major decisions for utilizing environmental resources and providing social services.

Food-gathering societies did not develop individualistic proprietary aspirations connected with the ownership of land. Rather, the use of areas for hunting or foraging was conceived as a right to be held in common. The community possessed a strong empathy with the natural environment as a result of its immediately perceived economic dependence and its mythic view of reality. Ecological viability was also optimized by the minimal capability of existing technology to alter the landscape or to thrown out of balance the biosphere's life-support systems. Opportunity was available for every member to engage in meaningful employment and to be assured an equitable allocation of goods and services, as well as risks. Peer recognition was provided on the basis of mores that related status and values to kinship, not property.

This minor extent and role of private property lessened the need for government and enforcement of order. Communalistic societies with a small population could get along with little or no formal government; they were essentially democratic, with the adults participating in group decisions. These concerned distributing food or other resources, protecting the group from hostile external activities, acting to ensure or restore order within the community, and to mete out justice.

Justice for primitive peoples meant maintaining equilibrium. Although private property was limited, theft could occur, thereby wronging the victim. Where modern legal procedure calls for punishment of the thief, in simple societies justice was achieved by compensation, that is, restoration of what has been stolen or its equivalent. Acts of murder comprised crimes which deprived the victim's kinsmen of his economic and social support and called not simply for revenge but for as complete a replacement as possible of what the murdered man represented to his family and the group. Acts considered dangerous to society as a whole required punishment by the entire community. These included treason, witchcraft, and incest. Such acts were not settled by compensation; punishment could be death.

Food-gathering societies required specialized skills in order to subsist. Survival from one generation to the next called for the transmission of skills for working in flint, bone, and antler, manufacturing tools, weapons, traps and nets, boats, and clothing, and training the young in the techniques of hunting, fishing, and foraging. Similarly, the arcane knowledge of the shaman and medicine man had to be transmitted to apprentices if society was to continue to employ magic as a technology designed to control environmental forces and maintain or restore balance and well-being among members of the community. Opportunities were made available for self-expression in dances and ceremonials, the sculpting of masks and other ritual gear, the carving of totem poles and other artifacts. (Probably the most famous examples of artistic expression among ancient food-gathering societies are the Paleolithic cave paintings, possessing both an aesthetic and a religious significance.)

Magic and religion colored primitive man's outlook and penetrated his environmental and social technologies. That he possessed a mythic view of reality should not be interpreted as meaning he turned his back on reality. In our empirical tradition, we approach nature in terms of the existence of things as determined by general laws. But the mythic approach views the world in dramatic terms; as a world of actions, forces, and conflicting powers. Things are not viewed as dead.

Where scientific thought generalizes on the basis of objective, i.e., quantitatively verifiable data, mythic thought is subjective, immediate, and personal. Lithic man attached importance to his physical as well as psychical states, and entertained no dualism between matter and spirit. He was not devoid of a sense of individuality, nor did he fail to distinguish between subject and object. He possessed a wealth of zoological and botanical knowledge that extended far beyond the realm of stone-age economic necessity. Such knowledge was acquired to satisfy intellecutal curiosity and provide a meaningful view of reality. Careful observations and experimentations were undertaken by lithic peoples in connection with the cultivation of plants and the domestication of animals - processes which could yield profitable returns only after many generations.

The mythic tradition was not a rudimentary form of subsequent societal traditions, but was complete in itself, independent, and fully articulated. Mythic thought was geared to the present tense, in the sense that reality was conceived to be existing or occurring now, rather than as having occurred yesterday, or at the beginning of the world. Therefore, it could always be "tapped." Hence, while lithic man could functionally differentiate subjects from objects at one level of reality (a man is not a wolf), man and wolf alike embodied for him a life-force which could be expressed as a single value: "It is." In the mythic view, man could identify himself with any or all aspects of the phenomenal world.

Within such a perspective, "cause" and "effect" were not impersonal, as with us; every event had an individual character. Rites and symbols were viewed not as distinct from that which they signify or evoke, but as vital embodiments of those things. They were designed to tap the universal reservoir of power which enabled the desired action to occur. Similarly, the shaman's magic sought to bring about sudden alterations in the man-environment relationship. But its purpose was not to upset the overall order of things but rather to correct imbalances which have occurred in society's relationship with the external world, or in the psyche of the individual himself.

Rites and incantations were repetitive, as was consistent with a world order that was not seen as temporally "progressing," but rather as ever-repeating. Social services, values and goals were geared to reflect and sustain this world-view. Food-gathering societies regarded themselves as integral parts of a world that is self-stabilizing and permanent. Their values and goals were appropriate to maximizing its viability and continuity by means of social conservation rather than material devotion.

STAGE TWO

Primitive Food-Producing Societies: The Outer Dimension
The Paleolithic Age gave way to the Neolithic with the domestication of certain wild grasses and animals around 7-8,000 B.C. So far as we know, this New Stone Age occurred first in the grasslands east of the Mediterranean. It was paralleled independently in the Pre-Columbian Americas. It represented a massive breakthrough in mankind's capacity to manage and exploit its

terrestrial habitat. No longer did all members of the species have to remain food-gathering hunters or fishermen; an ever-increasing number could become farmers or herdsmen capable of producing, and therefore controlling as never before, basic foodstuffs. This increased technological capability permitted people henceforth to "stay put," that is, to become sedentary. A more reliable and greater food-supply enabled a larger population to be supported, accompanied by new settlement patterns - such as the village node - and a more complex division of labor. To the traditional duties of obtaining animal food and tool-making, Neolithic men added the crafts of hewing wood and carpentry in order to build village shelters and set up wattled fences to keep the domesticated animals from straying. Women worked in the fields and also acquired the skills of the potter and weaver. The congregating of several scores or even hundreds of people in a village called for new patterns of social organization and activities, including village headmen or matriarchs, healers and priests or shamans to propitiate the local spirit and attempt to induce favorable weather for the farmers.

Neolithic villages were small and self-sufficient, with limited interactions among them. They were connected by trackways or waterways but they did not depend on the satisfaction of their basic needs on the transport of people, resources or goods between villages. They produced the food stuffs which still feed contemporary mankind, and they also invented clothing made from wool and the fibres of domestic plants. They tanned leather from the skins of herd animals, built houses of wood, clay and stone, and made clay pottery on the potter's wheel.

However, although contemporary societies still exist on the kind of foodstuffs grown by Neolithic peoples, there were great differences in methods of food production in early and later agricultural societies. Of the three major categories of food production - horticulture, pastoralism, and agriculture - the first two are much simpler in social structures and technology than the last. Horticultural societies gained a livelihood from the cultivation of plants; pastoral societies from the care of herds of domesticated animals. The transformation leading to them occurred in various parts of the world more or less independently, such as in Southeast Asia, Western Asia (including such sites as Jericho and Jarmo), and in Middle and South America. As Paleolithic societies eventually spread into all continents (save Antarctica) as well as into the northern high latitudes as far as glaciation would permit, so the Neolithic Revolution emanated from its original locations and extended into the higher latitudes of the northern hemisphere in the wake of the retreat of the fourth glaciation. In doing so, it penetrated long-held Paleolithic preserves and either transformed food-gathering societies through inter-breeding, or compelled them to seek new milieus which could yield a subsistence to their hunters and foragers, but were either marginal or wholly unsuitable to farmers and herders.

Horticulture, and to a lesser extend pastoralism, was accompanied by significant advances in related technologies. Neolithic tool-making produced the polished stone-axe, an efficient implement for clearing the forest to plant crops as well as to fell trees large enough to build houses and pens to enclose animals. The advent of fixed settlements, represented by the Neolithic village, was accompanied by, and encouraged, the invention of a number of crafts and other technologies associated with sedentary life: pottery, alcoholic beverages). These new activities called for a further differentiation in the division of labor, which continued to have a sexual basis. Males cleared the forest and brush, tended the livestock, and continued to be responsible for hunting and fighting. Females cultivated the clearings and performed the various household tasks.

The basic social unit became the clan; the village comprised the basic residential unit. A horticultural society was composed of a number of villages linked to one another by means of clans. The larger populations resulting from horticulture made possible the creation of lineages beyond those that had composed the hunting band. But it became difficult or impossible to remember exact biological or ancestral relationships; nevertheless, the fiction of kinship was maintained, and it ensured social solidarity. The members of the clan believed that they were descended from a common ancestor through either a patrilineal or matrilineal line of descent. A social innovation to provide stability and continuity, it was an appropriate organizational device to assist the transition from a nomadic to a sedentary way of life.

The Neolithic organizational evolution did not stop with clans: they were in turn subsumed within tribes which possessed both economic and political autonomy. They did not comprise a state form of political organization: economic and political activities were organized without recourse to a superordinate centralizing agency. This situation remained true even in the chiefdom, in which the economic, social and religious activities were better coordinated than in the tribe. Such coordination was performed independently by a number of centers, each of which remained an autonomous nucleus.

The social services offered in Neolithic societies occurred - as in Paleolithic societies - at the local level where kinship relationships, rights, and rules continued to dominate. Technological advances improved the chances of physical survival - and by adding to the human lifespan, increased also the number of elders in the society. Government by the elders remained fairly simple and unstratified. For the most part, decisions were taken by a village council on the basis of common consent. Where chiefdoms existed, the chiefs exercised more authority - often of a sacral character - but still within separate social groups. Communal order was maintained not by consciously formulated set of laws but by rules of custom. These could take the form of tabus, i.e., social norms that prohibited certain actions and held them punishable by the community, or by supernatural forces and spirits.

Primitive Food-Producing Societies: The Inner Dimension

In food-gathering societies the overall concept of reality was suffused with animism and magic. The changeover from a hunting and nomadic to a cultivating and sedentary way of life conserved some aspects of the mythic world view and altered others. Conserved were the interest in magic as a means to attain objectives. Likewise continued was the worship of fertility goddesses, known to us from many carved female figurines with markedly exaggerated sexual features. Earlier goddess figures were supplemented by carved phalli and effigies made of clay, stone and bone. Some of the finest examples of the cult of the earth goddess were found in the megalithic tombs of Malta. These were associated not only with the earth-oriented cult of a mother goddess but with the idea of rebirth - a concept compatible with a way of life in the horticultural society in which a static seed is buried, to reappear later in a new and living form.

Changes that occurred with the advent of Neolithic food-producing societies include a new interest in the sun and in seasonal variations. Since the cultivator, unlike the herder, has to be patient and wait hopefully for his harvest, such interest is not surprising. (It is surmised that Neolithic man's understanding of the movement of the sun and other celestial objects was relatively sophisticated: Stonehenge, for example, may have been both a religious center and an observatory.) Important changes occurred also with respect to aspirations to own land. Hunters in Paleolithic societies possessed a territorial sense and competed for hunting grounds, but their sense of possession did not extend to the concept of ownership. Private ownership by individuals or families did not evolve even in Neolithic societies, but the aspiration to possess land for cultivation appeared. Arable lands belonged to the village community, along with pastures, but specific plots were consigned to a given clan or family. Families aspired to own and cultivate the lands, and increased in numbers in order to posses more land. In addition to having direct offsprings, they could adopt children, add relatives and form extended families. Such aspirations, and the family structures entailed by them, survive to this day in numerous traditional societies.

The social revolution that accompanied the move to fixed settlements also affected the relationship between the sexes. Some scholars argue that clan organization favored matrilineal forms of society where land descended through the female line. In contrast, fixed settlements (of the kind found at the next stage of societal organization) weakened the clan system in favor of male individual ownership as practiced by patriarchal systems. In any case, women appeared to have enjoyed an optimal status in Neolithic times, given the existing way of life, its functions, and values.

Like their Paleolithic foraging predecessors, the Neolithic horticulturists and herders lived in societies that were basically egalitarian, communal in organization and values, and which subordinated the individual to group authority, traditions, and decision-making. They were again fundamentally conservative societies, where the Earth Mother was worshipped as generator of life from womb to tomb and womb again through rebirth, and where the supreme purpose and value of human life was to maintain the cyclic balances of the natural universe.

STAGE THREE

Advanced Agricultural Societies: The Outer Dimension
By about 3500 B.C., advances in territorial size and control, new forms of generating and using energy, the growing size of populations, and the larger dimensions of typical settlements produced major shifts in economic, social and political organization. The localization of populations in the valleys of several major rivers in Africa and Asia and in various areas in the Americas permitted the utilization of large amounts of water throught the invention of appropriate "hydraulic" technologies. Large-scale intensive farming meant a vast increase in the population which could be supported. This called for a corresponding increase in the complexity of social organization: the rise of political elites and bureaucratic structures; the creation of towns, and a shift in economic and political decision-making from the countryside to the new urban centers. A stage of development has been reached to which the term "civilization" can be applied.

Early advances in cultivation did not occur in areas of broad and uninterrupted expanses of arable land. Cultivation of Northern Europe's forested plains, Russia's steppes, and the American prairies came long after the development of small tracts of land in narrow river valleys and other natural enclosures. Plains and other unbroken expanses permit people to disperse, as population growth exerts pressure on the available resources. Low population densities do not encourage intensive cultivation. The latter requires an important geographical characteristic: the area of cultivable land must be circumscribed, keeping the population dependent on a non-expanding area of land. Elongated valleys, hemmed in and delimited by mountains or deserts, provided the constraints that motivated the shift from hunting and foraging lifeways to horticulture, and, where feasible, later to a still more intensive form of cultivation: agriculture.

The first truly agricultural societies in the Old World emerged in the narrow valleys of the Tigris-Euphrates, Nile, Indus, Ganges, Huang and Yang-tze rivers. Each fluvial environment was constrained and delimited by some combination of steppes, mountains, deserts, and ocean expanses. Its chief physical resources were rich alluvial soils and large amounts of seasonally generated water, which could be harnessed to benefit the land beyond the river banks. Since rainfall was not usually adequate to meet the needs of intensive cultivation, river waters were used in complex and often long-enduring irrigation schemes.

On the American continent, Pre-Columbian agricultural societies were not as dependent upon major river systems. Yet each one was sharply delimited by physiographical boundaries and circumscribed in the amount of cultivable arable land - and all depended upon irrigation to exist. In Peru, for example, Inca agriculture became the most intensified in the western hemisphere through the development in coastal valleys of irrigated fields that were heavily fertilized. Irrigation proved again to be an indispensable factor in the subsequent emergence of urban societies in the Valley of Mexico. A closed basin with a series of lakes on the bottom, the region required a highly sophisticated system of public works and water transport to become an economic and political entity.

In agriculture, the farmer is no longer dependent upon the hoe; he makes use of the plow to turn over the topsoil. This requires the power of draft animals. Whereas the Neolithic horticulturists engaged in slash-and-burn tactics, and abandoned their fields when the soil had become exhausted, the use of riverine plots and draft animals called for a more permanent type of existence, with new social relationships to ensure maximal use of the land not only during the growing and harvesting seasons, but in periods of fallow when the livestock was pastured on the stubble. New social relationships were required to organize an increasing population, capable of subsistance on equal areas of cultivated land. Studies have shown that whereas in a slash-and-burn system a community of one hundred families requires 1,200 cultivable hectares of land in order to exist, it can do so with only 650 hectares of fallowed land and calmil gardens, or 86 hectares of a mixed system of fallowing and irrigation, and, most economically of all, with but 37 to 70 hectares in a completely irrigated agriculture (Chinampas). In other words, where 1,200 hectares of cultivable land could support only one hundred families in the most primitive food-producing societies, the same amount of land could support as many as three thousand families in advanced agricultural societies.

Technological advances were not limited to improved methods of cultivation, but included the use of metals such as copper and bronze, new methods of the measurement of land and use of boundaries and maps, new forms of time-reckoning by means of calendars and other devices, invention of new writing materials and notational systems, greater diversification and use of prime movers (energy), and advances in astronomy, geometry and mathematics. Moreover, the fact that larger populations were living off the land through more sophisticated agricultural methods was a basic factor in the evolution of more complex social structures. In simpler societies, the basic social unit was organized according to kinship - and hence ancestral - relationships. In agricultural societies, traditional localized groupings, such as related nuclear families, remained. However, they served as foundation for more complex and stratified structures embodied in a new type of polity, the <u>state</u>. For a long time, traditional kinship groupings survived the superimposition of state structures, but underwent adaptive change in meaning and value through the elaboration of various specialized functions. Traditional kinship relationships provided a framework for the development, employment, and retention of the skills and attitudes of specialized craftsmanship; and they served as units of labor management for state services and projects, as well as for military service. Such transformation was a necessary concomitant of the emergence of the early forms of the state, which comprised not only a social "community" but also a delimited "territory," both under the centralized control of a single ruler.

The institutions of agricultural societies transformed the tribal circle of the more primitive food-producing communities into religious, political, and administrative hierarchies. The new institutions meant a different conception of social reality: it was no longer that of a circle based on kinship and participation, but that of a stratified pyramid. The beliefs, values and goals connected with the new mode of social organizations likewise underwent basic changes.

Advanced Agricultural Societies: The Inner Dimension
An essentially theocratic world-view developed in the archaic agricultural societies of both the Old and the New Worlds. Each of these societies developed its own view of reality with unique variations, but they shared a common basic characteristic: an explicitly formulated and socially institutionalized religion, which was the central social force. Whereas the basic belief systems of the earlier food-gathering and food-producing societies were telluric (arising from and directed toward, the earth), the orientation of the more advanced agricultural societies was celestial: directed toward the given religious conception of heaven or heavenly ruler. The Earth Mother has been subordinated to, and in some instances replaced by, "sky gods" whose advent was depicted in the pantheons of the archaic civilizations. This god-ship found its earthly counterpart in kingship. In various societies the ruler himself was considered divine; in others he represented a deity. But in all cases, human life was regarded as part of a widely spreading network of connections which reached beyond man-made communities into the hidden depths of the cosmos. The state itself was an earthly extension of the cosmic state; the latter alone was truly sovereign.

Kingship had its mandate from "on high," was expressed in terms of an unquestioning authority, and called for strongly centralized bureaucracies to administer the state and its laws - which for the first time had been formalized or even codified. In Egypt, the pharaoh possessed all the land, could decide when the fields should be sown, how the irrigation should proceed, and received the surplus from crops produced by laborers on huge royal estates. This surplus supported a large body of specialists - administrators, priest, scribes, artists, and artisans - who continuously worked in the service of the divine pharoah. The people's welfare was considered to rest on absolute fidelity to the ruler.

In Mesopotamia, the ruler was regarded not as divine but rather as the agent of the city-god who owned the city as a whole. In ancient India, the Rig Veda contains the earliest reference to the divine appointment of kings. The ruler had obligations both to the divine law and to his people, the paramount one being to provide them protection and to ensure that they remained in their respective classes or castes (which had divinely assigned appropriate social duties). The Indian social structure was hierarchical, fixed, and theocratically legitimized. In China, society and government centered since Shang times on the person of the Son of Heaven who later became omni-competent and was regarded as more than human in performing his multiple roles.

Several of these archaic civilizations endured for thousands of years. During their span of existence they underwent transformations in both structure and goals. We are concerned, however, with extracting from their basic world-views a number of common conceptual denominators which, taken together, form the "celestial" orientation typical of advanced agricultural societies.

1. In each of these societies a well-defined concept of "world-order" has evolved, which provided the society in question with a conceptual model capable of explaining its historical origins and justifying its continued existence.

2. The view of reality began with the emergence of "cosmos" (order) or of "chaos" (disorder). The process was fully reconceptualized; it did not build upon previous constructs of reality.

3. The male principle had primacy in the myths of creation. (This helps explain why the new cosmogonies could not continue to build simply upon earlier myths with their emphasis upon the earth mother principle.)

4. The female principle (which had of course to be recognized because of its indispensable role in the generative process) was embodied either in the form of minor atmospheric or terrestrial goddesses or as consorts of major (male) gods.

5. The cosmos was viewed as a "state," i.e., as an organic polity. It possessed both sovereignty and power which made possible the maintenance of cosmic order and harmony. The attributes of the cosmic "state" have been created by a supreme being

(a male deity); although subsequently the powers were thought to be wielded by other deities as well.

6. The cosmos was envisaged as hierarchical in structure and behavior; the supreme being was at the top, assisted by a pantheon of lesser divine beings.

7. Since the cosmos was thought to be a divine state, its governmental and social structure on earth assumed the form of a theocracy. Consequently, terrestrial kingship existed by divine fiat in order to embody and legitimize celestially-derived authority and power.

8. The exercise of authority and power was absolute and unidirectional: it proceeded from "on high," with no provision for feedback "from below."

Advanced agricultural states regularized economic activities and work habits, formalized norms of conduct, and institutionalized social behavior. They were paternalistic and absolute in their government, and placed strong emphasis upon "right order." In Egypt this was expressed in the concept of maat, which the Pharaoh was under obligation to maintain. Both nature and society were ruled by maat which stood for "right, truth, justice, cosmic order." In ancient Mesopotamia the gods had decreed justice as the order of society, and the ruler was expected to be just and persecute injustice wherever it occurred.

In India, supreme reality came to be viewed as Braham or Being, a vast undivided whole. The identity of man with the whole--of Atman with Brahman--was expressed by Dharma, a principle of all-pervasive and all-binding harmony holding sway over cosmos and human existence alike. Rita is the dimension of Dharma which stands for cosmic order, rightness and oughtness, and Dharma itself stands for goodness and duty. Rightness and goodness were also combined in the teachings of the Bhagavad Gita. The Vedanta philosophy fused a concept of reality with an ethics for human behavior, while later, in Buddhism, Mahayana ethics set forth the ideal of universal compassion and solicitude for all forms of life together with love, altruism and service to one's fellow humans.

While Vedantic and Buddhist humanism and ethics are grounded in metaphysics, in ancient China humanism and ethics were psychologically oriented and derived from the inherent nature of man and his relationship with his fellow man. Nevertheless, as in other archaic civilizations, the Chinese developed a concern for order on an all-encompassing scale.

The shared "celestial" orientation of these civilizations influenced their social organization. They reflected as a mirror-image the pyramidal structure which their members attributed to the supranatural world. As a hierarchy of beings was thought to exist in heaven, so on earth classes were stratified, and people regarded as unequal, by birth, occupation, and sex. The ruler's fiat applied to all, but there was one standard for the noble, sacredotal, and rich, another for the common and the poor. Nevertheless, as in food-gathering and primitive food-producing societies, earthly justice was designed to reflect and sustain a universal balance, and restore the order of society whenever disturbed. Hence in the law codes we find not only the <u>lex talionis</u> ("an eye for an eye"), but also what has later been called <u>noblesse oblige</u>, namely, that privilege begets obligations. The justice of the cosmic order demanded that the privileged few be given heavier punishment for wrong-doing than the masses of common people.

At the bottom of the social hierarchy were the slaves. Slavery was considered a socially acceptable institution. Given the organization of society and its distribution of labor, it was socially essential: human muscle power was the main energy source in the construction of massive public works. Enemies captured in war, as well as debtors who could not pay, were taken as slaves. Ownership extended to things and land, as well as to slaves. The ruler held possession of large tracts of land for his own use, and in principle all lands belonged to him. By bequest and mortmain, temple communities also acquired large holdings in perpetuity. The ruler further assigned grants of land to his nobles and those whom he desired to reward. Classes of landowners were thereby created that acquired hereditary and finally absolute rights.

The possession of property was but one manifestation of a new way of life, involving greater physical security and material comfort. It was reflected in lodging, dress and ornament, food and drink, and the amenities provided by the advent of urban centers. Architects designed temples, palace complexes, and processional avenues for the enactment of theocratic rites during sacred holidays. Sculptors depicted divine rulers, often in monumental proportions, while painters decorated temple walls and columns, and covered tomb interiors with pictures of the times. Craftsmen in wood, ivory, metal, precious stones, and perfumes practiced their skills and contributed to a way of life that materially had soared far beyond the capabilities of Paleolithic and Neolithic societies.

Social mobility was still restricted. Opportunities for advancement became available to the skilled craftsman and the boy fortunate enough to be sent to school for training in the priesthood or in public service. But for the great masses of people, hereditary lifeways could not be changed. Agricultural societies continued to be conservative, both with respect to the social order and the intellectual and spiritual horizons. The social order was assumed to have been divinely ordered, and its ruler carried an authority which was accepted to be complete and absolute.

The great archaic civilizations of the advanced agricultural stage persisted for upwards of five thousand years. Those situated in the valleys of the Nile and the Tigris-Euphrates were eventually subjected to powerful alien intrusions, which finally led to the shattering of the Pharaonic civilization by the Graeco-Roman states. Mesopotamia was fought over by innumerable armies, who came down upon the plains "like a wolf on the fold": Assyrians, Hittites, Persians, Mongols and others. They all but destroyed the civilization created by the Sumerians and revitalized by Sargon, Hammurabi and other great figures. In time, the societies of this civilization were assimilated in the culture of Islam.

Greater continuity was the historical experience of civilizations in South and East Asia. The massive populations of India and China have applied a river-based agriculture to the valleys of the Indus, the Ganges, the Huang-ho and the Yantze for upwards of five thousand years. Basic strands of these methods and their associated lifeways survive to this very day.

STAGE FOUR

Pre-Modern European Societies: The Outer Dimension
While archaic fluvial civilizations in the Old World were exploiting their riverine environments, significant developments took place elsewhere in the second millennium B.C. Indo-European speaking peoples fanned out over much of southern and western Eurasia: into the Indian sub-continent, Iran, and what is now western Russia and Europe. Differences in environmental conditions in turn led to differences in social organization. Riverine agriculture was called for a large measure of social centralization and direction, as we have seen, whereas rainfall agriculture could be pursued without massive central and bureaucratic control. The new environments encouraged the growth of locally self-reliant, multicentered societies. The newcomers were equipped with an iron technology, while around the rims of the Black, Baltic, and Mediterranean Seas they developed sea-going vessels which went with the rise of a number of maritime states, such as the Helladic, Hellenic, Hellenistic and Roman (while Semitic-speaking thalassocracies arose in Phoenicia and Carthage). Noteworthy among the pre-modern European societies which evolved in the first millennium B.C. were city-states in the Greek and Italian peninsulas. They heralded the presence of a fundamentally new stage in the evolution of human societies: the fourth in our assessment.*

---

*We are not claiming that alternative classifications are not possible, or that subsidiary stages could not be distinguished. We consider pre-modern European societies as Stage Four, due to their common European evolutionary sweep and basic structural and behavioral differences in relation to all other previous or contemporary types of society.

Agricultural communities equipped with Iron Age technology spread beyond the river valleys, into the mainland of the European continent. Whereas the Bronze-Age technologies of earlier agricultural societies permitted the plowing of lands only in light soils, the plowshares and other agricultural tools of the Iron Age enabled agriculturists to open the fertile heavy soils of Europe. As a consequence, the agricultural varieties of Hellenic Greece--vines, olives, certain species of grain-- spread to all new Greek settlements around the Mediterranean and the Black Sea. With them went various breeds of domesticated cattle, horses, and sheep.

The new settlements engaged in increasingly intense commerce and communication with one another. The Lydians invented coinage which revolutionized commerce as well as investment in agriculture and mining. The Phoenicians contributed to the building of ships for trade as well as war. They also developed an alphabet of 22 consonant symbols which, together with the subsequent introduction of vowel signs, created a simplified method of writing which increased the volume and speed of the transmission of information.

Geography directly influenced the character and activities of Greek civilization. The Greek peninsula's strongly indented coastline, rocky soil, and limited natural resources stimulated seagoing trade and the establishment of overseas colonies. At the same time the numerous mountain ranges which crisscross the peninsula hampered internal communications and encouraged the development of independent and autonomous political units. These were the city-states.

The _polis_, or city-state, comprised a city and its surrounding plains and valleys, ranged in size from 50 to 500 square miles, and had a relatively small population. The compact size of the city-state encouraged men to participate directly in politics (the word itself derives from _polis_). Four major types of government evolved: (1) monarchy of limited sort, like that described in the Homeric epics; (2) oligarchy (rule of the few), arising when the aristocratic council ousted the king and abolished or restricted the popular assembly; (3) tyranny, imposed by one man who rode to power on the discontent of the lower classes; and (4) democracy (rule of the people), occurring if and when the tyrant was deposed and the popular assembly was revived and made the chief organ of government. Democracy, however, did not represent the end stage. After dissatisfaction with democratic government became widespread, many of the city-states returned either to oligarchy or to one-man rule.

By 600 B.C., the use of coined money had created a new class of merchants. Various city-states, such as Athens, began to produce specialized wares - vases, metal goods, textiles, and wine - for export in exchange for foodstuffs and raw materials. Although growing economic interdependence in parts of the Mediterranean area called for political consensus and organization beyond that of separated and autonomous city-states, the

Greeks failed to create institutions to govern inter-<u>polis</u> relations. Instead, Athenian imperialism arose and warfare broke out in the fifth century between members of the Spartan League and the Athenian empire. The Peloponnesian War resulted in fratricidal, mutual destruction. It came to an end with the imposed unification of the Greeks by Philip of Macedon. His son Alexander, employing brilliant military strategy, created an empire extending briefly from the eastern Mediterranean to India. Seeking to establish "concord and partnership in the empire" between Asians and Westerners, Alexander blended both elements in his army and administration, founded scores of new cities, opened new trade routes, and minted a standard coinage. But an early death destroyed Alexander's plans to consummate the "marriage of Europe and Asia," and his empire was divided among successors controlling the African, Asian, and European segments. These segments constituted the Hellenistic world which struggled on until Rome's annexation of Egypt in 30 B.C.

The Romans succeeded in establishing a level of sociopolitical organization above that of individual city-states. Although they were indebted to the Greek genius for many innovations, the Romans possessed a high order of ingenuity themselves. Starting inauspiciously as a small city-state on the Tiber, Rome had to struggle for survival against powerful enemies. By developing a superb military and naval capability, the Romans acquired hegemony first over the western basin of the Mediterranean, then the eastern basin. They penetrated beyond the Alps into Europe, and eventually established an <u>imperium</u> that extended from Britannia to Mesopotamia.

Unlike Greek attempts at empire-building, the Roman world endured for many centuries. It was created by a synthesis of new technologies and innovative institutions. In addition to developing the legion with its great mobility and striking power, backed up by a military establishment unprecedented in its efficiency, the Romans laid down roads and aqueducts to facilitate not only troop movements but also trade. Built over a period of five centuries, the Roman communication system extended into every province of the empire, and its roads covered a distance 10 times that of the earth's circumference. By eliminating curves and cutting through hills, Roman highways made possible a speed of travel not surpassed until the early nineteenth century.

The Romans engineered spectacular aqueduct systems as well. That of Rome itself comprised 14 aqueducts stretching a total of 265 miles. It could deliver 50 gallons of water daily for each inhabitant. In addition, the Romans applied agricultural, surveying, and related technics to maximize agricultural development and the exploitation of their regions' resources.

Accompanying these physical advancements were remarkable innovations in the administration of the empire. Roman political and legal principles influenced the later phases of the evolution of pre-modern European societies and were carried over into modern societies as well. The Romans created and maintained a farflung imperium comprising upwards of one hundred million diverse people inhabiting more than one and a quarter million miles. The inhabitants of the empire, although rebelling from time to time, shared common institutions and lived under what Pliny the Elder termed the "immense majesty of the Roman peace."

But decline, destabilization, and destruction set in eventually - the "fall" of the Roman world-state in the West. Several factors were responsible: decline in economic productivity, progressive loss of administrative efficiency, mounting social dislocation and psychological tensions, and destabilizing pressures exerted by peoples pressing in upon the imperial perimeter. With the great movement of Germanic tribes, known as the Volkerwanderung, the Western half of the empire was shattered. The resulting transformation represented a "downward" shift from a highly complex to a simpler level of social organization. The advent of the so-called "Dark Ages" was marked by a diminution in population, the breakdown of the Roman road and communication systems, the decline and, in some cases, the disappearance of towns and their commerce, and the end of a central administration governing an empire. The center of gravity of society shifted from the cities to the countryside, and from the Mediterranean and its coastal lands across the Alps and a number of river systems in western and central Europe. A similar shift occurred with the fall in 1453 of the Byzantine ("East Roman") Empire, when the focal point of development shifted from Constantinople to the river networks of Russia.

The cultural landscape had been transformed. The disappearance of a unified political system resulted in geopolitical fragmentation and the gradual emergence of feudalism - a type of government by which political power is exercised locally by private individuals rather than by the agents of a centralized state. This was the characteristic political system of the ninth to eleventh centuries, and had its economic counterpart in manorialism. The feudal system provided protection for a fragmented, agrarian society; the manor, or large estate, provided the necessary food-stuffs. During this period, the major institution was the Church which alone penetrated into every parish and whose teachings and mission gave meaning and direction to medieval men and women.

The thousand years that elapsed between the fifth and fifteenth centuries were not static or "backward." The first part of this turbulent millennium crystallized a new pattern of decentralized feudal and manorial life, while maintaining western civilization against invaders from the north and east. By the eleventh century the West's resurgence had shifted to the offensive, laying the foundations for subsequent advances in technologies and institutions. A large number of inventions spread from eastern Asia to western Europe, including the wheelbarrow, iron-casting methods, paper, printing, gunpowder, the stern-post rudder, and the magnetic compass. Another major area of technological advance occurred in the use of prime movers. Our medieval ancestors succeeded in maximizing the muscle power of draft animals by improving their harness and traction, the latter by means of a new type of horseshoe. They also developed horizontal and vertical watermills as well as windmills with rotating turrets to catch the variable Westerly winds. These developments were part of what has been described as the "eotechnic" or "dawn" stage preceding the later Industrial Revolution. It initiated not only a progressive exploitation of water and wind as prime movers but a shift from complete dependence on tools to crude machines which did not require constant human manipulation and were driven by animal or natural energies.

Other important advances occurred in the latter half of the Middle Ages. The increased tractive power of animals enabled a heavy-wheeled plow to break the sod in the fertile but damp clay bottom-lands of Western Europe. Medieval farmers invented a three-field system of crop rotation to replace the older two-field system employed by the Romans. Europe's food supply increased, and consequently its population. It is estimated that in 1300 A.D. Western Europe's population reached a level of 50 to 60 million - a four or five-fold increase in five centuries.

Commerce revived along with urban life. By the 16th Century many towns arose, together with merchant and craft guilds. In Italy there was Venice, Florence, Verona and Genoa, among others; thriving city-states ruled by their own princes and conducting their economic and political affairs independently of one another. In England, France, and Spain, the monarchies gained new power and independence from the Church and laying the foundation of the nation-state system (which was to dominate the political organization of the Fifth Stage). The Catholic Church itself was fragmented by the rising tide of reformation which had its first great triumph when Luther nailed his 95 theses on the door of the Castle Church of Wittenberg in 1517.

In effect, European societies had now evolved to the point where their political interests, economic motivations, social attitudes, and intellectual endeavors could no longer be contained by the Church-dominated medieval feudal system. As we shall see, these processes led to the creation of a further stage of sociocultural organization, centered on secular modes of thought, private interest, and the spirit of inquiry. Their advent was propelled by the force of the emerging middle classes in Europe's increasingly populous and important commercial towns.

Pre-Modern European Societies: The Inner Dimension
The remarkable sequence of cultural change that took place in pre-modern European societies, starting with the first millenium B.C. and ending with the advent of the modern age in the 17th Century, laid the foundations of modern Western civilization. It did not constitute a uniform, linear development but showed many internal discontinuities, peaks, and valleys. We may encompass these vast processes under the common heading of the

inner dimension of pre-modern European societies when taking into account that each phase grew out of the one before it, and continued to build both by utilizing basic elements and adding its own innovations. Although great relapses occurred--such as in the early Middle Ages following the "fall" of Rome in the West--each phase in the sequence had something new to contribute and each laid the foundation for the phase that followed. Thus the classical Graeco-Roman civilization gave way to the Medieval world-view and its lifeways, but elements of it were preserved in the synthesis of classical learning and Christian doctrine. The Medieval perspective in turn gave way to an upsurge of diversity and humanism with the Renaissance, yet its elements survived and were assimilated with the new concepts. A common if varied conceptual thread ran through the history of European societies from classical antiquity to the dawn of the modern age.

<u>The classical phase</u>. Greek thought laid the foundations of science, philosophy, and many of the arts. In its complex evolution we may distinguish four stages. It is convenient to name these in reference to the kind of 'mind' which they represented; the orientation of Greek civilization was intensely intellectual and spiritual.

The first stage has been termed that of the <u>Heroic Mind</u>. It was the epoch of Homer and the epics. Epics showed men a world made bright by vivid perceptions, where men came to hand-grips with destiny, struggling to win a noble reward. In this world there was no clear-cut separation between the realm of men and the sphere of the gods. Traditional myths were interwined with keen observations of the perceived world and of the ambitions of contemporary people.

The second stage is that of the <u>Visionary Mind</u>. Its development reflects the firm establishment of city-states and their more complex society and outlook. Ordering thought plays a stronger part than before, but in this stage ideas were still infused with the play of the senses. This outlook emerged chiefly through poetry and drama, in the works of Pindar, Aeschylus and Sophocles.

After the Persian Wars, when Athens became the strongest city-state and was transformed from a traditional market-town to a metropolis, a new emphasis was laid upon social attitudes and ways of thought. This is the stage of the <u>Theoretical Mind</u>. Analytical powers came into play, looking beneath the visible surface. Typical of this cast of thinking was the historian Thucydides, who represents a far remove from Homer when he wrote: "Lack of the mythical may rob my work of charm. But if those find it useful who will wish to scan the exact character of past events - events that by reason of human nature will recur in life or analagous form - that will suffice."

The final stage, the <u>Rational Mind</u>, is encountered in the fourth century B.C. with Plato and Aristotle. It marks the triumph of concepts of rational order. To understand it we might single out four items: <u>logos</u>, <u>aretē</u>, <u>metron</u>, and <u>telos</u>. <u>Logos</u>, perhaps the most characteristic word in the Greek language, is traditionally translated as "word" but it also represented the Greeks' instrument for finding out what is true and just. The Greeks held that everything in the world has a <u>Logos</u>. Everything says something, means something, and it is up to men to understand. According to Plato, to reach truth or justice, men must engage in dialogue. Likewise Aristotle said that the <u>polis</u> exists so that men may "live well" and find the "good life." This was to be made possible by <u>logos</u>, through thinking, and discussing issues with one's fellows.

Man is not only a reasoning creature but also possesses a special worth or virtue (<u>aretē</u>). His nature finds fulfillment in certain ends, and to do so he must develop his <u>aretē</u>, or inborn capabilities, so far as he possible can. This calls for knowledge and the full development of the individual within a society. Among free men, <u>aretē</u> requires the recognition of virtue and worth in other persons, and it thereby calls into play the concepts of equity and social recognition. <u>Logos</u>, as order and reason responsible for everything in the cosmos, and <u>aretē</u>, as the worth of man as a creature capable of understanding the cosmos and of making rational decisions, represent a view of reality - and body of values - radically different from the theocratic, pyramidal views encountered in previous agricultural societies.

The third term, <u>metron</u>, means "measure." From the same Indo-European linguistic root came two words, the Sanskrit <u>maya</u> and Greek <u>metron</u>. They represent a parting of the ways between Eastern and Western approaches to the nature of reality. The Eastern route has been described as <u>philousia</u>, the study of essential Being. It concerns itself with pure Being and continuity, defying categorization and measurement. In contrast, the Greeks involved themselves in <u>philosophia</u> which called for an emphasis upon knowledge of the phenomenal world. Hence the central value of <u>metron</u>; the measure applied to the world of phenomena. When we combine <u>logos</u> and <u>metron</u>, we obtain a basic key to Greek, and subsequent Western, thinking: reason applied to a cosmos that is bascially measurable. The emphasis was upon quantification, logic, and the scientific method of observation and description (with little regard, however, to actual experimentation and testing).

The Greeks also sought to account for the nature of the world and man's role therein, and this search for explanation led them to look for cause and purpose (<u>telos</u>) in physical phenomena and human behavior alike. Thus, Aristotle argued that the explanation of a thing must answer all the queries comprehended under the question "why." He developed his theory of the four causes: material, formal, efficient, and final. For example, in the making a a pair of shoes, leather comprises the material cause; the pattern which the shoemaker has in mind constitutes the formal cause; while the efficient cause is represented by the shoemaker's acts which transform the raw material into the finished product. The protection of the foot is the final cause, the end or purpose (<u>telos</u>) for which the shoe was made. Aristotle assigned final causes to nature which implies that everything is governed by an indwelling form working toward a definite end. In other words, Aristotle and other thinkers regarded <u>telos</u> as an essential attribute of the Greek world-view.

The four concepts, <u>logos</u>, <u>aretē</u>, <u>metron</u>, and <u>telos</u>, gave a new status and worth to man in the scheme of things. He was seen as independent, possessing virtue and dignity, and the capacity by his reasoning powers to understand himself and the world around him in terms of causes and purpose.

The evolution of the Greek mind from its myth-infused early stages to its full-fledged analytical powers had a major impact on interpersonal relations in Greek society. Emphasis was placed on the independence of the group or polity, whose citizens were conceived to possess innate political and legal rights, held in common. The ruler of the <u>polis</u> was first among equals, much as the chief in primitive food-producing societies. However, the Greek ruler held office by consent and did not have hereditary rights. He was bound, together with all citizens, by the rule of law. Laws were to be promulgated, trial was to be by one's peers, and civil rights and duties were to be accepted. Individualism was to be carried over into the various strata of society: the farmers, merchants and artisans were to be their own masters.

These Hellenic principles were not always practised, or even practised very widely. The liberties and rights of the <u>polis</u> were enjoyed by men, not women, and by citizens, not slaves. The history of Greek government represents a tortuous and peril-infested struggle between tyranny and democracy. And the ideal of individualism was continuously vitiated by a failure to remember the rule of <u>Mēden Agan</u> - moderation - and to avoid the pitfalls of <u>hubris</u> - insolence or excess. Nor were the values of the <u>polis</u> easily exportable either to Hellenistic monarchies or the Roman world-state - where in the case of both Alexander and Augustus we find a reversion to the theocratic concept of divine kingship. Nevertheless, laws were to guarantee liberty; the Greeks saw that only law and liberty combined could be a worthy foundation of human life. It was upon this basis that the Romans in turn created their <u>Pax Romana</u>.

Roman political thinkers, such as Cicero, contributed germinal ideas which were influential for many centuries. These include the theory that government originates as a voluntary agreement among citizens; that all power ultimately resides with the people; and that law must be paramount in the administration of government. Roman law - together with English common law - is the basis for jurisprudence in most modern nations. Roman legal principles have also affected the development of canon law and provided the principles for international law. The evolution of this body of ideas paralleled the growth of the Roman empire and its inclusion of many non-Roman peoples and cultures. Adhering to the concept of equity and influenced by Stoic philosophy with its concept of a "law of nature" common to all men and knowable by human reason, Roman jurists humanized and rationalized Roman law to meet the needs of a world-state. In the 6th Century A.D. the enormous bulk of Roman laws was systematized and codified in volumes that permitted it to be preserved for posterity.

The medieval phase. The cultural heritage of the classical phase of the evolution of pre-modern European societies came to us through transformations caused by the "fall" of the Roman empire, the rise of Christianity, and the advent of feudal and manorial societies. The latter were spiritually, intellectually, and esthetically dominated by the Christian world view. Graeco-Roman civilization was largely human-oriented and secular in its pursuits. By contrast, the Middle Ages were God-oriented and with justification called the Age of Faith. The fundamental purpose of life was not the search for knowledge or the control of nature, but rather the salvation of the soul.

This shift in the inner dimension of the pre-Modern European societies of the early Middle Ages can be characterized by the opening lines of the Fourth Gospel: "In the beginning was the Word (logos), and the Word was with God, and the Word was God ... And the Word became flesh, and dwelt among us ... ." The concept of logos as reason and as cosmic ordering principle remained, but the creator of the universe was revealed to be a single, divine source. Logos has been incarnated - God made man. Whereas the Greeks employed logos and metron in the service of philosophia and the search for impersonal laws governing the cosmos and man himself, the Christian view of reality shifted perspective from an objective "It" to a subjective "Thou," i.e., from natural philosophy to revelation. We perceive the transition in the early Church Fathers, many of whom were intellectuals who had come to Christianity by way of Neoplatonism and Stoicism, and who argued that Greek philosophy and Christianity were compatible. Because both reason (logos) and truth derive from God, "philosophy was a preparation," wrote Clement of Alexandria, "paving the way towards perfection in Christ," the latest and highest manifestation of God's reason.

To synthesize reason and revelation was the objective of the medieval schoolmen. According to St. Thomas Aquinas, "Sacred doctrine makes use of human reason, not to prove faith but to make clear (manifestare) whatever else is set forth in this doctrine." The synthesis enabled man to comprehend a divine telos. To employ Aristotelian terms, it was made possible by Christ (the "formal cause") and His sacrifice acting as the "efficient cause," and by a "final cause," the act of salvation.

The marriage of reason and faith, of Aristotle and scripture, was part of a synthesis that perceived the universe holistically, as a divinely created summa. In it, both the spiritual and secular orders were sustained by the power of God, and human existence had no meaning except insofar as it reconciled the temporal

with the timeless; man with his maker. The medieval world-
order, depending upon a divinely-ordained unity, claimed an
inner coherence and harmony which theologians and priests were
to articulate. Its values reflected the attributes of God:
the will and authority of the Father, the love and wisdom of
the Son, and the activity of the Holy Ghost. The emphasis was
upon a world order to which the individual is subordinated; upon
overarching justice tempered with a recognition of the frail-
ities of the human condition and the necessity to be charitable;
upon a work ethic directed towards collective ends; and upon
self-discipline dedicated to the greater glory of God.

The renaissance phase. The internally consistent and encompass-
ing culture of medieval societies persisted in Europe until the
advent of the Renaissance. The latter - a cultural 'rebirth' as
its name implies - constituted another major shift in the inner
dimension of pre-modern European societies. The perspective
changed from that whereby medieval man viewed himself as part of
a world-order in which God and His commandments comprised the
standard, to one which did not dispute the primacy of God but
came increasingly to judge events and problems by means of human,
progressively secular yardsticks.

We can perceive this conceptual and cultural shift in Petrarch,
the "father of humanism." Petrarch always carried a copy of
Augustine's Confessions while he was at the same time seldom
without a volume of the works of Cicero. The desire to recon-
cile the Church's dogmas with the outlook of classical civilization resulted in the emergence in fifteenth century Florence
of a school of Christian Platonism. One of its members, Pico
della Mirandola, assigned to man a special place in God's creation. He attributed to God these words: "The other creatures
have a defined nature which is fixed within limits prescribed
by me. You, unhampered, may determine your own limits according to your own will, in whose power I have placed you. I have
set you in the center of the world; from there ... like a free
and sovereign artificer, you can fashion your own form out of
your own substance."

The Renaissance phase in the development of the culture of pre-
modern European societies constituted a return to greater consideration of this world, with man at the center and free reasoning as an important attribute. The classical concepts of
logos, aretē and metron acquired new meaning. Logos emerged in
the repudiation of the "Age of Faith" and the reinstatement of
empirical inquiry as the source of knowledge. Rational man was
seen as being endowed with a new intrinsic worth (aretē) as
Pico della Mirandola proclaimed. Metron came into renewed prominence in the attempts to determine not only the limits of man
but of nature as well. There was a new impetus to explore the
earth, to measure and map it by compass and new navigational
aids and cartographical techniques. The telescope and the micro-
scope, newly invented, were trained to explore the macrocosm as
well as the microcosm. Logos and metron were combined to lay
the foundations for the subsequent emergence of a secular method

of inquiry and systematization of knowledge: modern science. Arete was present in the culture as an inspiration to artists and architects, who sought to give a new expression of the worth of man in the context of the perfection of the universe. Vitruvius argued that as a well-built man fits with extended hands and feet exactly into the perfect geometrical figures of circle and square, so the harmony of the human body should be reflected in the proportions of temples. There was a belief in the correspondence of man and universe, of God and geometric symbols, and of the microcosm and the macrocosm. The all-encompassing God-created telos was retained.

As the perspective shifted from God to man and from belief to inquiry, so it shifted from the group to the individual. In place of the values associated with the Church, the community, the guild and the family, Renaissance thought substituted the value of the individual. There was renewed concern for independence and sovereignty, and for minimizing social constraints. By the end of the fifteenth century, the medieval ideal of universal political unity had been irreparably shattered. Italian city-states such as Venice, Milan, Florence, and Genoa had grown prosperous from their thriving industries, lucrative trade, and banking houses, while national monarchies had gained supremacy in Spain, France, and England. In theory sovereignty might still reside ultimately in God and His divine law, but in fact the theory of supreme authority had been arrogated to legitimate the pretensions and interests of secular rulers. The medieval concept of a universal or "catholic" church had been in turn fragmented into competing sects with the advent of the Reformation, and Protestant insistence that each man must become his own mediator with God. In the economic sphere, individualism was laying the foundations of both mercantilism and capitalism. The private ownership of property and the use of specialized techniques such as banking, credit, and insurance developed concomitantly with the rise of the middle class and the territorial state. And whereas medieval artists had largely labored anonymously on monumental projects such as cathedrals, the Renaissance artist and architect came into their own as individuals, to be recognized and assisted by wealthy patrons in turn.

In effect, the values of the Renaissance emphasized the status of the individual together with such concepts as independence and sovereignty. A Renaissance ideal of greatness was embodied in virtù, a term not to be confused with virtue but employed to characterize natural ability and abounding vitality. In this atomistic societal environment, competition and war were regarded as the normal state of human relations. Machiavelli reflected the spirit of his times when in The Prince he provided the audacious leader with a strategy for survival and conquest. This state of rapid yet chaotic flowering was the springboard from which Western civilization would propel itself to the next major stage of social evolution: that of the modern industrial nation-state.

STAGE FIVE

Modern Industrial Nation-States: The Outer Dimension
The leap into the next stage of social evolution was made with the help of an impressive series of rapid technological innovations. Among them three are particularly important in prompting the changeover from the pre-modern to the modern world. These are the invention of printing, the discovery of gunpowder, and the compass. As Francis Bacon pointed out in his Novum Organum, these three inventions (all of which, incidentally, originated in China) have changed the appearance and state of the whole world. They affected literature, warfare and navigation. The innumerable changes that derived from them transformed the character of European societies and influenced all others, no matter how removed they were from Europe in space and culture.

Following Gutenberg's first effective application of the technology of printing (Mainz, in the year 1447), a revolution was set in motion that affected all spheres of life through the increasingly rapid and standardized spread of ideas. The medieval scribe transcribed one book at a time by hand. The printer could henceforth use machines that reproduced the same information rapidly and in large quantities. Ideas could leap-frog from one locality to another, circumventing earlier barriers of time and space. Printed literature created more homogeneous societies, increased interaction among them, acted to centralize government, and strengthened the forces of nationalism. It laid the foundations for a mass society. At the same time, it encouraged the spread of education and contributed to the development of the individual. The many-faceted effects of printing contributed to the destabilization of traditional norms and concepts and brought Europe into the age of technologically impelled change.

The invention of gunpowder made the enforcement of order and waging of war more effective. The power of larger and wealthier societies over weaker neighbors increased, as did the control of ruling classes over the masses. The influence of powerful European societies has been magnified through the parallel invention of the magnetic compass. Although the attraction of lodestone for iron was known from antiquity, and the earliest work in the West on the compass appeared in 1256, it was in the 15th Century that sailors first made wide use of a needle that pivoted on a card marked with the main compass points. Other aids to navigation appeared in this period: sailing charts using the Mercator projection, methods for obtaining accurate soundings, and astronomical instruments such as the quadrant and the astrolabe. Thanks to the subsequent invention of the chronometer, latitudes as well as longitudes could be accurately determined.

Sailing ships were significantly improved. They were equipped with superior rigging and sails, improved steering devices such as the stern rudder, and had butt-jointed planking which permitted an increase in size. (By the year 1700 the wooden sailing ship could carry 2000 tons of cargo or over one hundred persons). Equipped with cannon and increasingly effective navigation aids, sailing ships traversed the oceans and inaugurated the Age of Discovery. Columbus pushed westward to the New World; de Gama rounded the Cape of Good Hope and reached the Indian sub-continent, and one of Magellan's ships circumnaviated the globe. In the wake of these mariners came the <u>conquistadores</u> to carve out vast overseas colonial empires as a technologically superior Europe proceeded to enforce its will upon other continents, and also acquire bullion from the New World and other valuable metals and commodities from the East. Thus the advent of the Oceanic Age in mankind's expanding control of its terrestrial environment is intimately associated with European hegemony, and the transplanting to the New World of its culture, languages, and human stock. Capitalism in turn had acquired inter-continental dimensions to the West's advantage, and the reinforcement of its traditional normative standards.

This oceanic and societal expansion had occurred when wind and water were the major energy sources. Then a technological leap occurred in the late eighteenth century when steam provided a new source of energy for ships as well as machines of production - and subsequently for land transportation. The "Industrial Revolution" which erupted on the world comprised three basic achievements: the replacement of hand-tools by machines; the invention of the steam engine; and the creation of the factory as a system of mass-production. The steam-engine was a mobile as well as new source of energy: it made industrialization possible in areas lacking wind- or water-power. It was perfected in the first half of the 19th century, when the theory of heat evolved into the science of thermodynamics. With it came the emergence of factories and factory towns, transforming both the natural and sociocultural landscapes.

By increasing the production of energy and using standardized interchangeable parts, the Industrial Revolution made available goods and services in unprecedented quantities. The result was a rapid increase in economic activity and the number of cities, the re-structuring of social relationships, and the transformation of living standards. The advent of steam made it possible not only to consolidate the oceanic stage of two-dimensional environmental control but to open the hinterlands of all the continents to the mass exploitation of raw resources and to mass settlement as well. Railroads intersected Europe, penetrated South America and Africa, and spanned the continents of North America, Australia, and Asia. This "conquest" of space was accompanied by the subjecting of space and time to precise measurement in the form of steamship and railroad timetables and the division of the globe into 24 one-hour time zones of 15 degrees each. In the medieval town, the church tower had struck the hours and provided the common time reference for the whole community. By the 19th century, the clock was ubiquitous and had also been miniaturized to the portable watch, so that temporal order - once the hallmark of monastic rule and order - had been brought into the everyday world to regulate the movement of machines and peoples alike.

The application of new technologies to physical resources on a worldwide scale, coupled with advances in public health, resulted in turn in an exponential increase in global population. Thus, in 1650 the estimated population was some 470 millions; a century later the figure had climbed to just under the 700 million mark. By 1850 the world population stood at an estimated 1,091 millions, and fifty years later had attained 1,500 millions, or more than a threefold increase in two and a half centuries.

Technological breakthroughs in modern European societies were carried over into the economic and political spheres. <u>Laissez-faire</u> capitalism raised the middle class to new levels of wealth and power. Political individualism manifested itself in the advent of representative government. A new sense of nationalism was born with the establishment of the nation-state system. According to the Treaty of Westphalia (1648), nation-states are sovereign and equal. They accept no authority superior to themselves (early acceptance of Church authority was not effective, and was later renounced even in principle). They claim unfettered proprietorship and control of their territory and populations. They wage war, carry out defense or aggression, and allow free or restricted trade, travel, and information in their own interests. Their attributes include a defined territory, a permanent population, a government, and a capacity to enter into relations with other nation-states. By virtue of the "logic of Westphalia," the nation-states are equal in status though dissimilar in stature, and the maintenance of international order has to rest upon the volition of governments with their very different interests, powers, and goals.

The concept of the nation-state was born in Europe and exported abroad. But European nations with their superior technology came first to dominate other peoples rather than accord them equal nation-state status. Where the demographic ratio favored the Europeans, as in North and South America and Austrialia, the indigenous populations were either liquidated or subordinated to the European powers and their transported culture. Here new nation-states emerged, built on the European mold with regional variations. Elsewhere, where the demographic ration favored the indigenes, territorial enclaves were created for trading purposes which were later taken over as colonies or dependencies. The territorial property of European societies expanded from the three and a third million square miles of the Continent to some 20 million square miles on five continents.

By the turn of the 20th Century, mankind had virtually completed its conquest of habitable space. Some geographically favored and technologically developed states had overseas empires on which the sun never set; others developed economic and political structures on a continental scale. During this period, which lasted until World War I, new technologies gave European and American nation-states increasing power and a steadily climbing standard of living. By its end, the economic order of capitalism and the political order of nation-states had climaxed. Individualism and nationalism were dominant. But there were many undesirable side-effects. Due to the economies of scale the operatives were mechanized in large scale mines, mills and factories. People had become subordinated to machines; their vlaue was calculated in terms of profit. The excesses of the Industrial Revolution included the creation of slums in which people toiled for inhumanly long hours, children and women were exploited, and health conditions deteriorated.

The reaction to these conditions had been, in the one hand, the revolutionary call for an alternative social order, issued by the Socialists led by Marx and Engels, and, on the other, the gradual institution of humanistic reforms, assuring social welfare, minimum wages and civil liberties.

With the institutionalization of Socialism in Russia following the 1917 uprising, and the geopolitical aftermath of World War II, which shifted Eastern Europe under Soviet influence, the industrial nation-states of the 20th Century were effectively split into two opposing ideological and socioeconomic camps. Subsequently, with the liberation of former colonies, a host of new nation-states irrevocably altered the membership of the United Nations against Western dominance. The new nation-states have overwhelming preferred to remain non-aligned but, instead, to develop their own economic and political strategies in international forums. Together, they comprise what is now seen as the Third and Fourth Worlds, one consisting of developing but resource-rich countries (such as the OPEC nations), the other made up of underdeveloped but disadvantaged countries suffering in various degrees from an imbalance between population and resources. Given the increasing deprivation and poverty which the resource-poor nations face, the 1970s witnessed a vectoring of tensions and confrontation from an East-West to a North-South axis, that is, from the ideologically polarized but jointly affluent countries of the liberal and socialist camps to a mounting socio-economic polarization between the "haves" in the temperate zones and the "have-nots" in the lower latitudes.

The inner dimension of contemporary nation-states has not remained unaffected by these developments.

Modern Industrial Nation-States: The Inner Dimension
The transformation of medieval European societies into globally expanding modern industrial nation-states was impelled by breakthroughs in technology. As we have seen, technology cannot be applied without producing major changes in the outer dimension of social existence. As we shall now see, such changes come about also in the inner dimension.

Technological breakthroughs themselves are the outcome of innovative thinking which reflect the evolution of a society's culture. Such new modes of thinking became widespread in European societies in the Renaissance. It was in liberation from doctrine based on tradition and accepted on faith that modern science was born and the arts were reborn. Once born, modern science transformed the lifeways and institutions of human societies. Even before its concepts acquired technological applications, science began to revolutionize people's views of the world.

The medieval schoolmen employed reason to exalt the primacy of God and did not question the truth of received dogmas. The new scientists and natural philosophers, renouncing truth based on faith, employed reason to observe, experiment, and systematize knowledge about the physical universe. This change of emphasis is shown, for example, by Francis Bacon's attitude towards Aristotle's doctrine of the four causes. Bacon, famous for advocating the method of induction, argued that while metaphysics "handleth the formal and final causes," it was the function of physics and other sciences to concern themselves only with material and efficient causes. In other words, the inner dimension had shifted its focus from "why" to "how."

Galileo published his Il Saggiatore (The Assayer) in 1642. In it he laid the foundations of the worldview which was later to penetrate all facets of the inner dimension of modern industrial societies, explicated by philosophers and implicitly accepted by the man on the street. Galileo distinguished between qualities of objects that can be exactly measured and those which cannot. The measurable qualities he termed primary; these were size, shape, quantity, and motion. The nonmeasurable qualities were called secondary, and comprised properties such as whiteness or redness, and bitterness or sweetness. Primary qualities were held to be the real furniture of the world. Secondary qualities were said to be what our mind attributed to real things when we perceive them. Science was only to investigate the world known by its primary qualities.

The object of modern science was thus a universe composed of properties it could measure. Size, shape, quantity, and motion were elements of a world that resembled a giant mechanism: it had definite parts, definite motions, but the model constructed by science was devoid of feelings or attributes such as justice, dignity, goodness, or worth - nor did it concern itself with any formal or final cause, in other words, with any ultimate purpose. Galileo has been called the prime mover in the development summed up in the phrase Science is Measurement. The mechanical paradigm, brought to a definitive synthesis by Newton, employs logos in order to demonstrate the potency of metron. But it has nothing to say on the score of aretē and telos. The physical world was studied in this perspective with remarkable success. But its consequences for the study and understanding of human affairs was less beneficial, as our generation has come (belatedly) to recognize.

One effect of the new mode of scientific thinking was to dethrone man, and rob his existence of meaning and significance. In the medieval conception God was at the center of the universe, yet man was his highest creation and the only living being with an immortal soul. Man's salvation was of direct concern to God, who sent his own Son to deliver him. In the modern conception God was dismissed as an article of faith that was not capable of proof: it could not be measured. Man could have been placed at the center, as certain scientists and philosophers advocated except for the success of modern science in its explanation of the Universe, evolution, and the mind. Copernicus produced his 'revolution' in explaining the motion of the planets, including the earth, as revolving around the sun. No longer did the universe revolve around our habitat; instead, men found themselves inhabitants of a small planet revolving around a very ordinary sun. Darwin produced his Origin of the Species, wherein he traced man's descent from primates such as the apes. The privileged nature of man had to be dismissed as well. Finally, Freud plumbed man's unconscious states and found that many of the processes which we thought of as free creations of our autonomous personality had explanations in the submerged mechanics of the mind. Man found himself in a universe made up of variously shaped bodies in motion, wherein he occupied the surface of a small planet. He now believed himself descended from the apes, and the plaything of forces that acted on his mind even without his knowledge. This was far removed from the medieval concept of man as a privileged being made in the image of God; or from the Renaissance concept wherein man is a free and rational agent.

Newton's brilliant synthesis of natural phenomena in reference to a few basic 'laws' seemed unassailable. Physics could explain the fall of an object to the ground, the motion of the pendulum, the behavior of the gyroscope, and trajectory of a moving object with the same simple laws that explained the motion of the planets around the sun. The world appeared to be a giant and complex machine given an impetus sometime in the past, and producing fully knowable and determined motions in obedience to eternal laws.

The inner dimension of modern industrial societies became immersed in this world view. The social sciences had no tested conceptions of their own, and society was already being molded by the technological applications of physics. Social scientists sought to emulate their natural science colleagues in being objective and value-free. They began to look upon their objects of inquiry either as mechanisms or as organisms. Political scientists sought to reduce the interaction of states to matter and motion. Power was regarded as the indispensable means for control in the political system, and its application in the form of physical force was the ultimate rationale in international relations. Individual nation-states were seen to seek the maximization of their power and territorial size, thereby producing forces which affect the international system and provoke countervailing forces that move the system back toward equilibrium.

Balance of power in the social world was modelled on the balance of forces observed in the physicist's laboratory.

Darwin's theory of organic evolution provided an alternative model for picturing societies. The concept of the survival of the fittest was broadly applied to human affairs. Herbert Spencer, a friend of Darwin, thought of society as a living organism which must be allowed to develop naturally, untrammeled by state interference. Marx himself spoke admiringly of Darwin and sought to apply the principle of struggle to the relationship of classes. During the Third Reich, German political scientists developed the theory of the 'organic state' to legitimize Nazi Germany's striving toward new territories and world domination.

The application of modern scientific concepts to society was internally inconsistent but nevertheless powerful. It combined notions of Newtonian classical mechanics with those of Darwinian theory of evolution. (The resolution of the seeming inconsistency between these scientific paradigms was not to come until the advent of nonequilibrium thermodynamics, evolutionary systems theory, and related disciplines in the mid-20th Century.) Economic processes within and between states were viewed mechanistically: they were seen to be regulated by immutable laws of supply and demand. The great classical theories of the capitalist economy were given a humanistic assurance by Adam Smith's doctrine of the 'invisible hand.' It was presumed to harmonize individual interest and public benefit through the law-like processes of the economic system. Consequently individuals could be left free to pursue their own interests; state-regulation was bound to be oppressive and unnecessary.

Classical sociology evolved similar laws concerning the circulation of elites, the relation of classes, and the relations of power and authority. Concepts such as 'price,' 'status' and 'power' were used in a similar way to the concepts 'gravity,' 'weight' and 'force.' Man was reduced to an 'economic man' and a 'political man' - automata that could be manipulated by a correct application of the new knowledge of society and its economy.

Competition between individuals, businesses and states was either interpreted by the Darwinian concept of 'struggle for survival' or found justification in capitalism's assurance of the harmonization of public and private interests. Thus, whereas great fortunes were made and the average standards of life rose rapidly, there was also great poverty. Unprecedented gaps were created between the extravagant mansions of the new 'captains of industry' and the humble abodes of toilers in the 'dark satanic mills' of industrial towns.

The Churches attempted to infuse concepts of man's dignity and value into social processes but suffered from an increasing credibility gap. The physical sciences excluded all ethical and value considerations from their concept of reality, and philosophers, impressed by the success of science, relegated values to subjective elements, ephermeral and disputable as matters of taste. Social scientists claimed to have discovered laws of social, economic, and political processes; psychologists made similar claims with respect to the laws of thinking and behavior. Much of organized religion remained at loggerheads with science in key areas: whether man was God's creation or descended from the apes; and whether the world was created in six days or was the product of billions of years of cosmic evolution. The Protestant Reformation did indeed reinterpret many traditional Christian doctrines and made them more acceptable to the spirit of the times. It directly contributed to the unfolding of certain aspects of the industrial-national worldview by emphasizing a work-ethic, and the subjugation of the earth for human benefit.

Secular movements and ideologies emerged forcefully. The ideal of a socialist society was present in Europe since before the French Revolution. It surged powerfully when Marx and Engels, horrified by the inequities of early capitalism, rejected the mechanistic as well as the religious concept of man and society, and replaced them with a dialectical philosophy. Here the struggle of opposites was recognized in the existing class-struggle, while a movement toward synthesis was also perceived. Dialectical and historical materialism's laws of evolution pointed toward the inevitability of a higher stage of social organization. All progressive people were to join forces in helping to bring it about through a revolutionary overthrow of the existing order.

Reformist rather than revolutionary movements gained dominance in Western societies in the late 19th and early 20th Centuries. Its fruits were universal male and, later, also female suffrage, recognition of civil liberties, guarantees of the free expression of opinion, and the institution of free and compulsory elementary education together with social welfare services. Whereas in the Soviet Union social inequities were transformed through the socialist revolution, in Western industrial nation-states the reformist movements succeeded in containing social and economic pressures.

The inner dimension of the modern nation-state stage of social evolution reflected, as well as motivated, the vast and rapid processes of its outer dimension. It manifested immense faith in modern science by generally accepting its mechanistic and organismic assumptions. It motivated the application of science through technology to achieve material power and benefit. It gave free reign to individual national enterprise and self-interested activity. It did respond to corrective tendencies when inequities and tensions grew beyond bounds. Despite a few warnings, such as those by Malthus and Mill, it did not reverse the prevalent belief in progress, measured by economic and material indicators. And it did not include a widespread recognition of actors in the human world other than individuals and nation-states.

These worldviews, values, and beliefs were well adapted to prompt the unfolding of the remarkable transformation of essentially agricultural and feudal, tradition-bound societies, into increasingly urban and industrial progress-motivated nation-states. Yet the economic, ecologic, and demographic outer-dimensional processes thus engendered cannot continue indefinitely. As new transformations are shaping up in the outer dimension of contemporary social existence, so major transformations are likely--and in the human interest, desirable--in its inner dimension. Stage five is now being transcended. Stage six looms before us, as a challenge and an opportunity.

BEYOND NATION-STATES

We have undertaken to develop a historical framework for thinking about the future in the expectation that it will help us answer the question: where are we headed? The answer now appears to be: toward stage six, beyond the stage of modern industrial nation-states. But what evidence do we have that we are already moving beyond stage five? And if so, what is the nature of a stage six society?

An answer to these questions can be hazarded by reviewing the salient features in the patterns of development of past and present societies in their two dimensions.

Patterns in the Development of the Outer Dimension

Growth of technological sophistication. The shift from each stage to the next has been marked by innovations in man's ability to cope with his environment. The first human inventions were the fashioning of flint and bone tools and the controlled use of fire. These set off man from all other species and gave him unparalleled survival advantage. Inventions thereafter included specialization, miniaturization, and efficiency-enhancement of tools, and the shift to metals (such as copper, bronze, iron, and steel, and other alloys). Innovations encompassed not only the making of tools to work the land, but to produce goods, increase the yield of crops, create means of transport, and produce, transmit, and receive information.

The Industrial Revolution devised new tools and machines to convert the energy of coal, gas, and oil for purposes of human consumption. Tools were made to make other tools and progressively sophisticated machines. A new quantum leap has occurred in our century; we have entered into a "Second Industrial Revolution" of automation and cybernetics, information-gathering, and communication. Technological innovations have spawned entire new industries such as aircraft, electronics, computers, and plastics, all based substantially upon scientific research and depending on continued applied science for their advancement. Whitehead's phrase, "the invention of the method of invention," has been carried to a new stage of conceptualization and development.

Increase in the use of energy. Each shift from one stage to the next was likewise marked by a radical increase in the production and use of energy. Daily per capita energy use among primitive food-gatherers was some 2,000 kilocalories: this included only the energy of the food they ate. Among hunters the figure doubled: it included the use of fire. In primitive agricultural societies the rate rose to 12,000 kilocalories - now the energy of some domesticated animals entered the calculation. Among the advanced agricultural societies energy use reached about 24,000 kilocalories, including the use of coal for heating, some water and windpower and animal transport. During the First Industrial Revolution daily per capita energy use reached 70,000 kilocalories: to the previous energy sources industrial fossil energy was added. Present energy use in the United States is estimated to be 230,000 kilocalories per day per person - and is still increasing.

Increase in the use of materials. Neolithic man used only the rock from which he chipped his primitive tools. With the harnessing of fire for cooking and heating, man began to use wood in increasing quantities. Metals came in turn: bronze, iron, copper, and more recently steel and the many base materials for modern alloys. Coal and gas came to be used in large quantities in the industrial age, together with oil. Some of these materials are in finite supply and may soon be exhausted. Since 1920, the United States alone has burned one-half of the total amount of coal ever consumed. Since 1940, its use equalled nearly half of the world's total consumption of oil and gas. It is presently estimated that most of the presently used raw materials of industrial societies, such as fossil fuels, metals and minerals, will be exhausted within a century. The rate of their use still increases from year to year.

Extended environmental control capability. Stone-age man's environmental control was limited to an ill-defined hunting territory. In simple horticultural societies, the territory comprised a village and its immediate surroundings. Control over these territories was constrained by the kinds and numbers of animals hunted, and the distribution of the plants eaten. In more advanced agricultural societies, the territory was extended along river valleys. Here the river washed down the silt and provided periodic irrigation through flooding; human control was still minimal. Irrigation systems later extended human control over the natural environment. Roads and larger, more permanent settlements were imposed on the landscape.

The early classical societies extended environmental control over vaster distances. Armies travelled over much of the known world, changed existing settlement patterns, cut down forests, built roads, and created towns. Sailing ships crossed the Mediterranean, the Black and Baltic Seas, and travelled the Indian Ocean.

Further expansion of environmental control capability had to wait until the late Middle Ages. Then larger ships were built, better means of navigation discovered, and as a result human settlements spread over much of the habitable globe.

The First Industrial Revolution radically advanced man's control over the environment. Large urban centers arose, the land around them was paved under, vast networks of roads were created, and fertilizers and heavy machinery forced the land to accommodate a large variety of crops independently of the natural ecology.

Currently man's reach extends also into the air, thereby creating a three-dimensional environmental control capability. Planes and missiles transport people and weapons across the atmosphere; electromagnetic waves carry information in code, sound and image. The depths of the oceans are subjected to progressive exploration and exploitation. The natural environment begins to feel the adverse effects of human control. Pollution spreads over the atmosphere, in the water-systems of the continents, and in the coeans. The land shows signs of overexploitation: topsoil is vanishing and more fertilizers are needed for equal sizes of yield. In our world there is no more terra incognita, and there are no longer any totally 'natural' environments.

Population growth. Total world population prior to Neolithic times is estimated at around five millions. At that time it took 1,500 years to double the human population. By 1650 the total population was approximately 470 millions and the doubling time was reduced to 200 years. It was in 1850 that for the first time one billion people were alive on this planet. Today over four billion people share the earth, and the population doubling time is under 35 years. Of the 60 to 100 billion humans who have ever lived, roughly 4-5 percent are alive today. (And, while human numbers mount, the populations of other species decline. Hundreds of species are on the endangered list today, and more are expected to join them in coming decades.

Increasing interactions. Food-gathering societies formed local mosaics, relatively self-sufficient within their environments. Food-producing societies were still self-sufficient but were less isolated: semi-permanent roads and waterways connected their villages. The advanced agricultural societies of Mesopotamia, Egypt, India, and China comprised large districts or regions each with numerous villages and centers. Interaction among these units intensified as a central role was imposed from above. But interaction between the scattered empires and civilizations was still limited.

With the rise of the maritime civilizations of early classical times, trade developed between culturally and geographically diverse peoples. Conquests by Alexander and Romans brought destruction as well as a new unity ('Pax Romana') to widely divergent cultures.

The early Middle Ages constituted a return to relatively isolated and self-sufficient communities. Interactions among these units increased gradually as technologies became more sophisticated, travel more comfortable and safe, and cultural influences more widespread.

The Industrial Revolution brought a sudden increase in trade and commerce. European empires were formed with large overseas colonies. Energies and raw materials were shifted from extraction to manufacturing site and from there to locations of consumption. One society had raw materials, another the capital and the technology, and perhaps a third a cheap and large labor force. Industry created global interaction. The ideological, social and economic conflicts and rivalries of states created a precarious balance of power.

Currently interaction has bred interdependence. Rather than self-sufficient and isolated communities, we have economically, politically and ecologically interdependent nations, and regional and international blocs and organizations. This is a new stage in societal evolution.

<u>Increasing information flows</u>. The transfer of information was by word of mouth in food-gathering and primitive food-producing recorded and carried by messengers. Inventions in writing technologies made possible the formation of libraries, like that at Alexandria, which comprised a significant portion of human ideas hitherto committed to paper. But information flows increased slowly, and knowledge was often lost - as in the case of the destruction of the library at Alexandria itself.

The explosion of information started with the invention of the printing press in the 15th Century. It was followed by the next explosion due to the invention of electronic communications media in the 20th Century. The first scientific journal (<u>Philosophical Transactions of the Royal Society of London</u>) was published in 1665. By the beginning of the 19th Century, 100 such journals were published, and by 1900 about 10,000. Currently close to 100,000 scientific publications are produced and distributed. Even these are but a fraction of the total flow of information in our times. This includes personal conferences, electronic conferencing, cables, phones, typed and printed materials of all kinds, private and public radio and television networks, and the rapidly accumulating stores of information in books, magazines, newspapers, microfilm, audio and video tape, and computer cards and tape.

<u>Increasing levels of complexity</u>. Neolithic man lived in communal bands with a simple division of labor. The size of basic social units and their complexity have increased with each stage. First more extended kinship systems, then sedentary village systems brought about a greater division of labor, more specialization, and increased social complexity. The emergence of the

theocratic civilizations of antiquity added unprecedented organizational levels in the form of a social hierarchy extending from ruler to slave. The administrative and legal structure of the Roman empire reached new heights in complex and coordinated social organization.

Following a reversion to simpler societies in the early Middle Ages, the size and complexity of social units began anew its unrelenting growth. It passed through the stages of still relatively independent princedoms, to reach integrated nation-states in the modern age. These in turn evolved regional organizations, for economic, political and security purposes. They came to be criss-crossed by non-governmental organizations on sub- as well as supra-national levels. Multinational corporations have further complicated the picture. They have entered as major forces on the world scene: of the 100 wealthiest actors in the contemporary world, nearly half are corporations.

A consequence of increased levels of complexity is the multiple role and allegiance of the average person. He or she may be a member of a family, community and nation, and also of a corporation, fraternal organization, or professional association. These may operate on the local, national, or international levels. In previous stages of social development, most people had a clear (though not always accurate) idea of social structure and roles. Today, sophisticated sociological inquiry is required to unravel the strands of interconnection among diverse roles and structures, and nobody has a clear and adequate knowledge of anything but a fraction of the structures and roles in his society.

Patterns in the Development of the Inner Dimension
We are beginning to perceive a pattern in the evolution of the outer dimension of human societies. Does an analogous pattern exist in the inner dimension?

The outer and inner dimensions are not mutually exclusive but form two dimensions of a single reality: the evolution of sociocultural systems with conscious human members. We find that the inner dimension of societies reflects their outer dimension, as well as providing the direction for the latter's further evolution. Yet development in the inner dimension is not linear but rather helical. Aside from the constant improvement in man's understanding of the world around him, there are few factors that are maintained or maximized. Emphasis in the inner dimension tends to shift back and forth between man and cosmos, the individual and the collectivity. However, it never returns to previous stages but discovers new factors and elements in ancient concerns and interests; it forms not a repeating circle, but an advancing spiral.

Food-gathering and hunting societies at the dawn of sociocultural evolution were mythic and collectivity-oriented. They worshipped the world they perceived together with the forces and spirits they attributed to it. They believed in a timeless cosmic order with its own justice and equilibrium. Interaction with this mythical world took place not only through everyday actions but also through magic. The forces of the world could always be tapped through the appropriate rites and rituals.

Food-producing societies conserved their interest in the earth and its spirits, but they contributed a new interest in the heavens. The earth was still the source of life and occupied the center of attention. Yet the horticulturist and the herdsman, to an extent not matched by the hunter, were subject to seasonal variations for gaining their livelihood. Hence their particular interest in the sun, in celestial bodies, and the seasons. New permanent settlements created a sense of ownership and family accomplishment in working the land. While Neolithic societies were still communalistic, individualism was slowly on the rise.

The more advanced agricultural societies fully shifted their gaze from the earth the heavens. Man was still subordinate to the cosmos, but now both the cosmic and the human realms formed a vast pyramid. As above, so below: human society was stratified in the image of the heavenly spheres. The unity of the two spheres was expressed in great religious systems of thought. Man sought to fit himself and his society into the patterns of order he perceived; his worldview was both an image of the world and a compulsory moral code.

The classical phase of the great sweep of development which occurred in Europe between the first millenium B.C. and the advent of the modern age placed man at the center of the stage. At its inception the world of men and of gods was still not separated, and the mythic worldview continued to dominate. But then came great breakthroughs in rational thinking with emphasis on reason, measure, and virtue. Man became the measure; he no longer merely reflected a heavenly order. Yet the order of the cosmos and the order of human society were still seen as harmonious. Greek thinking tread a fine line between the celestial and the telluric orientations, with Plato emphasizing eternal forms and cosmic harmony, and Aristotle centering attention on earthly things and processes. The Romans continued Greek thought in a pragmatic vein. They evolved a sophisticated concept of government and founded the basis of modern systems of jurisprudence.

The destruction of the Roman Empire in the West was followed by a renewed emphasis upon celestial beliefs. Man had been made in the image of God, and the function of reason was but a preparation paving the way towards perfection in Christ. The City of God was the supreme goal and value; human societies were temporal reflections where souls are prepared for union with their maker.

The Renaissance shifted attention once more to man as man. Reason and feeling came to dominate in place of faith and tradition; the world was again held to be knowable, and enjoyable, through human experience. In place of the group, the individual occupied center stage. Independence, freedom, and individual spiritual and artistic expression came to be valued above all other values. In this spirit of secular inquiry, modern science was born.

Modern science advanced empirical knowledge without precedent, but it also created a rift in the inner dimension of modern European societies. The objectively knowable and the immediately experienced were separated. The measurable was the knowable, and the knowable was held to be the real. Human perceptions, sensations, feelings, and abstract ideas such as goodness, justice and virtue, were not measurable. Hence they came under the authority of the spiritual tradition, whereas size, shape, quantity and motion belonged to the sphere of the scientific. Although the early modern scientists were devoutly religious, the spread of their theories and concepts in society infused a worldview that extended scientific concepts into the realm of human affairs and reduced the credibility of traditional religions.

In modern times, man was no longer subordinated to the cosmos on mythical grounds, but he was cut down to almost insignificant size through the scientific recognition of his place in the scheme of things. Nature emerged as part of a mechanistic universe, which man, however small, was free to exploit for his own benefit. Human society itself was often viewed as expressing the Darwinian struggle for survival, with ruthless conflict and competition - seen as the natural order of things.

The power of societies over the environment, their members, and other societies constantly increased through the technological applications of modern science. It gave rise to dominant beliefs, goals, and values which made technological-industrial progress possible, and which were reinforced by such progress. These can be summarized under the following headings:

Belief in the Feasibility And Desirability of Economic Growth

Economic growth was seen as contributing to the rise of the material standard of living of all people. Higher material standards were thought to be a precondition of happiness and well-being. Science and technology were considered to make almost unlimited economic growth possible. Hence science and technology were to be applied to produce continuous economic growth.

Technological Imperative

Technology was considered to be a human benefactor. Almost any technological invention was thought to provide some human benefit. Consequently if something proved to be technologically feasible, it was thought to be morally obligatory. ('Can,' said Ozbekhan, implies 'ought.')

Harmonization of Individual and Public Interest

The climate of _laissez-faire_ economic liberalism was undergirded by the comforting belief that private gain well-nigh automatically produces public benefit. Adam Smith's 'invisible hand,' which harmonized public and private interests, was assumed to be a fact, and free license was given to self-interested economic activity, as long as it did not conflict with the broad basis of business laws.

'Economic Man' Image

Human beings came to be seen as economic actors, reduced to roles of producers and consumers. The laws of economic systems were thought to regulate human behavior. Through appropriate manipulation of prices and supplies and the inculcation of demands, behavior could not only be calculated but also manipulated.

Irresponsibility for Long-Range Consequences

People have generally assumed responsibility for the perceived consequences of their actions, for example, when they have harmed somebody or interfered with their freedom. But in modern industrial societies, the range of consequences of people's actions have exceeded their preceptions of them. Actions have come to affect peoples in remote parts of the world as well as in generations yet to come. Moral responsibility was generally not assumed for such consequences.

'Infinite Earth' Image

The earth was regarded as practically infinite in regard to the resources and space it could offer. Global limits to nonrenewable resources, to pollution from production and consumption, to food-growing capability, to population carrying capacity, and to recoverability from large-scale war, were either ignored or only rendered lip-service. The earth was treated as if it were unlimited in its ability to support continual industrial and demographic growth; as if it had an unlimited source of safe, usable energy, and unlimited reservoirs of resources and pollution sinks.

'National Independence' Image

The emergence of nation-states as central actors, together with a belief in unrestrained competitive struggle for existence and advantage, fuelled the belief that nations are sovereign and independent of one another. Autonomy in decision-making was interpreted as freedom from constraints in the context of the decisions. Yet such constraints increasingly determine the possible response of nations, as economic, political, and ecologic factors of control are removed from their domestic jurisdiction into the international arena.

What does this review of the processes of the inner and outer dimensions of human societies tell us about the questions we asked at the beginning of this paper? Can we conclude that we are now moving beyond stage five societies? And can we perceive the likely shape of a stage six society?

I. Our review suggests that sociocultural evolution is an ongoing process, with no known return to previous stages. (Even the relapse into the 'Dark Ages' was not a return to archaic civilizations but had its own inner and outer dimensional characteristics.) The process unfolds unevenly, with long periods of stability alternating with epochs of radical change. We see that the rhythm of change has accelerated. Each stage of social organization is shorter than its predecessors.

Current processes of the outer dimension include new levels of technological sophistication, energy and materials extraction and consumption, population growth, information flow, social complexity, and interactions issuing in interdependence. All these processes have grown considerably since the advent of sovereign nation-states. The latter appear no more able to contain the further unfolding of these processes than the feudal structure of medieval Europe could contain the advent of the Renaissance and the dawn of the First Industrial Revolution.

The ideologies of the industrial nation-state - its inner dimension - seem similarly incapable of coping with recent developments. Until recently, faith in science and technology, and the mechanistic-organismic view associated with Newtonian and Darwinian theories, were still dominant. They were expressed in the belief that infinite economic growth is both feasible and desirable; that what is technologically possible is also humanly beneficial; that individual interest and public good coincide; that man is basically an economic actor; that no responsibility attaches to long-range consequences; that the earth is practically inexhaustible and unspoilable; and that nations are independent and autonomous.

In the perspective of the last few years, it is safe to say that the representative majority of people in industrial nation-states no longer hold such views, or at least no longer hold them without question and doubt. The inner dimension of stage five society is collapsing.

II. If the classical paradigm of modern industrial nation-states no longer corresponds to reality but is being left rapidly behind, can we foresee the nature of the next stage of social evolution?

Here we encounter the problem of prediction concerned with social determinism. We have already suggested that human sociocultural systems have an inner dimension which determines their choices among the options allowed by their outer dimension. Hence if predictions are to be made, they have to be based on the options available in the outer dimension, combined with a knowledge of the relevant aspects of the inner dimension.

What are our options as we head toward the 21st Century? One option may be to continue current trends. But can we expand technological sophistication <u>ad infinitum</u>? New breakthroughs are still likely. Yet the technological age itself may be a temporary phase in mankind's long-range evolution. Can we expand our energy resources and use? Given appropriate technologies, energy use-rates could increase for a long time to come. Yet they cannot be based on primary sources of fossil fuels, and they must stop short of surpassing the thermal and radiation pollution thresholds of the biosphere.

Similar considerations apply to the extraction and use of raw materials. Recycling and substitution can extend the life expectancy of nonrenewable materials, but upper thresholds will be reached before long unless the very crust of the earth can be processed. Our environmental control capability could, and clearly should, expand further. But it should now turn from unreflective exploitation of the lifesupport systems of the biosphere to a calculated harmonization of limit cycles and human interests. A simple continuation of existing trends would lead to the destabilization of ecosystems and the drastic reduction of the carrying capacity of the planet.

Population growth curves cannot be indefinitely set forth. Even if we used all available lands, produced foods in factories and laboratories and farmed and harvested the oceans, the increasing density of human populations and their reliance on vulnerable high technology would make life unpleasant and put it at risk. Short of the colonization of other planets, population growth curves must soon flatten out. From the vantage point of our present understanding of human advantage, they should flatten out sooner rather than later, at lower rather than higher levels.

We are already suffering from information overload. The historical curve of the information explosion is not infinitely sustainable. Our information production, transmission, and storing facilities have grown exponentially, but our brains - the receivers of information - are still roughly those of our Neolithic ancestors. They cannot continue to be overloaded without adverse consequences. Even the amount of information that man-machine systems can process in society has upper bounds, notwithstanding growing sophistication in electronic technologies.

For the above reasons, complexity in social organization also has upper bounds. Beyond foreseeable levels, complexity is no longer able to generate order but threatens to break down into chaos.

The humanistic options of our epoch do not include the simple and convenient one of letting things move ahead as they have in the recent past. Realistic calculations must take into account both the evolution of the outer-dimensional processes in history, and the conditions which these have created for contemporary mankind.

We began with Santayana's aphorism that those who cannot remember the past are condemned to repeat it. At this point we might adapt it to read: "Those who cannot envisage the future may be condemned never to experience it." If this sounds dramatic, we mean it to be so - because we live in a thermonuclear, and hence the most lethal age, in history, and in the midst of its costliest arms race. We have, in effect, argued that within the overall continuum of societal evolution there peridocally occurs accelerated and far-reaching transformations - or quantum shifts - and we have adduced a cluster of historical indicators to show that we are today in the midst of such a quantum shift, one that embraces both the outer and inner dimensions of mankind, and simultaneously upon a global scale. Given the evidence that mankind has evolved not only its technologies but its values and beliefs in the past, there is surely no reason why it should be incapable of doing so again within the time-span of the next few generations. We are at a crucial juncture. It is in our lifetime that mankind for the first time has reached the global stage of societal development. It can no longer grow without thought and qualification, but must henceforth carefully chart its own evolution. People everywhere need to recognize this ecumenical state of mankind and adjust their goals, beliefs, and values accordingly. History has led us to where we are. We ourselves must find the way to a sustainable - and humane - future.

SELECTED BIBLIOGRAPHY

Adams, Robert McC., *The Evolution of Urban Society, Early Mesopotamia and Prehispanic Mexico*, Aldine, Chicago, 1966.

Benedict, Ruth, *Patterns of Culture*, Houghton, Mifflin, Boston, 1961.

Bowra, C.M., *The Greek Experience*, Weidenfeld and Nicolson, London, 1958.

Brierly, J.L., *The Law of Nations*, Clarendon, Oxford, 1949.

Campbell, Bernard, *Human Evolution: An Introduction to Man's Adaptation*, Aldine, Chicago, 1966.

Carneiro, R.L., "Slash-and-Burn Cultivation Among the Kuikuru and Its Implications for Cultural Development in the Amazon Basin," *Antropologica*, Supplement No. 2, September (1961).

Cassirer, Ernst, *An Essay on Man, An Introduction to a Philosophy of Human Culture*, Yale University Press, New Haven, 1965.

Clark, Grahame and Stuart Piggott, *Prehistoric Societies*, Penguin, 1976.

Cohen, Yehudi A. (ed.), *Man in Adaptation: Vol. I, The Biosocial Background*, Vol. II, *The Cultural Present*, Aldine, Chicago, 1968.

DeBary, W.T., Wing-tsit Chan, Burton Watson (compilers), *Sources of Chinese Tradition, Sources of Indian Tradition, Sources of Japanese Tradition*, Columbia University Press, New York, 1958-1960.

Dictionnaire Archeologique Des Techniques, Editions de l'Accueil, Paris, 1963.

Eisenstadt, S.N., *The Political Systems of Empires, The Rise and Fall of Historical Bureaucratic Societies*, Free Press, Glencoe, 1963.

English, P.W., and R.C. Mayfield (eds), *Man, Space, and Environment*, Oxford University Press, 1972.

Fairbank, John (ed.)., *The Chinese World Order*, Harvard University Press, Cambridge, 1968.

Falk, Richard A., *A Study of Future Worlds*, Free Press, New York, 1975.

Farb, Peter, *Man's Rise to Civilization as Shown by the Indians of North America From Primeval Times to the Coming of the Industrial State*, E.P. Dutton, New York, 1968.

Finley, Jr., John H., *Four Stages of Greek Thought*, Oxford University Press, 1966.

Forbes, R.J., *Studies in Ancient Technology*, E.J. Brill, Leiden, 1955--.

Frankfort, Henri, *Kingship and the Gods: A Study of Ancient Near Eastern Religion as the Integration of Society and Nature*, University of Chicago Press, 1962.

Frankfort, Henri et al, *Before Philosophy: The Intellectual Adventure of Ancient Man*, Penguin, 1968.

Giedion, S., *Space, Time and Architecture*, Harvard University Press, Boston, 1962.

Haas, William S., *The Destiny of the Mind*, London, 1956.

Hawkes, Jacquetta and Sir Leonard Woolley, *History of Mankind, Vol. I: Prehistory and the Beginnings of Civilization, Un Esco*, George Allen and Unwin, London, 1963.

Hodges, Henry, *Technology in the Ancient World*, Knopf, New York, 1970.

Jantsch, Erich, *Design for Evolution: Self-Organization and Planning in the Life of Human Systems*, George Braziller, New York, 1975.

_____ and Conrad H. Waddington (eds.), *Evolution and Consciousness: Human Systems in Transition*, Addison-Wesley, Reading Mass., 1976.

Kluckhohn, Clyde K., "The Special Character of Integration in an Individual Culture," *The Nature of Concepts, Their Inter-Relation and Role in Social Structure*, Stillwater Conference, Oklahoma A. & M. College, 1950.

Koestler, Arthur, *The Lotus and the Robot*, Macmillan, New York, 1961.

_____, *The Ghost in the Machine*, Pan Books, London, 1971.

Kroeber, Alfred L., and Clyde K. Kluckhohn, "Culture: A Critical Review of Concepts and Definitions," *Papers of the Peabody Museum of American Archaeology and Ethnology*, Harvard University, Vol. XLVII, No. 1, (1952).

Kuhn, Thomas S., *The Structure of Scientific Revolutions*, University of Chicago Press, second edition, 1971.

Laszlo, Ervin, *Introduction to Systems Philosophy: Toward a New Paradigm of Contemporary Thought*, Gordon and Breach, New York, 1972.

_____ A Strategy for the Future: The Systems Approach to World Order, George Braziller, New York, 1973.

_____ (ed.), The World System: Models, Norms, Applications, George Braziller, New York, 1973.

Levi-Strauss, Claude, The Savage Mind, University of Chicago Press, 1970.

Levy, G. Rachel, The Gate of Horn: A Study of the Religious Conceptions of the Stone Age and Their Influence upon Europeon Thought, Faber and Faber, 1948.

Margenau, Henry (ed.), Integrative Principles of Modern Thought, Gordon and Breach, New York, 1972.

Matson, Floyd W., The Broken Image: Man, Science and Society, Doubleday, New York, 1966.

McLuhan, Marshall, The Gutenberg Galaxy, New American Library, New York, 1969.

Meadows, Donella H., Dennis L. Meadows, Jorgen Randers, William W. Behrens III, The Limits to Growth: A Report for the Club of Rome's Project on the Predicament of Mankind, Potomac Association, Washington D.C., 1972.

Mesarovic, Mihajlo and Eduard Pestel, Mankind at the Turning Point: The Second Report to the Club of Rome, E.P. Dutton, New York, 1974.

Mukerjee, Radhakamal, The Way of Humanism, East And West, Academic Books, Bombay, 1968.

Mumford, Lewis, Technics and Civilization, paperback edition, 1963.

_____ The City in History, Harcourt, Brace & World, New York, 1961.

_____ The Myth of the Machine: Technics and Human Development, Harcourt, Brace & World, New York, 1967.

Murray, Gilbert, Hellenism and the Modern World, George Allen and Unwin, London, 1953.

Needham, Joseph, Science and Civilization in China, Cambridge University Press, 1959--.

Nimkoff, Meyer F., and Russell Middleton, "Types of Family and Types of Economy," America Journal of Sociology, Vol. 60, (1960).

Northrop, F.S.C., The Meeting of the East and West, Collier, New York, 1966.

Oliver, Symmes C., "Ecology and Cultural Continuity as Contributing Factors in the Social Organization of the Plains Indians," University of California Publications in American Archaeology and Ethnology, Vol. 48 (1), (1962).

Palerm, Angel, Irrigation Civilizations in Mesoamerica, Social Science Monograph 1, Pan American Union, Washington D.C. (a selection of which is reprinted as "The Agricultural Basis of Urban Civilization in Mesoamerica," in Cohen (ed.), Man in Adaptation: Vol. II: The Cultural Present, Aldine, Chicago, 1968.

Radin, Paul, The World of Primitive Man, Grove Press, New York, 1960.

Raphael, Max, Prehistoric Pottery and Civilization in Egypt, Bollingen Series VIII, Pantheon, New York, 1947.

Read, Sir Herbert, Icon and Art: The Function of Art in the Development of Human Consciousness, Faber and Faber, London, 1955.

Redfield, Robert, The Primitive World and its Transformations, Cornell, 1968.

Ritchie, James, The Influence of Man on Animal Life in Scotland: A Study of Faunal Evolution, quoted in the Year Book of the Royal Society of Edinburgh, 1959.

Sahlins, Marshall D., "The Segmentary Lineage: An Organization of Predatory Expansion," American Anthropologist, Vol. 63, (1961).

Service, Elman R., The Hunters, Prentice-Hall, Englewood Cliffs, 1966.

Singer, Charles, and Others, A History of Technology, Clarendon Press, Oxford, 5 volumes, 1954-1958.

Singer, Charles, A Short History of Scientific Ideas to 1900, Clarendon Press, Oxford, 1959.

Tax, Sol (ed.), Evolution After Darwin, 3 volumes, University of Chicago Press, 1960.

Taylor, Alastair M., "Evolution-Revolution, General Systems Theory, and Society," in R. Gotesky and E. Laszlo (eds.), Evolution and Revolution, Gordon and Breach, New York, 1971.

_____, "A Systems Approach to the Political Organization of Space," Social Science Information, International Social Science Council, (1975) (XIV-5).

_____, "The Present Quantum in Societal Evolution: An Analysis of Historical Indicators," Proceedings of the Fourth International Conference of the Unity of the Sciences, Volume II, New York, (1975).

_____ "Process and Structure in Sociocultural Systems," in E. Jantsch and C.H. Waddington (eds.), *Evolution and Consciousness: Human Systems in Transition*, Addison-Wesley, Reading Mass., 1976.

Thomas, W.L., (ed.)., *Man's Role in Changing the Face of the Earth*, University of Chicago Press, 1956.

Wallbank, T. Walter, Alastair M. Taylor, Nils Bailkey, *Civilization - Past and Present*, two volumes, seventh edition, Scott Foresman, Chicago, 1976.

Wallerstein, Immanuel, *The Modern World-System: Capitalist Agriculture and the Origins of the European World-Economy in the Sixteenth Century*.

Webb, Walter Prescott, *The Great Frontier*, University of Texas Press, Austin, 1964.

Wertheim, W.F., *Evolution and Revolution: The Rising Waves of Emancipation*, Penguin, 1974.

White Jr., Lynn, *Medieval Technology and Social Change*, Oxford, 1962.

Whitehead, Alfred North, *Science and the Modern World*, Free Press, _____ 1967.

Whorf, Benjamin, *Language, Thought, and Reality*, Cambridge Mass., 1956.

Wittkower, Rudolf, *Architectural Principles in the Age of Humanism*, Random House, New York, 1965.

Yi-Fu Tuan, *Topophilia: A Study of Environmental Perception, Attitudes, and Values*, Prentice-Hall, Englewood Cliffs, 1974.

CURRENT PROSPECTS OF SUSTAINABLE ECONOMIC GROWTH

Thomas E. Jones

The multi-faceted topic of global economic growth can be viewed from many different perspectives.* This chapter focuses on ecological problems brought about by industrial growth, on ways of coping with these problems, on an appropriate global goal, and on several subsidiary objectives. More specifically, the main problems concern depletion of non-renewable fuel and metal resources and environmental pollution.** Certain technological breakthroughs and the reduction of ecologically inadvisable practices ("social and cultural constraints") provide opportunities for increasing the amount of sustainable global economic growth that is permitted by the limits of depletion and pollution. The global goal, which is formulated in the light of these problems and opportunities, is sustainable economic growth. The successful pursuit of various interconnected objectives would promote world-wide selective economic growth oriented toward the satisfaction of human needs and protected against the production of ecological consequences that would precipitate its own decline.

ECOLOGICAL PROBLEMS OF INDUSTRIAL GROWTH

Recent Problems of Economic Growth
By opening avenues to new types of production and services as well as to economies of scale, technological progress stimulated

---

*Regardless of the perspective selected, the problems posed by such growth constitute one of a number of interrelated sets of global problems (Harman, 1970). Efforts to ameliorate these sets of problems could be facilitated by the intelligent, cooperative formulation and adoption of interconnected global goals.

**Related problems that are mentioned -- for instance, the plight of resource-poor developing countries and the instability of the international monetary system -- cannot here be given attention proportional to their importance, nor can their relations to ecological problems be fully analyzed. The problem of nuclear proliferation is, however, so integral to the energy debate that recommendations for coping with it are treated in some detail.

the rapid economic growth of the developed world. Large-scale operations lowered unit costs and increased productivity. Higher productivity boosted income, which in turn created a demand for greater quantities of products. Thus a self-reinforcing, product proliferating economic spiral was generated.

Despite fluctuations of the business cycle, this spiral continued almost uninterrupted from the end of World War II to the early 1970's. A consequence was the highest rate of global economic growth ever known: approximately four or five per cent each year. Concomitant increases in the material standard of living expanded opportunities in developed countries for leisure, education, and other cultural pursuits.

During the seventies, however, an unanticipated anomoly arose: economic stagnation accompanied by inflation. The Arab oil embargoes of 1973-1974 caused energy shortages in many developed countries. The four-fold increase in oil prices led to serious balance of payments deficits in these countries and contributed to the instability of the international monetary system. The prices of a number of other industrially important nonrenewable natural resources were also raised by organizations of producing and exporting nations. As raw material and energy costs rose, inflation took an upswing, labor became more expensive, demand diminished, and economic growth slowed down in most industrialized countries.

To produce increasing quantities of material goods, the industrial process has depended on high rates of energy and resource use. One factor underlying the upsetting changes of the seventies is the unequal geopolitical distribution of the remaining high-grade deposits of fossil fuels and metallic ores all nations require for the maintenance and growth of their economies. The concentration of these resources in a few nations puts these nations in a position to raise prices and restrict supply. Another factor is the enormous demand placed on the limited supply of fossil fuel and metal resources that can be extracted at low costs by current technologies. As high-grade deposits that are easily extractable have been progressively depleted in many localities, more effort has been required for extraction and prices have increased.

Not only have nonrenewable resources -- particularly, fossil fuels -- become somewhat depleted, less accessible, and higher priced, but production and consumption have begun to pollute the environment. The earth's mineral deposits and pollution-absorption capacity are finite. Is there a danger that rapid global industrial growth might undermine its own foundations during the next century? Answers to such questions must be formulated in view of the principal physical limits to industrial growth as well as the technological and socio-cultural ways of promoting growth that is less restricted by them.

Physical Limits to Industrial Growth*

Resource depletion. Fossil fuels, metallic ores, and other ores are used primarily by industrialized societies. Ten nations accounted for 75 per cent of the world energy consumption in 1968 (Cook, 1976). Not only are the percentages of resources consumed by such nations extremely high, the quantities are enormous. For instance, about 40,000 pounds of new mineral materials -- including 8,300 of petroleum, 5,300 of coal, 5,000 of natural gas, 1,300 of iron and steel, and 60 of aluminum -- are required annually for each United States citizen. The total U.S. use of mineral supplies exceeded four billion tons in 1973 (Bureau of Mines). Such large-scale use, especially when unaccompanied by extensive recycling, tends to deplete resource deposits.

Depletion of fossil fuels. At the present time, the global economy is heavily dependent on energy produced by burning petroleum, coal, and natural gas. In 1970, petroleum provided about 36 per cent of the world's energy use, coal 30 per cent, and natural gas 18 per cent.

Of the world's 569.5 billion barrels (in 1971) of proven petroleum reserves recoverable with current technologies, 346.8 billion (61 per cent) are in the Middle East. If present trends and policies continue, by 1980 the United States will import about 10 or 11 million barrels of oil per day -- almost 50 per cent of its projected oil consumption. The bulk of these imports would have to come from the Middle East (Surrey and Bromley, 1973).

Though only five per cent of the world has been thoroughly searched for oil deposits, geological comparisons can be used to make rough estimates of the amount of oil in other regions. M. King Hubbert, a reputable research geophysicist employed by the U.S. Geological Survey, has estimated that presently recoverable global oil reserves range from 1,350 to 2,100 billion barrels (Hubbert, 1969, 1971, 1972). Assuming the higher figure and a continuation of production trends, the rate of world oil production would peak around the year 2000 (Bethe, 1976). Production would thereafter decline rapidly as reserves become depleted. Though prospects would be considerably improved by an appreciable reduction in the rate of oil consumption, the arrival and departure of the short but spectacular oil age will nonetheless mark one of the great discontinuities in human history.

Coal reserves are considerably more extensive than oil reserves. The world's estimated seven and six-tenths trillion metric tons

---

*Three general physical limits are insufficient energy, depletion of raw materials, and pollution. In regard to the first two, we concentrate on major depletion issues today: depletion of conventional fossil fuels and of metallic ores.

of mineable coal could remain a major energy source until about
the year 2300, provided that present coal production does not
double more than three times (Averitt). Peak production might
be reached between the years 2100 and 2150.

The geopolitical distribution of coal reserves, like that of
oil, is quite uneven. Most of the world's estimated reserves
of hard and soft coal are in the USSR (62.7 per cent). Large
amounts, however, are also located in North America (18.1 per
cent) and China (11.5 per cent).

Use of coal instead of oil or natural gas leads to increased atmospheric pollution as well as higher costs of extraction and
transportation. However, the increased dependence of many nations on coal as an energy source is necessitated by the absence
of tenable alternatives, though the degree of increase can be
reduced by commitment to additional fission reactors.

Natural gas causes relatively little air pollution and is fairly
easy to handle. Though natural gas reserves are much harder to
estimate than coal reserves, accessible, competitively priced
natural gas is generally thought to have distinctly less potential than coal as a future energy source. Production of natural
gas in the United States has already begun to decline. An estimate of proven world reserves (in 1971) locates approximately
40 per cent in Eastern Europe and the USSR, and about 20 per
cent in North America (Ridgeway, 1974; and World Oil).

Thus conventional fossil fuels,* the primary source of harnessed
energy today, do not exist in sufficient quantity to sustain the
global industrial system more than perhaps 400 to 500 years.
Prices will probably rise as reserves are depleted. The unequal
geopolitical distribution of reserves will continue to alter the
world balance of power. Already, the possession of needed petroleum has elevated some nations like Saudi Arabia in the international hierarchy of power and influence, and lack of it has
lowered others. Western Europe and Japan are extremely dependent on developing countries for petroleum. As is evident from
the possibility of further politically motivated oil embargoes,
equitable access to fossil fuels is by no means guaranteed.

In view of such considerations, the pressing need for conservation and new energy sources should be obvious. Unless efforts
to meet this need prove successful, exhaustion of conventional
fossil fuels will limit industrial growth.

---

*Non-conventional hydrocarbons, such as tar sands and oil shales,
are treated subsequently, as is uranium. Also considered is the
possibility that there may be huge deposits of methane gas mixed
with salt water at depths of several miles. Furthermore, fission reactors, solar converters, and other current and prospective energy technologies are discussed.

Depletion of metallic ores. Easily accessible high-grade reserves of many nonrenewable metallic ores are being, or have already been, quickly depleted. By considering only proven land reserves of relatively high-grade ores and present usage rates, one can wrongly conclude that the reserves of practically all industrially important metals -- aluminum, chromium, copper, gold, tin, and so on -- will be virtually exhausted within 150 years (Meadows, et al., 1972). The problem of resource availability is much more complicated (Cole, et al., 1973).

Estimates of extractable natural resources beyond proven remaining reserves diverge widely. Moreover, known reserves of ores tend to increase with further exploration. The figures for iron ore rose from 19,000 million metric tons in 1950 to 251,000 million in 1970, an increase of 1,321 per cent. Known reserves of such minerals as chromite, copper, lead, and zinc have grown rapdily since 1950. Abundant manganese nodules on the seabed have been found to contain copper, nickel, and many other minerals as well. Furthermore, minerals present in seawater may become increasingly extractable by new technologies, thought it is doubtful, for instance, that the extraction of uranium will provide the basis for more energy than is needed for the separation.

In his analysis of potentially available resources, physicist Gerald Feinberg points out that all chemical elements are present in different but nonetheless large quantities in the earth's crust (Feinberg, 1972). Though this crust is from 25 to 40 miles thick, the depth of present-day mines is generally measured in hundreds of feet. (Holes drilled for oil sometimes go down six or seven miles.) Deep mining and the extraction of low-grade deposits do, however, require major increments in energy input. Apart from the question of the availability of this extra energy, additional high-grade deposits near the surface remain to be discovered. Even the first few hundred feet of the earth's crust have not been well explored for minerals in large areas of the world.

Forecaster Herman Kahn notes that more than 95 per cent of the world metal demand is for five metals that are, for all practical purposes, inexhaustible (Kahn, et al., 1976). These are iron, aluminum, silicon (a semi-metal), magnesium, and titanium. Kahn concludes that the application of advanced technologies and extensive recycling to the extraction of seven other metals -- copper, zinc, manganese, chromium, lead, nickel, and tin -- would probably make them inexhaustible. (According to Feinberg (1972) this conclusion is questionable for lead, which is a relatively minor constituent of the earth's crust.) Provided that enough energy is available, the long-range resource problems center on metals that constitute less than 0.1 per cent of the total demand (Kahn et al., 1976). Extractable mercury, for instance, might be practically exhausted in less than 50 years. Yet substitutes are available for each of its chief uses.

For many metals that are used today, other metals or synthetic materials such as plastics could be substituted (Goeller and

Weinberg, 1975). As John and Magda McHale point out, industrialized nations have built up large stocks of scrapped and relatively unused materials (McHale and McHale, 1975). Two-thirds of the copper in the United States is available for recycling if required.* Yet the lack of sufficient amounts of economic energy would pose a barrier to widespread substitutability and recycling.

However, the conclusion that adequate supplies of metallic ores can in principle be made available in the future does not guarantee that they will be. Hence this conclusion by no means justifies complacency. Availability presupposes extensive exploration, development of improved extraction and processing technologies, and enough reasonably priced energy to operate these technologies. <u>Thus the key question is not whether global reserves are in themselves adequate to meet foreseeable human needs, but rather whether a sufficient quantity of them can and will be located and extracted from accessible areas, by available technologies, within a given period of time, at acceptable prices, without significant environmental deterioration, and without depriving future generations of needed resources.</u> One crucial aspect of this question is whether the necessary capital, transportation, energy, water, and land resources will be available; another, whether institutional arrangements will be developed to analyze choices, make the appropriate trade-offs, and rationally manage resources in the interests of future as well as contemporary generations.

As reserves of easily accessible high-grade ores are becoming depleted, higher prices, limitations of present technologies, and unequally distributed locations of known reserves are putting increasing pressure on a number of metallic ores. To avoid shortages, resource-poor developed nations may intensify their competition for these ores as well as for fossil fuels.

<u>Environmental pollution</u>. When deposited on the ground or dumped into rivers and oceans, huge amounts of solid wastes from the production and consumption processes contaminate natural environments (Kneese and Schultze, 1975; MIT, 1970; Ward and DuBois, 1972). Annual solid waste in the United States amounts to approximately 5,340 million tons: 3280 million from agricultural sectors, 1,700 million from mining, 250 million from household, commercial, and institutional sources, and 110 million from industries. The world total is far above 50,000 million tons each year.

The principal water pollutants are garbage, food processing by-products, pulp and paper, processing effluents, human wastes, other organic materials, and toxic chemicals. The major sources of air pollution are automobile combustion, industrial combustion

---

*Paradoxically, shortages of fresh water and firewood -- renewable natural resources -- may be more serious during the next few decades than shortages of most nonrenewable resources.

(emissions from these sources including carbon monoxide, nitrogen oxides, hydrocarbons, and particulate discharge), and to a lesser degree, noncombustion emissions from refining and from the preparation of volatile chemicals. Transportation accounts for about 42 per cent of all air pollution, while 21 per cent comes from fuel combustion in stationary sources, 14 per cent from industrial processes, and the rest from solid waste, forest fires and other miscellaneous sources.*

Pollution is by no means limited by national boundaries, for trade winds diffuse pollutants over the globe, and oceans as well as rivers carry pollutants from nation to nation. In short, pollution is a global problem.

Man-made eco-disasters that have occurred on a relatively small scale include explosions in the atmosphere, oil spills in the sea, and contamination of bodies of fresh water. Among large-scale dangers is a sufficient build-up of particulate matter in the atmosphere to instigate a cooling trend by filtering out sunshine. On the other hand, a warming "greenhouse effect" might eventually result from the carbon dioxide released by the burning of fossil fuels. The widespread, prolonged use of any type of energy other than earth-based solar energy poses the threat of eventually increasing the temperature of the atmosphere enough to melt the Antarctic icecap and flood coastal cities.** If the Western part of this icecap continues to split and slides off the continent, the water level of the oceans would rise substantially. Furthermore, industrial pollutants discarded into the ocean have already begun to reach levels at which they impair its important oxygen-generating capacity and poison marine life. Major increases in such pollution could bring disastrous consequences. Thus pollution could inhibit industrial growth by degrading the biosphere.***

---

*Extreme acidity and alkalinity can occur in both air and water. Nitrogen oxides and sulphur oxides in air mix with water vapor and turn into nitric and sulphuric acid, thus dangerously lowering the acidity-alkalinity level. Some inorganic wastes dumped in water show either high acidity or high alkalinity. Extreme acid or alkaline wastes endanger human health when they fall with rain, destroy aquatic life in water and damage metal as well as concrete structures, boilers, and piping.

**Most of the icecap at the North Pole is already submerged in water. Hence the melting of this icecap would not raise the level of the oceans nearly as much as the melting of the Antarctic icecap.

***Typically, pollution would limit industrial growth not by making it impossible, but by rendering its environmental and social costs so exorbitant that it would be discontinued. The ultimate physical limit to industrial growth may prove to be rising temperature of the atmosphere.

Moreover, technologies whose adverse ecological consequences are not fully understood or anticipated could drastically limit growth. For instance, the ozone layer of the atmosphere might be seriously reduced by large fleets of supersonic transport planes, extensive use of aerosol sprays containing fluorocarbons, or global war. Ozone screens out part of the ultraviolet radiation which otherwise would increase the number of skin cancers and induce genetic mutations in fetuses. Subsequently, we argue that the environmental and social costs of implementing the "breeder reactor" -- so-called because it produces more fissionable plutonium fuel than it burns -- apparently outweigh the economic benefits of extra energy.

A dangerous subtlety of many forms of pollution is the time required for them to exert their full impact on the environment. An example is provided by mercury which, once introduced into aquatic ecosystems, becomes concentrated in the food chains from small organisms to large fish. In time, it produces a toxic effect in the final consumers, human beings. By the time the danger of a pollutant is recognized, crisis or even catastrophe may have become inevitable. Cancers, for instance, can arise years after contact with carcinogenic chemical compounds.

Recent evidence points to the impending threat of the harmful chemical contamination of biological systems (Epstein and Grundy, 1974). The proliferation of chemicals manufactured and used in mass-consumption societies has not been preceded by careful analysis of the ways in which these chemicals interact to form compounds that induce cancers, other degenerative diseases, and harmful mutations. The incidence of cancer has been shown to be significantly correlated with the output of the chemical industry. Workers in many chemical plants are particularly susceptible to cancer. Furthermore, animal experiments indicate that many chemically-laden consumer products, such as nearly all commercial hair dyes, may induce cancers in human beings. Medical authorities generally agree that between 60 and 90 per cent of all human cancers are probably due to environmental factors (Norman, 1976).

Studies conducted in the United States suggest that asbestos, which is carcinogenic, is now present in much of the nation's fresh water. Another carcinogen, PCB, has been detected in a number of bodies of water, from which it may eventually find its way into human beings. Furthermore, rising levels of radiation are associated with increases in cancer and genetic defects (Epstein and Grundy, 1974).

Many other examples of biological contamination could be cited. Some competent forecasters estimate that within a decade or two, longevity in mass-consumption societies may decline by several years. Although the severity of this threatened trend could be mitigated by prospective medical breakthroughs, the most pressing need is the protection of human physiological well-being by extensive research concerning the production and release of polluting chemicals into the biosphere.

Dirty technologies coupled with the practice of discharging wastes into the environment produce consequences that could decrease human life spans and limit the quantity of industrial growth. A polluted environment, moreover, detracts from the overall quality of life. Adequate responses to pollution problems require enough relatively clean energy for recycling, an ability to pay the costs, and a willingness to forego certain technologies and practices.

COPING WITH PHYSICAL LIMITS

Appropriate Technological Breakthroughs

A common response to the threat of encountering physical limits to economic growth is to devise new technologies that make growth less restrained by these limits. For instance, the use of cleaner technologies increases the growth that will be unhampered by environmental pollution. Likewise, technologies that harness new energy sources and efficiently extract lower grade ores reduce the extent to which the depletion of fossil fuels and metallic ores hinders current growth. How much sustainable growth can current and prospective technologies make possible?*

Such questions evoke conflicting answers from technological optimists and from proponents of growth stabilization. The former envisage a world in which technological breakthroughs result in plentiful wealth; the latter, a world in which natural limits induce disaster unless industrial growth is soon stabilized. For instance, R. Buckminster Fuller maintains that "the comprehensive introduction of automation everywhere ... will generate so fast a mastery and multiplication of energy wealth ... that we will be able to support all of humanity in ever greater physical and

---

*For simplicity sake, we often write as if there were a specific, yet variable level of sustainable growth that is compatible with the limits of depletion and pollution. Actually, these limits can be encountered separately at different levels in diverse geographical localities. Besides, they interfere with exponential growth to various degrees, usually not making it impossible for growth to continue but posing trade-off problems. For instance, when pollutants discharged into a lake begin to poison fish, decisions must be made as to whether the polluting industry should be closed down, be required to invest in pollution-control technology, or be permitted to continue its practices unabated. The quality of life and long-term consequences should be taken into account.

Hence the concept of a sustainable level of global growth is complex. Moreover, the amount of growth that is sustainable is quite indefinite, not only because of the conceptual complexities that it involves but also because it depends on such uncertain factors as which prospective technologies will become economically feasible.

economic success (Fuller, 1969). Conversely, Dennis Meadows and his co-authors argue: "If the present growth trends in ... industrialization, pollution, ... and resource consumption continue unchanged ... the most probable result will be a rather sudden and uncontrollable decline in ... industrial capacity ... within the next one hundred years (Meadows, et al., 1972).

As we will show in the subsequent treatment of existing, feasible, and possible technologies for generating energy, much sustainable global economic growth -- including considerable industrial growth -- appears to be feasible. Such growth depends significantly on an adequate resolution of the energy problem.* If enough relatively clean energy is harnessed, extensive recycling can be performed to yield new resources and to diminish pollution. Such hypothetical statements express the uncertainty that pervades the long-term energy outlook. Yet in view of the many energy technologies now being researched and developed, a sizeable increment to the world's energy supply appears likely.

The next two or three decades, however, will require energy conservation and may involve some shortages of high-priced energy and slow industrial growth. Fuel derived by emulsifying coal, oil, and water may take up much of the slack left by the progressive depletion of petroleum and natural gas. Some increases in the safer types of fission reactors (including specially designed heavy-water reactors but not breeder reactors), will be needed to fill the gap between expected supply and reasonable demand. Additional growth in the service sectors of the economy can be stimulated by the use of energy-efficient electronic information technology which can also save energy by taking over many of the activities now carried out by energy-wasteful transportation.

Loosening Unnecessary Social and Cultural Constraints
The opportunity for technologically induced sustainable growth does not imply the wise utilization of current technologies and the prompt development of the most beneficial feasible technologies. The amount of global economic growth that is sustainable depends not only on physical limits and technologies, but also on human abilities and practices (Jones, 1975a, 1975b; Falk, 1971). In other words, the particular growth level at which a physical limit would be encountered is a consequence of such factors as the kinds of economic growth that are sought and the extent to which fuel and metal resources are conserved. The primary barriers to sustainable growth today are social and

---

*On the one hand, technological options for energy generation need to be mentioned before socio-cultural constraints; on the other, such options had best be treated in detail in the subsequent section on energy objectives. Hence claims made in this section possess the character of promissory notes that will be redeemed.

cultural -- especially, economic and political -- constraints.*
Cultural perceptions, beliefs, value-priorities, goals, institutions, and policies that produce ecologically inappropriate types of growth unnecessarily restrict the amount of appropriate growth that would otherwise be attainable. Moreover, they could cause growth to become unsustainable, as might happen if an attempt to maximize growth by using dangerous technologies produced disastrous pollution.

Difficulty in quantifying or pricing these constraints does not make them any less real. Nor does their prominence imply that physical limits are unimportant and that all current forms of industrial growth may safely proceed full speed ahead.

Constraints on R & D projects. Social and cultural factors, including present-day political and economic goals, restrict the amount of sustainable quantitative and qualitative growth far below the amount foreseen from the strictly technological viewpoint. There is no guarantee that human beings will promptly devise and implement those technologies that would be most beneficial to the human race in the long run. Among the socio-cultural factors that interfere are the following.

Two major barriers to the rapid research, development (R & D), and implementation of new technologies are "lead time" and cost. These barriers can never be removed, but they can often be surmounted by easing the socio-cultural constraints that artificially limit what is humanly possible. Inferior design, unanticipated problems that could have been foreseen, and other unnecessary constraints prolong lead time from research to development to extensive implementation. Insufficient funding is often the result of an unwillingness to rechannel substantial sums of money that are spent in more immediately gratifying ways.

Once technology has been developed, costs of implementation -- both initial outlay and maintenance costs -- constitute further barriers. The rapid implementation of a new technology may be opposed by powerful vested interests, to whom such implementation would mean depreciation of present capital as well as loss of

---

*Constraints that stem from institutional arrangements constitute "social" constraints. "Cultural" here refers to symbolic systems (for instance, directives of capitalism and of the nation-state system), to lifeways (largely divided from such systems) that have been learned and may be transmitted, and to various products of human creation.

The statement that the primary barriers today are social and cultural constraints is compatible with the previous statement that substantial sustainable growth depends significantly on an adequate resolution of the energy problem. Not only is the first statement about the present and the second about the future; the barriers to such a resolution appear to be primarily social and cultural constraints.

developed sources of income and political interest. As in the
case of R & D programs, a commitment to long-range goals may
prove mandatory for overcoming constraints. To make an appropriate new technology competitive in price with the existing
technologies that it is intended to replace, gradated taxes may
be imposed on the outmoded technologies or tax benefit conferred
for adoption of new ones.

The "problem of the commons". Thus non-technological problems
that have no technological solutions must be resolved to facilitate the rapid research, development, and implementation of
feasible technologies. One type of non-technological problem
of growth arises in situations in which individuals, corporations, and nations promote their own short-term growth interests
at the expense of others and of the longer-term future. Garrett
Hardin graphically depicts the structure of such situations in
terms of "the tragedy of the commons" (Hardin, 1973).*

A "commons" is a situation in which a group shares an environment from which benefits are extracted by its members, each of
whom is allowed to keep what he extracts. For instance, when
each herdsman in a publicly owned pastureland keeps adding animals to his own herd, the pasture becomes over-grazed. Thus
actions that temporarily benefit each herdsman lead to the subsequent ruin of all. The tragedy arises from the irresponsible,
unrestrained private use of a publicly owned resource. Even if
such use -- or rather, abuse -- of the commons can be justified
when population density, production and consumption are low, it
cannot when they have become high. The tragedy of the commons
can function as a socio-cultural constraint on growth in such
diverse areas as food gathering, farming, depletion of nonrenewable natural resources, and pollution.

Outmoded beliefs, values, and goals. Many constraints can be
traced to interrelated cultural beliefs and value-priorities
(for short, "values") from which economic and political goals
arise. Which beliefs, values and goals govern the behavior of
economic and political elites -- and thus to a large extent the
behavior of societies -- regardless of ideological differences?
The most basic value and corresponding goal is that of maximizing both economic growth and the growth of political power.
This presently challenged goal has been achieved principally by
maximizing the growth of technology. Hence technological development constitutes a partially derivative, but nevertheless com-
pelling, value and goal. Growth-oriented economic optimism is
rooted in the belief that science and technology can continually
improve the material standard of living. To expand their own
political power in the competitive arena of international politics, nations rely on increasingly destructive weapons derived
from technological sophistication as well as on economic growth.

---

*Recognition of the insightfulness of Hardin's analysis of such
situations does not imply general agreement with his views on
coercion, population, and food.

Whereas Easterners historically valued harmony with nature, Westerners have been culturally oriented toward controlling nature by technology. Rational bourgeois capitalism and the nation-state, both of which arose in Europe during early modern times, relied on competitive self-interest to supply the motivational power for economic and political growth. Adam Smith's "invisible hand" seemed to guide private self-interest to unwittingly serve the common good. In spite of warnings by Thomas Malthus and John Stuart Mill, the principles that governed business and politics treated the global system (technically the earth-sun system) as if it were an unconditionally "open system." Such a system would have an unlimited source of usable energy, unlimited reservoirs for resource extraction and unlimited sinks for pollution absorption. Technological breakthroughs were counted on to push back any limits to growth. Regardless of whether this belief was explicitly articulated, in practice the earth was treated as if it were unlimited in its ability to support continual industrial growth. Thus little responsibility was assumed for the consequences of economic and political behavior on people harmed by it, on future generations, and on the exploited environment.

These increasingly outmoded beliefs, values, and goals direct present-day economic and political systems toward crisis-prone growth and away from emphasis on safe growth. Though new technologies might even make possible much sustainable industrial growth by harnessing an economic source of plentiful, non-polluting energy, this by no means implies that the earth-sun system is unconditionally open. Recognizing that it is not makes wasteful behavior intolerable, and efficient design necessary to do more with less energy and resources. Not only could such inappropriate beliefs and values be changed; several that have long characterized industrial societies have begun to change rather dramatically.* One is the "open system" belief. Another is the value expressed by the "technological imperative" -- the assumption that what can be done technologically should be done. This imperative, which ignores any limits to growth, has recently been largely replaced by "technology assessment," a method employed to evaluate feasible technologies in order to choose between them.

The need for a global economic goal. The social sciences and history furnish convincing evidence that what happens in societies depends significantly on the character of their goals (Polak, 1961). Rapid change can render once functional goals outmoded and the formulation and adoption of new goals appropriate. To an appreciable extent, the ecological problems encountered by today's industrial growth have arisen from continued

---

*For instance, a switch from "linear" toward "circular" economies (figure 1, p. 139) -- a switch that embodies basic changes in beliefs and values -- has started in the industrialized world, though much further progress is needed.

pursuit of goals that are becoming increasingly inappropriate in our technology-shaped, diverse but progressively interconnected world. Adoption of an ecologically appropriate global economic goal and its accompanying objectives would minimize the ecological dangers inherent in a continuation of the current type of industrial growth. In addition, it would stretch the elastic socio-cultural constraints that now unncessarily but effectively restrict the level of sustainable growth as if they constituted a straight-jacket. This will become clear as the global goal of sustainable economic growth is proposed in the context of an analysis of the growth controversy, and as subsidiary objectives and certain strategies for implementing them are discussed.

SUSTAINABLE ECONOMIC GROWTH

In the early 1970s, the tendency in the growth controversy was to advocate extreme positions: either continued exponential economic growth or its rapid cessation. Both positions have since been subjected to cogent criticism (Gordon, 1976).

The maximization of quantitative, relatively undifferentiated growth* by a "business as usual" orientation is dangerous. Nearsighted exponential industrial growth could excessively deplete fuel resources and overpollute the environment. Consequently, the global industrial system might exceed its sustainable level and begin to move or even plummet downward. Hence fundamental changes are needed -- and to an appreciable extent are now being made -- in the concept of growth, in the character of the current industrial system, and in technologies.

Not only has the continuation of past trends of rapid quantitative industrial growth been put in doubt by economic and ecological considerations; the desirability of such growth has been questioned on the basis of social considerations. Among its undesirable side-effects are urban congestion, alienation, invasion of privacy, unemployment, and inflation. Moreover, it has widened the gap between countries that are affluent and those that are resource-poor. Even in typical industrialized countries, it has failed to resolve the problem of core poverty. Though the standards of living of the poor have typically increased despite widening gaps, these gaps do not go unnoticed. Rather, painful perceptions of relative deprivation result.

However, attempts to stop all industrial growth are unrealistic, unnecessary, and undesirable (Kahn and Bruce-Briggs, 1972). In view of the worldwide desire for at least some industrial growth

---

*The key term in this expression is "relatively." In the past growth was, and in the present is, differentiated. Our point is that growth is not yet sufficiently differentiated in certain ecologically significant respects. Likewise, though growth has not been sufficiently qualitative, it has been qualitative as well as quantitative.

and the widespread aversion to extensive, rigid political control of economic activities, aspirations to stabilize global industrial growth before the end of the twentieth century appear to be quite unrealistic. Since the threat of a breakdown of the world economic system during the next century stems principally from entrenched socio-cultural constraints that are evident in today's goals and behavior, this threat can be minimized by appropriate changes in those institutions and lifeways which are now incongruous with a global future of sustainable, beneficial economic growth. Thus it is unnecessary to restrict all kinds of industrial growth or to reduce the world's growth rate to zero during the next few decades. Indeed, large-scale capital expenditures are required to develop new energy sources, substitutes for diminishing raw materials, better extraction and recycling technologies, and cleaner, more efficient machines. Selective industrial growth is particularly needed to raise material living standards in poor countries. Therefore, cessation of all industrial growth is undesirable.

Even more inappropriate would be attempts to terminate economic growth, not only industrial growth but growth in the service sectors* of the economy. Growth in these sectors is much less limited by resource depletion and environmental pollution. Hence extensive sustainable growth is possible in the service sectors. Moreover, it constitutes a mandatory objective. Without such growth, the services needed to provide basic minimum living standards for hundreds of millions of people in poor countries and for appreciable numbers of poor people in rich countries cannot be supplied. Sufficient reserves of free capital would not be available to create educational, health, and transportation systems that are responsive to human needs. Furthermore, a no-growth economy could easily lead to stagnation and weaken work incentives.

Hence economic growth is still a goal highly desired by nations and business corporations. In the wake of debates on limits to growth, this goal has often been questioned, sometimes modified, but not abandoned. The real issue is not whether to grow or not to grow. Rather, it is how to grow: with which technologies, in which sectors of the economy, for which social purposes, at what rates, and to what extent. As opposed to the extreme positions of maximizing or stabilizing economic growth, this emergent

---

*Service sectors can be divided into tertiary (transportation, utilities), quaternary (trade, finance, insurance, real estate) and quinary (health, education, research, government, recreation) sectors. In affluent developed countries (for instance, the U.S.), that are moving toward "post-industrial" society, quinary services are gaining increased importance. As distinguished from the service sectors, the primary sector is extractive (agriculture, fishing, mining, timber) and the secondary sector is goods - producing (manufacturing, processing), (see Daniel Bell, The Coming of Post-Industrial Society, N.Y.: Basic Books, 1973).

intermediate position seeks to identify feasible changes that would guide the human race toward a rewarding global goal: a future of sustainable economic growth (Madden, 1972; Mesarovic and Pestel, 1974; National Goals Research Staff, 1970).

Economic growth must continue, but must not be allowed to generate consequences that would trigger its decline or collapse. To be sustainable in the long run, it must proceed only in ecologically safe ways that employ appropriate technologies. And growth, instead of being sought merely for its own sake, must be increasingly aligned to meeting the basic needs of all people and to improving the quality of life.

Thus today's insufficiently differentiated growth must become decidedly more selective. Types of growth that have excessively high ecological, social, and personal costs must be discouraged; types that promote human well-being, encouraged. Each policy designed to induce economic growth must be evaluated not merely on the basis of such classical quantifiable factors as profitability and growing market-share, but also in reference to qualitative factors that include social responsibility, environmental quality, cultural continuity, and personal and job security.

OBJECTIVES TO PROMOTE SUSTAINABLE GROWTH

Selective growth is so integral to sustainable growth that it is here regarded as part of this global goal rather than as a subsidiary objective. To attain this overall goal, a number of interrelated objectives must be successfully pursued. Especially crucial among them are the following:

1) Growth concentrated in the service sectors of developed countries (thus using relatively little energy, consuming few resources, and causing little pollution) and aided by the use of electronic information technology (especially computers linked with communications media);

2) Growth in developing countries to meet the basic needs of all their citizens; includes, but does not necessarily emphasize, industrial growth, which must be selective;

3) A transition from wasteful "linear economies" toward conservation-oriented "circular economies,"* which are based on recycling and on producing quality goods that last rather than on maximizing GNP (thus increasing the safety of industrial growth and raising its level of sustainability);

    a) Increased availability of resources, achieved through conservation, technological progress, and political agreements;

---

*See Figure 1, page 139.

b) Protection of the environment against excessive pollution, attained by monitoring, legislating and taxing, recycling, and switching to clean technologies;

c) Safe growth of the world's energy supply, including: wise utilization of fossil fuels, with emphasis on emulsification; rapid development of ecologically and economically acceptable alternative energy technologies, among which will be a source of clean, abundant energy; careful, limited use of selected fission technologies (as needed while vigorous efforts are made to implement emulsification rapidly and to develop clean energy technologies), but refusal to implement breeder reactors;

4) Open, non-dictatorial use of "motivational resources" to promote rapid, widespread, effective implementation of the objectives.*

Growth Concentrated in the Service Sectors of Developed Countries
Developed countries could safely enter a new stage of major industrial growth during the next century if a source of relatively clean, abundant energy becomes available at economically acceptable costs. But in the meantime, industrial growth in these countries should proceed more slowly and selectively, in full awareness of limitations imposed by the environment and with due regard for the local and global quality of life. For at least three major reasons, a reduction of the industrial growth rates of the 1960's appears to be the most realistic aim -- if not a necessity -- for developed countries in the near future:

First, restrictions are imposed by the diminishing amounts of currently available fossil fuels and high-grade ores. The problem of energy shortages is exacerbated by increased energy costs and by the long lead times needed to devise and implement new energy technologies.

Second, it is necessary to guard against the possibility that the vision of abundant, clean energy at reasonable prices will

---

*These objectives are not, of course, exhaustive of all needed objectives, nor is this the only plausible categorization. Each objective involves more specific recommendations. Some of the objectives overlap others. While overlaps could be eliminated from a list of objectives, awareness of them elucidates ways in which the objectives are intertwined. Since '3c' is so integral to other objectives and so crucial today, it is here selected for extensive, detailed treatment. Apart from certain controversial features of '3c' which were too important to bypass, an effort was made to center attention on those prospective global objectives that promise to be acceptable to people of divergent ideological persuasions. Though disagreements are indeed treated by this study, much further research must be conducted to analyze controversial issues.

turn out to be a chimera. Maximized industrial growth of developed nations might even exceed the sustainable regional or global levels, precipitating subsequent collapses of industrial systems. Slow-growth policies would facilitate the transition to the virtual global stabilization of industrial growth (but not all economic growth) that will eventually be needed unless abundant, clean, economic energy is harnessed (Daly, 1973). Yet selective rapid growth in certain industries would still be feasible. Moreover, the increasingly efficient design of machines, a variety of energy sources, and substitutes for diminishing resources might permit some continuing global industrial growth.

Third, as human needs for manufactured items become satisfied, further supply of such items is usually valued less. In the parlance of economics, "Diminishing marginal utility" has set in -- in other words, enough is plenty. Increases in the quantity and quality of services become more important than the exponential growth of manufactured goods. Fortunately, much safe, sustainable growth is possible the service sectors of the economy.

Thus somewhat slower selective industrial growth in increasingly circular economies is an appropriate objective for developed countries during the next two or three decades. The focus of economic growth should shift more to the service sectors. This is in line with the general direction in which the most developed countries are already headed. As computerized automation takes over the task of production, the labor force shifts increasingly into the service sectors. Already, over 60 per cent of the workers in the United States have jobs in the service sectors.

The most developed countries have begun to become "post-industrial societies" (Bell, 1973; Kahn and Wiener, 1967): service-oriented "information societies" which, while still industrial, are increasingly organized around the production, collection, dissemination, and use of information. Growth in the service sectors depends on increasing the quantity and quality of information and its uses. Information plays crucial roles in such services as education, health care, and government. The information revolution is marked by the use of computers and communications media as well as "intellectual technology" -- the substitution of explicit rules for intuitive judgments in the practical problem-solving process. One example is "technology assessment," which provides systematic techniques for estimating the consequences of various feasible technologies for which research and development funds could be allocated. Efforts to develop the services could significantly contribute to the quality of life by increasing the quantity and quality of such services as education, medicine, job training, and cultural and recreational activities. An accompanying benefit for the labor force would be the creation of new jobs. Another advantage of selective growth in the services and in related technologies would be more efficient uses of energy and materials, together with reduced pollution. Increasing emphasis on electronic information technology -- particularly, computers and television -- would open new doors to much safe, beneficial economic growth in the services. Though the manufacture of the components of electronic information technology consumes energy as well as raw materials and generates pollution, the use of such technology is extremely efficient and non-polluting. The net ecological gain as compared to many other kinds of technology is substantial.

The linking of computer technology with telecommunications promises to replace many of the activities now carried out by wasteful transportation vehicles with parallel ones requiring only efficient electronic communications media. For instance, instead of using private automobiles to do shopping, comparative shopping by videophones and computers along with delivery by small fleets of efficiently operating trucks could result in extensive savings of energy, resources, time, and money. Travel to and from conferences could be partially replaced by television -- and later, perhaps, by the three-dimensional images of holography -- installed in offices and laboratories, and connected through telecommunications networks.

Communicating is not only more efficient and quicker than commuting; it also reduces traffic congestion. Improvements in flows of information will make it increasingly possible to decentralize crowded urban areas.

Electronic information technology can also facilitate the educational process. Since the knowledge needed to live and work in today's world is steadily growing, its acquisition is mandatory for all people who wish to live rewarding, useful lives. A growing need for socially relevant, meaningful information is being felt in countries where existing values and goals are being questioned and few new ones have yet been firmly established. Education in the developed world -- and in the developing world as well -- must be free as well as compulsory on elementary levels. It must be accessible on the basis of need. In technical and advanced areas accessibility should depend on merit.

In the overburdened school systems of most of the developed world, face-to-face teaching in crowded classrooms may not be sufficient. Selective use of computers and television, which schools of industrialized countries could adopt without major financial strain, could expand the capacity of classrooms. Although electronics cannot always substitute for the presence of a teacher, much useful information can be taught with the aid of new learning technologies. This is especially true of basic skill-training programs in which the essentials can be communicated rapidly and efficiently. Assimilation can be impartially tested by electronic means.

Communications media can be used for broad public information programs that would help relatively uninformed people to become more aware of the dangers and opportunities of the current world situation. Hopefully, their sense of social responsibility would be enhanced, resulting in beneficial behavior in such areas as consumer preferences, preferred lifestyles, career choices, and selection of political leaders.

Electronic information technology could even be used to promote broader public participation in political processes. While watching television programs on which elected experts debate alternative courses of action on policy issues, viewers could make their preferences known by pressing keys attached to their television sets and connected to a central computer that instantly tabulates the results.

Potential developments and uses of electronic information technology are vast and progress is rapid. For instance, the miniaturization of mass-produced telecommunications and computer components will probably make it possible for many families in the United States to buy computerized telecommunications consoles well before the end of the century.

However, electronic information technology can also be put to undesirable uses, such as the invasion of privacy through electronic surveillance and the compilation of extensive electronic files on individuals. In such matters control is essential. The mere quantitative growth of flows of information in the developed world does not guarantee that humane objectives are being considered and implemented.

Growth to Meet Basic Needs in Developing Countries
The benefits of industrialization include many of the things which the developing world needs most, including housing, clothing, and material goods. Half the total urban population of developing countries does not have housing equipped with toilets or even drinking water. The World Bank has estimated that about 750 million people live in absolute or relative poverty, which is defined as having an income per capita below $50 a year or below one-third of the average income in their country. Most of these people have few if any of the major benefits conferred by industrialization. Even many of those at relatively higher income levels remain far behind standards that are considered minimal in the developed world.

Therefore, selective industrialization, including substantial increases in wise energy usage, constitutes a commendable objective for developing countries that elect to pursue it. Such growth needs to be linked with concern for the conservation of natural resources and of the environment. The long-term aspiration is to enjoy the fruits of sophisticated technology and high productivity without making some of the historical errors that have been made by developed countries.

In view of the importance of employment for the many people who are living in abject poverty, special attention must be given to creating satisfactory jobs in large numbers. Selective industrial growth should employ those technologies that are best adapted to provide jobs appropriate to the skills of the labor force.

When industrial output rises in poor countries, industrial employment normally increases at a rate much below that of the increase in population. Frequently, even family members of industrial workers have no alternative to low-paying jobs in the service sector. Hence an objective must be to raise the level of remuneration for services. Such increases would proceed from the menial services that require little qualification, to the middle level of commercial and clerical services, and finally to the level of technical and professional services. Thus special employment policies must be pursued in tandem with industrial growth policies.

Although industrial growth may be emphasized by developing countries, it need not be. The primary objective, regardless of the various means that can be selected to achieve it, must be to meet the basic needs of all citizens. All people should have access to adequate food, housing, clothing, employment, health care, and education. Countries with a large rural population and potential for agricultural development should consider following the Chinese model of self-help by sustained agrarian development. This strategy provides food, widespread employment in jobs for which the workers are prepared, and a way to combat excessive rates of urbanization (Omo-Fadaka, 1975).

The developed and developing worlds should conjointly explore new investment, trade, and resource policies by which both can grow more harmoniously in a common world (Brown, 1973, 1974; Falk, 1972). On the one hand, absolute gains in per capita income ought to be more important to poor countries than reduction of the gap that separates them from rich countries. Growth in developed countries benefits developing ones by providing expanded markets for raw materials and labor-intensive manufactured goods. On the other hand, as Lincoln Gordon (1976) points out, the developmental effects of income gaps between countries work best for middle income nations that are not far behind the leaders, while the poorest nations may be left to stagnate in poverty indefinitely.

Accordingly, adequate assistance to poor countries must be provided by governments of both developed and resource-rich developing countries, by the world scientific community, by direct foreign investment, by financial institutions, and by individuals. Aid must be predicated on mutual compacts. Developing countries must adopt strategies of development that do not exacerbate global problems but put the fruits of aid to humane, responsible uses. Such countries must be allowed to choose between a number of tenable development strategies.

Poor countries that are excessively dependent on outside assistance need to become less dependent. In the long run they will benefit most from foreign aid that helps them to help themselves.

Conservation-Oriented Circular Economies
A crucial objective that must be adopted to guide the world's industrial growth into channels that are safe and beneficial requires a fundamental change in contemporary industrial systems.

Not only are they unnecessarily wasteful of energies and materials; they also threaten the balances of the environment. Figure 1 shows how their linear mode of operation, which treats the earth-sun system as if it were unconditionally "open," consists of extracting natural resources without adequate attention to conserving them, using them to maximize production and consumption, and discarding wastes from the productive process and from consumption into the environment (Boulding, 1966).*

Since increasing material production and consumption constitute an overriding goal of present-day economies, the flow of materials through them is maximized. The measurement of industrial growth in terms of total sales encourages demand for expanding quantities of products. Inasmuch as major enhancement of the durability of products would decrease sales, it is generally perceived as contrary to the interests of such a system. Thus the built-in obsolescence of products in the "throw-away society" promotes sales. Yet it also brings about much unnecessary waste of natural resources as well as accelerated pollution. Concern about resource use and environmental quality would at least initially raise the costs of production and consumption and result in diminished output.

As long as resources are only mildly depleted and the environment is relatively unpolluted, raw materials and disposal of waste may be inexpensive or free. Hence in an era of excess capacity of water, air, land, resources, and pollution absorption, limits to growth may seem irrelevant. But the situation has changed everywhere. Pollution has accumulated and resource shortages coupled with price increases have begun.

Because of their excessively linear character, our industrial systems have started to encounter limits to growth. The goal of maximizing quantitative production is being rendered increasingly obsolete by the ecological consequences of its attainment. When an economic system reaches its current energy, resource, and pollution limits, <u>what is perceived as good in the short run for producers and consumers may become disastrous for the whole system -- and thus for all who participate in it -- in the long run</u>. Pursuit of individual short-term self-interest in an exploited common environment can easily trigger collective catastrophes.

Actually, linear economic systems artificially restrict the amount of sustainable global industrial growth by imposing unnecessary socio-cultural constraints. <u>A switch from relatively</u>

---

*As depicted in Figure 1, linear and circular economies are diammetrically opposed conceptual models that present and future economic systems approximate to various degrees. What is required is a movement from current relatively linear economies to increasingly circular ones.

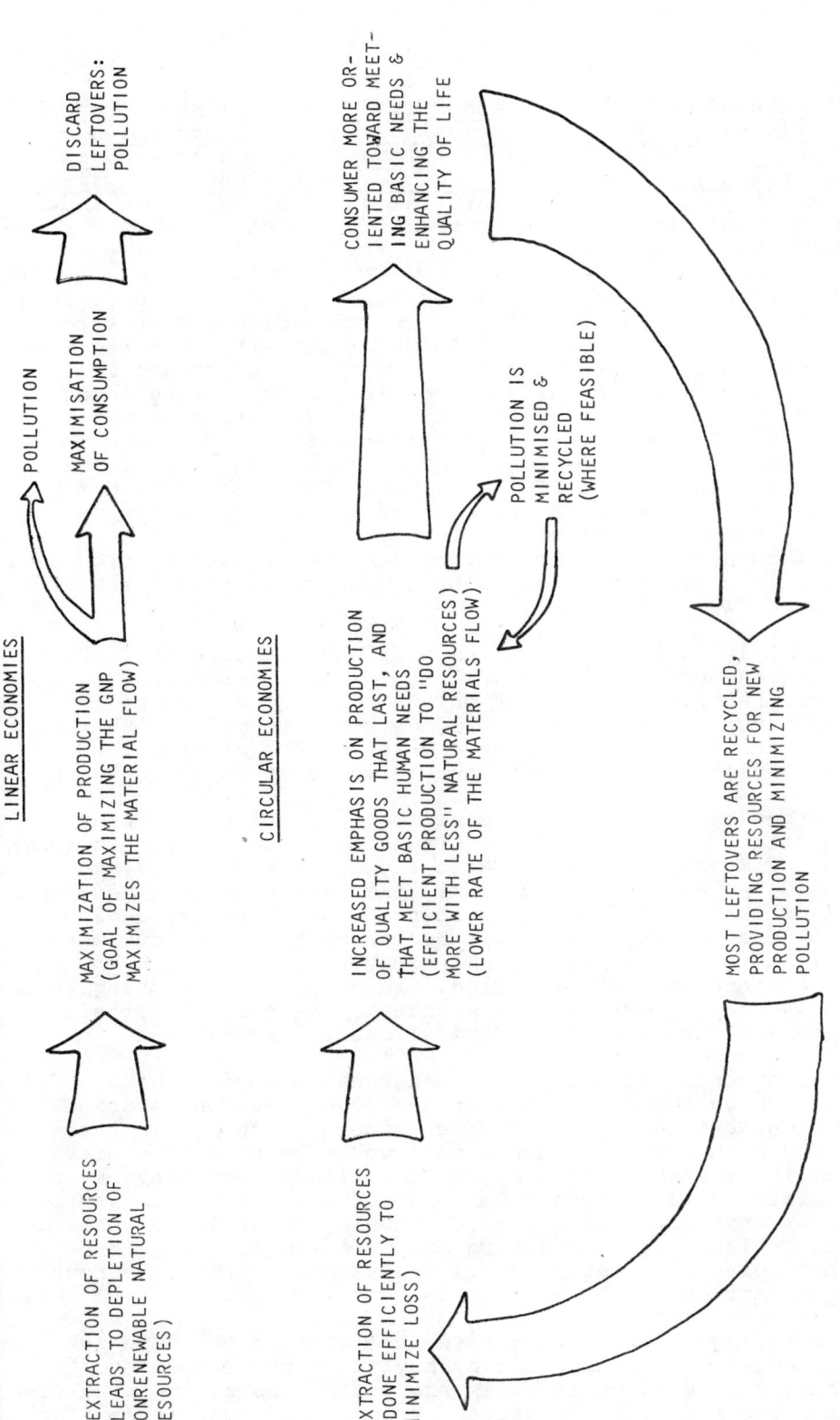

Fig. 1. Linear and circular economies.

undifferentiated quantitative economic growth in linear economies to selective growth in increasingly circular economies would permit much more sustainable global economic growth, including substantial industrial growth, unrestrained by physical limits (see Figure 1). To satisfy the need for selective industrial growth, a reasonably rapid transition must be made to such conservation-oriented economies.

The key to circular economies is recycling. Glenn Seaborg, former chairman of the U.S. Atomic Energy Commission, notes that the "recycle society" can safely do much more with less raw materials and energy (Seaborg, 1975b). Wastes from production and consumption would be extensively recycled, thus cutting down drastically on harmful emissions and discarded trash as well as providing recycled materials for further production. Moreover, recycling usually consumes less energy than that needed to mine and refine new materials. For instance, aluminum produced from discarded cans conserves 95 per cent of the energy otherwise consumed by the costly electrolytic reduction of aluminum to the metallic form. About 75 per cent of the energy used to produce steel from iron ore can be saved by producing it from scrap iron (Executive Office, 1972).

Since the early 1970's, some industrialized countries have begun to make genuine progress in recycling. Yet much remains to be done. For instance, at present only about 26 per cent of the recoverable used steel in the world is being recycled. Furthermore, many junked cars remain as eye-sores that clutter land, though in reality they constitute reservoirs of metals.

Seaborg suggests how recycling could be facilitated. Products would be built with standardized, replaceable parts so that they could be easily repaired with basic tools. All products and parts would be labeled in such a way that their use, origin, and material content could be easily identified. Many household items would have parts that could be assembled in various ways to perform different functions. A consumer could return an old item for a standard trade-in price. Inasmuch as everything would be coded and tagged for material content, the cost of materials separation would be greatly reduced (Seaborg, 1975a).

Resources and energy can also be conserved through limited, efficient use. Doubling efficiency in energy conversion, storage, distribution, and use would provide twice as much power at the same energy cost. Though such a goal would be hard to achieve, substantial gains in efficiency are definitely feasible. Even more progress could be made toward reducing unimportant, wasteful uses of energy. John and Magda McHale (1975) argue that, in many areas, high energy consuming countries could maintain or enhance their present standard of living with half their current energy consumption.

Consumers living in areas that have cold winters can save substantial amounts of heating oil by buying storm windows and doors, adding insulation in walls and roofs, installing weatherstripping, and replacing furnaces. Further savings result from such behavioral changes as turning down thermostats and closing off unneeded rooms (McHale, 1976).

A chief aim of circular economics would be to create quality goods that last rather than to maximize production. Substantially increasing the lifespans of products would conserve resources by decreasing the resource flow through the economy, and would save much energy otherwise required for extensive recycling. An efficient economy could even bring about an increasing material standard of living with a slightly decreasing gross national product. Hence the craze for the newest types and models of resource-consuming and pollution-generating consumer goods needs to be discouraged and replaced by pride in well-designed, lasting products capable of easy maintenance and repair (Papanek, 1972).

To be more specific, suppose that by 1980 the service-life expectancy of all appliances in the United States were increased by one-third. This could reduce both annual appliance purchases and annual appliance discards by 25 per cent. A reduction in resource use would result, Robert Lund observes, to the extent that consumer savings from increased product life are not channeled into other goods purchased. Steel production could decrease by about 1.1 million tons; copper, by 7,000 tons; and aluminum, by 35,000 tons. Among the policies that might promote longer consumer product life are the following:

- reduce the cost of appliance repair, so consumers would be less inclined to discard an appliance;

- reduce servicing costs relative to purchase costs;

- encourage remanufacturing;

- provide extended service contracts to diminish the uncertainty of future repair expense;

- insure a continuation of parts even for older appliances;

- make life-cycle cost information freely available in understandable, useful forms (lund, 1977).

Admittedly, the aim of producing long-lasting quality goods that meet basic human needs is rather vague. Yet the existence of twilight does not mean that there is no difference between day and night. Likewise, the vagueness of the terms in question fails to justify the conclusions that all products are of equal life span or quality and that all needs are equally basic (Masloro, 1962). Rather than being dismissed, these terms must be carefully defined in order to promote the formulation of action-guiding principles that are ecologically tenable and acceptable to a wide spectrum of people in a society. Within general limits, various societies could justifiably opt for different trade-offs.

Attempts by a small, powerful group to define these terms in ways that would promote their special interests could easily result in arbitrary definitions and stringent, ultimately counterproductive, restrictions on advertising. What is needed is voluntary change of societal value-priorities. Such change would issue from an increasing ecological consciousness and a willingness to work out warranted guidelines by the give-and-take of argumentation.

In the process of such argumentation, exceptions to general principles would be specified. For instance, insistence on maximum life spans of products that are easily recycled and have little impact on resource depletion and environmental pollution could raise production costs excessively. Besides, it could minimize the variety of products and discourage improvements in them.

Thus circular economies are oriented toward the conservation of energy and resources and toward the protection of the environment from pollution. Intimately related to the general objective of circular economies are more specific objectives, some of which are partially or totally identical with various aspects of this objective. We have selected the following objectives as crucial ways of coping with the physical limits of the depletion of fossil fuels and metallic ores and of environmental pollution. The conservation objective has just been treated as the essence of the objective of circular economies. Though the objective of environmental protection could be accorded a similar treatment, we single it out for special attention. Compatible with, and partially dependent on, the objective of resource conservation is the objective of increased resource availability.* The objective of safe growth of the world's energy supply must be pursued in ways that are conducive to, or at least harmonious with, the transition to circular economies. First, we set forth the resource availability objective, then the environmental protection objective, and finally the safe energy growth objective.

<u>Increased resource availability</u>. It would be unwise to maximize the extraction and use of those nonrenewable natural resources whose known reserves are being depleted rapidly. Moreover, economic incentives that favor the rapid exploitation of virgin materials and discriminate against recycled materials must be changed. This cautionary note is sounded because of such resource-restrictive factors as the following:

- the time required for further exploration as well as for the development and implementation of needed extraction and processing technologies;

- socio-cultural resistances to the implementation of appropriate changes;

---

*Since the availability of fossil fuels is considered in conjunction with the safe energy growth objective, the increased resource availability objective here is concerned primarily with metallic ores.

- the possibility of being unable to harness plentiful, clean, economic energy for the large-scale use of low-grade ores, or resource substitution, and of recycling.

However, <u>resource conservation must go hand-in-hand with the increased availability of resources</u>. Although nonrenewable natural resources must not be wasted, they should be made more widely available to satisfy basic human needs. Attainment of this objective depends in part on international political agreements. Nonetheless, its sustainability presupposes a transition to selective growth in relatively circular economies. Of special importance is the recycling of discarded capital and consumer goods to replenish the stock of resources (Barnea, 1976b), as is the production of quality goods that last to avoid waste of available resources. Also important are:

- extensive mineral exploration with better techniques;
- invention of technologies for mining mineral deposits that are not currently extractable;
- mining and processing low-grade ores to extract minerals (where feasible and not excessively damaging to the environment);
- efficient methods of extraction, processing, and production that reduce the loss of minerals;
- creation of substitutes for those nonrenewable resources that are being rapidly depleted;
- generation of enough relatively clean energy for extensive recycling and for resource extraction and processing;
- international access to nonrenewable natural resources that are concentrated in a small number of nations;
- official recognition of submerged mineral resources on the continental shelf outside a narrowly defined zone of national jurisdiction as "the common property of mankind"; institutionalized procedures by which poor countries would share the profits made by those who extract these resources.

The last three items on this list deserve special consideration. The objective of increased resource availability is intertwined with the objective of safe growth of the world energy supply. As the preceding section indicated, energy expended to provide resources can be conserved in three basic ways: by recycling used materials rather than mining, transporting, and processing virgin minerals; by limited, efficient use; and by making products more durable so that they do not have to be produced and recycled so frequently. The pressing need for energy conservation places some limitations on resource availability, though they can be partially overcome by these energy-saving procedures.

If in the future a source of abundant, non-polluting, relatively inexpensive energy were harnessed to power circular economies, resources could become and remain plentiful. Such energy could be used to derive resources from low-grade ores. Since industrially important high-grade ores constitute but a small fraction of the chemical elements in the outer layers of the earth's crust, a technology that would permit utilization of the content of common rock as a source of materials could greatly diminish the problem of resource scarcity. A number of competent physicists maintain that "plasmas" (hot ionized gases) made at much lower temperatures (5,000 to 10,000°) than fusion plasmas (100,000°)* could be used to vaporize common rock, thereby obtaining industrially important metals that are present in low-grade concentrations in such rock. Indeed, the "plasma torch" needed for resource extraction could be fed from any source of electricity. Yet an abundant, clean, reasonably priced source would permit large-scale extraction, thus providing a key to extensive sustainable industrial growth. Gerald Feinberg's calculations indicate that the amount of mining, disposal, and pollution involved in this "earth-burning" would not be exorbitant (Feinberg, 1972).** Abundant, inexpensive energy would also make extensive reclamation by recycling economically feasible.

Access to geographically restricted natural resources needs to be guaranteed. A global future of sustainable economic growth requires relatively harmonious international interaction that avoids politically motivated embargoes on important resources. Producing and exporting countries must be paid adequate prices, but not prices that would create unmanageable balance of payments deficits in resource-dependent developed countries or would seriously disrupt the international monetary system. Since the economic well-being of nations, corporations, and peoples has become so dependent on the international economic system, top priority must be attached to devising and instituting mutually beneficial policies to guide the economic interaction of developed, resource-rich developing, and resource-poor developing nations (Brown, 1973, 1974). The unequal distribution of energy fuels and other resources calls for cooperation that transcends the principles now governing nation-states in this increasingly interpenetrating world.

The severe problems of resource-poor developing countries could be alleviated by enabling them to share in the mineral wealth about to be extracted from the ocean floor. Not only would the development of these countries reduce the widening economic gap

---

*Since fusion plasmas must be kept exceedingly clean, they would not be used to process common rock or recycle solid wastes.

**Though harnessing such energy would be advantageous, it would not resolve all problems. Beyond a certain point, for instance, the overall costs of extensive earth-burning would outweigh the benefits.

between them and developed countries; it would promote international trade by providing new markets for the products of developed countries. An International Seabed Authority could establish a dispute settlement system. These changes would be conducive to a peaceful world.*

Environmental protection. Just as a sustainable increase in resource availability necessitates a movement toward selective growth in circular economies, so does the protection of the environment from excessive pollution. Like resource availability, environmental protection can be attained by recycling and by the fabrication of enduring quality products that would diminish the flow of materials through the economy and into the environment. Both the resource and the environmental objectives depend on the production of sufficient amounts of relatively non-polluting, economic energy to permit large-scale recycling. In addition, environmental protection requires that:

- a transition be made to generating energy by means of clean technologies (which can also promote energy conservation by producing fewer by-products that need to be recycled), or at least to preventing any dirty technologies from triggering environment deterioration;

- pollution levels be monitored, both regionally and globally, in regard to long-range as well as short-range dangers;

- environmental policy be exceptionally comprehensive;

- such sanctions as universally enforced laws and taxes be invoked to encourage the widespread implementation of relatively expensive clean technologies and pollution-control technologies; and to restrict: 1) the emission of effluents from technologies used by producers and consumers, 2) the marketing of products containing chemicals that have not been adequately tested for their environmental impacts, and 3) the indiscriminate discard of capital and consumer goods.

These last three requirements call for further treatment. During the early and middle 1970's, steps have been taken to monitor such long-term global threats as partial destruction of the ozone layer of the atmosphere and unintentional climate modifications. The enhancement of systematic monitoring is imperative, as is its increased institutionalization and its application to policy formulation. Analytic models must be devised to improve the forecasting of changes in the biosphere produced as unintended consequences of various human activities.

---

*The last section of this chapter suggests how the changes in motivation required for such cooperation could occur, thus removing some of the obstacles that have been encountered by the ongoing United Nations Conference on the Law of the Sea.

Such needs make it clear that environmental policy must not confine its focus to the rectification of a few specific problems. Comprehensive policy must be formulated to provide a coherent, systematic approach to the environment as a whole.

In regard to the last of these requirements, significant progress toward controlling air and water pollution has been made in many industrialized countries during the 1970's. There is, however, a genuine possibility that the previously mentioned chemical contamination of biological systems is becoming far more serious than is generally recognized. Aside from this, evidence suggests that reasonable protection against local or regional air and water pollution can be attained at costs not exceeding two or three per cent of the gross national product of rich countries (Gordon, 1976). "Reasonable" here refers only to protection against major health hazards and impairment of productivity.

Somewhat higher standards of environmental quality, though more costly, are worth achieving. For instance, nearly everyone would benefit from major breakthroughs leading to the economically feasible reduction of the air pollution caused by automobiles. Among the various suggested approaches that should be investigated more intensively are the following: modifications in fuel composition; engine redesign; the treatment of exhaust emissions through an afterburner; readjustment of the internal combustion engine; use of the gas turbine and the diesel engine; sulphur dioxide suppression and fuel desulphurization.

When air and water were regarded as "free resources" that producers could pollute with impunity, competing businessmen in a free-market economy could not be expected to invest in expensive pollution-control technology. Despite definite progress in environmental protection, new incentives and institutions should be created. The self-interest of individuals, business, and nations needs to be increasingly harnessed to socially desirable environmental objectives.

The rigor of controls should vary directly with the toxicity of the pollutants. Universally enforced laws with severe penalties attached are required to combat the most dangerous forms of pollution. Relatively mild pollutants can be discouraged by graduated pollution taxes and by tax benefits for investing in pollution-control technology and for switching to less-polluting modes of production.

Before new synthetic chemicals are placed on the market, they must be tested -- both by themselves and in combination with other chemicals -- for harmful effects on people. Prompt, decisive legislative action must be taken to forestall the chemical contamination of biological systems. Even if the dangers turn out to have been somewhat exaggerated, the safer course will have been followed. Human life is too precious to be subjected to potentially disastrous chemical effects than can be averted by human forethought.

A few concluding remarks about the energy requirements for effectively combating pollution dramatize the importance of another objective: safe growth of the world's energy supply. Although major increases in recycling are mandatory, its energy costs are rising. Hence methods of pollution control that are more energy-efficient must also be emphasized, including a shift toward long-lived products in order to curtail the pollution that stems from manufacturing excessive numbers of quickly obsolescent items that are soon thrown away.

If enough energy were to become available, plasmas could be employed for the extensive recycling of discarded material goods. Among those who have argued for this use of plasmas are James Eastland and William Gough of the former U.S. Atomic Energy Commission. According to their conception of a plasma torch, plasmas would be made to vaporize, dissociate, and ionize solid wastes in such a way as to permit recovery of valuable elements and compounds for reuse (Gough and Eastlund, 1971).

Safe growth of the world energy supply.* By now it should be clear that circular economies powered by abundant, non-polluting, relatively inexpensive energy would make possible a new stage of safe global industrial growth. Such energy could be used to control pollution by means of recycling and to expand the resource supply by recycling used materials as well as by extracting low-grade ores. Thus the amount of sustainable economic growth allowed by the limits of pollution and resource depletion would be greatly increased.

Regardless of whether such an energy source or combination of sources can be made available eventually, a number of new energy generating technologies need to be developed quickly (Technology Review, 1972; Wilson, 1972). Adoption of energy conservation**

---

*For an overview of the energy situation, see:

Anton B. Schmalz, ed. Today's Choices, Tomorrow's Opportunities, Washington, D.C.: World Future Society, 1973.

Sam H. Schurr, ed., Energy, Economic Growth, and the Environment, Baltimore: John Hopkins Press, 1972.

Glenn Seaborg, "Opportunities in Today's Energy Melieu", The Futurist, Feb. 1975.

Glenn Seaborg, "Finding a New Approach to Energetics", Saturday Review/World, Dec. 14, 1974.

Resources for the Future, U.S. Energy Policies: An Agenda for Research, Baltimore: Johns Hopkins Press, 1968.

**The energy plan recently set forth by President Carter constitutes an important step toward the implementation of the objectives proposed in this section.

methods and a shift in rich countries toward energy-efficient electronic information technology, while clearly necessary, are not sufficient by themselves to provide the further increments of energy required for continued world economic growth. To promote safe growth of the world energy supply, at least three subsidiary objectives need to be achieved. First, presently and potentially available fossil fuels must be utilized wisely. Second, new technologies for generating safe energy from other energy sources at acceptable prices must be researched, developed, and implemented as quickly as proves feasible. Hopefully, at least one of these technologies will harness a source of clean, abundant energy. Third, the projected gap between reasonable demand for energy and its supply during the next two or three decades leaves no feasible alternative to the expanded -- though cautious -- use of those fission technologies that are less dangerous.

<u>Wise use of fossil fuels</u>. Petroleum, natural gas and coal must be used more efficiently and conserved wherever possible. Energy-saving public transportation systems, for instance, could be expanded and enhanced to reduce the need for private automobiles in urban areas. Moreover, automobiles burn less gas if they are reduced in size and equipped with more efficient engines.

Coal, which will have to be employed extensively, poses moderate health hazards. To reduce these hazards substantially, coal-burning power plants should be located far from population centers and be equipped with "scrubbers" or other pollution-control technology. The resulting health benefits far outweigh the higher prices.

High priority should be accorded to the conversion of coal into synthetic gas and oil. Much further research and development of conversion technologies is required.

So-called "secondary" and "tertiary" deposits of fossil fuels need to be tapped through the development of extraction and processing technologies that can operate at acceptable costs without excessively adverse environmental consequences (Barnea, 1976a). Since the extraction, processing, and use of fossil fuels will always have undesirable side-effects, careful cost-benefit analyses must be made. A previous commitment of research and development funds must not be allowed to result in the implementation of a new extraction or processing technology that would seriously degrade the environment.

Strip mining as usually practiced is environmentally damaging; deep mining is dangerous and costly. Yet the German reclamation of strip mines makes them much less damaging, and deep mining may subsequently be performed by robots.

The unused reserves of non-conventional hydrocarbons -- including heavy oil deposits, tar sands, oil shales (Schramm, 1970), and methane natural gas mixed with salt water -- are many times larger than those of conventional oil, natural gas, and coal.

Further technical advances and higher prices for conventional fossil fuels could make the use of some of these hydrocarbons economical.

Assuming a 50 per cent recovery rate from estimated global oil shale deposits and a yield of ten gallons of oil per ton of shale, recoverable reserves would be three to six times larger than M. King Hubbert's (1969, 1971, 1972) estimated range of total crude oil reserves. Apart from unforeseen technological breakthroughs, however, the net energy gain would probably be small and the environmental impact, considerable. Yet the extraction of oil from shale deserves extensive investigation, as does the process of deriving petroleum from heavy crude oil. Methane gas can be collected on a small scale from coal mines and from the putrefaction of organic wastes.

If very recent reports by Paul H. Jones of the Louisiana State University Department of Geology and by William M. Brown of Hudson Institute prove to be correct, huge deposits of methane gas mixed with salt water are present far beneath the Gulf of Mexico off Texas and Louisiana (P. Jones, 1975; Brown, 1976a & b; Science, 1976). Prospectors drilling for oil have repeatedly struck methane in the Cenozoic deposits that in places are 50,000 feet thick. In some localities, the methane deposits begin about a mile below the surface. According to some estimates, there may be more energy-generating capacity (expressed in "quads") in these deposits than in the remaining petroleum reserves of the Middle East or in the coal reserves of the United States. Despite the great uncertainties concerning the size of the deposits and the cost of extraction and separation, the genuine possibility of large deposits of methane warrants serious investigation. The U.S. Energy Research and Development Administration (ERDA) has begun to fund such investigation.*

One fossil fuel technology is quite promising. Emulsification, a method of mixing immiscible substances such as oil and water, is a longstanding technology that is now being applied to fossil fuels with promising results. Compared to more recent exotic technologies, it is simple and inexpensive. Research on the applications of emulsion technology to various energy problems is now being supported by ERDA. Within a few years, it should be possible to estimate the potential contribution of emulsification technology to meeting world energy needs. In the meantime, industries, utilities, and other large energy users are privately

---

*Apparently, gasoline could even be grown on hydrocarbon plantations. Nobel Prize-winning chemist Melvin Calvin of the University of California has discovered a cactus-like tree, genus Euphorbia, which produces a latex sap convertible to hydrocarbons. He estimates that 10 to 50 barrels of oil per acre could be produced annually in dry areas of the U.S. Southwest for between $5 and $15 a barrel. While the potential of this new technology is highly conjectural, it warrants scrutiny (S.J.N. "Grow Your Own Gasoline", Technology Review, December 1976, p. 17).

investigating the costs and benefits of emulsified fuels for specific applications.

An emulsion is a form of colloidal suspension in which one or more substances is suspended in another substance by means of mixing. Emulsification of fuels makes possible the synthetic composition of fuel oil substitutes that may be burned in conventional furnaces and, in addition, can be made with various other properties according to the needs of the user. The main types of emulsions being considered today as fuels are coal/water/oil (Dooher, 1977; Essenhigh, 1976), water/oil, and water/gasoline, but they are by no means the only ones. Many potential fuels that are difficult to burn or environmentally objectionable in pure form -- such as residual oils, wood oil, sewage sludge, and industrial or other wastes -- are now being considered as candidates for emulsification with fuel oil or dispersed coal and water.

The primary advantage of all colloidal fuels over other synthetics is simplicity and economy of manufacture. Emulsions in particular can be prepared by a variety of means including mechanical mixing, pumping, and dispersion by ultrasound. Tables 1 and 2 give a rough estimate of comparative costs per BTU for coal/water/oil emulsions of different qualities at present oil and coal prices. Rising oil prices have made coal/water/oil emulsions an attractive substitute fuel. Even if rising coal prices would eventually cancel out most of these advantages, emulsification technology is sufficiently flexible that more expensive fuel components may be replaced or extended by hydrocarbons that today are classed as waste products, such as wood oil or sewage sludge.

TABLE 1 Comparative Prices of Fossil Fuel per MM BTU

	Heat Content	Price	Price/MM BTU
coal (low qual.	a) 24 MM BTU/ton	$23.00/ton	$0.96
coal (high qual.	b) 24 MM BTU/ton	35.00/ton	1.46
oil	6.3 MM BTU/bbl	12.00/bbl	1.90
oil	6.3 MM BTU/bbl	15.00/bbl	2.50
coal/water/oil emulsion		(coal at 23.00/ton) (oil at 12.00/bbl)	1.36
coal/water/oil emulsion		(coal at 35.00/ton) (oil at 12.00/bbl)	1.46
coal/water/oil emulsion		(coal at 23.00 ton) (oil at 15.00/bbl)	1.62
coal/water/oil emulsion		(coal at 35.00/ton) (oil at 15.00/bbl)	1.91

(a) - high sulfur - high ash
(b) - low sulfur - low ash

TABLE 2 $ Savings Resulting from the Use of Coal/
Oil/Water Emulstion Compared with Oil

Coal Price	Oil Price	Savings per MM BTU	Savings per Barrel of Oil Equivalent	Savings in %
$23.00/ton	$12.00	$0.54	$3.40	28%
23.00/ton	15.00	0.88	5.54	37%
35.00/ton	12.00	0.25	1.57	13%
35.00/ton	15.00	0.59	3.74	25%

An important advantage peculiar to emulsions is that they can be prepared with suspended water in them. Suspended water produces exploding drops that cause a secondary super-fine fuel atomization as trapped steam blows apart the confining oil droplets, thus improving combustion thoroughness and reducing soot production. Calcium carbonate, soda ash, and other additives to remove SO_2 can be dispersed in the emulsion or dissolved in the water.

This may make possible the use of many high sulfur coals and oils that cannot be burned in conventional systems.

Another advantage of emulsions as fuels is the great range of characteristics that can be produced by varying their composition and method of preparation. It may be possible, for instance, to "tailor" emulsions to existing engines and boilers, thus avoiding many costs and problems of retrofitting. A potential that remains to be explored is the possibility of creating feasible emulsion fuels for fossil-fuel-poor nations by emulsifying currently unburnable hydrocarbon wastes with small quantities of oil or coal.

Despite this optimistic outlook, there are some problems in the use of emulsion fuel technology. Depending on the application, an emulsion fuel should have some minimum stability, that is, resistance to breakdown or settling out by which free water could extinguish the ignition flame. In industrial and institutional applications, stability is less crucial than in home heating applications and private cars, because of faster fuel turnover and because of the practicality of storing emulsion components separately and operating emulsifiers on the fuel-feed lines to the boilers.

The ultimate impact of emulsification technology on the world energy problem depends largely on the design and manufacture of a small, reliable, low-cost emulsifier. Such equipment could make the use of presently feasible fuels more economical and, more important, could make feasible potential fuels that cannot be exploited by conventional means because of problems with combustion or emissions. Included in this category are high sulphur and ash coals and oils, biomass fuels and hydrocarbon wastes. Emulsion technology can also significantly reduce the burden of oil purchase at the currently high world market price. For nations possessing or having access to coal reserves, such technology can serve as a short-term "poor man's coal liquefaction".

In the longer run, the oil component of coal/water/oil emulsions might even be replaced by liquefied coal, creating an all-coal-and-water fuel. The great range of applications of emulsion fuel technology rather than the promise of any one form of emulsion makes this technology such an attractive alternative in an energy-deficient world.

Though new technologies that are conducive to the wise use of fossil fuels are urgently needed, the advisability of extensively burning fossil fuels well into the next century is questionable. As already noted, this practice might, by increasing the amount of carbon dioxide in the atmosphere, create a warming "greenhouse effect." Moreover, fossil fuels that have been burned can no longer perform their valuable functions in the petrochemical industry or be employed to make fertilizers that boost food production. Hence it would be wise to conserve these nonrenewable resources by rapidly devising and implementing technologies for harnessing alternative sources of safe energy.

Development of alternative energy sources. New technologies for producing relatively nonpolluting energy from sources other than fossil fuels, uranium, and uranium isotopes should be thoroughly researched. If economically feasible, they must be rapidly developed and implemented. From among these new technologies, the following have been selected as especially important:

1. Controlled fusion reactors. Controlled nuclear fusion is widely regarded as the best candidate for the procurement of abundant, clean, economically priced energy (Gough, 1972; Rose and Feirtag, 1976). Fusion is quite different from fission. Fission is the splitting of the nuclei of heavy elements, such as uranium and plutonium, to form lighter elements and free neutrons. Conversely, fusion is the combination of two hydrogen nuclei to derive a single helium nucleus, a neutron, and a radiation loss of mass, which is converted into a large amount of energy.* Fusion requires the confinement of "heavy" hydrogen at extremely high temperatures similar to those in the sun's interior.

Presently, scientists working on fusion projects are experimenting with two major technologies -- magnetic "bottles" and laser beam implosion -- to reach and go beyond the "break-even point" in the fusion reaction. This is the point at which the output of energy equals the input. Encouraging progress is now being made.

A recent breakthrough -- "neutral beam injection" -- has made break-even power production from a new magnetic fusion reactor quite likely. Neutral beam injection makes it possible to fire a high energy beam into magnetically bottled "plasma" (hot ionized gas) to heat and enrich the plasma fuel. The new reactor,

---

*A more precise definition of fusion, including the use of tritium derived from lithium, is rather complicated.

to be built at Princeton University, is of the Russian "tokamak" design. The reactor is constructed to fuse two forms of heavy hydrogen: deuterium and tritium. Tritium plasma will be confined inside a magnetic bottle, into which a beam of deutrium will be fired. This will heat the deuterium-tritium mixture to the fusion point at about 100 million degrees, provided that the mixture remains confined. The extent to which the break-even point may be surpassed is not known.

If technological feasibility is demonstrated by this reactor, crucial remaining tasks will be the engineering of such a reactor for commercial use and the demonstration of its economic feasibility. Each of these tasks will encounter problems that are completely unsolved at present. It is possible that the enormous difficulties inherent in converting a source of neutrons into commercially useful electricity will never be resolved.

The current U.S. fusion timetable calls for operation of a large commercial fusion-power generating system in the mid-to-late 1990's (The Futurist, 1976). Its purpose will be to demonstrate the engineering and economic features necessary to introduce fusion power into the world's energy economy. Extensive use on a worldwide scale would, however, take several more decades.

Laser fusion involves the implosion of hydrogen-containing fuel pellets by converging laser beams that form extremely hot, dense plasmas. Commercial feasibility of laser fusion may be demonstrated early in the next century.

Like laser fusion, electron beam fusion or heavy ion induced fusion converges beams on fuel pellets. Soviet experimenters recently reported producing fusion reactions by means of electron beams, though the neutron production was far below that required for a practical energy source. Recent considerations suggest that high energy heavy ions, like gold ions, might induce fusion in hydrogen fuel pellets.

The fuel problems and environmental risks of fusion are far less than those of fission. Deuterium, which is the main fuel in fusion reactions, is plentiful in sea water. The other fuel is tritium. Tritium is not a natural element but is derived from lithium, deposits of which are somewhat limited. Yet once the fusion plasma is surrounded by lithium, tritium can be produced in the fusion reactor itself, at least to the same extent that it is consumed. In other words, the fusion reactor is a breeder.

Though tritium is not fissionable, it is radioactive and would be used in large amounts. Yet the energy of the particles it emits is very small and its half-life is only about 12 years. Nevertheless, great caution will have to be exerted in handling tritium, for by entering water molecules it can get into biological systems. Hopefully, tritium release can be kept sufficiently low.

Other radioactive nuclei will be formed in the walls of a fusion reactor because the fast neutrons, which are the main operating ingredient of the reactor, will partially change any element into radioactive species. However, the designer can to a large extent control the radioactive species that will be produced by choosing appropriate wall materials. Thereby, he can avoid radioactive elements that have very long lifetimes as well as those that are biologically most damaging. Hence the radioactivity problem, despite its persistence, can be managed in ways that make it far less serious than it is in fission reactors.

Other advantages of fusion reactors are the impossibility of an explosion or a runaway process and the greatly reduced risk of sabotage or theft. Such reactors could, however, become sources of inexpensive neutrons, which in principle can be used to make nuclear explosives. Moreover, fusion energy would probably be appreciably more expensive than fission energy, though hopefully less than twice the cost of the latter.

For a long time to come, tritium will have to be employed to attain a controlled fusion reaction. Eventually, however, the deuterium-tritium reaction may be replaced by the cleaner deuterium-deuterium reaction, which would require neither tritium nor lithium. If this kind of fusion becomes technologically and economically feasible, a source of clean, abundant energy that could be used for millions of years will have been harnessed. Accordingly, a new stage of safe global industrial growth will have become possible.

2. <u>Solar energy converters</u>. Heat from the sun is already used in certain sunny locations for space heating. Maintenance costs are reported to be low. Installation costs are as yet considerable, though they could be mitigated by government incentives for investment in this renewable, non-polluting form of energy. During the next few years, solar heating seems likely to be economically competitive with present energy sources for only limited parts of the United States occupied by about ten to twenty per cent of the population. However, expected increases in the costs of fossil fuels and decreases in the costs of solar heating promise to make the latter competitive for most of the U.S. within 40 or 50 years.

Eventually, solar energy could -- and should -- replace the use of large quantities of fossil fuels for the heating and cooling of buildings. This difficult but worthy undertaking would, however, require decades. Moreover, the increasing percentage of total energy consumption released from dependence on fossil fuels in industrially advanced societies would be quite small. Suppose the United States were to convert ten per cent of its seventy million homes to solar heating and cooling by 1990. The solar energy used would only total about one per cent of the national energy demand, for home heating and cooling account for a mere ten per cent of this demand. Nonetheless, the total demand is so great that this switch from heating by means of fossil fuels to solar heating would make a noticeable difference in dependence on imported oil and in environmental quality. Moreover, for tropical or subtropical developing countries that will be able to afford the installation costs, solar heating will be an appropriate technology. Harrison Brown (1954) has argued that, in "a well-designed world", perhaps 20 to 25 per cent of the total energy needs could be supplied by solar heating and cooling.

From a purely technological viewpoint, the largescale conversion of solar energy into electrical power is feasible. Utilization of the sun's energy would provide ultraclean, safe power. Solar converters on the earth's surface would be unique among energy generating devices insofar as they would not ever increase the temperature of the earth's atmosphere. Local heat pockets would, however, remain a problem.

The question of whether solar energy can be made economically feasible is hotly disputed. Murray and LaViolette project such feasibility by 1986. Many others are more skeptical. The problem is that sunlight is diffuse and requires large areas of collection devices. Ten square miles or more would be needed to collect the energy required for a modern electric power station of one million kw capacity. To cover such an area with solar collectors is very costly, even after savings by development, inexpensive materials, and mass production have been taken into account. The crucial problem is that of producing workable elements cheaply. The intermittence of sunlight further accelerates costs. Moreover, maintenance costs would be substantial. Hans Bethe estimates that solar electricity would be at least five times as expensive as nuclear energy. The goal of generating more reasonably priced electrical energy than the energy consumed in the construction and maintenance of a solar installation could only be achieved, Glenn Seaborg argues, in the very long-term -- and possibly not at all -- by methods presently under consideration. According to them, there is no such thing as cheap solar electric energy in the foreseeable future.

William Pollard, who presents evidence against the economic feasibility of central-station solar electricity, maintains that small, self-contained solar energy systems seem destined to play an increasingly important role in the total world energy system (Pollard, 1976). These small systems, located in rural or remote areas and in developing countries that could afford them, would have limited storage and transmission capacity. They would be supplemented by at least one other energy source, such as bioconversion of wastes.

The economic problems encountered by present-day efforts to produce large-scale solar electricity do not justify the conclusion that research programs oriented toward inventing better technology and reducing costs should be abandoned. Rather, they should be vigorously pursued. Though current costs of solar conversion technologies discourage or prohibit implementation, eventual costs of improved technologies are somewhat conjectural. Whether, when, and just how solar energy will be harnessed for large-scale electrical power generation at an acceptable price is difficult to forecast.

Among a number of relatively small-scale projects, several of which are sponsored by ERDA, different approaches to the large-scale generation of electrical power by solar energy converters can be distinguished. We here select four types of converters that are receiving attention today:

(1). One approach is to build "solar farms" in sunny desert regions that are within 35 degrees of the equator. Hundreds of thousands of motor-driven mirrors covering a large area would focus the sun's widely dispersed rays to produce high temperatures in a central solar furnace and boiler atop a tower. The steam produced would be used to generate electrical power. An energy storage system could be based on the hydrolysis of water. The energy could be distributed from such farms through conventional high-voltage lines or perhaps be shipped as compressed hydrogen.

(2). Another approach utilizes the ocean as the world's greatest solar energy collector (Schmidt, 1976). Ocean thermal energy conversion would generate large amounts of energy by exploiting the temperature difference of some 35 degrees between the upper layers of ocean water within about 1000 miles of the equator and the much colder lower layers. Heated by warm ocean water, ammonia will boil and reach high pressure that could then drive turbine power generators. The exhaust gas can be cooled and reliquefied by cold water pumped from the ocean depths. Then the liquid ammonia would start the cycle anew. ERDA intends to build a floating "ocean thermal energy conversion" ammonia plant by 1984. Subsequently, plant-ships could produce hydrogen by electrolysis, liquefy it, and transfer it to tankers.

In a hydrogen economy, hydrogen would function as a means of converting, storing, and transmitting energy over long distances from power plants to distribution centers. After transmission, hydrogen could be efficiently reconverted to electricity by fuel cells. Clean-burning hydrogen would also be the basic fuel for almost all purposes. In its liquid form, it could be used for airplanes and probably also for automobiles. Some Japanese researchers expect a hydrogen economy to become competitive with the petroleum economy by 1990.

Pollard (1976) argues that capital investment in an ocean thermal energy system would be very large and the maintenance costs formidable. Yet costs are being reduced considerably. For instance, a concrete hull, which now appears feasible, would be only one-seventh as expensive as a steel hull; and the large investment in heat-exchangers could be cut in half by making them from aluminum. The case against the economic feasibility of this type of solar electrical system seems less conclusive than against the first and fourth types here discussed. Ocean thermal energy conversion certainly deserves much investigation.

(3). Alternatively, sunlight shining on silicon cells produces electrical current at about 20 per cent efficiency. Although this photovoltaic technology has been used to power most spacecraft, it is still far too costly for general use. Recent breakthroughs, including the British substitution of glass coated with cadmium sulfide for silicon, promise to lower prices substantially. In addition, costs would be cut by utilizing much of the unused 80 per cent of incoming energy to produce heat and then electrical energy. If costs are decreased sufficiently to make the large-scale implementation of photovoltaic technology economical (Barnea, 1976c), the need for a vast utility power grid network would be reduced. Solar cells could be employed not only for large-scale power generation but for electricity generation within buildings.

(4). Peter Glaser and Gerard O'Neill have suggested that solar energy converters be stationed in orbit above the earth (O'Neill, 1975). Approximately five square miles of a lightweight panel of solar cells installed in a space station would be needed to supply New York City's current power needs (10 GW). Radiant energy collected by the cells would be converted to electricity with a 15 to 20 percent efficiency. Then the electricity would be converted electronically to microwave energy with an 85 per cent efficiency. Microwave beams would be narrowly focused on antennas at selected earth locations. Finally, the microwave energy would be converted to electrical energy with an efficiency ranging from 70 to 85 per cent.

However, the economic feasibility of this proposal is highly dubious (Riegal, 1976). With any foreseeable cost of establishing space stations and providing microwave beams of high power, Hans Bethe maintains, the cost of such a solar energy satellite would probably be at least 1,000 times the cost of an equivalent power station on earth. Even the technological optimist Arthur Clarke (Richardson, 1976) doubts that orbiting solar power plants assembled in space could compete economically with ground-based installations. (Clarke, incidentally, speculates that space travel may eventually become inexpensive and that heavy, polluting industries may subsequently be located on metal-rich Mercury where there is ten times more solar power available per square meter than in earth's orbit.)

While concerted efforts are made to reduce prices and improve solar energy conversion technology, the world's people might asses the trade-offs of paying more for clean, perpetually renewable solar heating and cooling and even solar electricity. At what price levels and over which timespans could various groupings of people switch to solar energy without excessively disrupting their economies? Such questions are worth considering, even though the prospects for achieving economically feasible conversion of solar energy to electric power do not appear encouraging. After all, the ideal energy source for the world would be abundant surface-based solar energy at prices that people would afford.

3. <u>Geothermal wells</u>. Much of the energy expanded by hot springs and geysers is not yet harnessed (Hess, 1976). Geothermal exploration is taking place in a number of countries, both developed and developing, partly with the assistance of the United Nations. It seems likely that reasonably safe geothermal energy will be tapped locally at acceptable prices to provide increasing energy self-sufficiency for some areas that lack fossil fuels, have inadequate sunshine and wind potentials, and are either financially unable or otherwise disinclined to invest in nuclear technologies. Seaborg maintains that geothermal energy can realistically be expected to produce some of the United States' future energy requirements, but not a very large fraction.

It may be unnecessary to limit geothermal power plants to the few areas that have hot springs and geysers. The deeper holes are drilled, the higher the temperature rises. Despite the lack of extensive empirical data -- petroleum drillers have indeed gone as deep as 35,000 feet, but only in sedimentary areas -- it is safe to conclude that the potential for deriving energy from the hot interior of the earth is great. Geothermal energy could be obtained by drilling holes wherever there are hot rocks relatively close to the surface and then piping water down. The water would return as steam, which could be harnessed to drive turbines for electrical power generation.

However, such geothermal wells might cause enough disturbance inside the earth to trigger subsidence and possibly earthquakes. To be widely used, the energy would have to be transported or transmitted over long distances. Though the geothermal wells technique deserves much further research, a number of leading energy experts seriously doubt that it will provide energy that is plentiful, safe, or inexpensive.

4. <u>Modern windmills</u>. Windmills have been used in Europe by the tens of thousands since the Middle Ages to mill grain, pump water, and perform other tasks. In the past hundred years, knowledgeable engineering has promoted the invention of more efficient machines. Sharply increasing fuel costs and energy shortages during the past few years have led to renewed interest in wind power, which involves the harnessing of wind to generate electrical energy. The types of windmills now being devised would be radically different from those of the past (Barnea, 1976d).

Windmills generate electricity relatively efficiently. The theoretical maximum of power extraction is equal to 60 per cent of the kinetic energy of the wind passing through the blades or rotating devices of the machine. About three-quarters of this limit has been reached, and further improved efficiency is expected in coming years.

Not only is wind energy non-polluting; its sources are inexhaustible. Yet like solar energy, it is an intermittent energy source. The problem of storing energy for use when the wind subsides has hampered many applications. Although wind energy cannot supply the world's energy needs even when selective growth and conservation practices are in effect, it could diminish the rate of use of more exhaustible, polluting, or dangerous energy sources.

The National Aeronautics and Space Administration in the United States has estimated that 1.5 trillion kilowatt hours of electricity could be produced annually by the year 2000 -- between 5 and 10 per cent of the country's total electric power needs -- from wind power sites in Alaska and the Great Plain and Great Lakes regions, as well as off the New England, Eastern Seaboard, and Texas Gulf coasts. By contrast, the Energy Research and Development Administration has argued that a few per cent of U.S.

electrical power needs -- not nearly as much as 1.5 trillion kilowatt hours -- may be supplied by windmills. Like ERDA, Seaborg and Bethe agree that the NSF-NASA estimate is too high. At any rate, wind power generators should be developed and implemented while the potential contribution of such generators to the total energy supply is being carefully investigated.* Regardless of the U.S. potential, many smaller countries with good wind sites and lesser energy needs might be able to meet their electrical power needs primarily by the use of wind generators.

5. Bioconversion. A number of other energy technologies are being researched and developed.** For instance, a few attempts are being made to devise technologies for extracting usable power from the movement of ocean tides. A particularly important example is that of bioconversion technologies, whereby organic matter can be converted into fuels or power by a number of processes. On the one hand, trees or crops that convert sunlight efficiently might eventually be grown on "energy farms." On the other, dry organic wastes from urban and rural areas can be used to generate power. Organic wastes can be burned directly as fuel or can be converted first to oil or gas. Garbage is already being burned to fuel several large furnaces in North America and Europe (Kahn et al., 1976).

Bioconversion provides a useful technique for facilitating the transition toward increasingly circular economies. Not only is pollution controlled; it is used to generate new energy.

Careful interim use of selected fission technologies. The rest of this century constitutes a major transition for the human race from cheap petroleum to a highly uncertain, promising but perilous future. As reserves of conventional fossil fuels are

---

*Marshal F. Merriam argues that, assuming the energy grid can absorb all energy at the time it is produced, wind power generators could eventually supply about 15 per cent of present U.S. energy use. He believes that a determined national effort could produce the large-scale use of wind energy during the 1880's. ("Wind Energy for Human Needs", Technology Review, January, 1977, pp. 28-39). Also consult:

"Proceedings of the Second Workshop on Wind Energy Conversion Systems", Frank Eldridge, editor. Workshop held June, 1975, Washington, D.C., Proceedings published by the Mitre Corporation, McLean, Va. Document NSF-RA-N-75-050; MTR-6970.

"Wind Energy Conversion Systems - Workshop Proceedings", J.M. Savino, editor. Conference held June, 1973, Washington, D.C., National Science Foundation Document NSF/RA/W-73-006.

**Physicist - inventor Joseph C. Yater has been funded by ERDA to explore the capability of tiny microcircuits to light, heat, and cool a typical home, thus tranforming it into a self-sufficient power plant. He will also investigate applications outside the home.

diminishing, the amount of energy generated by nuclear fission reactors is increasing rapidly. Yet during the next two or three decades, some energy shortages are likely to occur. The directions and rates of economic growth will be affected. This outlook is due not merely to the decreasing reserves of fossil fuels and high-grade uranium ore coupled with their disproportionate geopolitical locations, but also to the long lead-times -- often about three decades -- needed for the research, development and widespread application of compelx new technologies.

Despite the many uncertainties that characterize the best energy forecasts, existing and seemingly feasible technologies tend to support expectations that the period of energy crunch need not be more than temporary. Yet the only new technologies that appear to have potential for supplying a sizeable percentage of the world's commercially generated energy during the rest of this century are fission reactors, coal/oil/water emulsification and, to a lesser extent and more conjecturally, some of the other new fossil-fuel technologies. Energy experts Hans Bethe and Glenn Seaborg argue that fission is the only major nonfossil power source that the United States can rely on for at least the next quarter of a century (Bethe, 1976). The need for fission energy to fuel the economies of industrialized countries that lack fossil fuel deposits is even greater.

However, the prospective, widespread use of fission reactors threatens adverse consequences that transcend national boundaries (Weinberg, 1971). More specifically, it poses problems that are part and parcel of the interrelated global problems of energy supply and demand, pollution, and the danger of nuclear war. Hence no nation can afford to treat fission energy as a distinctly domestic issue to be dealt with outside the framework of foreign policy and defense. No nation acting independently can resolve the nest of problems inherent in this issue. To cope with these problems, intelligent international cooperation is mandatory.

Such cooperation is not easily achieved, for these knotty problems provoke controversy. Attempts to formulate specific objectives encounter pointed criticism. Yet the problems are so important and the need for constructive policies is so great that this study must not avoid them. The objectives that grow out of the following analysis of three different types of fission reactors are reasoned suggestions that remain open to revision.

1. _Conventional fission reactors_. Fission reactors are already used in many parts of the world. In the United States, for instance, they supply about 9 per cent of the electrical power needs. The most common fission reactor is the light-water type. As uranium atoms are split inside a reactor's long, thin rods, energy is produced to heat water that circulates through the reactor. The steam produced by the water is carried to a turbine generator, which spins to produce electricity.

The wisdom of major increases in the use of conventional fission reactors has been questioned on four major counts: accidents, waste disposal, proliferation, and limited uranium reserves.*

First, serious accidents could occur in the operation of standard fission conversion facilities. Radioactive materials (fission products) released from a reactor that underwent a core meltdown and a failure of the Emergency Core Cooling System could be spread by wind over a wide area.

The probability of such accidents was studied in great detail by a group of scientists and engineers under the leadership of Professor Norman C. Rasmussen of MIT (1975). After investigating the probability of failure of all the parts of a fission reactor and assessing their findings in terms of known industrial practice, the Rasmussen group concluded that the probability for a serious reactor accident is exceedingly small: about one in a thousand years when 100 reactors are operating. This group also assessed the damages that would occur in an accident. The worst consequence is delayed cancers in the population affected by the fallout -- about 1000 cases in the serious accident mentioned. The total could rise to several thousand, depending on wind direction and population density. Nevertheless, the average risk for the entire population of the United States is only 2 casualties per year.

Critics of the Rasmussen report estimate higher probabilities and worse consequences.** However, even the most pessimistic claims are generally not more than 100 times the Rasmussen result. The maximum average risk of 200 casualties per year compares to 100,000 casualties from other types of accidents.

---

*Since several criticisms levelled against fission in general apply most forcefully to the breeder reactor, this essay focuses on them subsequently while evaluating breeders.

**Professor Joel Yellin of MIT aruges that the Rasmussen Report's assessments are unreliable because of many uncertainties in calculating the likelihood of accidents, and the failure to account for long-term fatalities from a nuclear accident in comparing nuclear and non-nuclear risks (Bell Journal of Economics, Spring, 1976). Opposing Yellin's claim that there is no evidence of a large gap between nuclear and non-nuclear long-term latent health risks, Professor Richard Wilson of Harvard contends that studies show nuclear plants to be much safer than coalfired plants in the long run (Bell Journal of Economics, Fall, 1976). Yellin also maintains that the Rasmussen Report is inapplicable to problems of plant siting, neglects effects of the aging of components of nuclear plants, and makes a very weak case for assumptions underlying its "fault-tree analysis". Wilson agress with these criticisms, but argues that Yellin overstates them. The upshot of the Yellin-Wilson debate appears to be: "The analysis of health risks from energy production has undoubtedly moved far beyond the narrow scope of the [Rasmussen] report, but the report still represents a firm base on which to build" (D.M., "Rasmussen Report Revisited", Technology Review, January, 1977, pp. 24-25.

Yet according to one competent estimate, a single accident might kill as many as 45,000 people (including long-term cancer victims), cause $17 billion property damage, and contaminate an area as large as the State of Pennsylvania. Hence extreme care must be taken to avoid faulty design and minimize human error, either of which could greatly increase the likelihood of a major accident. Already, partial core meltdowns have occurred at the Fermi reactor near Detroit and at the Windscale reactor in England. The Union of Concerned Scientists (UCS, Cambridge, Mass.) concluded from a careful examination that disaster was narrowly averted in the 1975 mishap at the Brown's Ferry TVA plant near Athens, Alabama. The reliability of the Emergency Core Cooling System has not yet been satisfactorily demonstrated by small-scale models. Moreover, the Atomic Energy Commission and its successor, the Nuclear Regulatory Commission have withheld information from the public about nuclear power plant safety. Henry Kendell, an MIT physics professor who heads the UCS, argues that the nuclear power program is still troubled by mismanagement, design weakness, and poor operating procedures. Thus the advisability of plans to build as many as 1,000 nuclear plants in the United States before the year 2000 is indeed dubious. Despite required delays and increased costs, the Emergency Core Cooling System must be demonstrated to be reliable and operating procedures must be improved.

A second area of concern is the disposal of toxic, long-lived radioactive wastes. As the amount of wastes requiring almost perpetual isolation from the environment increases, much more care must be taken to construct fail-safe management systems. Concern has been stimulated by repeated leakage of tanks at Hanford, Washington, which contain radioactive wastes from reactors that were used to produce plutonium for nuclear weapons. However, this type of tank is no longer used for storage of wastes from power-producing reactors. New tanks, which have double walls, are much more carefully constructed. After five years, the wastes will be converted to solids. After five more, they will be shipped to a national repository.

Though careful research concerning different methods for the final disposal of radioactive wastes has produced promising results, no definite decision has yet been reached. The favorite method is to incorporate the wastes in a very tough type of glass, to insert the glass cylinders in steel containers, and to dispose of these containers deep underground. The preferred disposal medium is salt that has not been touched by any mining operation. Though experts are confident that this method will permanently remove the radioactive materials from contact with living beings, it has not yet been demonstrated by actual operation. Hence there are many skeptics.

A related problem that has caused much concern is the transport of highly radioactive materials and of nuclear fuel. Transportation appears to be the most vulnerable link in the chain that unites the various components of a fission system. To strengthen this link, special vehicles have been designed to remain intact even after a head-on collision at 60 mph and a subsequent oil fire. Vehicles for the transport of nuclear fuel can be patterned after those used to transport nuclear weapons. The latter vehicles are highly protected against highjacking or other theft (Willrich and Taylor,). Excessive risks would occur, however, if other countries fail to follow the example of the United States, which has developed these techniques.

The third type of objection centers on the serious danger that the spread of fission reactors will promote the proliferation of nuclear weapons. Approximately 30 countries have begun to install reactors. Within another 15 years, most countries will have the technical ability to produce plutonium bombs from used reactor fuel. Twenty years from now, about 100 countries may possess both the knowledge and the raw materials necessary to build such bombs. Though the primary motivation behind nuclear development is economic rather than military, the international dissemination of reactors will markedly increase the danger of war and terrorism. This is the strongest argument against the movement to a world fission economy.

The plutonium contained in the used fuel of light-water reactors can be separated by a chemical procedure. This plutonium, while distinctly less potent for the manufacture of explosives than the plutonium of breeder reactors, could be used by a nation just beginning nuclear weapons technology to construct rather crude bombs. A much greater threat is the international sale of breeder reactors and of plants for the reprocessing of spent fuel and for the enrichment of uranium. This could easily lead to the widespread availability of weapons-grade material.

The fourth major concern about conventional fission reactors is that the supply of uranium ores of high concentration is quite limited.* Such ores in the United States have been estimated to be sufficient to fuel all domestic nuclear reactors that will be built until the year 2000. Each of these reactors could be fueled for its lifetime of 30-40 years. Beyond that time, ores of very low concentration would have to be mined -- unless reactors had previously been made more efficient than current light-water reactors (LWRs) in burning uranium. The need to extend the supply of high grade uranium ore has led to the search for alternative types of reactors, of which the following two are especially important.

---

*Since the geographical distribution of the limited quantities of high-grade uranium ores is quite uneven, political as well as economical considerations could restrict international trade. Moreover, as high-grade deposits become depleted, prices will rise. Indeed, a ton of rock in the earth's crust contains an estimated average of 600 kwh of uranium energy that could be produced by light-water reactors. Yet extraction of uranium from such low-grade ore would probably not become economically feasible in the absence of a source of plentiful, low-cost energy.

2. _Avoidance of breeder reactors_. The first type, which is generally favored, is the fast-breeder reactor (Cochran, 1974). Demonstration breeder reactors have operated in France and the Soviet Union for several years. The United States and a number of other countries are engaged in extensive research and development of this kind of reactor.

Breeders are so called because they generate the very fuel they burn, thus adding to their own energy source. They employ the isotope Plutonium^{239} as fuel in conjunction with the abundant isotope Uranium^{238}. As plutonium is "burnt," neutrons are absorbed in the uranium, thereby producing more plutonium.

The astonishing advantage of a generator that produces its own fuel is unhappily counterbalanced by the explosive, toxic character of Plutonium^{239}. It is highly fissionable. Roughly, ten pounds are sufficient to build a nuclear weapon that could destroy a medium-sized city or a few city blocks, according to the skill of the bomb designer. A minute particle of plutonium -- a fraction of a milligram -- can cause lung cancer. The amount of plutonium in a single large breeder reactor would be about three tons.

The great toxicity of plutonium exists only if it is inhaled in the form of small particles, not if it is ingested with water or food. For this reason, contamination of soil with plutonium is not very dangerous. Only if strong winds cause some of the soil to become airborne could there be danger of inhalation of plutonium particles.

The problem of preventing plutonium from contaminating the environment is worsened by the consideration that its "half-life" (the amount of time required for half of it to decompose) is 24,400 years. Since it will remain toxic for about a quarter million years, it will have to be carefully guarded during that time. Critics argue that this requires a kind of political and social stability that the human race has never experienced. Moreover, attempts to impose tight security measures could infringe on civil liberties. It is not clear that either the Scylla of radioactive pollution or the Charybdis of authoritarian controls would be avoided.

Many individuals and groups, including the National Council of Churches of the United States, have expressed concern about a plutonium economy. In the United Kingdom, Sir Brian Flowers headed a Royal Commission which concluded that all the problems of a plutonium economy would have to be carefully considered before the U.K. embarked on an extensive program of fast-breeders. Concern about plutonium is typically twofold: inadvertent release of plutonium into the environment and the misuse of plutonium for the illicit manufacture of atomic weapons.

During normal operation, reactors do not release plutonium. Such releases could come from the chemical reprocessing and the fuel fabrication plants. Yet the current practice of designing and operating these plants makes it possible to restrict the release of plutonium to 1 part in 10 trillion of the plutonium throughput. Experts argue that further improvement by a factor of 1,000 is in sight. Therefore, in spite of the large amount of plutonium that a future plutonium economy would involve, the release from reprocessing and fabrication plants could be restricted to minute quantities.

In the highly unlikely case of a reactor accident, only a small fraction of the plutonium would be released. Since plutonium oxide is highly refractory, even a severe accident would vaporize very little of it. Estimates made in the Rasmussen report on present-day LWRs indicate that the hazard from plutonium release is extremely small compared to that from the release of fission products like iodine and cesium. Hans Bethe maintains that this will not change very greatly in the case of a plutonium reactor.

The risk of plutonium release during transportation might generally be slight, though vehicles -- as well as reactors, reprocessing plants, and fabrication plants -- would be vulnerable to attack by other nations, to sabotage with powerful weapons, and to such accidents as being hit by a crashing airplane. Light-water fission reactors are exposed to similar dangers. To reduce such risks, future fission facilities could be built underground and transportation of nuclear fuels and radioactive materials kept to a minimum. Consequently, security would be appreciably increased. Construction costs would be higher but nonetheless manageable.

The danger of theft of plutonium from reactors is also very small because such plutonium is contaminated by a great amount of radioactivity. This would make it virtually impossible for any group of people to steal the plutonium. The danger of theft exists at the chemical reprocessing and fabrication plants, but can be reduced by always keeping the plutonium diluted with larger amounts of uranium. Nevertheless, the material in these plants will have to be guarded with extreme care. Experts maintain that technological methods have been found to accomplish this.

If plutonium were stolen, the possible consequences would be very serious. Given a sufficient amount of plutonium and a group of perhaps 25 highly competent scientists, engineers and technicians, nuclear weapons could probably be built.* Such a bomb would presumably not be able to destroy a city, for the plutonium in reactors is not of so-called "weapons quality." Yet the bomb would nonetheless be a powerful weapon in the hands of terrorists. While a fishing boat, for instance, carried the bomb undetected, a nation might be warned that one of its cities would be attacked unless certain non-negotiable demands were quickly met.

---

*The number 25 comes from a careful Swedish study of this problem.

The theft of plutonium could lead to the establishment of a black market and to the smuggling of plutonium into other countries. If further plutonium reactors are constructed, they should be confined to countries with high degrees of societal stability.

A new laser technology for separating uranium isotopes appears feasible, though it has not yet been developed. Such separation, which could be carried out independently of fission power, would make it relatively easy to construct inexpensive atomic bombs. One variant of isotope separation requires such sophisticated technological expertise that it will not be imitated easily in developing countries. Another variant might be simpler but its workability is far from proven. Although much more uranium would be mined, transported, stored, and burned in a fission economy, the very serious problem of laser separation of uranium isotopes would remain even if fission power were not developed further.

Since the adverse consequences of theoretically unlikely mistakes could be so adverse in a plutonium economy of breeder reactors, critics object that human errors may not be sufficiently designed out of the overall system. Nobel Laureate Hannes Alfren is quoted by the Union of Concerned Scientists:

> The technologists claim that _if_ everything works according to their blueprints, atomic energy will be a safe and very attractive solution to the energy needs of the world. This may be correct. However, the real issue is whether their blueprints will work _in the real world_ and not only in a technological paradise.

In the long run and on a large scale, the risks involved in breeder reactors may well outweigh their benefits. The argument against breeders is strengthened by the prospect of harnessing safer alternative sources of energy.

3. _Heavy-water fission reactors_. One alternative method for extending the life of the uranium supply is to switch to the heavy-water* reactor (HWR). Developed in Canada, this HWR, known as CANDU, has operated extremely well. In place of ordinary water, heavy water is used to slow down neutrons in order to cause enough fission to sustain a chain reaction. Natural uranium, in which the concentration of fissionable U-235 is only 0.7 per cent, can be used in place of the enriched uranium required by light-water reactors.

Despite its advantages, the CANDU technology makes it possible to extract fuel that, having burned for only a short time, is more suitable for the construction of nuclear weapons than fuel extracted from light-water reactors. With an HWR, India produced the plutonium for its recent nuclear explosion.

---

*Heavy water is a type of water formed with deuterium, an isotope of hydrogen with twice the atomic weight of ordinary hydrogen.

In contrast to present Canadian practice, this reactor could be operated with enriched uranium and with thorium added to convert into the separable isotope Uranium^{233}. The Canadian group has calculated that such a conversion device could be a near-breeder. This means that the reactor would not actually breed additional fuel but it would almost hold its own. This heavy water-enriched uranium-thorium reactor could extend the supply of uranium at least ten-fold without encountering some of the troubles that beset the fast-breeder.

One problem that can be overcome is posed by the consideration that U^{233} is almost as suitable for making weapons as plutonium. To prevent easy extraction, U^{233} and thorium could be diluted with enough non-fissionable U^{238}. The result is a useful nuclear fuel that is inoperable for use in a nuclear explosive. Even if the uranium is separated chemically from thorium, the resulting mixed uranium is not weapons material. To extract the U^{233} would require isotope separation that is technically very difficult.

The presence of U^{238} means, of course, that some plutonium will be made, but at least five times less than in normal light-water reactors which in turn produce much less than breeder reactors. Therefore, the use of the thorium cycle as a substantial replacement for the uranium-plutonium cycle, which includes the cycle of light-water reactors, is being recommended by some experts concerned with the nuclear proliferation problem (Feiverson and Taylor, 1976).

In view of the need for fission power and the global problems posed by its widespread use, what tentative conclusions seem warranted? Substantial implementation of fission reactors during the next two or three decades appears necessary -- especially in resource-poor developed countries such as Japan and those of Western Europe -- to provide a sufficient amount of energy independence for political stability and to forestall unemployment, recession, and possible depression. Developed countries could save much wasted energy, but generally not enough to fill the energy gap.

Yet recognition of the need for a limited amount of the safer types of fission reactors as an interim necessity is by no means equivalent to a blanket endorsement of a rapid, full-scale transition to a global fission economy oriented toward maximizing energy production. As long as there is reasonable hope of obtaining an economically acceptable, cleaner source of abundant energy within a reasonable period of time, extensive investment in fission reactors would hinder a quick transition to this source should it be proven feasible. Besides, if very large numbers of the more dangerous kinds of fission facilities are implemented indiscriminately without adequate safeguards, risks will be enormously increased and civil liberties would probably be jeopardized by attempts to make an unsafe system of energy-production safe.

The objective of selective slow-growth in the use of energy in developed countries requires wise choice among technologies and the progressive elimination of wasted energy in ways that would not lower living standards. Such an orientation is appropriate for the rest of this century, regardless of whether abundant, non-polluting, economical energy will be harnessed subsequently. In case the vision of such energy turns out to be an illusion, the selective slow-growth world would be safer and would have preserved more options for future generations. In the light of such considerations, the following policy recommendations appear appropriate:*

- Concentration upon implementation of light-water reactors.

- Increased safety by demonstration of safe methods for transporting and disposing of radioactive wastes, by decreasing the likelihood of release of radioactive materials into the environment from reactor accidents, and by building all future nuclear facilities underground.**

- Insofar as possible, prevention of proliferation of nuclear weapons.

- Extensive search for further uranium deposits and development of better extraction techniques, in order to make light-water reactors feasible for a longer period of time and fuel-reprocessing plants unnecessary during that time.

- Assurance by nuclear powers of adequate supplies of enriched uranium to other countries, thus discouraging the construction of uranium-enrichment and plutonium-reprocessing plants by those countries.

- Leasing of enriched uranium fuel by nuclear powers to customer countries with the requirement that all of the used fuel from which plutonium might otherwise be separated for the construction of bombs, be returned.

- Export controls reached by agreement of nuclear exporting countries, multinational control over dangerous nuclear materials, and improved, more frequent inspection by a stronger, better-funded International Atomic Energy Agency (IAEA).

---

*A somewhat similar analysis that proved helpful in formulating these recommendations is contained in: Nuclear Energy and National Security, A Statement on National Policy Committee of the Committee for Economic Development, U.S.A. Georgian Press, Inc., 1976.

**Switzerland, Sweden, and Belgium have found that building a nuclear power plant underground adds only four to eight per cent to the initial capital cost. The increase in safety is significant.

- Refusal by nuclear exporting countries to sell uranium-enrichment and plutonium-processing plants and breeder reactors.

- Implementation of certain types of heavy-water fission reactors, such as CANDU, and of the thorium-converter reactors that are being developed, but only with the isotope U^{233} diluted with non-fissionable U^{238}.

- To avoid the enormous risks of a world plutonium economy, refusal to construct any commercial breeder reactors in the near future.

- Continued attention to breeders only for possible future implementation if enough energy cannot be extracted from cleaner sources (including heavy-water fission reactors) by the time high-grade uranium is almost exhausted, if sufficient safeguards have by then been provided to assure probable safety without excessive infringement on civil liberties, and if people generally decide that the economic benefits of the energy outweigh the risks.

- Well-funded, extensive international cooperation to research, develop, and implement a cleaner technology -- controlled fusion or solar electric -- for economically generating sufficient energy.

- While such policies are being pursued within the framework of current political and economic systems, extensive investigation of feasible, voluntary, internationally cooperative, systemic, structural changes (that is, basic rearrangement of the institutional and authority patterns that now shape international relations) to promote increasing military denuclearization that may require non-military denuclearization.

This last recommendation is inserted because of the extremely serious consequences of the spread of nuclear technology in our divided world, which has already been rendered unsafe by the threat of global nuclear war. Since exclusive devotion to the most desirable goals sometimes interferes with achievement of good ones, this recommendation is preceded by more feasible proposals that require less extreme change. Yet even if these proposals were effectively implemented, global security would diminish at least temporarily.

In view of the energy prospects and the conditions of the economies of many nations, non-military denuclearization -- without which military denuclearization would be difficult to achieve -- is feasibly only on the basis of unprecedented international cooperation (Falk, 1976). Instead of each nation-state seeking to maximize what it now perceives as its own short-term national self-interest, nations would have to work together for a better world in which the energy needs of each nation were met while new energy technologies were being developed as rapidly as possible.* Thus the approach here suggested is to work constructively within the existing constraints of the complex global economic-political-military system while simultaneously exploring the extent to which those constraints might be lessened.

The world energy picture appears far from bleak when all the available options are considered. Yet it is fraught with uncertainties and dangers when one takes into account, for instance, the adverse consequences of the threatened proliferation of breeder reactors or of the failure to rapidly develop adequate alternatives to conventional fossil fuel technologies. The development of new technologies to extract, process, and use fossil fuels and other hydro-carbons effectively is mandatory, as is the development of safe alternative energy technologies. Cautious, selective use of the less-dangerous types of fission technology is also needed to respond constructively to the interim threat of energy shortages.

If a source of abundant, clean, reasonably priced energy can be harnessed, the long-range problem of energy shortages could be resolved. The technological prospects of obtaining such energy are rather encouraging, yet economic feasibility is still conjectural. The lead times from research to development and then to widespread commercial use will probably be long and cannot be estimated easily. Hence energy policy for the coming decades should also be oriented toward the investigation of a range of less spectacular energy technologies and the implementation of some of them well before the end of this century. This would constitute an extension of current "mixed-energy economies".

Refusal to proceed with the breeder reactor would, however, constitute a worthy, feasible global policy objective. Though an interim period of relatively high-priced energy with some shortages would apparently be unavoidable, the long-term benefits and the decreased risks would more than justify this objective. As long as there is reasonable hope of obtaining plentiful energy -- and perhaps even if this hope becomes shattered -- a plutonium economy of breeder reactors is just too dangerous to warrant implementation. Enough energy can probably be provided by the emulsification of fossil fuels; the efficient use of nuclear fuels in heavy-water and thorium converter reactors; herculean efforts toward energy conservation, bio-conversion, and a hydrogen economy; a willingness to pay very high prices for solar electrical power; and other available options.

Investments in alternative energy technologies have grown enormously since the four-fold rise in oil prices. Yet much of the money has been earmarked to provide relatively short-term energy

---

*The kind of perceived situation that could motivate such a change is analyzed in the last section of this essay.

solutions that could easily create serious problems, especially in the more distant future. The lead times of some of the prospective technologies that promise to be most beneficial could probably be reduced substantially by expensive crash programs, but sufficient funds have not yet been made available. Admittedly, problems are not solved just by well-funded programs. This is particularly true of the indispensible stage of pure research that must precede development. However, the enhancement of various incentives would attract more of the best qualified scientists to work on pure research.

The long-term global gains of quickly acquiring clean, economical technologies for large-scale energy generation would far outweigh the short-term sacrifices required. By shifting but a small percentage of the approximately $300 billion in public funds that is channeled each year to world military expenditures, several crash programs could be financed. Consequently, the period of scarce, expensive energy could probably be significantly shortened. Thus the successful pursuit of the global goal of sustainable economic growth hinges in part on the achievement of the goal of world security.

"Motivational Resources" for Implementing Objectives
Despite the pressing need for much further analysis of appropriate objectives for sustainable global economic growth, the most crucial problems concern the implementation of these objectives. Feasible strategies for lessening socio-cultural constraints in acceptable ways must be devised. Among the obstacles to be surmounted are political-ideological opposition, the self-centered defense of vested interests, and the ubiquitous problem of the commons.

While the author only touches on strategies in this chapter, he has sought to select objectives that cannot properly be dismissed as the product of wishful thinking but could -- at least to a significant extent -- be implemented in the real world. Yet these rather abstract objectives must subsequently be given "cash value." In other words, they must be shown to be adequately realistic by being joined to plausible implementation scenarios that take fully into account the potential for constructive change as well as expected opposition by vested interests and by any conflicting political-ideological orientiations.

As previously mentioned, non-technological factors hinder the rapid research, development, and implementation of needed technologies. The adverse effects of such factors can, however, be substantially reduced. Skillfully coordinated research and development programs -- particularly, "crash programs" for development after pure research has been successfully completed -- can sometimes produce remarkable results in relatively short periods of time. Such projects must be properly funded, though waste of funds can and must be curtailed. Lack of sufficient investment capital for many needed R & D projects confronts present-day mass-consumption societies with a major barrier. Yet if energy, resource, and pollution constraints are to be satisfactorily reduced, cooperative saving is required as is investment of the money saved. This in turn presupposes shared commitment to desirable long-range goals. Clearly, motivation is a crucial factor in the existence and success of R & D projects.

Though the lessening of socio-cultural constraints can involve the use of technologies, much of it centers on changes in outmoded or otherwise inappropriate policies, institutions, incentives, economic and political systems, cultural beliefs and values, and ultimately, perception and conception of the world and of one's place in it.* Major institutional reforms to combat entrenched socio-cultural constraints should not be oriented toward unrealistic aspirations, but rather toward making enough progress in reducing these constraints to bring about a future of sustainable growth. To attain this objective, many present government institutions would have to be revitalized and a number of new ones created. The role of governments in coordinating the transition to sustainable growth would go far beyond the establishment of R & D projects. During disruptions stemming from the termination of ecologically unsound practices and the transition to better technologies, governments would be called upon to protect affected business from bankruptcy, to help manufactures convert to different kinds of production, and to retrain displaced workers as well as locate jobs for them. Though such tasks require increases in some types of centralized governmental decision-making, electronic information technology could be employed to decentralize decision-making wherever feasible. Effective government leadership might be possible without a massive swelling of government budgets. Such leadership could also foster popular willingness to endure necessary disruptions. In democratic societies, a successful transition cannot be made without public cooperation.

New international institutions and agreements are needed to: manage international dislocations occasioned by huge transfers of assets to oil-producing countries; guarantee equal access to scarce resources; check any mad scramble for such resources and for export markets; establish a world food reserve for aiding famine-stricken areas, rectify the diversified manifestations of the problem of the commons, and perform many other tasks. Though a full-fledged world government would probably be unnecessary, strong international institutions would be needed. Decisions

---

*The maze of difficulties inherent in efforts to cope with non-technological problems of growth, such as the problem of the commons, calls for extensive exploration. This chapter briefly treats only one aspect of the responses needed to cope with these problems, namely, appropriate institutional changes. Appropriate revisions of cultural beliefs, values, and goals that are becoming increasingly outmoded are analyzed by the author in two other essays, "Outmoded Aspirations" and "Toward a Future of Selective Growth" (Jones, 1975a, 1975b; Falk, 1971).

regarding world-interest should doubtless be influenced by a broad-based assessment of popular sentiments. Yet in the final analysis, international institutions would make and enforce such decisions. These institutions must be designed to be both efficient and representative.

At the heart of implementation difficulties lies the problem of motivation. The successful ongoing pursuit of the global goal of selective, sustainable economic growth and of the subsidiary objectives requires extensive local, national, and international cooperation. How, if at all, can people be motivated to cooperate intelligently in ways that will lead them to produce and accept the needed changes? How limited are "motivational resources"?

The open, non-dictatorial use of motivational resources to facilitate implementation of the other objectives is itself an objective. To achieve this objective, a three-fold motivational task needs to be performed. First, objective payoffs must be changed -- for instance, by laws and taxes -- so that they encourage ecologically sound behavior and discourage the opposite. Second, self-interest must be reconceptualized to overlap more with cooperatively sought collective well-being. Third, commitment to collective well-being must be viewed as subjectively rewarding.

A motivational orientation based on the accomplishment of these three tasks provides a master key for overcoming unnecessarily restrictive socio-cultural constraints, such as the problem of the commons. Appropriate changes in policies and institutions can arise from the underlying changes in perception and motivation.

An example of how the first part of this task can be accomplished is provided by the aforementioned changes in rewards and punishments required to combat pollution in a market economy. On the international level, international institutions would be needed to enforce necessary regulations.

To perform the extremely important second part of this task, one must show how self-interest is becoming increasingly intertwined with the well-being of the human race. The common interests that unite people must be interpreted as more important than present divisive interests. <u>Repeatedly, history has demonstrated that rapid, effective shifts from action governed by conflicting self-interest to collective action directed toward common goals is influenced by this shared perception of a changed situation: Only by cooperation can mutual disaster be avoided and mutually beneficial goals achieved. Evidence supports the claim that only by intelligently working together can human beings avert unprecedented collective suffering and successfully make the transition to a rewarding future of sustainable global economic growth.</u>

This kind of cooperative orientation usually arises only <u>after</u> a crisis has come about. The subtle danger of interrelated global problems is that they may not be perceived as constituting a crisis demanding unprecedented cooperation until after disaster can no longer be averted. Will human beings anticipate likely consequences of these problems vividly enough to mobilize constructive collective action before these problems become unmanageable? This is the primary challenge of the next few decades.

The third part of the task requires recognition that a morally good person can have a satisfying life. Such a person is willing to do his duty even if refusing to do it would bring him more objective gain. He can view his subjective gain as outweighing an objective loss, for self-actualization is frequently enhanced by constructive commitment to the well-being of a collectivity. A person's empathetic acceptance of the obligation to contribute to human well-being can bring the feeling of unity with a meaningful whole. Thus people can find purpose in life by choosing to be responsible members of the global system. Such people possess integrity, having become valuable "moral resources".

Performance of this threefold task by leaders and by people generally would make duty and perceived self-interest coincide more extensively than they do today. Societal rewards and punishments, likely objective gains and losses, and subjective gains and losses would encourage cooperative behavior oriented toward sustainable economic growth and discourage behavior that conflicts with this global goal. Instead of continuing to be dominated by the "zero sum game" mentality according to which some nations must be losers if others are winners, national leaders and citizens might explore the possibility of synergistic exchange agreements between developed and developing countries (Brown, 1972, 1976). For instance, the former might provide scientific and technical assistance, economic advice, clean technologies and personnel. In exchange for these benefits, developing countries might agree to supply natural resources at mutually acceptable prices, to sign trade agreements, to renounce possession of nuclear weapons, and to make major efforts to increase their food producing capacities as well as to reduce their birth rates rapidly. Actual agreements would, of course, have to be far more specific, detailed, and complex. Yet a plurality of complementary exchange agreements, whether formal or relatively informal, could help to resolve interconnected global problems and to usher in a global era of sustainable economic growth.

ACKNOWLEDGEMENTS

The author wishes to express his gratitude to the following reviewers whose constructive comments helped him to improve the quality of this essay: Hans Bethe, Glenn Seaborg, Anthony J. Wiener, John Harwood-Jones, Burns Weston, Andrew J. Lipinski, Joelle Brink, Gerald Feinberg, John Dooher, Thomas W. Wilson, Margaret Mead, O.W. Markley, Clark Souers, Ervin Laszlo, Judah Bierman, C.P. Wolf, and Anthony J. Fedanzo.

REFERENCES

Averitt, P. "Coal", United States Mineral Resources, ed. D. Brobst and W. Pratt, Washington, D.C.: United States Government Printing Office, pp. 133-142.

Barnea, J. "The Future Supply of Nature -- Made Petroleum", paper circulated by the United Nations Institute for Training and Research, Jan. 1976a.

_____ "Reclaiming and Recycling of Used Materials", Important for the Future, Vol. X, No. 6, 1976b, p. 7.

_____ "Towards Mass-Produced Low Cost Solar Cells", Important for the Future, April 1976c, New York: UNITAR, p. 2.

_____ "Windpower--Without Need for Storage", Important for the Future, Vol. 1, No. 2, New York: UNITAR, Feb. 1976d, p. 4.

Bell, D. The Coming of Post-Industrial Society, New York: Basic Books, 1973.

Bethe, H. "The Necessity of Fission Power", Scientific American, January 1976, Vol. 234, No. 1, p. 21.

Boulding, K. "The Economies of the Coming Spaceship Earth", Environmental Quality, ed. Henry Jarrett, Baltimore, Md.: Johns Hopkins Press, 1966.

Brown, H. The Challenge of Man's Future, New York: Viking, 1954.

Brown, L. In the Human Interest, New York: W.W. Norton, 1974.

_____ "Rich Countries and Poor in a Finite, Interdependent World", Daedalus, Fall 1973, p. 163.

Brown, W. "A $100 Trillion Energy Treasure?", HI-2541-DP, Croton-on-Hudson, New York: Hudson Institute, June 1976a.

_____ Fortune, October 1976b.

Cochran, L. "The Liquid Metal Fast Breeder Reactor", Resources for the Future, Inc., Baltimore: John Hopkins Press, 1974.

Cole, H., C. Freeman, M. Jahoda, and K.L.R. Pavitt, Models of Doom, New York: Universe Books, 1973.

Cook, E. Man, Energy, and Society, San Francisco: W.H. Freeman and Company, 1976.

Daly, H. "The Steady-State Economy", Toward a Steady-State Economy, ed. H. Daly, San Francisco: W.H. Freeman and Company, 1973, pp. 149-174.

Dooher, J. "Feasibility Study of Using a Coal Water/Oil Emulsion as a Clean Liquid Fuel", John P. Dooher, Garden City, N.Y.: Adelphi University, 1977, prepared for the United States ERDA.

Epstein, S. S. and R. Grundy, Consumer Health Product Hazards, Cambridge, Mass.: MIT Press, 1974.

Essenhigh, R. H. "Combustion of Oil/Water and Emulsions", presented at the Central States Section Meeting of the Combustion Institute, Battelle Memorial Laboratories, Columbus, Ohio, Apr. 5-6, 1976.

Executive Office of the President, Office of Emergency Preparedness, The Potential for Energy Conservation: A Staff Study, Washington, D.C.: U.S. Government Printing Office, Oct. 1972.

Falk, R. A. "Statist Imperatives in an Era of System Overload", paper presented to the American Association for the Advancement of Science, Dec. 28, 1971, Philadelphia, Pa. Also, see Falk's This Endangered Planet, New York: Random House, 1972.

_____ "A World Order Analysis of Nuclear Proliferation", Forum, Vol. 8, No. 2, Oct. 1976, pp. V-111 - V-116.

Feinberg, G. "Some Considerations on a Long-Term Future Materials Policy", paper for the Conference on Society and Growth, Minneapolis, Minn., June 1972.

_____ "Some Hope and Doubts About Technological Answers to Future Materials Problems", in G. Garvey, ed., The Political Economy of International Resources, in press.

Feiverson, H. A. and Theodore B. Taylor, Bulletin of the Atomic Scientists, December 1976, p. 14.

Forrester, J. World Dynamics, Cambridge, Mass.: Wright-Allen, 1971.

Fuller, R. B. Utopia or Oblivion, New York: Bantam Books, 1969.

"Fusion Power Comes Closer to Reality", unsigned, The Futurist, Feb. 1976, pp. 45, 46.

Goeller, H. E. and A. Weinberg, The Age of Substitutability, Eleventh Annual Foundation Lecture for presentation before the United Kingdom Science Policy Foundation Fifth International Symposium - "A Strategy for Resources" - Eindhoven, The Netherlands, September 18, 1975.

Gough, W. "The Promise of Fusion Power", The Futurist, Oct. 1972, pp. 211-215.

_____, and J. Eastlund, "The Prospects of Fusion Power", Scientific American, Feb. 1971.

Gordon, L. "Limits to the Growth Debate", Resources for the Future, Summer 1976, pp. 1-44.

Hardin, G. "The Tragedy of the Commons", Toward a Steady-State Economy, ed. Herman E. Daly, San Francisco, Calif.: W. H. Freeman and Company, 1973, pp. 133-148.

Hess, H. "Geothermal Energy: Prospects and Limitations", Sierra Club Bulletin, Nov./Dec. 1976, pp. 2-12.

Harman, W. Alternative Futures and Education Policy, Menlo Park, Calif., Educational Policy Research Center of Stanford Research Institute (Research Memorandum EPRC 6747-6), February, 1970.

Hubbert, M. "Energy Resources", Resources and Man, National Academy of Sciences -- National Research Council, San Francisco: W. H. Freeman and Company, 1969, Chapter 8.

_____ "The Energy Resources of the Earth", Energy and Power, A Scientific American Book, San Francisco: W. H. Freeman and Company, 1971, pp. 31-40.

_____ "Survey of World Energy Resources," paper presented to the 26th Annual Conference of the Middle East Institute, Washington, D.C., Sept. 1972.

Jones, P. contribution to The First Geopressurized Geothermal Energy Conference, Myron H. Doffman and Richard W. Deller, eds., Austin, Texas: University of Texas Center for Energy Studies, June 2-4, 1975.

Jones, T. "Outmoded Aspirations", paper delivered at the Fourth International Conference on the Unity of the Sciences, New York, 1975b, published in the conference volume.

_____ "Toward a Future of Selective Growth", The Next 25 Years: Crisis and Opportunity, ed. Andrew A. Spekke, Washington, World Future Society, 1975a.

Kahn, H., W. Brown, and L. Martel, The Next 200 Years, West Caldwell, N.J.: William Morrow and Company, 1976, pp. 101, 102.

_____ and A. J. Wiener, The Year 2000, New York: Macmillan, 1967.

_____ and B. Bruce-Briggs, Things to Come, New York: Macmillan, 1972.

Kneese, A., and Charles L. Schultze, Pollution, Prices, and Policy, Washington, D.C.: The Brookings Institution, 1975.

Lund, R. "Making Products Live Longer", Technology Review, Jan. 1977.

Madden, C. *Clash of Culture*, Washington, D.C.: National Planning Association, 1972.

Massachusetts Institute of Technology, *Man's Impact on the Global Environment: Assessment and Recommendations for Action*, Cambridge, Mass.: MIT Press, 1970.

Maszlow, A. *Toward a Psychology of Being*, New York: D. Van Nostrand Company, 1962.

McHale, J. M. "Incentives in Saving", *Technology Review*, December 1976, 32d.

_____, and M. McHale, *Human Requirements, Supply Levels, and Outer Bounds*, N.Y.: Aspen Institute, 1975.

Meadows, D. H., D. L. Meadows, J. Randers, and W. W. Behrens III *The Limits to Growth*, N.Y.: Universe Books, 1972.

Mesarovich, M., and E. Pestel, *Mankind at the Turning Point*, New York: E. P. Dutton and Company, 1974.

Norman, C. "Federal Safeguards on Industrial Chemicals: A Vote for Foresight", *Technology Review*, December, 1976, p. 7.

O'Neill, G. K. "Space Colonies and Energy Supply to the Earth", *Science*, Vol. 190, No. 4218, Dec. 5, 1975, pp. 943-947.

Papanek, V. *Design for the Real World*, 1972.

Polak, F. L. *The Image of the Future*, Two Vols., New York: Oceana, 1961.

Pollard, W. C. "The Long-Range Prospects for Solar Energy", *American Scientist*, Vol. 64, July-Aug. 1976, pp. 424-429.

Rasmussen, N. C., Director, Wash - 1400, Reactor Safety Study: "An Assessment of Accident Risks in U.S. Commercial Nuclear Power Plants", several volumes, Washington, D.C.: Atomic Energy Commission, October, 1975.

Richardson, J. "The New Era of Practical Space Programs", *The Futurist*, Dec. 1976, pp. 346-351.

Ridgeway, J. "Natural Gas", *The Last Play*, New York: New Age Library, 1974.

Riegel, M. "Space Debate", interviews with John Holt and Gerard O'Neill, *New Age*, Dec. 1976, pp. 44-47.

Rose, D. J., and M. Feirtag "The Prospect for Fusion", *Technology Review*, Dec. 1976, pp. 21-43.

"Natural Gas: U.S. Has It If the Price is Right", *Science*, February 11, 1976.

Schmidt, J. C. "Ocean Energy", *John Hopkins Magazine*, March 1976, pp. 32-35.

Schramm, L. W. "Shale Oil", *Mineral Facts and Problems*, Washington, D.C.: United States Government Printing Office, 1970.

Seaborg, G. "Opportunities in Today's Energy Milieu", *The Futurist*, Feb. 1975a.

_____ "Toward a Recycle Society", presentation to the Conference on Facing a World of Scarce Resources, Los Angeles, Calif., March 21, 1975b.

Summers, C. M. "The Conservation of Energy", *Energy and Power*, A *Scientific American* book, San Francisco: *W. H. Freeman and Company, 1971*.

Surrey, A., and A. Bromley, "Energy Resources", *Models of Doom*, H. S. D. Cole, C. Freeman, M. Jahoda, and K. L. R. Pavitt, New York: Universe Books, 1973, p. 95.

Technology Review, *Energy Technology to the Year 2000*, Cambridge, Mass.: Technology Review, 1972.

U.S. National Goals Research Staff, *Toward Balanced Growth: Quantity With Quality*, Washington, D.C.: Government Printing Office, 1970.

Ward, B., and R. Dubois, *Only One Earth*, New York: W. W. Norton & Co., 1972.

Weinberg, A. M. "Can We Live With Fission?", paper presented to American Association for the Advancement of Science, Philadelphia, Dec. 27, 1971.

Willrich, W. and T. B. Taylor, *Nuclear Theft: Risks and Safeguards*, International Research and Technology Corporation.

Wilson, T. W., Jr., ed., *World Energy, the Environment and Political Action*, International Institute for Environmental Affairs, New York: WEEPA, a workshop co-sponsored with the Aspen Institute for Humanistic Studies, 1972.

World Oil, Aug., 1972.

MOTIVATION AND GOALS FOR GLOBAL SOCIETY

K. B. Madsen
The Royal Danish School of Educational Studies

INTRODUCTION

An important hypothesis behind the present project, as stated by Ervin Laszlo, is: "Motivation for implementing changes might be elecited by reconceptualizing the global situation as one in which human beings can avoid undesirable futures and attain desirable ones by intelligent cooperation to reach mutually rewarding collective goals".* Before we analyse the truth-value of this hypothesis, we have to define some main concepts like "motivation," "value" and goal." We then present a survey of modern models of motivation, and in the last main section we analyse the posibilities of changing motivation as well as finding motivation to change. That section concludes with a survey of some empirical evidence for our guiding hypothesis.

The definitions of the main concepts may most conveniently be stated in relation to a psychological model (see Fig. 1). This model suggests that human behavior is determined by two different kinds of psychological processes:** dynamic and cognitive processes.

Dynamic (motivational and emotional) processes, have the function of energizing or activating the organism or person to action; these processes manifest themselves empirically as the intensity of behavior. Cognitive processes have the function of steering the person's behavior on the basis of information received from the environment; these processes manifest themselves empirically in the direction of behavior. In addition to these

---

*Ervin Laszlo: Goals for Mankind -- A Third Generation Project for the Club of Rome (Forum 1975).

**From an epistemological point of view the "psychological processes" are hypothetical processes located in the brain. From an ontological point of view the psychological processes may be conceived as identical with the brain processes, such as these are known to neurophysiologists. They may also be conceived ontologically as the person's "consciousness" which depends on the brain processes.

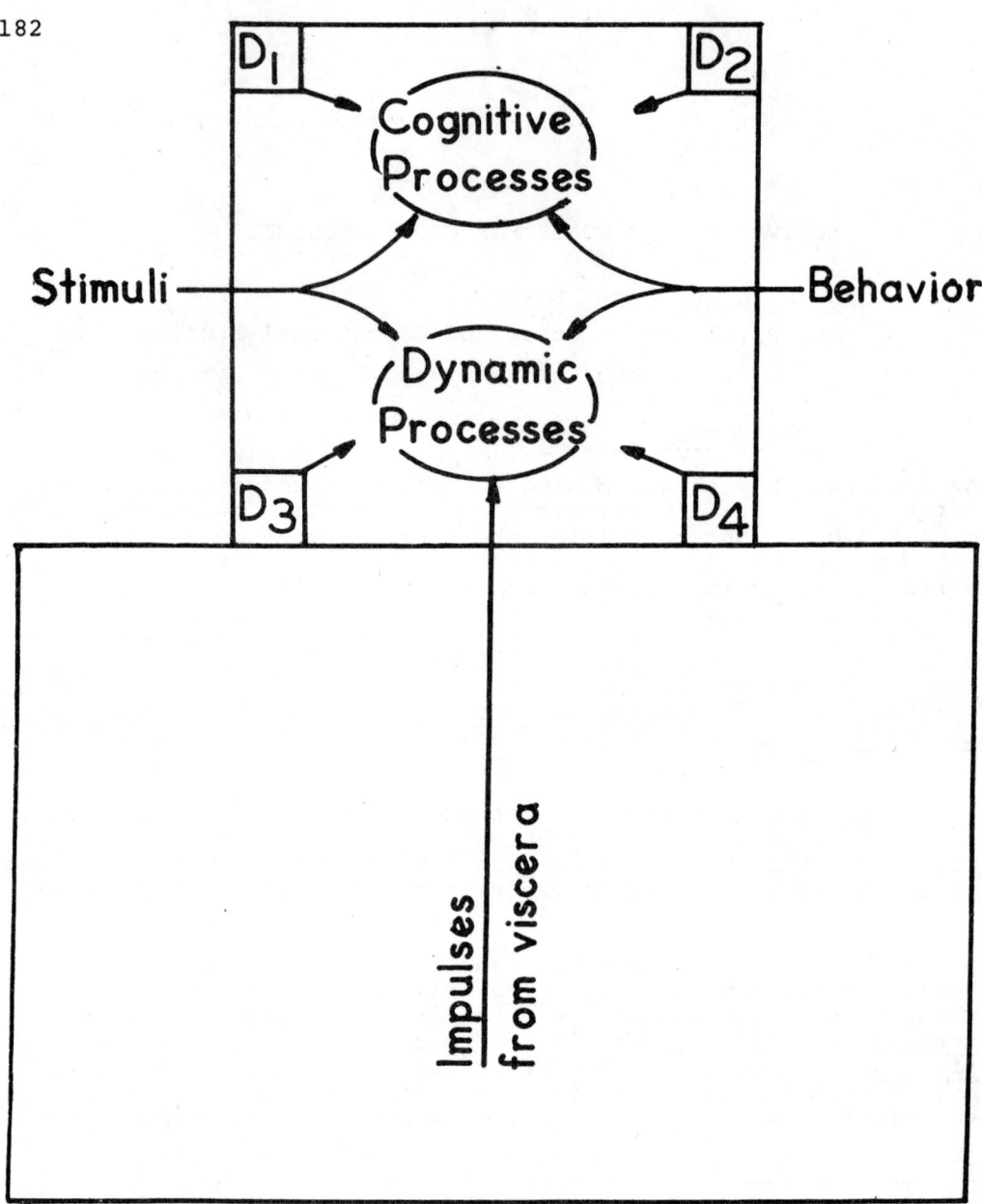

Fig. 1. B is determined by cognitive and dynamic processes in interaction. These processes are determined by external stimuli and internal impulses from the viscera, and the processes are also influenced by dispositions, which cause individual differences.

D_1 and D_2 are acquired and constitutional intellectual dispositions (intelligence factors, etc.).

D_3 and D_4 are constitutional and acquired dynamic dispositions (personality factors).

psychological processes there are some (hypothetical) psychological structures ("factors" or "dispositions"), which influence the course of the processes and determine the individual differences manifested in behavior. These structures can be classified into cognitive and dynamic structures. Furthermore, the structures may also be classified into inborn and acquired structures (although this is a difference of degree rather than an absolute difference). As examples of (mainly) inborn cognitive structures we can mention "intelligence factors"; and among the acquired cognitive structures we have "knowledge," "beliefs," "skills," etc. The inborn dynamic structures are the "temperamental factors," while the acquired dynamic structures are "sentiments," "attitudes," and "value-systems."

These relationships may be presented in a classification table (Table 1):

TABLE 1 Classification of Hypothetical Psychological Variables According to the Behavioral Effects and the Ontological Forms.

Effects in Behavior: Ontological Forms:	Dynamic Variables (Effect: intensity of behavior)	Directive Variables (Effect: direction of behavior)
Structural variables ("Dispositions", "Factors" or "Structures")	Temperamental dispositions, personality factors, attitudes, values, sentiments, etc.	Cognitive structures, intelligence factors, beliefs, concepts, skills, etc.
Process Variables ("Processes" and "States")	Motivational and Emotional processes and Affective States	Cognitive processes (Perception, Thinking, Problem solving, Planning).

After this representation of our psychological model, we are able to present a set of definitions of the main terms occurring in this report.

The term "goal" refers either to "Goal-object" defined as "the object or end-state toward which behavior is directed," to "Goal-cognition" defined as "the common term for all cognitive processes (perceptions, images, thoughts, plans etc.), which refer to the goal-object and direct behavior in the direction of attainment of the goal object."

Closely related to these terms are two others: "Belief", which may be defined as "the acquired, cognitive structure in which the goal-cognitions occur", and "Value", which may be defined as "the acquired dynamic structure which manifests itself empirically by selective activation of behavior (preference, choice, etc.)". Thus "value" and the related "attitude" are structures which supplement the motivational structures and processes: they are more or less generally activating, although the motivating factors may have some specific activating function. For the sake of completeness, we also present definitions of motivational terms.

"Motivation" is a common term that includes the motivational (dynamic) processes as well as the motivational structures. In addition, the term "motivation" also includes the external motivating stimuli ("incentives") and the internal motivating needs. (cf. our model). The different conceptions and theories of motivation are surveyed in our next main section, based upon the author's metascientific study of 42 theories of motivation Madsen 1959, 1973, and 1974).

MODELS OF MOTIVATION*

We have found it convenient to classify the basic hypotheses -- axioms or postulates -- of motivation into four categories. We call them "models of motivation" because they are often systems of interrelated hypothetical variables, which can be represented by a "model." These models may be concrete, diagramatic models, but in many cases they are only verbal analogies. In some cases, they are mathematical models. According to the main content of the basic hypotheses in the models, we can classify them into four categories: 1) The "homeostatic" model, 2) the "incentive" model, 3) the "cognitive" model, and 4) the "humanistic" model.

The Homeostatic Model
This is the oldest model in the history of motivational psychology. The concept of "homeostasis" was formulated by the famous American physiologist Walter B. Cannon in 1915 (Cannon, 1915). He was inspired by the French physiologist Claude Bernard's conception of the "internal milieu." A similar conception was formulated by Freud at the same time (Freud, 1915).

The special feature of the homeostatic model is that all biological processes -- including behavior -- are determined by a disturbance of "homeostasis," i.e., the optimal conditions of equilibrium in the organism. And the biological processes -- including behavior -- go on until homeostasis is restored (or the

---

*This section is borrowed from K.B. Madsen: Modern Theories of Motivation (Copenhagen and N.Y.: Munksgaard and Wiley, 1974).

organism is dead). Formulated in more familiar psychological terms, the homeostatic model indicates that: A disturbance of homeostasis constitutes a <u>need</u> which in turn determines a central <u>drive</u>. Together with cognitive processes, this drive determines <u>behavior</u>, which reduces -- or "satisfies" -- the need, and thus re-establishes homeostasis (see Fig. 2).

This homeostatic model is found in such influential theories as those of Freud and Hull. And many other psychologists have adopted this model, because it has several advantages. The most important are that 1) it is a <u>simple</u> model, always an important quality for scientists, and 2) it is a <u>biological</u> model, which was important for psychologists in the post-Darwinian period. The popularity of the model led psychologists to misuse it and to ignore, for a long time, facts which did not fit into the model. Finally, the homeostatic model was so severely criticized that it could not retain its position as the only valid motivational model. Other models were created as alternatives to the homeostatic model.

The Incentive Model
The "homeostatic period" lasted from about 1915 (the year of Cannon's first formulation) until about 1953 (the year of the first Nebraska Symposium on Motivation). There, H.F. Harlow criticized the homeostatic model as being too narrow. He pointed out that there were other biological primary motivations besides homeostatic drive. He was especially concerned with the existence of a visual exploratory drive (Harlow, 1953).

Later it was demonstrated by many experiments that even the so-called "homeostatic drives" especially hunger, thirst and sex cannot be completely explained by the use of a homeostatic model. The earliest and strongest experimentally based attack on the narrow homeostatic model was made by P.T. Young. As early as the beginning of the 1940's, he presented experimental evidence regarding food preferences in animals which were <u>not</u> based on homeostasis (see Young, 1941 and 1961; also the chapter about Young in Madsen, 1968). According to the incentive model, certain external stimuli have a <u>dynamic</u> effect, i.e., they determine a state of activation or energy mobilization in the organism. This dynamic state determines -- together with cognitive processes -- the behavior of the organism. This behavior often results in a reduction of the external, dynamic stimuli (see Fig. 2). These stimuli have their origin in stimulus objects called "incentives", i.e., motivating (dynamic, activating, energy mobilizing) stimulus objects. In some theories, incentives include "reinforcers" and "goal objects."

There are two kinds of incentives: <u>primary</u> and <u>secondary</u>. The <u>primary incentives</u> are S-variables which have an <u>innate</u> dynamic effect. These primary incentives play an important role in the so-called <u>"hedonistic" theories</u>, among which P.T. Young's is the most elaborate we have studied. He claims that external stimulation has <u>affective</u> as well as sensory consequences, and that the

Fig. 2
Models of Motivation

Homeostatic Hypotheses

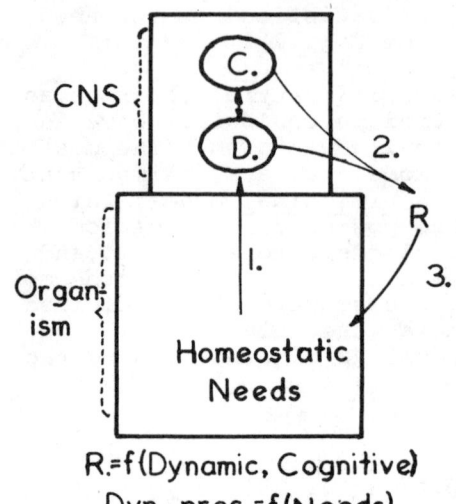

R.=f(Dynamic, Cognitive)
Dyn. proc.=f(Needs)

Incentive Hypotheses

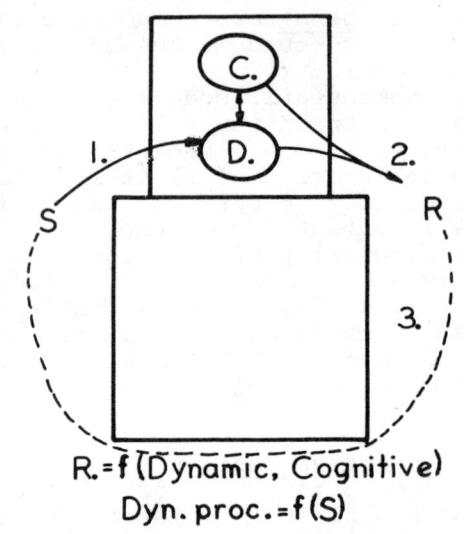

R.=f(Dynamic, Cognitive)
Dyn. proc.=f(S)

Cognitive Hypotheses

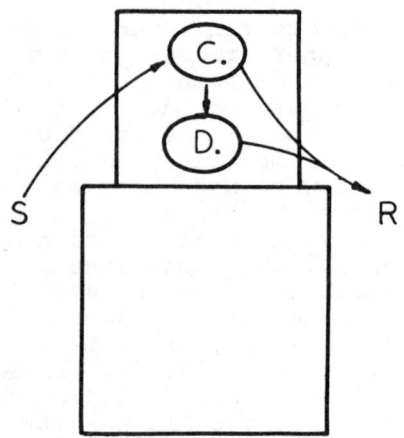

R.= f(Dynamic, Cognitive)
Dyn. proc.= f(Cogn)
Cogn. proc.=f(S)

Humanistic Hypotheses

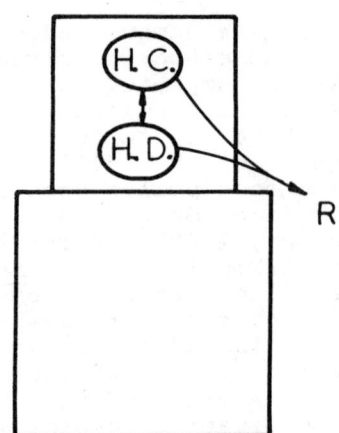

R.=f(Human Dyn., Human Cogn)
Hum.Dyn. proc.=f(?) Indeter-
Hum.Dyn. proc.=f(?) ministic

Fig. 2. Models of motivation.

affective "arousal" orients the organism towards or against the stimulus object, and thus influences choice and preference. Other well known hedonistic theories include Hebb's earliest theory (1949), McClelland's theory and Tinbergen's theory. We should mention that the hedonistic theory is very old -- even older than the homeostatic theory. It goes back to such ancient philosophers as Epicurus and appears in the so-called "Utilitarians" (e.g., J. Bentham) in the 1800's. The hedonistic conception is also inherent in Thorndike's "law of effect" and Freud's "pleasure principle."

The secondary incentives are S-variables which have an acquired dynamic effect. Therefore such incentives play an important role in modern learning theory. Thanks to K.W. Spence's incentive, motivation was included in Hull's theory (denoted by the symbol, K", together with "drive, D" and "habit strength, sHr" determine the "reaction potential, sEr" and the subsequent behavior. K is thus a hypothetical variable which is determined by the S-variable: magnitude and quality of the reward (e.g., food) used in the learning experiments to which the theory refers.

Spence developed the conception of incentive motivation on the basis of Hull's earlier concept of the "r_g-s_g mechanism" or the so-called "fractional antedating goal response." In Hull's theory, this "r_g-s_g mechanism" had only a directive effect, but Spence pointed to the possibility that the frustration of R_G -- the complete goal response -- has an activating effect similar to drive. This activating or dynamic effect of r_g-s_g was separated from the directive effect by the label "K". In Spence's later version of his own theory (see Spence, 1960), K was more important than D as a determiner of behavior. They were here supposed to interact in an additive way, so that Spence's version of Hull's well known formula reads:

$$sEr = f[sHr \times (D \times K)] \quad .$$

K is thought to be acquired by reinforcement, defined as drive reduction, while sHr is acquired, according to Spence, by contiguity.

Among the modern theories of motivation we have dealt with, we find Atkinson's to be the most elaborate one based upon an incentive model. Among the earlier theories we should especially like to mention K. Lewin's because it contained the "valence" concept. Atkinson has been strongly influenced by this concept. Freud's concept of "cathexis" is also similar to the modern incentive concept. After this survey of different incentive theories we now turn to the third model of motivation.

The Cognitive Model

This model of motivation was implicitly included in many earlier theories of perception and cognitive processes, but without being elaborated as a theory of motivation.

Thus there was -- according to Fritz Heider (Heider, 1960) -- a motivational hypothesis contained in the classic Gestalt theory. The "tendency to closure" or "to create the good figure" was treated by the classic Gestalt psychologists as a dynamic variable, a "force." This conception was never elaborated into an explicit motivational hypotheses and the "tendency to closure" was perhaps only intended to explain the motivation of cognitive processes. But the Gestalt psychologists inspired K. Lewin, who elaborated a general theory of motivation and personality, an incentive rather than a cognitive theory.

The Gestalt psychologists also inspired -- via K. Lewin -- E.C. Tolman. His original theory (Tolman, 1932) included both cognitive and motivational variables in order to explain purposive behavior in animals and man. And some of the variables -- especially Tolman's "Sign-Gestalt-Readiness" -- were mixed cognitive motivational variables. Later Tolman (Tolman, 1951) elaborated these mixed variables into his "Belief-Value Matrix," which together with his "Need System" and "Behavior Space" determined behavior. He has himself called his theory "A Cognition Motivation Model" (Tolman, 1952).

Modern theories of motivation contain two slightly different versions of a cognitive model. According to one version <u>cognitive processes determine dynamic processes</u>, and thus cognitive processes have both a <u>directive</u> and -- increasingly -- a <u>dynamic</u> effect (see Fig. 2). Festinger offers a good example of a clear and consistent theory of this type.

Another version of the cognitive model of motivation presupposes that <u>cognitive processes</u> have <u>their own "intrinsic motivation."</u> The best illustration of this we have found is Woodworth's theory. This theory contains a <u>generalization of the idea of "intrinsic motivation" into a "behavior primacy theory"</u>; it claims that the most basic kind of motivation consists of dealing actively with the environment. This theory does not exclude the fact that "extrinsic" motivation -- needs and incentives -- also may sometimes co-determine behavior. But the main idea is that even without these "extrinsic" sources of motivation the organism would be active.

In a very thorough and thought-provoking paper J.McV. Hunt (Hunt, 1965) presents a modern "information theory version" of earlier cognitive models of motivation. In the same paper he claims that Jean Piaget's theory contains an implicit hypothesis of intrinsic cognitive motivation. Hunt also claims that Karl H. Pribram's theory belongs to the same category. The present author believes, however, that the latest version of Pribram's theory is a broader and more comprehensive theory, although it comes nearer to the cognitive model than to any of the other models of motivation.

As the more complex cognitive processes are exclusively concerned with human beings, the cognitive model comes nearer to the following model of motivation.

The Humanistic Model
This model of motivation is not so clearly defined as the three others. But we think that there is a group of motivational theories which have so much in common that they can be differentiated from the other theories and classified together. They have two important features in common: 1) A humanistic conception of psychology, and 2) the hypothesis that a special class of human motivation exists. This class of motivation -- or human behavior as a whole -- is conceived of as being undetermined (see Fig. 2).

We have studied two theories which typify the above class. G.W. Allport presented his theory in his well known book, Personality (1937, rev. ed., 1961). In this book he made a distinction between idiographic and nomothetic science, which comes near to the two conceptions of "natural science" and "hermeneutic science." He also introduced the conception of the "functional autonomy" of motivation, which was inspired by an idea presented in Woodworth's first book (1918). According to this conception, there is evidence for a class of motivation in adult, mature and mentally healthy people which is functionally independent of the basic, primary motivation found in animals and infants. Allport claims that the motivational theories contained in learning theories are too narrowly based on animal experiments and that the motivation theory contained in psychoanalysis is too narrowly based on studies of neurotic people, who are more infantile in their motivation than healthy mature adults. (see our chapter about Allport's theory in Madsen, 1959, 4th ed., 1968).

Abraham Maslow's theory which we have studied and presented in Chapter 15 of Madsen, 1974, was inspired by Allport as well as others. He was the leader of the "humanistic psychologists" and exposed the necessity for another humanistic conception of science in opposition to the naturalistic, which dominated American psychology until recently. In connection with this he also defended a special humanistic conception of man in opposition to the prevailing biological one. Included in Maslow's conception of man is his hypothesis about a special humanistic adult kind of motivation, the so-called "growth need" or "metamotivation."

A less well known example of a humanistic theory is that of Thomas V. Moore (Moore, 1948), which we have studied as one of our earlier theories (Madsen, 1959). This theory is very much influenced by scholastic, Thomistic philosophy. It presupposes a humanistic conception of science and an indeterministic "free will" theory about human motivation.

We can conclude this section about models of motivation by presenting the results of our study in a classification scheme (Table 2). In this scheme we have presented the modern and earlier theories of motivation according to the dominant hypothesis

of motivation. But the reader must bear in mind that many of
the theories studied are so comprehensive that they include two
or three kinds of motivation.

TABLE 2 Classification of Basic Motivational Hypotheses

Basic Hypotheses	Homeostatic Hypotheses	Incentive Hypotheses	Cognitive Hypotheses	Humanistic Hypotheses
	Pavlov ?	Lewin	Tolman	Allport
	Freud	Young	Woodworth	Maslow
	Hull	Tinbergen	Koch	Buhler
	Murray (1938)	Helson	Festinger	Rogers
	Freeman	Hebb	McV. Hunt	
	Duffy	Olds	Nuttin	
	Eysenck ?	Murray (1959)	Leeper	
		McClelland		
		Atkinson		
		Heckhausen		
		Miller		
		Spence		
		Eysenck?		
		Brown		
		Logan		
		Berlyne		
		Skinner		
		Bindra		
		Bolles		

A Combined Model
The present author has considered the possibility of making a
synthesis of the different models of motivation. We have at the
moment integrated the first three models, but have not succeeded
in including the last one, the humanistic model.

Our synthesis is based upon a metatheoretical presupposition and
a hypothesis. The metaproposition states that all three models
are "partly true" as they correspond to different categories of
motivation. Or, in other words: the models of motivation are
all true, but have limited applicability. Thus each model is
supposed to be valid for a special category of motivation. Our
hypothesis states that each category of motivation involves a
specific structure in the brain (in addition to the Reticular
Arousal System (RAS) which is involved in all kinds of motivation). Thus we have the following categories of motivation.

The hypothalamic motives. This is the category of motivation
which is assumed to involve hypothalamic centers -- as well as

TABLE 3 Classification scheme representing our integration of the different models of motivation into one classification of motives according to the brain structures involved.

"Motive" or Category of Motivation	Brain Structures Involved.	Model of Motivation Applicable	Examples of Motives
Hypothalamic ("organic" or "homeostatic") Motives.	Hypothalamus and the RAS	Homeostatic Model	1. Hunger 2. Thirst 3. Sex Motive 4. Maternal Motive 5. Excretion Motives 6. Sleep Motive 7. Breathing Motive 8. Acquired "hungers" for tobacco, narcotics, etc.
Limbic ("incentive") Motives.	Limbic System and the RAS	Incentive Model	Emotional motives: 9. Fear 10. Aggression Social Motives: 11. Affiliation Motive 12. Achievement Motive 13. Power Motive
Cortical ("cognitive") Motives.	Cerebral Cortex and the RAS	Cognitive Motive (first version)	14. Curiosity 15. Dissonance Reduction
The RAS Motives (intrinsic activation motives)	Only the RAS	The Intrinsic Version of the Cognitive Model	16. Motives for: Motoric Activities Sensoric Activities Brain Activities Autonomic Activities

the RAS. This is the category of motivation for which the homeostatic model is most valid. But even in this instance we cannot regard the homeostatic model as completely true, for the homeostatic motives include, for example, the sex motive, which is not a completely homeostatic motive. Incentives may also determine this kind of motive as well as other organic motives: hunger, thirst, pain avoidance, cold avoidance, heat avoidance, etc. Thus we could call this category of motivation "organic motives," "homeostatic motives" or "hypothalamic motives."

The limbic motives. This is the category of motivation which is assumed to involve the limbic system as well as the RAS. We have adopted Konorski's hypotheses that "emotional motives" involve limbic "drive centers" and that "social motives" are conditioned to the emotional motives. We find that the incentive model is especially applicable to these motives. Thus the "emotional" and "social" motives could also be called "limbic" or "incentive" motives.

The cortical motives. The category of motivation which is supposed to involve the cerebral cortex -- as well as the RAS. These are the motives which function in accordance with the first mentioned version of the cognitive model: cognitive processes determine their own motivation. Consequently the category of motives could be called "cognitive" or "cortical" motives.

The RAS motives. This is the category of motivation which is assumed to involve only the Reticular Arousal System. These motives are those for which the intrinsic model -- e.g., Woodworth's behavior primacy theory -- is supposed to apply. Therefore, these could be called "intrinsic" or "activation" motives.

We can summarize this combination of the models in the form of a classification scheme (Table 3) and a brain model illustrating our integrated model of motivation (Fig. 3).

Conclusion. It has for many years been a well known fact that psychology is a science which produces many competing theories. We think that this will continue in the future. Therefore, it is important for psychologists to be able to cope with all these different theories in a rational way. We think that metascientific studies of psychological theories can be of great help to empirical and practical psychologists in their attempt to utilize theories rationally. Therefore, we have tried to develop systematology, the comparative study of theories, into a systematic and exact metascientific discipline. This can be done, among other ways, by the help of computers, which we have utilized in connection with our forthcoming "Modern Theories of Motivation," to which we can refer the reader who is interested in a more expensive and thorough presentation of systematology than we have been able to give here.

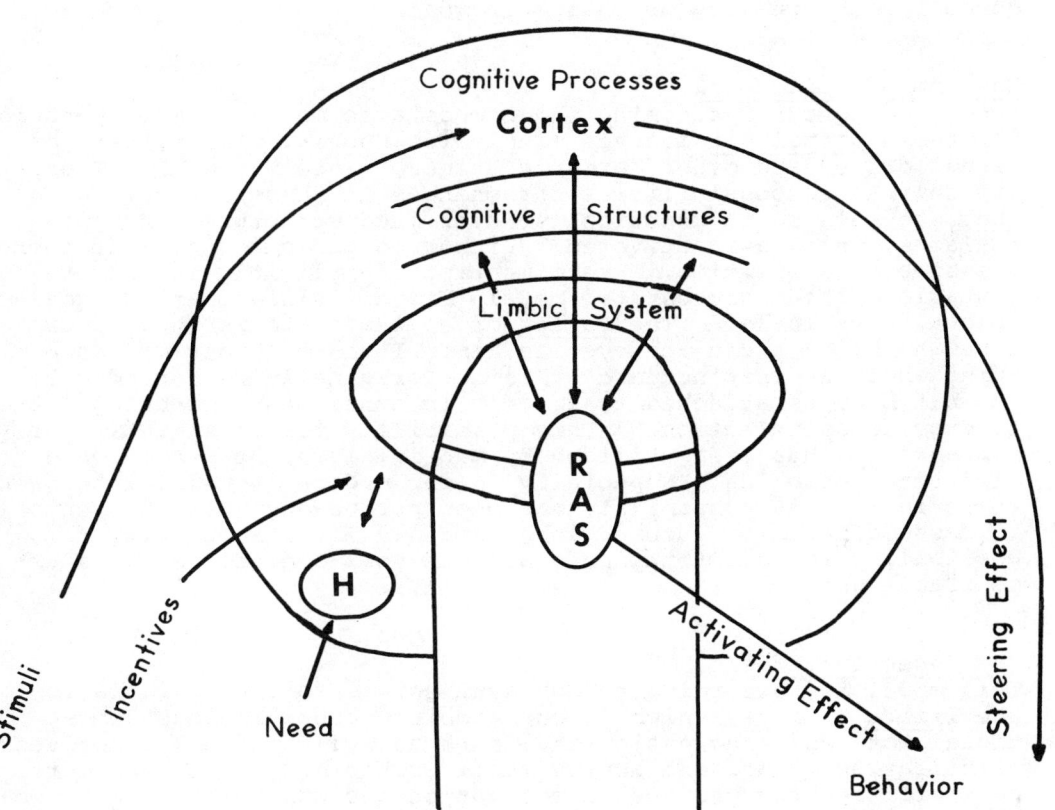

Fig. 3. Integrated model of motivation.

MOTIVATION AND CHANGE

In the preceding section, we presented the results of comparative studies of the main models of motivation together with our synthesis, "the combined model." In this section we shall present a survey of the possibilities for changes in goals, values and motivations. In the first part we analyse the possibilities for change in motivations according to the different models (including the combined model). In the second part of the section we discuss which motives to change of goals and behavior are the most useful driving forces behind such changes. In the third and last part we present some examples of empirical studies, as evidence for the reality of change of goals.

The Homeostatic Model

According to our synthesis, the homeostatic model is mainly valid for the hypothalamic motives (including hunger, thirst, sex, maternal drives and other "organic drives," (see Table 3). There are only a few possibilities for changes in these motives, as they are related to genetically determined structures in hypothalamus, which are activated by inborn organic needs. But there are some possibilities. Freud mentioned explicitly in his presentation of the homeostatic model (Freud, 1915), that the goal-object is variable: "The object of an instinct* is that in or through which it can achieve its aim. It is the most variable thing about an instinct and it is not originally connected with it, but becomes attached to it only in consequence of being fitted to provide satisfaction." This possibility for substitution of goal-objects has been utilized by man in different periods and different societies. Especially in the modern industrial "growth societies," this possibility has been pursued by advertisements in mass-media. The future global society may also utilize this possibility for substituting desirable goal-objects for more undesirable goals.

The Incentive Model

This model is, according to our synthesis, especially valid for the limbic motives, which in our combined model include "emotional motives" (aggression and fear) as well as "social motives" (affiliation, power and achievement). This model includes more possibilities for changes in motivation and goals than the homeostatic model does. According to the incentive model the independent motivating variables are the incentives, which include both rewarding and aversive stimuli-objects. These incentives are the goal-objects of behavior according to this model. The function of some incentives are primary (unlearned) and the function of others are secondary (learned). And according to the incentive model there are unlimited possibilities for learning new incentives by conditioning. This has in the past been utilized

---

*"Instinct" should have been translated as "drive," which is the most correct equivalent to the German word "Trieb."

by all kinds of approaches to influencing human behavior through childrearing, education, behavior modification and behavior therapy. And the learning of new incentives may also in the future global society be the main method of influencing people to change their goal objects (which are equal to incentives according to the incentive model).

The Cognitive Model
This is the model which, according to our synthesis, is valid for both cortical motives (including curiosity, dissonance reduction and other cognitive motives) and the RAS-motives (including "intrinsic" or activation motives). According to the theories, which are exclusively accepting the cognitive model as the only valid model, all kinds of motivation have a cognitive component. Although these theories do not deny the existence of inborn needs and external incentives, they postulate that their activations of behavior is mediated through some kind of cognitive variables like "expectation," "belief-value matrix" (Tolman), etc. Therefore this model contains more possibilities of changing motivation and goals than any other. Furthermore, this model allows for more influencing of adult people through written or oral persuasions and rational arguments. According to the cognitive model, the main rule for establishing a new "motive," "value" or "goal-cognition" is to make cognitive, rational or logical relationships to already established motives, values or goal-cognition (or to establish "means-end-expectations" in Tolman's terms). Thus the cognitive model has the advantage compared to the other models that it can be applied to the so-called* secondary socialization (formal education, information through mass-media) of adult people, while the homeostatic model and the incentive model are limited in application to primary socialization (upbringing or child rearing). Primary socialization can occur with adult people in psychotherapy.

We can summarize this section by presenting the main results of our analysis in a survey table. From the table it appears that a complete coverage of changes of all kinds of motivation has to apply all the models (equal to the combined model). But we emphasize again, that the change of motives in adult people is mainly possible with application of the cognitive model, which has the advantage of being effective through mass media.

---

*Here borrowed from Bente Lis Christensen and Jorgen Stig Norgaard: "Social Values and the Limits to Growth" (1974). To be published in Technological Forecasting and Social Changes.

TABLE 4 Survey of the Possibilities of Change in Motivation According to the 3 Main Models of Motivation

Model: Change:	Homeostatic Model	Incentive Model	Cognitive Model	Category of Motivation
Classical Conditioning (especially in Childhood)	Substitution of Goal-objects			Hypothalamic motives ("organic drives")
Classical and Operant Conditioning (Childhood and Adulthood)		New acquired Incentives		Limbic motives (Emotional and Social Motives)
Cognitive learning (late Childhood and Adulthood)			Establishment of new mediating cognitive variables	Cerebral and RAS-motives (Cognitive Activity Motives)

Motives for Change

After having analysed the possibilities for change contained in the different models of motivation, we are now going to discuss which categories of motivation (="motives") may be utilized as driving forces behind the changes in values and goals. We are taking the classification of motives included in our synthesis (see table) as our starting point.

The hypothalamic motives ("organic drives") can be the driving forces behind changes in goals. Thus the pollution, lack of energy sources and food supply and other negative consequences of the industrial growth might be so serious that Man's biological needs cannot be satisfied. These unsatisfied needs via the hypothalamic motives would be strong driving forces behind striving for changing the society. But that might happen too late. Therefore we have to look for possibilities among the other motives.

The limbic motives include the "emotional motives" and the "social motives." The emotional motives are mainly "fear" and "aggression." The propaganda of the preceding years has primarily used fear as a motive for changing the goals for the global society. In order to motivate men to seek security by behavior in accordance with the desired or established norms, the easiest means for propagandists has always been to threaten human beings with all kinds of danger. But unfortunately fear has disadvantages as a motive for changing behavior. First, fear may be too strong, and then it has a tendency to activate flight or rigid defences; both obstacles to creative problem solving. Second, people may be accustomed and adapted to the threats from the moral propagandists to such a degree that the threats do not result in fear. Thus the old proverbial sentence: "Things are not always as black as they are painted."

The social motives may be much more effective as driving forces to changes in the global society. Many psychologists believe that the motive to social contact, the affiliation motive is one of the strongest driving forces behind human behavior. This motive is the cause of altruistic and even of heroic, self-sacrific behavior. The affiliation motive is closest related to the primary group. The incentives for the affiliation motive are the stimuli -- or lack of stimuli -- from family members and other primary group members. But it is possible to expand the range of this motive to the secondary groups, national institutions and organizations, and even to the whole mankind, perhaps to the whole living world. Thus there can be established a solidarity with all people -- perhaps with all living beings in the world. This solidarity may be attained by secondary socialization and formal education, through the mass media. These influences establish mediating cognitive structures that change and expand the original narrow affiliation motive to a global social motive.

If "cognitivation" of the affiliation motive succeeds in expanding it to a global social motive, then there are more possibilities for creating motives and changing goals to encompass the global society. Thus the other social motives, the power motive and the achievement motive could also be used as driving forces behind goals for global society. When people identify themselves with a group, the power of the whole group and the achievement of the group may be the goals for these social motives. And the group may be expanded to the whole mankind, thus the goals for the power motive and the achievement motive as well as the affiliation motive generalize to goals for a global society.

The cortical motives include "curiosity" and "cognitive dissonance" as well as other cognitive motives. The goals of these motives are knowledge, problem solving and cognitive balance. These goals may be related to and subsumed under the goals for global society by establishing a mediating structure. Thus these motives may also be driving forces, which may be integrated with the "global social motive."

The RAS-motives are the "intrinsic motives" or "activity motives" (the motives for sensory activity, motory activity, antonomic activity and brain activity). These motives are subsumed by the term "self-actualizing needs" by Abraham Maslow. If people really identify themselves with the whole mankind then there is established a mediating cognitive structure. Thus the goals for these RAS-motives ("the self-actualizing need") are also subsumed under the goals for the global social motive.

Conclusion: Thus we may conclude this section by the statement that the affiliation motive is the most useful driving force behind goals for global society, and this motive may be expanded to a "global social motive" by the development of a mediating cognitive structure. Furthermore: the other social motives (power and achievement) as well as the cortical motives and the RAS-motives may be subsumed under the same global social motive by the same mediating structure.

Empirical Evidence
In this last section we shall look at some empirical evidence for the possibilities for a change in motivation, values and goals. Within our limits of space it is not possible to present a complete survey of the pertinent empirical research, so we have to concentrate on a few representative investigations. One of the pioneers in the field of motivation and its social applications is Kurt Lewin. Under the Second World War, he made some experiments with changes in goals, values and motivation. The social problem was how to change the food "habits" of Americans, which were too luxurious under the war conditions. Lewin investigated several ways of changing the food-consumptions of individuals. He compared lectures to house-wives with group-decision-procedures and individual instructions. He found that group decision-procedures were the most effective in producing permanent changes in actual behavior (see K. Lewin: Field Theory in Social Sciences Tavistock Publications, London 1952 -- especially the paper: "Frontiers in Group Dynamics"). Lewin's experiments have inspired the later developments in "group dynamics," "sensitivity training," etc. Among Lewin's most well-known followers are Festinger and McClelland.

Leon Festinger and his co-workers have presented several experimental results which have relevance for the problems of changing motivation and goals. Like K. Lewin he has investigated the effect of decision. In addition he has made experiments with forced compliance and exposure to information. Especially the last subfield is very relevant to our main theme. Both exposure to information, compliance pressure, disagreement and conflicting alternatives determine a cognitive dissonance, which results in a motivating pressure. This is a motivation for change of behavior or cognition in the direction of dissonance reduction. (See Festinger, 1957 and Festinger et al., 1964.)

David C. McClelland and his co-workers have made a very comprehensive and thorough empirical investigation of social motives, especially the achievement motive (D. McClelland et al., 1953). Some of his co-workers -- especially J.W. Atkinson -- have later developed a highly formalized theory about human motivation (Atkinson, 1964, and Atkinson and Birch, 1970). But McClelland and other co-workers have been more interested in the practical application of the theory. Thus McClelland has demonstrated that the achievement motive is the main driving force behind economic growth in different societies at different times. Especially the leaders in industry and business have a strong achievement motive (compared to other groups in the society, such as scientists, artists and teachers). The strength of the achievement motive is determined by child rearing, and this is dependent on the values and ideals in the society (McClelland, 1961). Of special interest for our main theme is a later investigation by McClelland and co-workers,* which has demonstrated that it is possible <u>to increase the strength of the achievement motive in adult people</u> through a specially arranged training course. One of McClelland's more recent studies shows, that it is possible <u>to increase the strength of the achievement motive through a special educational effort</u>. McClelland has created a course for managers which is intended to increase the strength of the achievement motive in the participants. The content of the course is largely the same as those of other well-known courses for managers. But in this one the participants learn about the achievement motive theory and to see the whole course in the light of this theory. They are tested and taught how to make a content analysis of the stories. Finally they are trained to write stories with increasing amounts of achievement-oriented fantasies in them, bettering their previous scores. This may seem like a false effect, but the theory is that the subjects learn to think in terms of achievement orientation. In this way an associative context is created, a cognitive structure which is affectively charged, i.e., closely connected with the motivating structures (e.g., in the limbic system). As the achievement motive is acquired, according to McClelland, and as a motive is defined as an "affectively charged associative structure," it is in agreement with the theory that it should be possible to increase the achievement motive in adults. But how is this done practically? McClelland has investigated the economic activity of the participants for two years after the course. Their economic activity was compared to that of a control-group made up of participants in an ordinary course. The test group and the control group were both employed in the same large firm, giving two comparable groups. There were statistical differences between the test group (from McClelland's course) and the control group (from the ordinary course). The test group had a lasting increase in economic activity (e.g. increase of own working hours, starting new organizations, increase in economic investment, development of new products and/or methods, etc.). Later, McClelland repeated these experiments in connection with the U.S. aid to India. He has organized similar courses and compared the results with those of ordinary courses held in the same cities. The courses have also been used on drop-outs from high schools and colleges in the U.S., and for educating leaders in minority groups.

McClelland's work is extremely important for our main theme, because we think that <u>a similar educational procedure may be used to increase the affiliation motive and to change it to a global social motive</u>. Just as the industrial and business organizations increase the driving forces (especially the achievement motive) toward economic growth by training courses for their leaders, so

---

*See D.C. McClelland and D.G. Winter: <u>Motivating Economic Achievement</u> N.Y.: Free Press, 1969.

may the future global society also increase their leaders' driving forces (especially the global social motive) toward the goals for global society.

We shall conclude the survey of empirical evidence by summarizing an investigation conducted by Milton Rokeach and presented in his book: The Nature of Human Values (1973). Rokeach defines "value" in this way:

> A value is an enduring belief that a specific mode of conduct or end-state of existence is personally or socially preferable to an opposite or converse mode of conduct or end-state of existence. A value system is an enduring organization of beliefs concerning preferable modes of conduct or end-states of existence along a continuum of relative importance.

Rokeach presents a list of 18 "terminal values" together with 18 "instrumental values." Especially his terminal values may be compared to our list of motives (see Table 3 and 5). These values are presented in a test called "Value Survey" by which a person tested can arrange the 18 terminal values and the 18 instrumental values in the rank order reflecting their personal value system.

Using this instrument Rokeach has made many investigations among others in values and politics. The most relevant for this report is Rokeach's study of "Change in Values." Rokeach presents a "cognitive balance" or "inconsistency" theory which is rather similar to Festinger's theory. The main hypothesis is that an inconsistency between a value and the self-concept or between different values results in an affective state of self-dissatisfaction, which is a motivation for changes in the person's value system. On the guidance of this hypothesis Rokeach has made an experiment with change in the value system of several hundred students. The main method for inducing change is to expose a person to information about his own belief system in order to make him consciously aware of certain contradictions.

The experiment was conducted so that the subjects were tested before and after the inducing of change. The main results were that the experimental inducing of change resulted in changes both in the value system (measured by the "Value Survey") as well as in some attitudes related to the values (and measured by some attitude-questionnaires) and in some behavioral acts (e.g. participating in an organization for civil rights). And these changes were found to last several months (the latest test was conducted 21 months after the experimental session). So it can be concluded, that Rokeach has experimentally demonstrated the possibility of longterm changes in values, attitudes and behavior by creating a state of cognitive inconsistency and affective self-dissatisfaction.

TABLE 5   "Value Survey"

Terminal Value	Instrumental Value
A comfortable life (a prosperous life)	Ambitious (hard-working, aspiring)
An exciting life (a stimulating, active life)	Broadminded (open-minded)
A sense of accomplishment (lasting contribution)	Capable (competent, effective)
A world at peace (free of war and conflict)	Cheerful (lighthearted, joyful)
A world of beauty (beauty of nature and the arts)	Clean (neat, tidy)
Equality (brotherhood, equal opportunity for all)	Courageous (standing up for your beliefs)
Family security (taking care of loved ones)	Forgiving (willing to pardon others)
Freedom (independence, free choice)	Helpful (working for the welfare of others)
Happiness (contentedness)	Honest (sincere, truthful)
Inner harmony (freedom from inner conflict)	Imaginative (daring, creative)
Mature love (sexual and spiritual intimacy)	Independent (self-reliant, self-sufficient)
National security (protection from attack)	Intellectual (intelligent, reflective)
Pleasure (an enjoyable, leisurely life)	Logical (consistent, rational)
Salvation (saved, eternal life)	Loving (affectionate, tender)
Self-respect (self-esteem)	Obedient (dutiful, respectful)
Social recognition (respect, admiration)	Polite (courteous, well-mannered)
True friendship (close companionship)	Responsible (dependable, reliable)
Wisdom (a mature understanding of life)	Self-controlled (restrained, self-disciplined)

The empirical evidence presented from Lewin's, Festinger's, McClelland's and Rokeach's experiments has the common feature that they all require isolation of the experimental subjects for a shorter or longer time in order to change their motives, values and goals. This leads to the question of the possibility of changing motives, values and goals in whole nations or the whole global mankind. The present author thinks that <u>there exists empirical evidence for changing motives, values and goals on a national scale via the mass media</u>. We shall briefly mention three examples.

In the People's Republic of China, the so-called "cultural revolution" started in 1966. This non-violent revolution had the purpose of changing motives, values, attitudes and goals in the whole Chinese people. It seems to have succeeded in obvious changes in education, and academic life as well as changes in organization of the productive work in factories and farms. And this enormous change has been initiated by using the mass media, especially the Chinese form of newspapers (the so-called "Wall papers").

Another example is a debate in the Danish mass media about the continuation of a spontaneous social experiment, which consisted in the establishment of a collective in some old military buildings in Copenhagen. This collective, which was called "the free town of Christiania" had many members who were former criminals or narcotics addicts. But the frequency of criminal actions as well as the use of drugs was reduced considerably. There was in the beginning a very strong opposition in the Danish population against this "revolutionary" collective, but after a year's debate in the mass media the attitude has changed in many people. This is demonstrated by the results from two measurements of opinion conducted by the Danish Gallup Institute. The per cent for and against Christiania were 21% and 59% in April, 1975 and 35% and 43% in February, 1976. Thus there was a considerable change in the attitude created by the debate in the mass media.

The third example is the debate in the mass media created by the publication of the first report for the Club of Rome: "Limits to Growth," which is translated into Danish as well as many other languages. In Denmark this has created a great interest in people in general for these problems, and this interest has resulted in many practical activities for solving the problems.

In the last mentioned example the whole change in motives, values, and goals was reinforced by the simultaneous occurrence of the so-called "Oil-crisis," which increased the interest in all energy-problems. But in the other examples the change in motives, values and goals was created by the <u>debate in the mass media reinforced by group discussions in homes, schools and all working places</u>. Together with the experimental results presented earlier in this section our three examples support our <u>main hypothesis: The social motives are the strongest driving forces behind change of goals for global society</u>.

REFERENCES

Allport, G.V.: *Personality: A Psychological Interpretation*. Holt, Rinehart & Winston, New York, 1937.

――――――: *Pattern and Growth in Personality*. Holt, Rinehart & Winston, New York, 1961.

Atkinson, J.W.: *An Introduction to Motivation*. Van Nostrand, Princeton, N.J., 1964.

―――――― (ed.) *Motives in Fantasy, Action, and Society*. Van Nostrand, Princeton, N.J., 1958.

―――――― and Birch, D.: *The Dynamics of Action*. Wiley, New York, 1970.

―――――― and Feather, N.T. (eds.): *A Theory of Achievement Motivation*. John Wiley, New York, 1966.

Canon, W.B.: *Bodily Changes in Pain, Hunger, Fear and Rage*. Appleton-Century-Crofts, New York, 1915.

Christensen, Bente Lis and Jorgen Stig Norgaard: Social Values and the Limits to Growth. (To be published in *Technological Forecasting and Social Change*).

Festinger, A.: *A Theory of Cognitive Dissonance*. Row, Peterson, Evanston, Ill., 1957.

Festinger, A., et al.,: *Conflict, Decision, and Dissonance*. Stanford U. Press, 1964.

Freud, S.: The Prospects for a Scientific Psychology. In Marie Bonaparte et al. (eds.): *The Origins of Psychoanalysis*. Imago, London, 1954.

――――――: Instincts and Their Vicissitudes. In S. Freud, *The Collected Papers*. Collier Books, New York, 1915 (paperback edition).

Harlow, H.F.: Motivations as a Factor in the Acquisition of Responses. In M.R. Jones (ed.), *Nebraska Symposium on Motivation*. Nebraska University Press, Lincoln, 1953.

Hebb, D.O.: *Organization of Behavior*. John Wiley, New York, 1949.

――――――: Drives and the CNS (Conceptual Nervous System). *Psychological Review*. 1955, 62, 243-54.

Heider, F.: The Gestalt Theory of Motivation. In M.R. Jones (ed.), *Nebraska Symposium on Motivation*. Nebraska University Press, Lincoln, 1960.

Hunt, McV. Incentive Motivation and its Role in Psychological Development. In David Levine (ed.) Nebraska Symposium on Motivation. Nebraska University Press, Lincoln, 1965.

Laszlo, Ervin: Goals for Global Society. (In Forum for Correspondence and Contact N.Y. 1973).

Lewin, K.: A Dynamic Theory of Personality. McGraw-Hill, New York, 1935.

————: Principles for Topological Psychology. McGraw-Hill, New York, 1936.

————: The Conceptual Representation and the Measurement of Psychological Forces. Duke University Press, Durham, N.C., 1938.

————: Field Theory in Social Science. D. Cartwright (ed.). Harper & Row, New York, 1952.

McClelland, David C.: The Achieving Society. Van Nostrand Reinhold, Princeton, N.J., 1961.

————————, Atkinson, John W., Clark, Russel, A., and Lowell, L.: The Achievement Motive. Appleton-Century-Crofts, New York, 1953.

————————, and Winter, D.: Motivating Economic Achievement. Free Press, New York, 1969.

Madsen, K.B.: Theories of Motivation, 4th ed. Munksgaard, Copenhagen, 1959, 4th ed., 1968.

————: Theories of Motivation. In B.B. Wolman (ed.): Handbook of General Psychology. Prentice-Hall, Englewood-Cliffs, 1973.

————: Modern Theories of Motivation. Munksgaard, Copenhagen, and Wiley, New York, 1974.

Maslow, A.H.: Motivation and Personality. Harper & Row, New York, 1954, 2nd ed., 1970.

Moore, T.V.: The Driving Forces of Human Nature. Grune & Stratton, New York, 1948.

Pribam, K.H.: Languages of the Brain. Prentice-Hall, Englewood Cliffs, N.J., 1971.

Rokeach, M.: The Nature of Human Values. Free Press, N.Y., 1973.

Spence, K.W.: Behavior Theory and Conditioning. Yale University Press, New Haven, Conn., 1956.

_____: *Behavior Theory and Learning*. Prentice-Hall, Englewood Cliffs, N.J., 1960.

Tolman, E.C.: *Purposive Behavior in Animals and Men*. Appleton-Century-Crofts, New York, 1932.

Tolman, E.C.: *Drives Toward War*. Appleton-Century-Crofts, New York, 1942.

Tolman, E.C.: A Psychological Model. In T. Parson and E.A. Shill (eds.), *Toward a General Theory of Action*. Harvard University Press, Cambridge, Mass., 1951.

Woodworth, R.S.: *Dynamic Psychology*. Columbia University Press, N.Y., 1918.

_____: *Dynamics of Behavior*. Henry Holt, N.Y., 1958.

Young, P. Th.: *Motivation of Behavior*. Wiley, N.Y., 1935.

_____: *Motivation and Emotion*. Wiley, N.Y., 1961.

PERSONALITY TRAITS AND PROBLEMS OF GLOBAL PLANNERS

R. Felix Geyer

In the following, an effort will be made to describe the relevance for global planning of a systems theoretical approach to alienation theory -- especially insofar as it may lead to an ideal-typical description of the desirable personality characteristics of the global planner. In principle, the global planner will share this "profile" with all others who are professionally engaged in what might be termed the "reduction of man-made environmental complexity": politicians, managers, intellectuals, and business leaders -- particularly when they are working on an international level.

First, a short overview of a systems theoretical approach to alienation theory will be presented, specifically with regard to the "modern" forms of alienation. Second, the desirable personality characteristics of the global planner will be derived from it. Third, the global planner's dilemma -- having to perform a continuous balancing act between "involvement attitudes" and "planning attitudes" -- will be analyzed in more detail.

A SYSTEMS THEORETICAL APPROACH TO ALIENATION THEORY*

Over thirty different kinds of alienation are distinguished in the literature by authors who represent several social science disciplines and who are, moreover, often committed to widely varying schools of thought.** In spite of this proliferation, Melvin Seeman seems to have grasped the five most basic dimensions of alienation. These are powerlessness, meaninglessness, normlessness, social isolation, and self-estrangement. _Powerlessness_ refers to information processing problems in the individuals's _output_, or behavior; it implies that his alternatives for action are limited by an outside source. _Meaninglessness_ can similarly be correlated with the individual's _input_: meaning is -- or is not -- ascribed to incoming information. _Normlessness_

---

*See R.F. Geyer -- Alienation and General Systems Theory, _Sociologia Neerlandica_, 10(1):18-42, May 1974 for a more detailed explanation of the contents of this paragraph.

**See Richard Schacht -- _Alienation_, London, Allen & Unwin, 1971.

refers to decisions to steer, i.e. to transform certain inputs (environmental stimuli) to certain specified outputs (reactions) rather than others, and can therefore be conceptualized as a problem in the system's decision functions. These include <u>environment mapping</u>, <u>value hierarchy</u>, and <u>procedural rules</u>, the latter indicating how to reach a specific goal, once this goal and a certain environment mapping (or image of surrounding reality) are taken as given. <u>Social isolation</u> refers to a breakdown of interaction with the environment, i.e., an inhibition of both inputs and outputs; it is rarely total, except in artificially created laboratory situations of "sensory deprivation." <u>Self-estrangement</u>, finally, denotes a problem in the system's <u>state functions</u>, which contain a symbolization of his past internal states -- i.e., his memories of the concrete experiences he encountered in his life. When some of these memories are repressed (in a psychoanalytic sense), the individual is said not to be in contact with his "real self," which has repercussions for his decisional functions (e.g., "false consciousness" in a Marxist sense).

All five dimensions are highly interdependent and can be separated only for analytical purposes. A severe disturbance in the input, for example, will often "feed forward" and will thus come to include all the other dimensions. Now this is precisely what happens in "modern" situations of unmanageable environmental overcomplexity, where the individual is confronted with "information overload." If one is prepared to view alienation as a generic term, denoting various kinds of information processing problems of human individuals -- conceived as information-processing systems in interaction with their environment, -- then these dimensions can be correlated with the elements of the following simple model:

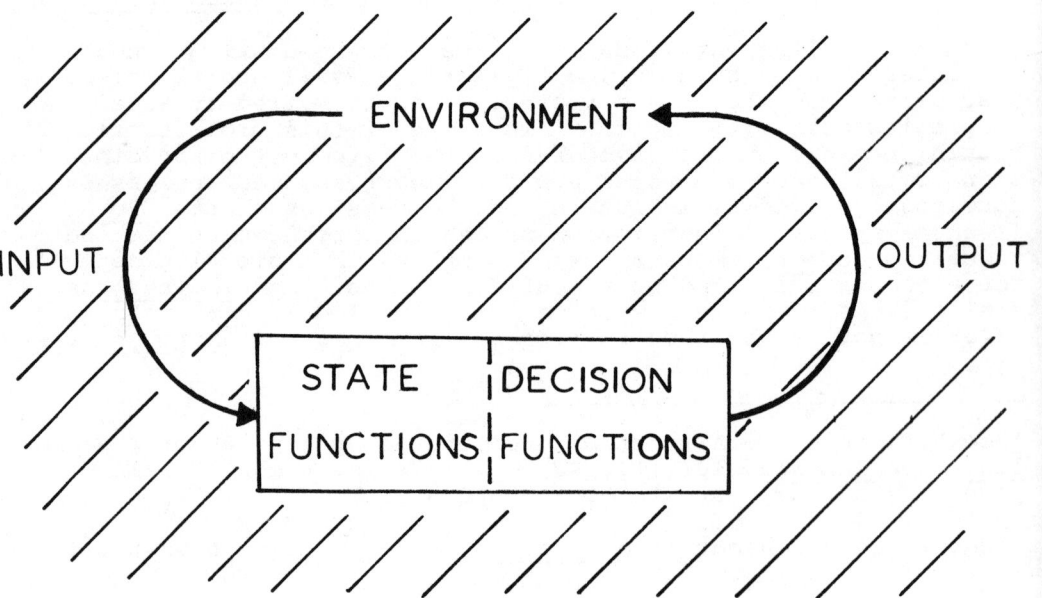

The German sociologist Niklas Luhmann has pointed to the accelerating "complexity differential" between the individual and his man-made environment in modern Western societies -- the latter, of course, show the greatest complexity. He views the reduction of environmental complexity as one of the main tasks of information-processing systems. This reduction is necessary in order to understand, hence predict, and ultimately influence the reactions from their environment. It is accomplished by the individual's gradually building up internal complexity. In modern environments, however, this buildup of internal complexity is disrupted: confronted with environmental overcomplexity (information overload), the individual's possibilities for iterative reality-testing of cumulatively formed hypotheses about environmental reality are severely hampered.* Learning becomes virtually impossible.

W. Ross Ashby covers much the same territory Luhmann does; his Law of Requisite Variety states that only internal variety within the system itself can force down the variety due to the system's environment. Whether an input contains information depends on the interaction between this input and the individual's pre-existent emotional and cognitive structure, (as laid down in his state functions, respectively his decisional functions); and these, in turn, are the result of previous interaction-loops. This situation of an ever accelerating complexity differential between the individual and his man-made societal environment often leads to typically modern forms of alienation.** The individual tends to feel he is being ruled by impersonal forces he cannot control, rather than by "bad" ones: large-scale societal and economic processes, institutions, bureaucracies, etc.

Seeman's alienation dimensions, which are relatively time-independent, can be translated into the more specifically modern forms of alienation. It will be clear that global planners, since they are professionally entrusted with the reduction of macro-societal complexity, should try to bridge the complexity differential with their environment by developing a high degree of internal complexity, and should consequently score low on these modern forms of alienation. Some problems are worth noting.

Meaninglessness (an input-problem in our model) becomes focussed on information overload. Alienation can be viewed as a selection problem with regard to taking in a small percentage of all information offered, and as a scanning problem with regard to the information one must actively find for oneself in the environment,

---

*I.e., forming a hypothesis on the basis of a (limited) environmental mapping, acting on it, ascertaining whether the environmental reaction conforms to predictions, and subsequently forming a revised and usually more complex hypothesis, which is tested too.

**See R.F. Geyer, "Alienation and Stress," in Clair Blong (ed.): The Quality of Life, Washington, Society for General Systems Research, 1975, pp. 72-83.

because it is needed for problem-solving. In this respect, global planners should not have the usual economic bias, but should develop a high sensitivity to the non-economic feedbacks to their planning activities, i.e., the ecological consequences and the social-psychological reactions of the "subjects" for whom they are planning.

Self-estrangement (state functions) turns into alienation as an assimilation problem: many new codes or categories must be developed to contain new and more complex experiences, while multiple coding (i.e. storage of information in a combination of partially overlapping categories simultaneously) is necessary for "holistic" storage of high-complexity experiences and for learning from them later. Multiple coding decreases the "random access time" of a particular memory, and therefore increases the chances it may be available whenever functional on a future occasion. In this respect, "unwelcome information," e.g., the activities of pressure groups resisting the global planner's ideas, should not be repressed. In general, the global planner should try to be fully aware of the multivariate nature of his environment, and should constantly guard against oversimplifying it.

Normlessness (decisional functions), translated into the modern forms of alienation, can be reconceptualized.

As a flexibility problem: one's environment mapping, or image of external reality, must be overhauled frequently in a fast-changing environment. This requires a capacity for tolerance of ambiguity, and for unlearning as well as relearning. Especially since he is usually engaged in long-term planning in an environment which is in constant flux, the global planner should not be rigid, but should develop the flexibility to change his plans in mid-course whenever environmental reactions make this imperative.

As an identification problem: the individual confronted with environmental overcomplexity tends to regress to a kind of semi-closed system state. This regression disturbs the normal process of identification with ever-widening horizons in the course of his life -- in principle from the primary group to the world community. This is the most obvious point of all: evidently the global planner should have a strong identification with, and commitment to, the world community which forms his backyard. If his identifications have not widened beyond his own (professional, class, or national) interest groups, this would disqualify him automatically as an effective global planner.

As an overchoice problem, an inability to make ever more complex decisions: the individual's capacities to choose have not kept pace with the increasing possibilities to do so which exist under conditions of information overload from a highly complex environment. Not only do more alternatives have to be evaluated, but each of these alternatives involves more variables, and more unknown consequences, which also stretch further in time. Since he is trying to influence such an extremely complex macro-environment, the global planner should have a well-developed aptitude for multivariate thinking and decision-making under conditions of uncertainty. His required internal complexity should, in this respect, alleviate the overchoice problems he would otherwise encounter; the greater it is, the less he is confronted with overcomplexity.

Powerlessness (output) becomes a self-actualization or self-realization problem (Maslow) under modern conditions. The number of possibilities for feeling, thinking, and especially doing is far greater than the individual can ever realize in a lifetime. The percentage of unrealized individual possibilities increases with the complexity of the environment. This is not merely a matter of relative deprivation, nor a sheer problem of multiplicity. Confronted with the communications explosion, individuals in Western societies realize they not only can often have a better deal (i.e., the freedom-limiting Marxist alienation of underprivileged groups), but also a very different deal. Within expanding limits, they can choose a different environment -- qua friends, job, wife or husband, religion, geographical location, ideology, etc. -- thereby leading a different life and even becoming a different person. In this respect, the global planner should be sensitive to the new goals, values, and aspirations that tend to emerge as a result of changing economic and social-structural conditions, and, consequently, he should try to be continually alert to the implicit ideological premises on which his planning activities are based.

THE DESIRABLE PERSONALITY CHARACTERISTICS OF THE GLOBAL PLANNER

Some desirable characteristics of global planners already mentioned will now be spelled out in more detail. The planner's specific task is to reduce the environmental complexity of the modern world system to (literally) manageable proportions. Many politicians, business leaders, and intellectuals are also doing the same in their own fields, but usually in a more limited, less comprehensive way.

Adequate planning on any scale, and certainly on a global scale, has a number of prerequisites. These are largely determined by the specific type of environment global planners have to cope with: the macro-societal environment, consisting of abstract, large-scale institutions, structures, and processes -- partly interdependent and partly competing. The societal environment, in contradistinction to the individual's interpersonal environment (his primary group members, colleagues, friends, etc.) has become extremely complex in modern societies, while it is also subject to accelerated change. Not all knowledge is "eternal" anymore, but it has a "half-life" like uranium. Real insight into societal processes is increasingly hard to come by -- not only because it tends to be outdated by the time it is arrived at, but especially because the process of learning itself becomes progressively more difficult in a complex and fast-changing environment. As stated before, learning is based on reality-testing of continually developed hypotheses about environmental reality. Whenever action (output) on the basis of some hypothesis does not produce the desired results in the form of environmental inputs -- i.e., does not conform to predictions -- new hypotheses are developed by the individual in a temporarily "off-line" phase of theorizing, and are subsequently reality-tested in turn. This iterative process is thwarted when environmental responses are <u>ambiguous</u> or <u>contradictory</u>, or when they simply <u>arrive too late</u> to be seen as reactions to one's own previous outputs. Unfortunately, all this tends to be the case in a complex environment.

For example, the <u>ambiguity</u> of environmental response is caused by the fact that <u>the planner</u> usually has a lower internal complexity than the environmental subsystem or system he is trying to steer -- a logical impossibility according to Ashby. Therefore, the environmental feedback on his planning activities has more variety than he can contain in his conceptual categories. Further, the <u>contradictoriness</u> of environmental response is due to the fact that <u>the planner's</u> actions, although directed at a specific segment of the environment, may also have (completely opposite) effects on other segments. Finally, the <u>unrecognizability</u> of environmental response is the result of <u>the fact that</u> information in a complex environment has to travel a longer way between output-emission and subsequent input-registration. The chance for unpredictable "quantum leaps" is thus increased, while the contingency (immediacy) of reinforcement, in Skinner's terminology, is lost.

Although the above is true for any individual in a complex society, it has added relevance for global planners. Their personality profile should therefore be such that it counteracts these inherent difficulties of interacting with a modern, fast-changing, high-complexity environment.

On the basis of the above, the following ideal-typical criteria could be formulated. Since global planners operate specifically with regard to the modern, macro-societal environment -- with its connotations of information overload -- global planners <u>should score low on the abovementioned forms of alienation</u>.

On their "<u>input-side</u>", they should be able to make an adequate <u>selection</u> of all inputs offered to them: neither too narrow, nor too wide, nor too biased in any direction. Moreover, they should be well-trained in <u>scanning</u> the environment for whatever information they need to update their environment mapping in areas relevant to their decision-making; i.e., they should know how to act on their environment to obtain the information they need with a minimal expenditure of time and energy.

In their <u>state functions</u>, they should be able to truly assimilate new experiences by continually enlarging their category system and by making a habit of multiple coding, thus developing an information-network with the high degree of interconnectivity conducive to free associations and hence to creative solutions for complex problems.

In their decisional functions, they should have a high degree of flexibility and the psychological predisposition to sustain it: a high tolerance of the ambiguity that comes with overcomplexity and a willingness to unlearn and relearn continually. Their knowledge about the macro-societal environment should not only be detailed and reality-adequate, but it should also reflect environmental change with a minimal time-lag: if their planning is not to become rigid, if their proposals are not to be overtaken by environmental change before they are fully worked out, they should engage in a continuous process of reality-testing, scrutinizing not only their basic assumptions about environmental reality, but also their own goals. These, after all, were the result of previous interaction with their environment and are likely to change when essentially novel information becomes available.

As to a global identification, planners will be more likely to have such an orientation when they are fully aware of the interconnectivity of events on a global level, and thus are convinced that group- or even national loyalties should not take precedence over global ones -- even in their own long-term interest. Furthermore, global planners will have to be able to make complex decisions under often inevitable conditions of incomplete, perhaps even biased, and generally unverifiable information. Their capacity for fast scanning and selection of environmental feedbacks should give them more confidence in this respect: although they may take the wrong decisions, they will very soon be alerted to the fact.

As far as their "output-side" is concerned, they should be aware of both their own and their subjects' capacities for self-realization. Without allowing Durkheim's "anomic passion for the infinite" to influence their day-to-day decisions, they should yet be sufficiently open to incorporate the emerging aspirations of subgroups of the population, in their overall planning designs.

Not surprisingly, global planners should score high on what we have termed elsewhere* "planning attitudes." To a large extent, these are opposed to the "involvement attitudes" discussed below. Planning attitudes imply the following characteristics.

To engage in successful planning, the planner must be able to manipulate his environment, i.e., to initiate actions that result in predicted and desired environmental inputs. Consequently, he should have a fair knowledge of the "input-output matrices" of the goal systems in his environment: he need not know their internal structure, but he should know the outputs they are likely to give when stimulated in a specific way.

Planning attitudes are especially required with respect to interaction with systems of higher internal complexity (societies),

---

*To be published in proceedings, annual meeting Society for General Systems Research, Boston, February 1976: "Interpersonal vs. societal alienation."

while involvement attitudes are a prerequisite for interaction with systems of roughly equal complexity (one's fellow men).

Especially where complex, modern societies are concerned, the societal environment is often an <u>input-environment</u> rather than an <u>interaction-environment</u>: it exerts pressure on the individual, but offers extremely limited possibilities for feedback. Global planners should, for this reason alone, have a high capacity for environmental complexity reduction -- which means they must have developed a high degree of internal complexity themselves.

Aspects of such a high degree of internal complexity are, amongst others the capacity to engage in <u>multivariate thinking</u>, i.e., to renounce simpler forms of linear cause-effect thinking in favor of thinking in terms of multivariate correlations and circular causality (e.g., systems thinking in terms of feedbacks and feedforwards); the capacity to simulate internally ("off-line") the hypothetical secondary, tertiary, etc. consequences of certain planned actions before actually committing oneself to a chosen course.

More complexity means that one's environment is filled with more objects, with more attributes of these objects, and especially with more interactions between them.

An individual with a high degree of internal complexity can obviously produce more variety for his environment than an individual with a lower internal complexity. This means concretely that: he has more alternative ways of reacting to a certain output, i.e., he has more degrees of freedom, is less determined by his environmental inputs; he can, moreover, produce outputs that are <u>apparently</u> (i.e., to his simpler-minded environment) <u>unrelated</u> to his previous inputs. These outputs may be based on <u>any</u> of his previous inputs, some of which entered so long ago that the environment fails to see any connection with his present outputs. These consequently become more active than passive, more manipulative than adaptive. The environment does not just receive his reactions, but is also forced to decipher his actions. Evidently, this kind of creative manipulation of, and active orientation towards, one's macro-environment is an asset for global planners.

Thus, the higher the internal complexity of the individual, the more he can increase the <u>input-unpredictability</u> for his environment. Precisely the same is true the other way round: a complex environment presents the individual with more unpredictable inputs than a simpler one -- either because the individual's originating actions (outputs) are transformed with more degrees of freedom, which makes the planner's task more difficult, or because a complex environment produces more variety than a simpler one anyhow, even without being stimulated by the individual's previous outputs.

Now, it is already unlikely in a complex environment that an individual will have a well-integrated and non-contradictory value hierarchy. This means that he is often unsure whether a certain input should be viewed as a reward or a punishment, it all depends with which of his values a certain input is correlated. This situation is further aggravated by a high input-unpredictability; it results in a punishment/reward ratio that approaches randomness. A complex environment does not necessarily present the individual with more punishments and fewer rewards that a simpler one -- in some cases, even the opposite may be true -- but both punishments and rewards progressively lose their relationship with the individual's own efforts. Evidently, this is an unpleasant and meaninglessness-increasing situation; better to receive more punishment, but know at least what one is getting if for, than to go through life as if it were one big game of roulette.

The only remedy against this (objectively) increased input-unpredictability of modern macro-societal environments is to increase one's own internal complexity, and thus develop such an insight to societal processes that inputs become more predictable again. This is obviously desirable for anyone, but it is an absolute conditio sine qua non for global planners.

The more complex the sector of the societal environment the global planner is interacting with -- e.g., the global model of the Club of Rome -- the more the chains of consequences stretch out synchronically (i.e., more persons, institutions, and processes are involved simultaneously in complex decision-making procedures -- the decision-chains become "wider") as well as diachronically (decisions made now make their consequences felt much longer, and often in unforeseen ways). Indeed, as Meadows and others have pointed out, large-scale societal systems often seem to behave in a counter-intuitive way. Goal-directed actions based on intuition and common sense may not only fail to reach their goals, but may even have the opposite effect. On the other hand, actions that seem diametrically opposed to certain goals at first sight turn out to bring them closer to realization.

The secret lies, of course, in the complexity of the causality-chains involved, and especially in the unanticipated feedback mechanisms that are built into them. Particularly regarding large-scale societal systems, almost everyone's systems thinking is defective. Even the sharpest analytical minds can register only some of the causal links and some of the feedback mechanisms. In this respect, the "modal" global planner certainly does not conform to the ideal-typical description presented here. Moreover, these links and mechanisms are often probabilistic rather than deterministic, while they may be counteracted again by other and hitherto undiscovered feedback mechanisms. As a result, whatever course of action one embarks upon tends to have unanticipated consequences (synchronically), or latent ones (diachronically) that take a while to become manifest.

We have drawn an exceedingly gloomy picture here, and, indeed, planning the societal environment on a global scale, though admittedly necessary for a variety of reasons, is extremely difficult. Moreover, insight to all the relevant variables is not enough: the planner must also be able to influence their values. In all probability, this means that a system of equal complexity (e.g., a globally-integrated power structure) should be developed before the planning of societal processes on a global scale can be implemented -- whether the world economy as a whole, or problems like food supply, depletion of resources, manpower, or even cultural development. Such a system should be flexible enough to be able to absorb essentially novel environmental inputs that might induce it to change its planning goals in mid-course. Needless to say, this frequently presupposes a thorough re-evaluation of implicit premises, as exemplified on a global scale by the proposals for a transition from a growth economy to a zero-growth economy.

The Global Planner's Dilemma: Balancing Between "Planning Attitudes" and "Involvement Attitudes"

In the above we have sketched the elements comprising the complex of planning attitudes, which constitute a professional prerequisite for global planners. However, as hinted before, these planning attitudes conflict with the involvement attitudes that are necessary for optimal interaction with a different kind of environment: the direct-interpersonal one.* In interaction with the interpersonal environment <u>involvement</u> is more important than <u>planning</u> -- although the reverse is true for interaction with the societal environment, especially on a world scale.

Evidently, interpersonal interaction requires involvement: being concentrated in the here-and-now while receiving the other's message, whatever it may consist of. Unalienated interpersonal interaction is <u>im-mediate</u>: it is direct, and does not need the medium interposed between the decision to emit a certain output and the actual output itself of first internally simulating all the expected possible consequences of one's output. It denotes, at its ideal-typical best, an "Ich-Du"-relationship (Martin Buber), or a capacity for B(eing)-cognition in the partners involved (Abraham Maslow). It implies truly <u>meeting</u> the other person: i.e., allowing his message to enter without defensive or otherwise motivated distortions, even if it is not exactly what one wants to hear. It also means <u>seeing</u> him: i.e., realizing that the other, in a Talmudic sense, is a complete universe in his own right, and not just another input-providing object in one's environment.

---

*In principle: face-to-face interactions with primary group members that are not functionally-specific; this in contrast to the indirect-interpersonal environment: for example, writing a letter to an official, not a primary group member, non-face-to-face, and functionally-specific. These concepts are developed by Norbert Elias in <u>Über den Prozess der Zivilisation</u>, Basel, 1939.

Thus, the stress is on <u>uniqueness</u>, in contradistinction to the planning attitudes where the focus is on subsuming the unique under more general categories. Seeing someone else, in the above sense, makes one realize that the other has an internal structure that may be completely different from one's own, based on different experiences, premises, and environmental conditionings -- and therefore not reducible to one's own categories. In unalienated interpersonal interaction, one should evidently acknowledge this difference, and not try to minimize it by making the other into an extension of oneself, out of the misplaced conviction that the other is thus made "harmless" as a potential source of unexpected environmental variety. In global planning, on the contrary, it is important to manipulate and ultimately reduce the unexpected environmental variety that emanates from lower-level (e.g., national) systems.

Interpersonal interaction should thus indeed be immediate; that is, it should not involve any planning or simulation in trying to decide how to translate one's message in the other's supposed frame of reference. Otherwise, one would enter Laing's "spiral of reciprocal expectations": "I think, that you think, that I think...," etc., and in this way <u>probabilistic</u> and <u>future-oriented planning</u> would replace <u>discrete</u> and <u>present-oriented</u> <u>involvement</u>.

It will be clear that planning attitudes imply operating procedures that often run directly counter to those required in interpersonal interaction: prudence rather than spontaneity; disciplined and often cumbersome thinking in terms of multi-order correlations rather than intuitive and associative feeling in terms of immediately recognizable inputs from the interaction-partner; internally simulating intended outputs on all their possible consequences and one's probably future evaluation of these consequences, in terms of one's continually updated knowledge about the environment, rather than simply acting out the way one feels at the moment.

To some extent, every individual in a high-complexity environment has to engage in some forms of planning, if only to give minimal direction to his own life. Professionally planning on a global scale, however, evidently poses much higher demands. What is true for the inhabitants of the Western world in general, therefore, is all the more true for the global planner: the more an individual is educated for, or engaged in, planning segments of the macro-societal environment, and the more complex these segments are in themselves, the larger the chance that he will "introject" the operating procedures characterizing the planning syndrome as self-evident norms, that will <u>also</u> permeate his interaction with his interpersonal environment.

Thus we come to the relevance of the distinction between interpersonal and societal environment for alienation theory -- and, <u>mutatis mutandis</u>, for the professional dilemma of the global planner: our hypothesis is that alienation towards the interpersonal environment and alienation towards the societal environment tend to be inversely related.

Interpersonal alienation. Those who have a low capacity for dealing with societal complexity (amongst others: the educated, the intellectuals), especially when they make much use of this capacity in their daily lives (the organization men, the managers and planners) tend to be unable to prevent an "overflow" of their planning attitudes in their interpersonal contacts. They are prone to interpersonal alienation and often see simple interpersonal relations as more complex than they actually are. They are insufficiently attuned to the present, because they cannot drop the habit of constantly thinking and planning ahead.

Societal alienation. Those who have a low capacity for dealing with environmental complexity (the uneducated, amongst others), especially when their lowly position in complex hierarchical structures does not require much planning regarding their wider societal environment (e.g. the unskilled), on the contrary, tend to be unable to prevent an overflow of their involvement attitudes in their societal interaction-loops. Unlike the first group, they do not dehumanize interpersonal relations, but on the contrary tend to anthropomorphize their societal interactions: large-scale societal, economic, and political issues therewith become oversimplified. They tend to see complex social relations as less complex than they actually are. They are, in direct opposition to the first group, insufficiently involved in the future, not because they cannot kick the habit of being involved in the here-and-now, but because they never developed the "broadsight" and "longsight" that characterizes the interpersonally alienated.

Thus, the two groups are not entirely symmetrical opposites. The interpersonally alienated do have an experience in interpersonal interaction, although overgrown by later acquired "planning subroutines." The societally alienated never develop a sufficient sophistication in societal interaction. They suffer from a societal alienation that is, paradoxically, based on withdrawal, apathy, and non-participation, in other words, on non-involvement in wider societal structures. They are the alienated described in much of the empirical alienation research, and at the same time the often unwilling subjects of the global planner. They are all the frustrated, under-privileged minorities -- low on income, education, status, power, and what not -- who together form the manipulated majority in a world in which the ability to handle the complexities of the societal environment guarantees top positions in all the intercorrelated hierarchies. Unfortunately, these descriptions are often highly alienating in themselves. They are based on alienation scales whose items clearly do not tap any real feelings of alienation. They frequently miss the point so completely that one cannot help but wonder if the empirical social scientists who developed them do not belong themselves in the first category: the interpersonally alienated reducers of societal complexity who view their "subjects" largely as providers of inputs that corroborate their world view, but are unable to empathize with them in their societal alienation.

This paradox poses a double dilemma for the global planner. He himself should take care not to become interpersonally alienated as a result of his professional planning activities; he must retain the values that lie at the basis of the involvement attitudes described above. Otherwise, the results of his planning may create unliveable conditions for his subjects: a one-sided mania for "hard" economic indicators or for "efficient" urban planning may already result in deplorable living conditions on a national scale, while the consequences on a global scale may be even worse. On the other hand, the global planner faces a dilemma with regard to his subjects, many of whom will belong to the societally alienated. How can he explain the rationale behind his plans to an audience that tends to oversimplify the complex societal problems he is trying to solve? How can he motivate them to go along with his plans, to see their necessity and give their cooperation?

Behind these dilemmas there is another problem, already implicit in the above argument. If it is indeed true that the interpersonally unalienated tend to be the societally alienated who clamor for a larger share of the societal pie, while the societally unalienated (such as the global planners) tend to occupy the power positions precisely <u>because</u> they are best able to reduce societal complexity, and consequently are interpersonally alienated, then the question becomes: "Can a high-complexity society ever be a non-alienating society, if it is led by those (politicians, managers, planners) who score highest on interpersonal alienation?" Or must it by definition be "non-responsive to basic human needs," as Etzioni claims? Or, rephrasing it in Mannheim's terminology, can the planners be planned in such a way that they have the required high capacity for complexity reduction, but at the same time can prevent an overflow of "planning attitudes" into their interaction with, and perception of, fellow human beings?

When global planning will become institutionalized the way national planning is already, with planners often entrenched in monolithic bureaucracies, interacting more with like-minded politicians and with each other than with their subjects, the prevalence of planning attitudes over involvement attitudes seems inevitable. To prevent this danger of professional myopia, it might be desirable for at least some of those engaged in global planning to operate outside the established bureaucratic structures, e.g., in independent think tanks, or as advisers to action groups.

The same danger exists in socialist societies as in capitalist ones. The societally alienated proletariat cannot fulfill the savior's role envisaged by Marx, who did not live to see the revolution and its crop of interpersonally alienated apparatchiks. The majority of the proletariat, though better off economically, is <u>still</u> proletariat influence-wise, while the new "red bourgeoisie" that rose from it turned gradually and inevitably into bureaucrats, just as in capitalist societies. As in the West, these new bureaucrats could not but lose their former, more simple underdog-feelings about the alienating way the establishment was run by their predecessors by the time they had to steer it themselves. One can observe this process very often in those who start from humble origins and eventually rise to positions of power. They could only arrive at these positions because they developed not only a high capacity to reduce societal complexity, but also an ability to produce a high amount of variety for their environment. They learned to take fast, complex, nonroutine decisions which take more variables into account that the average man does and therefore come unexpected for him and often seem counterintuitive, i.e., running counter to the implicit assumptions of the "involvement attitudes" developed in interaction with the interpersonal environment.

Involvement attitudes derived largely from interpersonal interaction cannot be applied unchanged to societal interaction which requires planning attitudes. Anthropomorphizing the societal environment can be just as dangerous and dysfunctional as dehumanizing the interpersonal environment; widespread political alienation, for example, may endanger the very fabric of society. This is also one of the less evident reasons why education is so important: not everyone can have power, but everyone can certainly receive a reasonable amount of education that enables him to view societal issues on the complexity level on which they should be viewed. Thus, tendencies to anthropomorphize and oversimplify complex political, economic and cultural issues can be counteracted effectively.

When large segments of the population engage in oversimplification of complex societal problems, they almost invite manipulation by planners and politicians. Manipulation is not merely the fault of the "dirty manipulators" -- this would be an anthropomorphic viewpoint in itself -- but it is the result of an interaction, a supply-and-demand process. No global planner in his right mind would even contemplate explaining the intricacies involved in certain policy decisions -- giving foreign aid while "so much remains to be done at home," to give a popular example to a future worldwide TV-audience. From there to outright manipulation is only a small step.

Summarizing the above, the global planner should be continually aware of his double dilemma: how not to become interpersonally alienated himself as a result of his professional activities -- with a resulting tendency for both dehumanized planning and overmanipulation of his subjects, the more likely since he is, after all, primarily engaged in the manipulation of his environment; -- and how to decrease the societal alienation of many of his "subjects" so that they will not exhibit irrational resistances against his hopefully rational solutions for complex societal problems -- which is a prerequisite for successful global planning and can be accomplished by giving due priority to certain types of education.

ASSESSING THE SOLAR TRANSITION

Robert H. Murray and Paul A. LaViolette*

The most desirable energy source and delivery system for the future of Oregon, and the World, would be permanent, indigenous, safe and reliable. The conversion equipment for processes would be adaptable to mass production, permit gradual integration of the newest technological breakthroughs, use abundant material resources, involve no secrecy or security precautions, and would not impose irreversible changes on our natural ecosystems or culture.

We are, in fact, within one generation of the realization of such a system, which we call the Solar Alternative.

State of Oregon, U.S.A.
<u>Transition</u>
January 1, 1975

Humankind has come to a fork in the road. A choice must be made. Should we choose a nuclear future, or should we choose a future primarily based on solar energy? Should we continue to pursue the almost unregulated expansion of energy guided only by market demand and resource availability, or should we undertake a carefully thought out energy policy which stresses such factors as long term energy availability, environmental and social impact, and prudent usage? This decision is very important, for it will influence the course of human civilization and all life on this planet. Primarily, it is a choice between mutually exclusive energy strategies, a choice of means.

---

*The authors share responsibility for the evidence and the conclusions presented in this essay. Mr. Murray took primary responsibility for the sections dealing with technical and economic analysis, choice criteria and the mapping of solar pathways and technologies. Mr. LaViolette took responsibility for the later sections relating to the possible new role of government in the commercial development of photoelectric solar technology. The authors are grateful to Professor Laszlo for the opportunity to present a documented inquiry into the desirability and feasibility of a global solar energy transition and to Professor Bierman for editorial assistance in developing the presentation.

Lovins (1976a, p. 65) refers to these alternative strategies as the "hard path," which leads inexorably to a centrally controlled nuclear future, and the "soft path, which is increasingly solar powered and decentralized. He observes that government policy has been pursuing the former, the nuclear path extrapolating from the recent past and relying on the rapid expansion of centralized, highly sophisticated technologies to increase supplies of energy, primarily in the form of electricity. On the other hand, the solar path, a whole greater than the sum of its parts, diverges radically from these incremental past practices to pursue long-term goals. It involves making a prompt commitment to use energy efficiently to develop solar technologies matched in scale and in energy quality to end-use needs, and to utilize special fossil-fuel technologies for transitional purposes.

Our purpose in this paper is to demonstrate that this choice is not a matter of scientific understanding or technological potential or capacity, but wholly a matter of political commitment. We present here documented scientific and engineering evidence in a systems analysis framework to demonstrate that we can choose the solar alternative to achieve a permanent clean source of abundant energy in a fully ordered and economically feasible global transition. Solar energy will prove to be economically the least expensive and socially the most affordable path.

The difficulties involved in choosing the nuclear pathway are familiar; these include economic and socio-political problems similar to those we already know, growing increasingly complex and perhaps eventually insurmountable. For example, as Lovins articulates, in an electrified society the monolithic nature, gargantuan scale, and exacting requirements of hard technologies tends to homogenize the social infrastructure; from the viewpoint of the consumer, diversity becomes a vanishing luxury. Everyone's lifestyle is frustratingly shaped by the economic imperatives of the energy system.

Choosing the solar path involves the difficulties of direction change, of doing something differently from the way we are accustomed to, and this difficulty should not be underestimated. However, the solar path offers us many advantages: social, economic, and geopolitical. As a soft technology, solar energy carries the advantage of being structurally less coercive and more participatory, compared to hard technologies such as nuclear energy. The soft path is an affirmation of human rights and freedom of expression. As Lovins states,

> ...in a soft path each person can choose his own risk-benefit balance and his own energy systems to match his own degree of caution and involvement. People who do not care to partake of the advantages of district heating will be free to reject them -- and, if the system is thoughtfully designed, to change their minds later. People who want to drive big cars or inhabit uninsulated houses will be free to do so -- and to pay the social costs. People can choose to live in city centers, remote

countryside, or in between, without being told their lifestyle is uneconomic. People can choose to minimize their "consumer humiliation" -- their forced dependence on systems they cannot understand, control, diagnose, repair, or modify -- or can continue to depend on traditional utilities... (1976b).

Finally, and perhaps most important, solar energy offers the virtual elimination of nuclear proliferation.*

Why we must now give serious thought to the question of our energy future needs little explanation. It seems clear enough that we are near the end of the fossil fluid age. Whatever the differences in estimates of remaining reserves of coal, gas, and oil, these are relevant only to the exact timing of the transition. No expert now argues that fossil fuel can continue as our primary global energy resource. The time has come to take a global, long-range view, to consciously define those criteria that must be met in choosing the world's permanent energy source, and to make the choice: The future of mankind hangs in the balance.

<u>Criteria for choosing the world's permanent energy source</u> cannot be stated briefly. The source must be abundant, accessible, and affordable (economically, environmentally, etc.). Moreover, the form of energy that makes human society possible on this globe must be part of, and make a contribution to, what can be called global solidarity. We explore below some of these criteria briefly within each of several categories to provide an understanding of the broad impact involved in the transition we recommend.

Abundance means that the source must be available at an adequate rate for the indefinite future, in a geographical distribution that permits and indeed favors the lesser developed regions of the world. Abundance means that one region's use will not diminish the amount available to another region and that the use by both will not diminish the resources bequeathed to our children throughout time.

---

*Dr. Joseph M. Ha, a professor of international affairs, states it this way (Ha, 1977): "We observed previously that states seek to develop nuclear power because they desire to use relatively inexpensive forms of energy to facilitate economic development and because they fear dependence on imported oil. Perhaps, then, one of the wisest nonproliferation strategies the United States, in concert with other major powers, can adopt is a very substantial effort to assist Third World nations in the assessment of their energy needs and the development and application of the various new, often inexpensive [solar] energy technologies. In this way, the United States should be able to reduce the political and economic incentives for the proliferation of nuclear power and, thus, nuclear weapons."

Accessibility, beyond the abundance criteria, means that the source must be accessible to a wide range of cultures and applications; this requires versatility. The choice must permit a diverse array of technologies to fit local climatic conditions and development stages. It must permit flexibility of energy characteristics to match user processes efficiently. It must be applicable through various technologies on a wide array of scales, from household to central power generation, and it must provide the potential for wide public participation in applying the technologies themselves.

Affordability takes into consideration human health and weighs environmental costs and benefits, social costs and benefits, and economic costs and benefits against one another. There are obvious overlappings among these categories, but we can list some conditions of affordability under each of those headings. Thus, environmental affordability criteria include safety from threats of genetic damage, from birth defects, from contaminants releaseable under ordinary or abnormal conditions, and from the larger dangers of global or local thermal pollution and heat balance problems. These all need to be explored in more realistic long-range terms.

Social cost-benefit affordability includes criteria related to social stability and harmony in an enhancement sense. The choice of an energy source should <u>reduce</u> nuclear proliferation and thus the threats of nuclear attack. It should reduce the pressure for global weapons. It should reduce the possible threat to civil liberties involved in security measures needed to protect a vulnerable and hazardous technology. It should reduce dependence on a technological elite. More positively it should promote decentralized control, local self-reliance, easy transferability, and harmonious rather than exploitative relations.

Affordability also involves the criteria of direct economic cost and benefit. Here we could consider a predictable fuel price, the freedom from unpredictable generic design problems, minimum maintenance requirements, longer equipment and plant life, learning curve massproduction cost improvements, and small scale low cost incremental investment patterns to permit flexible planning and immediate integration of technological breakthroughs.

Finally, the criteria must include the contribution that the energy source makes to global solidarity. The source must be free of secrecy requirements to permit full and open sharing of technical and economic information. The source must be such that regional differences in climate, culture and development invite, in fact <u>require</u>, the full participation of scientists, engineers, and economists from all nations and regions.

This lengthy list clarifies the conditions of choice: Careful consideration of these criteria compels the conclusion that <u>the world's permanent future energy source must be solar energy, the "soft path."</u> This must be humankind's destiny.

What kind of energy future will solar energy bring? First, a solar future would be characterized by a much more efficient use of energy. Significant energy efficiencies are possible and needed in all areas of the world, but particularly in the high consumption countries. A study by the American Institute of Physics (AIP, 1975) shows that most energy uses in the developed economies could be greatly improved. Second, this future would have a more dispersed energy usage pattern than is now exhibited in the developed world.

Third, in those centralized energy systems that do persist, chemical energy will occupy the primary role, utilizing hydrogen and other synthetic fluids for their storage capability and long-distance transmission advantage. Since electricity cannot be stored without converting it into a different form, such as chemical or gravitational potential energy (hydroelectric storage), and since its long range distribution involves substantial losses, electrical networks will come to play a secondary role. They will be increasingly confined to local area distribution, permitting cascading and district heating at the point where the electricity is generated.

Integrated energy systems designs, involving a blend of solar technologies, should be the objective. As both the developed and the emergent regions converage to decentralized, diverse, appropriate solar-based economies, they will, in effect, "meet in the future." The development gap will not be closed by confrontation and economic or military terrorism, but by each nation converging in the future to a common level of well-being, a humane, global society which will be rich in diversity and opportunity, and increasingly equal in the satisfaction of basic human needs. That is where the soft path leads.

Once it is agreed that the solar future, the soft path, is a desirable choice, what should be done to realize this goal? Lovins (1976a & 1976b), Commoner (1976), Clark (1975), and Schumacher (1973) offer valuable insights. Appropriate action depends on the type of society considered. As indicated above, in high consumption societies there is an immediate requirement to increase energy efficiencies by investing in well-documented conservation technologies.

In the U.S.A., positive conservation actions may be occurring at last. The Alliance to Save Energy, a coalition of some of the nation's most prominent politicians, academics, and industrialists has just been formed to tap the richest, cheapest, cleanest energy source: "Conservation energy." The goal is to make the development of conservation energy a national goal, and to achieve zero energy growth (ZEG) by 1985. President Carter has congratulated the Alliance, stating that: "Conservation will be the centerpiece of our national energy policy" (United Press International, 1977).* This is the type of understanding and commitment needed to create a "window-in-time;" time to create the solar transition.

A different strategy from this should be adopted by the emerging nations, which are now using much less energy. They should incorporate and integrate technologies of the developed world which are appropriate to their current needs and infrastructure, discarding those which are unsuited, disruptive and/or vulnerable to external actions. These societies cannot and should not follow in the footsteps of the high consumption societies because the latter were built with cheap fossil fluids which are nearing their depletion. It would be a tragic mistake to convert to an unsupportable technology and consumption pattern just when the developed nations are at the point of abandoning it. Developing countries should <u>anticipate the future</u> ane even lead the way by developing their own solar-based technologies, capabilities, and human resources.** Help will be available in the form of educational and training assistance; but due to local climatological, cultural, and economic differences, a large proportion of what has been developed in Japan, Oceania, North America, Russia, and Europe will not be appropriate*** (Abelson and Tinker, 1977).

The energy-choice criteria presented earlier reveal the desirability of a solar future, but will the solar transition actually come about? Since solar technology has no war potential, massive backing from military R & D budgets will not occur. <u>If solar energy is to be promoted, it will be for peaceful reasons</u>. But first, certain misconceptions concerning the economic costs of solar technologies must be addressed.

The section that follows examines a number of prominent solar-electric technologies and projects their respective costs. An examination of these cost projections will reveal that it is not always more research and development that is needed, nor even more

---

*A detailed 20 year energy scenario developed for the Northwestern U.S.A. illustrates, in a regional context, concrete examples of the dramatic benefits that a comprehensive, conservation-based energy policy can produce (Beers & Lash, 1977).

**Brazil provides a good example. Hammond (1977b and 1977c) reports that the Brazillian government has launched a program to replace most of their imported oil with ethyl alcohol produced from sugarcane and other crops. Brazil's blend of land, water and climate make an energy strategy based on biomass production ideal. Brazil has the potential to become the world leader in renewable-solar-energy utilization, and to become the first developing country without significant oil resources to achieve energy self-reliance.

***For a brief survey of solar technologies being developed internationally, see Appendix A.

demonstrations, but some type of temporary <u>catalytic</u> intervention on the part of government (i.e., the public) to allow these fledgling industries to become self-sustaining. This new role for government is developed in the last section by reference to a specific example of a pivotal solar technology.

The essay concludes with a challenge: <u>That we must face the choice, make the decision, and take all necessary actions</u>.

AN ASSESSMENT OF 20th CENTURY SOLAR TECHNOLOGY

The transition to a solar based economy is not a trivial matter like making the decision to switch from leaded to non-leaded gasoline. To conceptualize what we mean by a 'solar transition', one must be prepared to embrace a broad scope of technologies and their relationships. Just as a river is formed from an integrated plurality of tributaries, so too the pathways for capturing solar energy are many. This is fortunate, for, with this inherent diversity, the various solar capturing technologies may be thermodynamically matched to the large variety of end-use processes existing in modern society. But, besides being aware of the great multiplicity of technologies and their matching potential, one must be aware that solar energy, although abundant, is unevenly distributed in time and space. Receivable sunlight varies with time-of-day, season, weather, latitude and local terrain. Thus, the utilization of solar energy requires prudent management, energy banking and exchange, so that temporal and spatial discrepancies between energy supply and demand may be evened out. Finally, and most obviously, for each of the available solar technologies, one must consider engineering and economic factors to determine whether the technology is reasonably competitive with conventional nonsolar approaches.

This section will endeavor to treat each of these topic areas in this general order.

The Diversity of Solar and Solar-Related Energy Technologies

Solar energy can provide for every energy-demanding process now in use. There exists a reassuringly diverse variety of pathways and technologies for receiving and using the sun's energy. Solar energy can be received, transformed, and delivered in the following energy forms: electromagnetic, thermal, chemical, food, mechanical, kinetic, electrical. It can also be delivered in a "canned" form in chemical feedstocks, wood for structural use, and high energy-requiring products like fertilizer. This versatility is a great asset; for it allows a matching of delivered-energy characteristics (energy form, quality or temperature, rate, power density) with the characteristics of the intended use. Table 1 displays the rich web of solar and solar-related energy pathways and technologies which can be used to deliver energy in the form, rate, and quality appropriate to the full spectrum of human activities in all regions of the world.

TABLE 1 A Classification of Solar and Solar-Related Energy Conversion/Delivery Technologies

SOLAR

Solar-Electric
- Photoelectric (photovoltaic):
  - Central power stations,
  - Dispersed (rooftop)
- Solar-thermal-electric
- Wind-electric:
  - Central power stations,
  - Dispersed
- Ocean thermal gradient-electric
- Biomass-electric:
  - Waste resources (domestic waste, agricultural residues),
  - Energy plantations (land or marine)
- Hydroelectric
- Other terrestrial (ocean wave, salinity gradient,...)
- Earth satellite systems:
  - Sun/Earth, power satellite,
  - Earth/Earth, transmission relay satellite

Solar-Thermal and Lighting
- Domestic water heating
- Building space heating:
  - Passive only,
  - Active/passive
- Building space cooling (air conditioning):
  - Passive only,
  - Active/passive
- Cooking
- Clothes drying
- Agricultural processes:
  - Livestock shelter heating,
  - Water heating,
  - Crop drying,
  - Food dehydrating
- Industrial processes:
  - Steam generation,
  - Process heating,
  - Furnace applications
- Water purification (desalination)
- Daylighting

SOLAR-RELATED

Solar-Chemical (Fuels and Materials)
- Biomass-to-fuels and feedstocks:
  - Waste resources,
  - Energy plantations
- The Solar-Hydrogen Economy

Solar-Mechanical and Kinetic
- Wind propulsion (sailing ships, sailboats, sailplanes)
- Wind pumpers (irrigation and water lifting)
- Watermills (grinding, weaving)
- Windaerators (sewage treatment)
- Draft animal power

Solar-Food and Fiber
    Agriculture/Forestry:
        - Agribusiness, remote,
        - Family farm, remote,
        - Urban fringe integrated complexes
    Urban gardening
    Urban attached greenhouses

Thermodynamic Matching of Energy Sources and Uses

Any optimally designed energy system should attempt to match the quality of the energy source with the desired use. This means (1) designing each process to use energy of the lowest quality (i.e., lowest characteristic temperature) that is economically feasible, and (2) providing the energy at a temperature just above that quality. But due to the historic availability of fossil fluid fuels, designers have not been overly concerned with this quality matching (Berg, 1974). As an example, typical 2nd Law efficiencies* in U.S.A. processes are quite low: 25-30% is the highest achieved, and that only in certain industrial processes. Transportation, residential, and commercial sector processes show 4-10% (American Institute of Physics, 1975, p. 50).

Figure 1 displays the energy uses typical in the U.S.A. The percentages express each function's share of total energy consumed (regardless of quality). The temperature range shown would be typical for the corresponding application.**

Solar energy technology can make direct thermal energy available at any temperature between ambient and 3800°C through appropriate concentration or by combining solar-thermal preheating with a high-temperature fuel, also of solar derivation (see for example, Trombe & Royere, 1974; or Anderson, 1976). In addition to providing thermal energy, solar energy can be converted to electricity, fuels, and biomass-for-materials-use; it can provide natural lighting; and through solar furnaces (e.g. Odeillo, France), it can produce temperatures above anything required in industry. Therefore, all our present energy functions could be met with solar energy, although complete reliance on solar energy would probably not be realized before the year 2025-2050.

---

*The 2nd Law of Thermodynamics allows a calculation of the physical efficiency limits of key energy uses. The 2nd Law efficiency is defined as the ratio of the least available work that could have done the job to the available work actually used. The theoretical limit of this ratio is 100%. Available work is defined as the maximum work that can be provided by a system (or a fuel) as it proceeds (by any path) to a specified final equilibrium state (AIP, 1975, pp. 28-29).

**Agricultural uses such as crop drying, livestock shelter heating, and food preservation would fall in the range of hot water and space heating. The solar input to food and fiber production is not included in Figure 1.

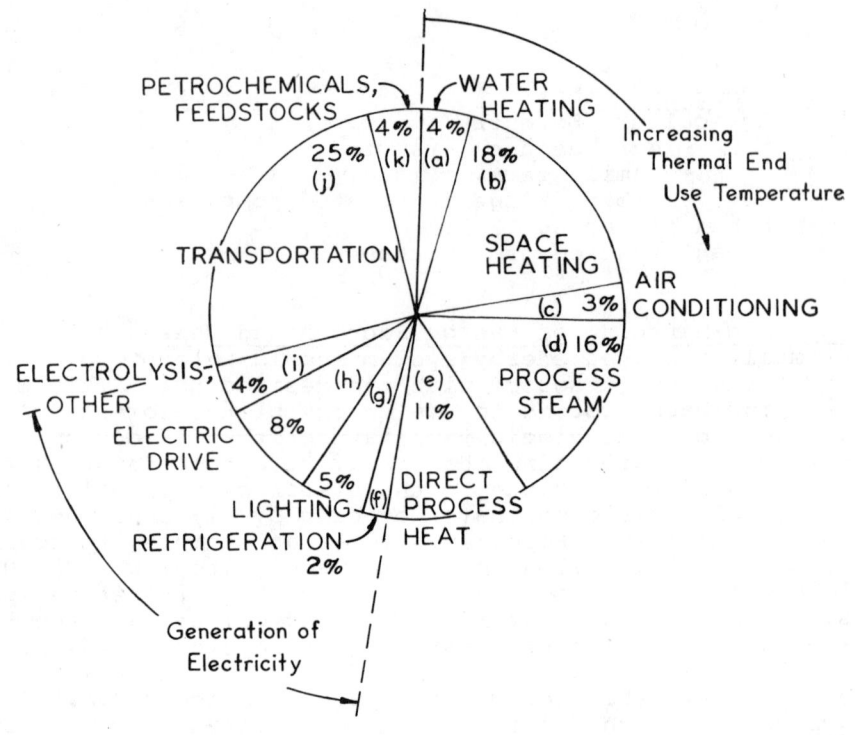

Fig. 1. Amount and quality of energy uses, U.S.A.

Functional Energy Uses	Percentage of (1968 USA Energy Use (1) (%)	Terminal Process Temperature Required (2) (°C)
Thermal Effects:		
a) Water Heating	4.0	50- 85
b) Space Heating	17.9	40- 75
c) Air Conditioning	2.5	77- 96 (3)
d) Industrial Process Steam	16.7 (87%) (13%)	100-200 200-250
e) Industrial Direct Heat	11.5 (80%) (20%)	<350 >350
f) Refrigeration	2.2	150-175
i) Selected Materials Refining (Conventionally by Electrolysis (4)	1.2	>350 (6)
[Clothes Drying	0.3	20- 65]
[Cooking	1.3	100-250]
Total Thermal Effects	= 57.6	
Lighting Effects	= 1.5	(6)

Functional Energy Uses	Percentage of (1968 USA Energy Use (1) (%)	Terminal Process Temperature Required (2) (°C)
Motion-Mechanical Effects:		
h) Electric Drive	7.9	(6)
j) Transportation (Conventionally by Fuels)	24.9	(6)
[Misc. Electrical Equip. and Appliances (5)	2.6	(6)]
Total Mechanical Effects =	35.4	
k) Material Properties (Non-Energy Uses) =	5.5	(6)
GRAND TOTAL =	100.0	

Figure 1 Notes:

1) From Stanford Research Institute (SRI) 1972, pp. 6-7. The use of electricity in each application was converted to a BTU-equivalent on the basis of the average heat rate for thermal power plants.

2) These temperature estimates are based primarily on research by Anderson (1976) and Reistad (1974).

3) The temperature range for solar air conditioning.

4) Constant temperature thermal processing is the requirement. Electrolytic processing is only one method, and perhaps not the best one in 2nd Law efficiency terms.

5) The "Other" category given in SRI (1972) was allocated into "Lighting" or "Miscellaneous Electrical Equipment and Appliances," thus slightly over stating the electrical share of usage.

6) Although functions traditionally performed with electricity have been expressed as thermal energy at 540°C. a standard temperature for thermal power generation (Anderson, 1976, p. 2), this is meaningless for photoelectric (or other non-thermal) generation technology. The same is true for fuels and feedstock usage. We prefer the restricted practice of associating temperature only with thermal effects.

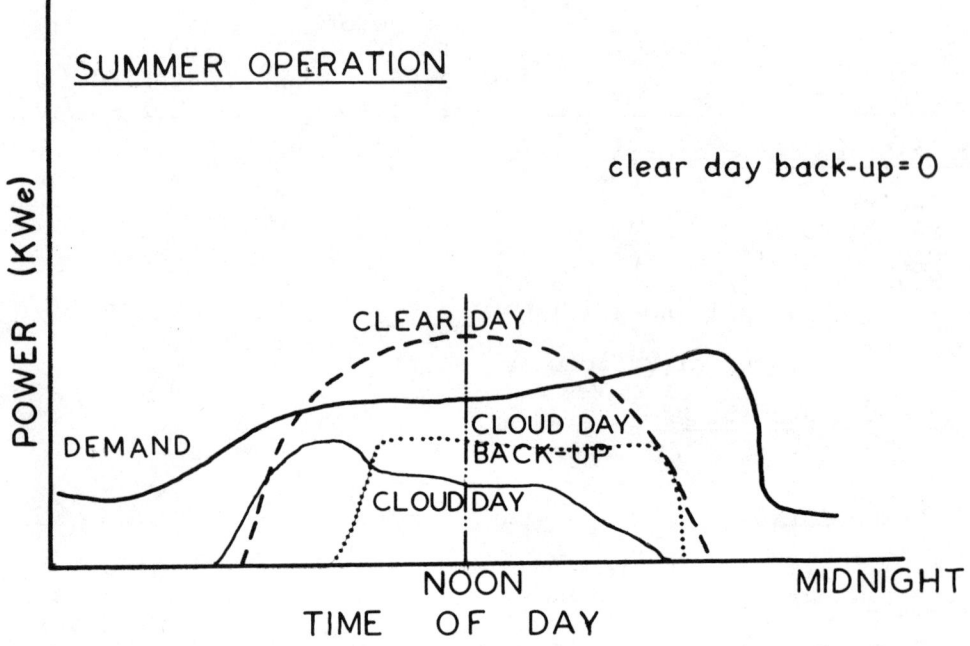
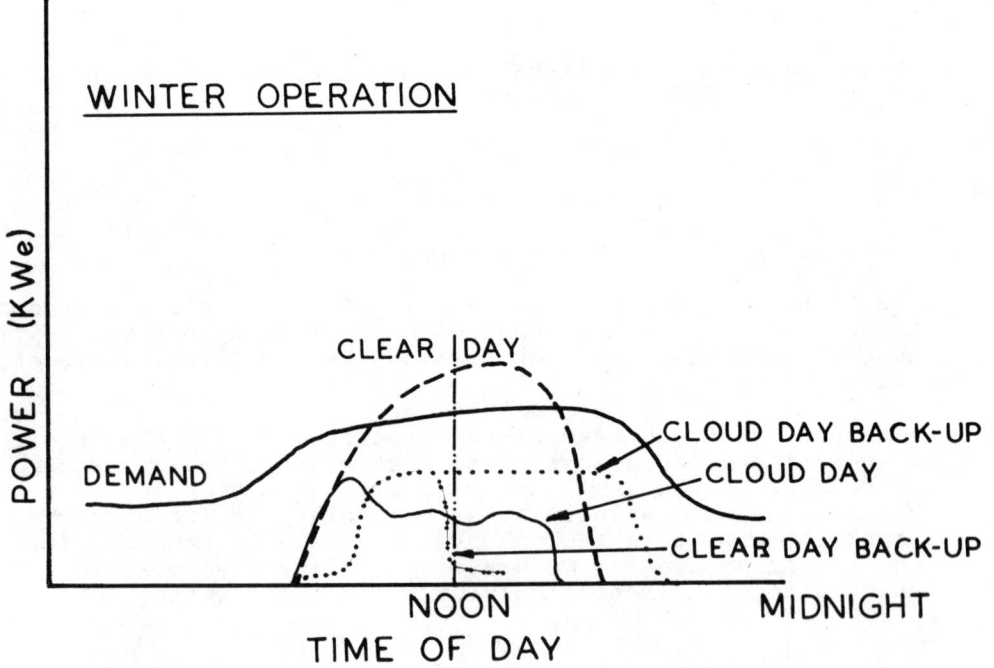

Fig. 2. Power profile curves for solar-electric generation.

The know-how for matching, in particular, solar-thermal system design and end-use thermal process design is still rudimentary. Even the prerequisite systems analysis procedures are not yet developed. Nevertheless, Elmer (1976) has made an ambitious beginning toward 2nd Law efficiency analysis of the full range of energy sources and uses in a metropolitan area; Lovins (1976a) has provided the context and goal for such analyses; and Berg (1974), Reistad (1975) and the American Institute of Physics (1975) have made additional contributions. In general, this work is just getting started.

Supply-Demand Power Matching

Central station solar-electric technologies of the type which must deal with daily variations in source availability require in general, a power backup and storage system (with the exception of ocean thermal gradient-electric, refuse-electric, or hydroelectric). Figure 2 shows one such combination although many configurations are possible. This arrangement, requires limited on-site storage (e.g. battery, flywheel, compressed air; about 6 hours at the daily average power level), plus a low capital costs, chemical-fueled backup generator (e.g. fuel cell, combustion turbine) for cloudy days. The combination shown happens to be optimized for summer.

On clear days in summer, the area under the solar-power curve is equal to the area under the power demand profile. Total daily kwhrs. electrical energy equals the 24 hour integral of the power vs. time profile, power being the energy delivered per unit time. The storage is adequate to capture the daily peak (noon) and to carry the load through the night. On clear days, the backup system is idle. However, any deficits due to cloudiness must be made up within a few hours by the backup generator. The backup generator can either be throttled (as in a fuel cell) or brought up in steps through the use of multiple units (combustion turbine). The length of operational time can also be varied, since the backup feeds into storage, rather than directly into the load. The constraint is that over each 24 hours, the area under the load curve must be equal to the combined areas under the solar power profile and the backup power profile.

Since this particular example is designed for maximum summer efficiency, for other times of the year, the backup system must operate for some time each day, with more energy required on cloudy days. As in the summer, an energy balance must be achieved each 24 hours.

Obviously, the concepts of baseloading, etc. must be updated, particularly in the context of gradually integrating these plants into a network of dissimilar generation technologies (see footnote at the end of Solar-Thermal-Electric Systems discussion).

Solar Energy Economics

The remainder of this section focuses on evaluating the economic

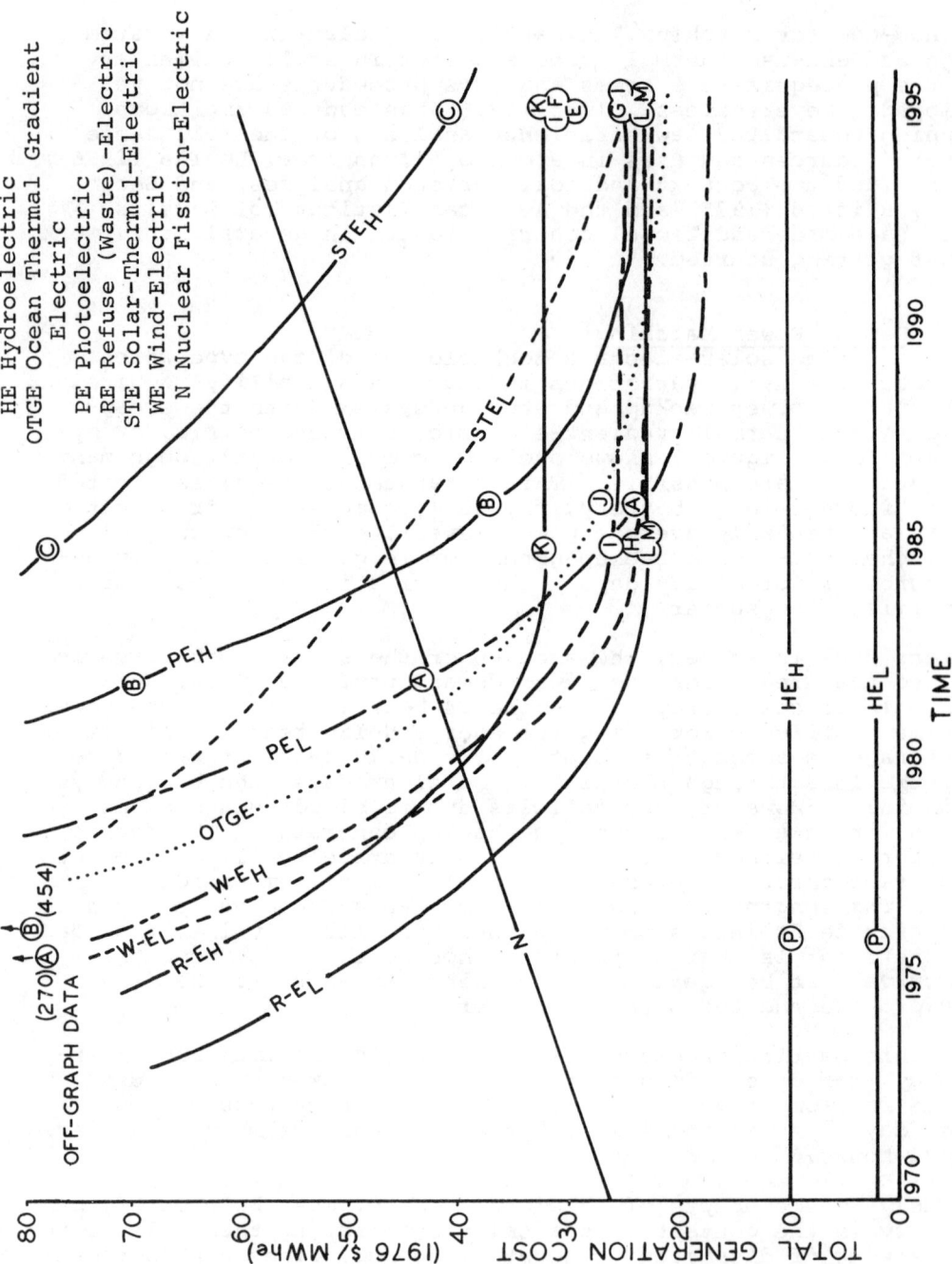

Fig. 3. Solar-electric cost comparisons.

Figure 3 Notes:

A) - Photoelectric, 1-axis concentration, no storage, Albuquerque. N.M., U.S.A.
B) - Photoelectric, 1-axis concentration, no storage, Blue Hill, Mass., U.S.A.
C) - Solar-thermal-electric, Southwestern U.S.A. (winter, 1976).
D) - Solar-thermal-electric, Southwestern U.S.A. (Duff & Shaner, 1976).
E) - Solar-thermal-electric, Southwestern U.S.A. (Smith, 1976).
F) - Solar-thermal-electric, Southwestern U.S.A., Intermediate loading (Aerospace Corp., 1975).
G) - Solar-thermal-electric, Southwestern U.S.A., base loading (Aerospace Corp., 1975).
H) - Wind-electric, 7 meter/sec wind speed, grid-stability storage (Coty & Dubey, 1976).
I) - Wind-electric, 8 meter/sec wind speed, no storage (Witwer, 1976).
J) - Ocean thermal gradient electric, U.S.A. Gulf Coast (Zener, 1976).
K) - Refuse-electric, baseloading, agricultural waste (Witwer, 1976).
L) - Refuse-electric, baseloading, municipal solid waste/coal (Witwer, 1976).
M) - Refuse-electric, baseloading, Purox system (Witwer, 1976).
N) - Nuclear, light water reactor, no storage (see text, following).
P) - Hydroelectric

Figure 3 Remarks:

The shape of these cost curves is based on our own judgement since most estimates are either specific to one or two dates, or are associated with any particular time period. Most of the cost improvements will occur before 1995 (1985 in some cases) assuming a vigorous commercialization effort (see discussion in the section entitled The New Role of Government).

Neither the amount or type of storage, nor the plant operational mode (e.g. baseloading, intermediate loading, peaking, fuel saver mode) have been treated systematically in the research we have reviewed. This probably reflects the fact that electrical network operations will be considerably different when solar technologies, and some of the newer transition technologies begin to be integrated into the power grids. This is particularly true of on-site (dispersed) generation. In any case, 6 hours of electrical storage only adds about $2/MWhe to the total generation cost (see Solar-Thermal-Electric Systems discussion). The operational mode has much more influence on the total generation cost, and the two factors, operation cost and storage cost, are not simply related. Base loading and fuel-saver operations enjoy a cost advantage in that the plant is operated anytime it is able to deliver energy, thus repaying its investment more rapidly (see footnote in Solar-Thermal-Electric Systems discussion).

feasibility of the solar energy transition. We describe and project the eventual economic costs of a number of solar technologies which are, or are likely to become, candidates for commercial use. These are summarized in Figure 3 which compares the costs of various solar-electric generation technologies to nuclear-electric generation.

Further, as we indicated, making the solar transition will involve two kinds of choices, socio-political and economic. The solar technology cost projections we analyze below need a contrast point for meaningful comparison. The obvious choice is the nuclear alternatives, and so we have used the typical light water reactor (LWR, "burner" reactor) to establish the needed reference.

Nuclear-Electric Generation

The format adopted here involves adjusting capital costs to the equivalent present worth in the initial year of operation (the year of initial operational capability, or IOC date) see Table 3. Money units are 1976 U.S.A. dollars, unless otherwise noted. Since nuclear plant capital costs are typically expressed in current year dollars and represent a cumulative time stream of payments through a protracted construction cycle, the Wholesale Price Index (WPI) was used as a dollar deflater, (1976 WPI = 1.0), and applied between the construction mid-point (halfway between the contract award date and IOC date) and the IOC date; the working assumption being that plant construction cash flow is concentrated at the mid-point of the cycle. The data base is the one presented by Olds (1975, p. 43). Plants under contract were eliminated.

Bupp, et. al., (1975, p. 21) found $31/KWe per year to be the average annual escalation in nuclear plant capital costs (in constant dollars) based on historical data and cost projections from early 1975. Since additional cost overruns are reported several times during the construction of nuclear plants, (Olds, 1974, pp. 39-40, charts 4 and f; and Olds, 1975, p. 44) the combination of actual costs and cost projections appears certain to yield lower escalation rates than will eventually emerge.

Historically, actual costs have averaged about twice the original estimates (Bupp, et.al., 1975, p. 19; and the preceding Olds citations). However, to be conservative (as seen from the solar perspective; optimistic from a nuclear viewpoint) we use the Bupp, et.al. escalation rate of $31/KWe per year for subsequent nuclear plant capital cost projections, rather than the $85/KWe per year from the linear regression on 1970-1976 historical costs.

To complete the calculation of nuclear generation cost, an annual fixed charge ratio (AFCR) of 15% is used;* operating and maintenance (O & M) cost plus fuel cost is taken as 1/3 of the total generation ("busbar") cost, (e.g., U.S.A. Atomic Energy Commission, 1974, p. 20, Table 1-5). Total generation cost is therfore

---

*Low for privately-owned utilities, high for those public-owned, due to profits and differential tax subsidies.

TABLE 3 Escalation of Nuclear Generation Costs

Initial Operational Capability Date (1)	Construction Mid-Point Date	Actual Cash Payments (1) Current $/KWe	Inflation Adjustments (2)	Present Worth at IOC Date (4)	
				Actual 1976 $/KWe	Linear Regression (3) 1976 $/KWe
1970	1967.67	143	1.965	281	252
1971	1968.40	164	1.921	315	337
1972	1969.00	241	1.880	453	422
1973	1969.64	248	1.835	455	508
1974	1970.25	308	1.799	554	593
1975	1971.08	415	1.752	727	679
1976	1971.64	451	1.707	770	764
1982					1277
1986					1618

TABLE NOTES:

(1) Data source: Olds (1975, p. 43). Since his data were published in September, 1975, the cost figure for 1975 IOC plants may not reflect the final cost overruns. The true 1976 IOC plant costs are almost certain to be higher than the values he shows, for the same reason.

(2) The inflation adjustment factor (for a given IOC year) is the Wholesale Price Dollar Purchasing Power in the construction mid-point year (for the given IOC year) divided by the value for 1976. For an example, plants coming on line in 1976 (the IOC year) were contracted for in 1967.28 (composite of all 1976 IOC plants). Therefore, the construction mid-point was 1971.64. The Wholesale Price Dollar Purchasing Power was 1.707 times higher at that time (interpolating between 1971 and 1972 values) than in 1976. The capital cost in Old's table $451/KWe (current $), when multiplied by 1.707, gives $770/KWe (1976 $).

(3) Linear regression over the 1970-1976 IOC time period gives an annual escalation, in 1976 $, of $85.43/KWe per year.

(4) IOC Date = the date of initial operational capability: the date when a plant first goes on line.

1.5 times annual capital costs. The latter assumption seems conservative, since nuclear fuel costs appear to be rising faster than capital cost. A plant capacity factor of 59.3% is used, which is the U.S.A.'s historical capacity factor for large plants (Komanoff, 1975, p. 1). Costs for de-commissioning and long-term guarding of dead plants have been ignored. (Although such costs may prove significant, only time will tell).

Combining these cost elements into one equation, the cost (in 1976 $) of electricity generated in a nuclear fission plant coming on-line in year T is:

Nuclear Generation Cost:

$$\frac{1976\ \$}{MWhe} = \frac{1.5 \times CC \times AFCR \times 1000}{8760 \times CF}$$

where, 1.5 = total generation cost/annual fixed charges;
$AFCR$ = annual fixed charge ratio = 15%/year;
1000 = KWe/MWe;
8760 = no. of hours/year;
CF = capacity factor = $\frac{\text{Actual (net) KWhe/year}}{8760 \times \text{KWe Nameplate}}$ = 0.593
T = year
CC = capital cost (1976 $/KWe) = $800 + 31 \times (T-1976)$

This equation projects nuclear generation costs as follows, in Table 4.

TABLE 4 Projection of Nuclear Generation Costs

Initial Operating Date	Capital Cost 1976 $ KWeNameplate	Effective Capital Cost 1976 $ KWeAverage	Total Generation Cost	
			1976 $/KWeAverage	1976 $/MWhe =1976 mills/KWhe
1976	800	1349	2020	34.70
1978	862	1454	2180	37.30
1980	924	1558	2340	40.00
1982	986	1663	2490	42.70
1984	1048	1767	2650	45.40
1986	1110	1872	2810	48.10

Dollar cost comparisons can provide useful insights; however, we emphasize that <u>dollar</u> cost must not be considered as the sole assessment criterion. It may not even be the critical one, as seen, for example, in the list of selection criteria suggested previously in this essay. A perceptive analysis of the social/environmental issues of solar energy development, just completed by Stanford Research Institute, observes that the future role of solar energy cannot be separated from other major societal issues; social policy choice involved must not be dominated by economic factors. Society's decision with regard to solar energy is best considered as part of a broad societal choice involving much more than selection of an energy technology (SRI, 1977).

SOLAR-ELECTRIC GENERATION

Photoelectric (Photovoltaic) Conversion
Direct conversion of sunlight-to-electricity through photoelectric solar cells has been routinely accomplished in the space program for 20 years. The reliability (no moving parts) and low weight of these devices are critical advantages in space probe and earth satellite applications, whereas cost hardly matters. The solar cell manufacturing technology that was developed to fill this vital but very limited need is, not surprisingly, very high-priced and not suited to mass production.

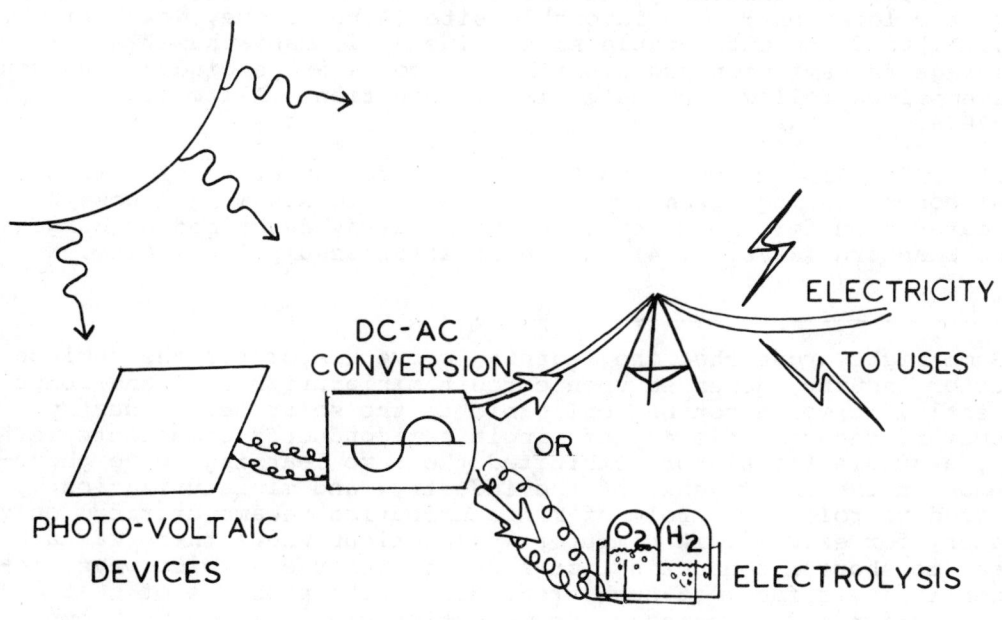

In the last few years, some modest efforts have emerged to modify the basic photocell technology for use in earth-based power stations. For example, solar energy R & D received U.S.A. federal funding for the first time in 1972 (3/10 % of the total U.S.A. energy R & D budget) with roughly 30% of the solar portion going to photoelectric conversion technology.

The photoelectric industry offers a textbook example of the rationale for making cost reduction projections for solar-electric technologies. In photoelectric technologies the cost of the solarcell itself plays a pivotal role in the overall system cost. Since a solar cell is essentially a semiconductor, it is reasonable to assume that, with specific production engineering improvements, the photocell industry, and hence, the photoelectric power generation industry, will essentially duplicate the "learning curve" history of the semiconductor industry (where large cost reductions consistently followed market increases).* A more in-depth analysis of these economics may be found in the next section (The New Role of Government), where it will be shown that these developments will depend to a large extent on whether government undertakes the responsibility to fill a critical new role (which will be later defined). The present discussion will concentrate primarily on providing specific cost estimates for photoelectric power generation.

Photoelectric generation costs are estimated below for a reference central power station of modular design utilizing silicon solar-cell technology and incorporating solar concentrators. Costs are calculated for initial plant operation in 1976, 1982, and 1986, for two locations: one favorable site (Albuquerque, New Mexico, U.S.A.) and one unfavorable site (Blue Hill, Massachusetts, USA). Storage transmission and distribution costs are excluded. Working assumptions follow each date/site combination. All costs are in 1976 $.

(1) 1976, Albuquerque: $3485 KWe Peak for an array of cylindrical concentrating geometry is equivalent to assuming a cost no greater than for the circular geometry array described by Burgess and Edenburn (1976, p. 4), a conservative assumption. Also, a

---

*Some might argue that the learning curve history of the semiconductor industry depended upon circuit miniaturization, and consequently, it would not be applicable to the solar cell industry. However, the cost history of single semiconductor components (e.g., a single transistor) exhibited the same learning curve phenomenon in the early years of the industry, and miniaturization played no role. The role of miniaturization became critical only later, for example, in computer applications where there was a need to shorten conducting paths due to the use of microwave frequencies. In fact, at such frequencies, the problems of heat dissipation and temperature compensation cause design problems and subsequent cost penalties which are much more troublesome at the microscale than at the macrosale typical of solar power generation.

value of 5.4 KWhe/m^2-day (annual average) for an east-west aligned, 1-axis tracking array of cylindrical geometry located in Albuquerque (Burgess, 1976, p. 3) gives a capacity factor of 5.4/24 = 0.225 (= 1/4.44); the ratio of annual average power to peak power (noon, clear atmosphere, normal surface). Peak solar power is assumed = 1 KWe/m^2, or 24 KWhs/m^2-day. Therefore, the $3485/KWe Peak (hypothetical 1976 initial operation) is equivalent to $15,490/KWe Average. (KWe Average always designates annual average.) An operational plus maintenance (O & M) cost of $5/MWhe (= 5 mills/KWhe) is assumed. Solar generation involves no fuel cost. Thus, variable costs for a solar plant, expressed in terms of KWe Average, are:

$$\frac{5(\$/MWhe) \times 8760 \text{ Hrs/year}}{1000 \text{ (KWe/MWe)} \times 0.15 \text{ (Annual Fixed Charge Ratio, yrs}^{-1})} = \$292/\text{KWe Ave.}$$

This effectively capitalizes photoelectric variable costs using 15%/year as the composite figure for all electrical utilities (U.S.A. Atomic Energy Commission, 1974, p. 20, Table 1-5). It subsumes various capital recovery periods and interest rates, taxes, insurance, etc. over an assumed lifetime of 30 years. It is assumed to remain constant in constant dollars.

Adding construction and capitalized variable costs, this give:

$\frac{3485}{0.225}$ + 292 = $15,780/KWe Average for total generation cost, or

$\frac{15,780 \times 0.15 \times 1000}{8760}$ = $270/MWhe.

(2) 1976, Blue Hill: $3485/KWe Peak and 3.2 KWhe/m^2-day (annual average) for an east-west aligned, 1-axis tracking array of cylindrical geometry located in Blue Hill (same references as above), with a capacity factor for Blue Hill of 3.2/24 = 0.133 (= $\frac{1}{7.5}$); gives a total generation cost of: $\frac{3485}{0.133}$ + 292 = $26,490/KWe Average, or $454/MWhe.

(3) 1982, Albuquerque: $500/KWe Peak is assumed for a concentrator array of cylindrical geometry as a 1982 projection (Magid, 1976, p. 6, Figure 2). This projection, based on U.S.A. ERDA data, is not a research and development goal, but, rather, a careful assessment of what can be achieved using presently developed technology. O & M costs are assumed to be constant (in 1976 dollars), thus the 1982 total generation cost at Albuquerque is $\frac{500}{0.225}$ + 292 = $2510/KWe Average, or $43/MWhe.

(4) 1982, Blue Hill: The total generation cost, using the same projection, is $\frac{500}{0.133}$ + 292 = $4050/KWe Average, or $69.30/MWhe.

(5) 1986, Albuquerque: $250/KWe Peak is assumed for a concentrator array of cylindrical geometry as a 1986 projection (Magid, 1976, p. 6, Figure 2). This yields a total photoelectric generation cost at Albuquerque of $\frac{250}{0.225}$ + 292 = $1400/KWe Average, or $24/MWhe.

(6) 1986, Blue Hill: At $250/KWe Peak in 1986, total generation cost at Blue Hill is $\frac{250}{0.033}$ + 292 = $2170/KWe Average, or $37.20/MWhe.

(7) 1986, Typical U.S.A. (Albuquerque - Blue Hill Composite): For the 1986 projection, the Albuquerque - Blue Hill composite (arithmetic average) is taken as representative of the U.S.A. and yields 250 x 0.5 ($\frac{1}{0.225}$ + $\frac{1}{0.133}$) + 292 = 250 x 5.98 + 292 = $1790, KWe Average, or $30.60/MWhe.

An advantage of photoelectric power generation is that solar array modules are no more costly at the scale of one rooftop than for several square miles (central power stations). Although installation costs would be higher for residential applications, as much as 25-50% of the total array cost could be defrayed if waste heat from the modules is collected and used for domestic water and space heating (solar cells are more efficient when cooled). Rooftop mounted solar arrays could substitute for the large-scale "solar farms" required for solar central power generation.

In addition to power generation capability, some provision would have to be made for energy storage. According to Morris (1976, p. 10) the cost of residential power storage using present lead-acid batteries would add $23/MWhe, assuming 36 hour storage capacity. This cost would be expected to drop with further developments in the battery industry. If the 1986 cost of photoelectric generation is taken ($30.60/MWhe), then total cost of electricity to the resident (in 1986) would be $53.60/MWhe, less expensive than the charge to consumers in many parts of the U.S.A. today. In areas where utilities agree to purchase electricity surplus to residential needs (back to the utility through the power grid) during the day while drawing power during the night, battery cost could be eliminated. Of course the utility price would be adjusted so that they would be compensated for providing "storage" (peaking capacity). The utility <u>should be</u> indifferent to their source of energy or their exact role, provided they are fairly compensated. This suggests a new role for utilities: The "energy bankers."

If the electric car becomes the primary means of personal (at least urban) transportation, the home photoelectric generator can charge batteries during peak solar hours and the car can exchange batteries at any time. Similarly, intercity automobile service stations of the future may be small solar farms, with swapping of batteries taking place more quickly than the present "fill-up." In this way, electrical network load levelling can be achieved by integrating the transportation and electric grid system designs.

No mention has been made of the use of either thin-film or integrated circuit technologies for photoelectric power generation. Recent developments are encouraging. The solar industry trade magazine, Solar Engineering (1976, p. 4), reports that thin-film solar cells, made of cadmium sulfide and copper sulfide, have exhibited 7.8% efficiency (sunlight to electricity), with an estimated materials costs of $1.12/m^2, which is negligible when added to processing and assembly costs. In the same citation, Solar Engineering reports the development of a new multi-layer, integrated circuit-type solar cell that converts 30% of the incident sunlight into electricity. Our cost estimates were based on the U.S.A. ERDA learning curve projections for conventional silicon solar cells. A breakthrough in the thin-film, integrated circuit technologies, or other competing approaches to photoelectric power conversion would further improve the cost estimates developed above.

Solar-Thermal-Electric Systems (Central Power Station)
Several basic schemes can be identified for converting sunlight to electricity by thermal generating technology. In the "central receiver" design, a field of heliostatically controlled mirrors reflect and focus sunlight on a tower-mounted receiver. This heats a working fluid which drives a conventional turbine-generator combination, thus producing electricity. In the "distributed collector" design, "point-focus" collectors are used to produce a hot working fluid at each of many collection elements in a large array. This fluid is collected in a piping network and used to drive the turbogenerator. A distributed, "line-focus" collector design is a variant of this. Within a category many different components and design alternatives are available.

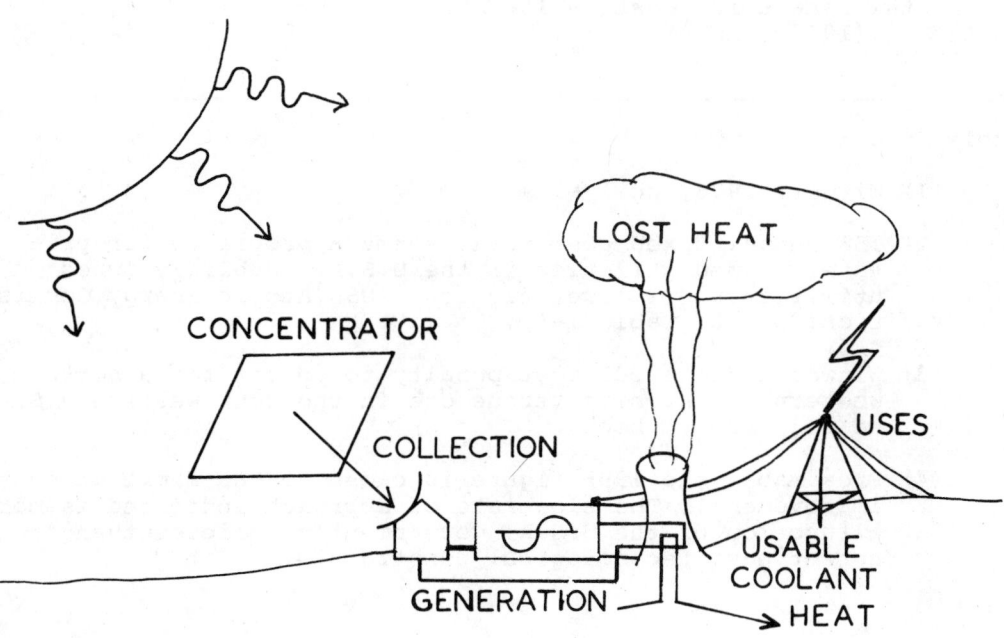

TABLE 5 Cost Estimates for Solar-Thermal-Electric Power Generation

---

Prototype definition:

    Central receiver design
    100 MWe rate power
    Southwestern U.S.A. location
    8 hour thermal storage (fused salt mixture)
    Intermediate load designation
    45% plant capacity factor

Cost Projections:	1985	1995[4]
Capital investment 1975 $/KWe northwestern U.S.A.	2200[1]	1100[1]
Adjusted to 1976 $ (@7%) southwestern U.S.A. location $\frac{1}{1.20}$ (3) (1976 $/KWe)	1960	980
Electrical Generation Costs Fixed costs @ 15% AFCR(2) (1976 $/Kwe)	74.6	37.3
Operating and Maintenance Costs Adjusted to 1976 $ (@7%) (1976 $/MWhe)	3.2	3.2
Total Generating Costs @ 15% AFCR[2] (1976 $/MWhe)	77.8	40.5

Table Notes:

(1) Witwer, 1976, pp. 7-12

(2) 15% annual fixed cost ratio seems appropriate for privately owned utilities in the U.S.A. Publicly owned utilities use a lower figure. (USA Atomic Energy Commission, p. 20, Table 1-5).

(3) Witwer added a 20% cost penalty to adjust for a northwestern U.S.A. site versus one in the southwestern U.S.A. We adjusted it back.

(4) Presumably the 1995 figure is close to the limit on cost improvement. The slow rate of approach indicated is more a function of the U.S.A. government's policies than inherent past technological constraints.

Since all three designs rely on tracking the sun, this technology is more effective when applied in regions of the world where clear skies are the rule. Other factors, such as the availability of hydroelectric systems for energy storage and responsive power-throttling, also play an important role in determining appropriate locations for this technology.

Duff & Shaner (1976, p. 245) quote a cost of $24/MWhe from a previous study (Colorado State University, 1974). This excludes storage, operating and maintenance (O & M) costs; and it is approximately the same for both a central receiver design and a point-focus, distributed collector design. They develop a capital cost estimate of $64/MWhe (Duff and Shaner, 1976, p. 269) for the best of the three alternative line-focus, distributed collector designs. The estimates could be adjusted to total generation cost by adding $3/MWhe for O & M (Witwer, 1976, p. 11). Six hours of storage, at the annual average power level, is estimated to cost 18.4 (1976 $/KWhe) (The Aerospace Corporation, 1975, pp. 175 & 180), which is equivalent to a storage cost of $1.89/MWhe.* Adding a 7% inflation factor to adjust the Duff & Shaner estimate from 1975$ to 1976$ yields (in 1976 $) $31/MWhe for the central receiver and the point-focus, distributed collector designs ($29/MWhe, without storage), for the line-focus, distributed collector design ($71/MWhe, without storage).

Smith, (1976, pp. 98-116), estimated a total generating cost of $29.6/MWhe (Smith, 1976, p. 113) for his 100 MWe central receiver design. This design includes an integrated storage capability which is sufficient to allow the energy equivalent of 53% of full power operation for 6.7 hours (Smith, 1976, p. 101), enough for 24 hour operations. Particular dollars (e.g. 1976 $) are not specified. O & M costs are included and the site is El Paso, Texas (Smith, 1976, pp. 112-113).

In a recent study performed at Stanford Research Institute, Witwer (1976, pp. 7-12), estimated solar-thermal-electric generating costs for 100 MWe intermediate load plants in the northwestern U.S. This study integrated material from industry sources and the following references: (1) the Aerospace Corporation, 1974; (2) Jet Propulsion Laboratory, 1975; (3) Federal Energy Administration, 1974; and (4) Solar Energy Intelligence Report, 1976, p. 35. The results, with normalizing adjustments, are shown in Table 5.

The Aerospace Corporation (1975) analyzed 100 MW electric conversion systems in each mode: base-loading, intermediate-loading, and peaking. The site was Inyokern, California, U.S.A. The projected total generation cost for intermediate-loading was $31/MWhe (1976 $), with six hours of thermal storage (Aerospace Corp., 1975, pp. 176-177). For base-loading, the projected cost was

---

$$*\frac{18.4\ (\$/KWhe) \times 6\ (KWhe/KWe\ Average) \times 0.15\ (1/years)}{8760\ (KWhe/year)/KW\ Average} \times$$

$$1000(KWhe/MWhe) = \$1.89\ \frac{1976\ \$}{MWhe}$$

246

$25/MWhe (1976 $), with a twelve hour thermal storage capacity
(pp. 174-175).*

Wind Energy Conversion
The kinetic energy of the wind in the lower 0.1 kilometers of
the atmosphere can be received in a variety of ways and converted
into different output forms. Some of these are: Electricity,
mechanical energy (for irrigation pumping, well water drawing,
aeration of sewage ponds, grain grinding, loom-weaving), chemical
energy (hydrogen gas through the electrolysis of water); and kinetic energy (sailing ships). Any one of these might be most use
ful in a given place, time and application. However, due to spac
limitations, the cost estimates below focus on wind-electric conversion.

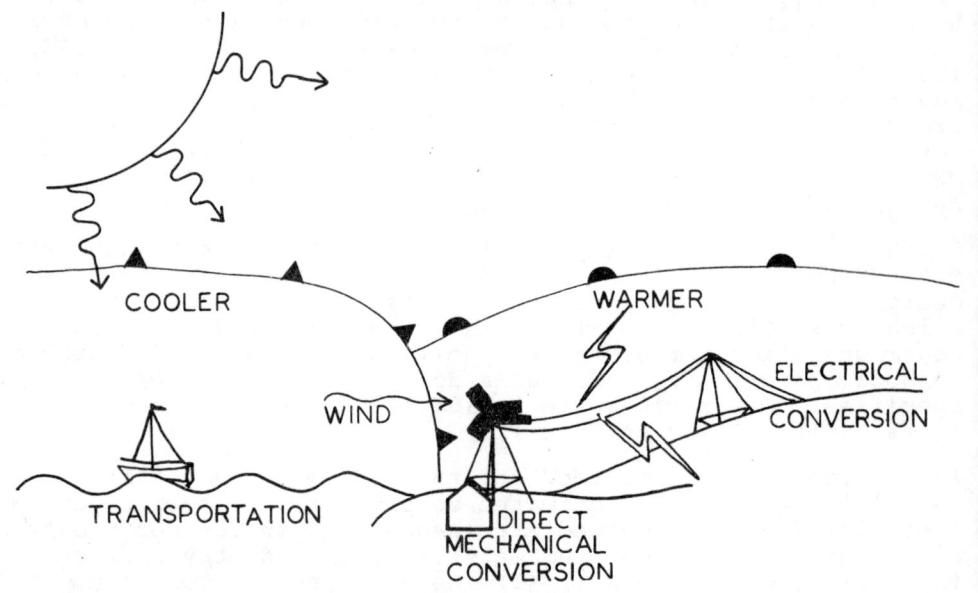

---

*At first glance, it may seem surprising that baseload generation
is more economical than intermediate-load operation. The explana
tion is that base-load plants are always placed on-line when they
are available. Intermediate and peak-load generators are shut
down when the load is inadequate. For example, coal-fired, plant
are shut down in deference to nuclear plants, which in turn would
be shut down when competing hydroelectricity or other solar-elec-
tricity is available. The highest variable cost plants are throt
tled back and then taken off-line as the load drops in a typical
network. Figure 2 shows how a solar plant would be managed to
match plant output to a typically varying load. The fact that nu
clear plants would no longer retain base load status is perhaps
one of the underlying reasons why utility and nuclear industry
representatives, and their government counterparts, have been opposed to solar-electric technology development. (See Metz, 1976,
p. 1256) for a recent U.S.A. incident.

The Lockheed-California Company recently conducted a comprehensive U.S. wind energy assessment for the U.S. ERDA.

> Wind energy is an abundant resource in the United States. It can be captured economically by large wind turbine generators and used to supplement electric energy provided from fossil fuel and hydroelectric resources. Today's technology is more than adequate for wind energy to make an immediate contribution to alleviating the energy crunch. A recently completed study sponsored by the Energy Research and Development Administration shows that the full potential of the wind is far greater than previously estimated. Full implementation would produce clean energy without pollution, and would make a significant contribution to the conservation of our fossil fuel reserves. (Coty and Dubey, 1976, p. 1).

Specifically, the study found that 35% of the 1995 electricity usage of the western U.S.A. could be provided by large wind-electric generators (mostly in the northwestern region because of the extensive hydroelectric system); for the entire U.S.A., the percentage would be 19% (p. 6). The study projects costs (in 1975 $) of $24/MWhe (grid-stability storage only) or $21/MWhe (no storage, "fuel-saver" mode). In an integrated wind-hydroelectric network, costs drop to $12/MWhe (Coty and Dubey, 1976, p. 6, Figure 10). These figures can be adjusted to 1976 $ by adding 7%. The optimum size rotor is approximately 350 ft. in diameter, almost without regard for the average wind speed. Their assumed average annual wind speed was 7 meters/second (15.7 miles/hour). Wind data from over 700 stations were analyzed. A 10,000 unit production run was assumed for their calculations.

Stanford Research Institute (SRI) performed a cost assessment of wind-electric generators for Bonneville Power Administration (Witwer, 1976, pp. 19-22), and reported an electric power cost (in 1975 $) of $18/MWhe in 1985, $17/MWhe in 1995 (at a 10% annual fixed charge ratio) or $31/MWhe in 1985, $29/MWhe in 1995 (at a 20% annual fixed charge ratio) (Witwer, 1976, p. 22). Both assume the "fuel-saver" mode of operation, i.e., electricity is fed into the grid when the wind blows, all storage and peaking is provided to the grid by other generators (the northwest U.S.A.'s hydroelectric system, in this case). When these estimates are normalized by adjusting to 1976 $ (at 7% inflation) and by using a 15% annual fixed charge ratio, the costs become $26/MWhe for 1985 and $25/MWhe for 1995. These projections were based on a wind-electric generator with a 180 ft. diamter rotor, and an annual average wind speed of 18 miles/hour (8 meters/second) (p. 21). Witwer offers no explanation on the selection of 180 ft. for the prototype diameter rotor. The curves presented by Coty and Dubey indicate an economic optimum at a 340-360 ft. diameter. It is instructive to compare Witwer's prototype with the cost curves of Coty and Dubey. Plotting Witwer's prototype on the generation-cost/power-rating curve in the Lockheed-California Co. study (Coty and Dubey, 1976, p. 4, Figure 4; also shown at an enlarged scale in Lockheed-California Co., 1975, p. 8-11) yields a generation cost of $25/MWhe (no storage, 1975 $).

The addition of storage capability (in areas lacking a hydro-electric system) adds about $1.9/MWhe for 6 hours of storage, according to the Aerospace Corporation study (1975, pp. 174, 180). However, geographical diversity can be utilized by locating "wind farms" in an appropriately dispersed pattern, once wind patterns and variations are better known (Justus, 1976, p. 268), in effect providing zero cost energy storage.

Sorensen (1976, p. 935) demonstrates that the storage capability of ten hours of annual average power output makes the dependability of a wind-electric generator comparable to that of a typical nuclear plant with no storage.

"Wind farms" will span a good deal of land: To avoid "wind-shadowing," the towers should be separated by 10 rotor diameters. However, very little land is pre-empted, i.e. closed to cultivation, grazing, or other rural uses.

Ocean Thermal Energy Conversion

Since the ocean is a rather large solar collector, and since its upper layers absorb most of the energy, a temperature gradient exists (deeper=colder) which can be harnessed to produce energy in other forms, including electricity, hydrogen, fertilizer (energy embedded in a useful, transportable product). All must be transported to land to ultimate use; the optimal locations exist in tropical oceans and the warm currents flowing from them (e.g., the Gulf Stream). Since the ocean is a "thermal moderator," no storage is required for continuous 24-hour operation, i.e., baseloading. Naef (1976, p. 939) states:

> The results of several studies indicate that solar energy collected by the surface layers of the ocean can be converted to electricity using contemporary technology, and with design and fabrication improvements, can be made economically competitive with fossil and nuclear-fueled plants.

The studies to which Naef refers are: Dugger and Francis, 1976; TRW, 1975; and Lockheed Missiles and Space Company, 1975. Naef adds that these ocean thermal plants would "utilize readily available materials and can be produced by existing industrial facilities and labor," (Naef, 1976, p. 393). He states that such systems "can be designed with a negligible environmental impact." A thorough analysis will be required to confirm this, once a basic design has been formulated and locations specified.

Zener examined the economics of ocean thermal energy conversion to electricity, taking a reference design plant beginning initial operation in 1986 for his example (Zener, 1976, pp. 535-540). He calculates a capital cost of $1,000/KWe Average at 80% plant factor; excluding O & M of fuel costs.

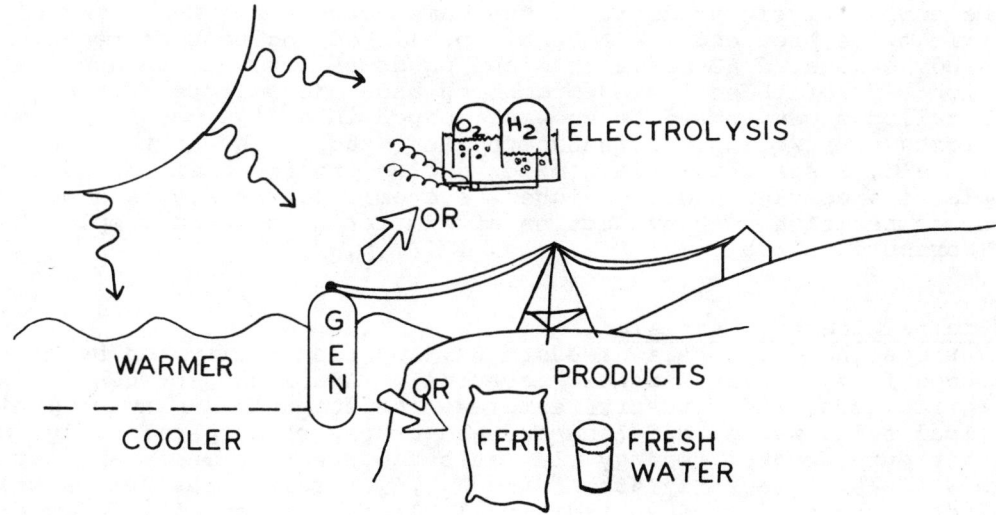

To express this in $/MWhe, a few working assumptions are needed. First, the ocean thermal plant has a $10/MWhe cost penalty for transmission to land; second, O & M costs average $5/MWhe; third, express Zener's estimate in current year (1986) $; fourth, a 15% annual fixed charge ratio applies; and fifth, inflation occurs at 7% per year between 1976 and 1981 (the mid-point of construction). Zener's estimate for a 1986 on-line date becomes (in 1976 $):

$$\frac{\$1000 \times 0.15 \times 1000}{1.07^5 \times 8760} + 5 + 10 = \$27.20/MWhe.$$

(Breakdown: Fixed cost = 12.2; O & M = 5; Transmission to land = 10)

Where the ocean thermal gradients exist too far from land for economical transmission through buried cables, conversion to chemical form for storage and transmission may be feasible. Hydrogen can be recovered from sea water by electrolysis or other means, stored, and transported to land by ship or pipeline. Alternatively, fertilizer can be produced at the ocean plant site and transported to land, thus releasing conventional energy for other uses. Zener speculates that when U.S.A. Gulf Coast ocean thermal-electricity capital costs are brought down to $500/KWe Average, it will be used to generate hydrogen at less than $3.million BTU, which will then become the basis for a new petrochemical industry in the southern U.S.A., as well as the basis for a synthetic fuels industry. He sees this beginning in the early 1990's (Zener, 1976, p. 545).

Going a step further, many energy-intensive chemical products can be competitively produced at the same ocean sites where the electricity is produced. A recently published engineering research study evaluated 62 major chemical products for such an application: 23 of these looked promising and were selected for more detailed study. Production was grouped into five possible complexes. Marketing and transportation studies showed that, of these 5, a sea-chemicals complex and an organic chemicals and plastics complex had the highest economic potentials, and would be competitive with production at similar land-based complexes (Hornburg, Lindal, and El-Ramly, 1976, p. 413).

Biomass Energy Conversion
Various chemical fuels, feedstocks, and electricity can be produced from biomass (organic material). Available sources include agricultural and forestry residues, feedlot animal manure, municipal solid waste, and land and sea crops grown specifically for this purpose (the "energy plantation" concept). These are not new ideas: presently 45% of the U.S.A. forestry residue is collected and sold, and an additional 21% is used on-site for fuel (Witwer, 1976, p. 34). Crop or forestry residues and municipal solid waste (with metals removed) can be combusted singly or in combination with other fuels for the production of heat and/or electricity. The large number of possible combinations of source location, energy form, and conversion technology makes generic cost estimating difficult.

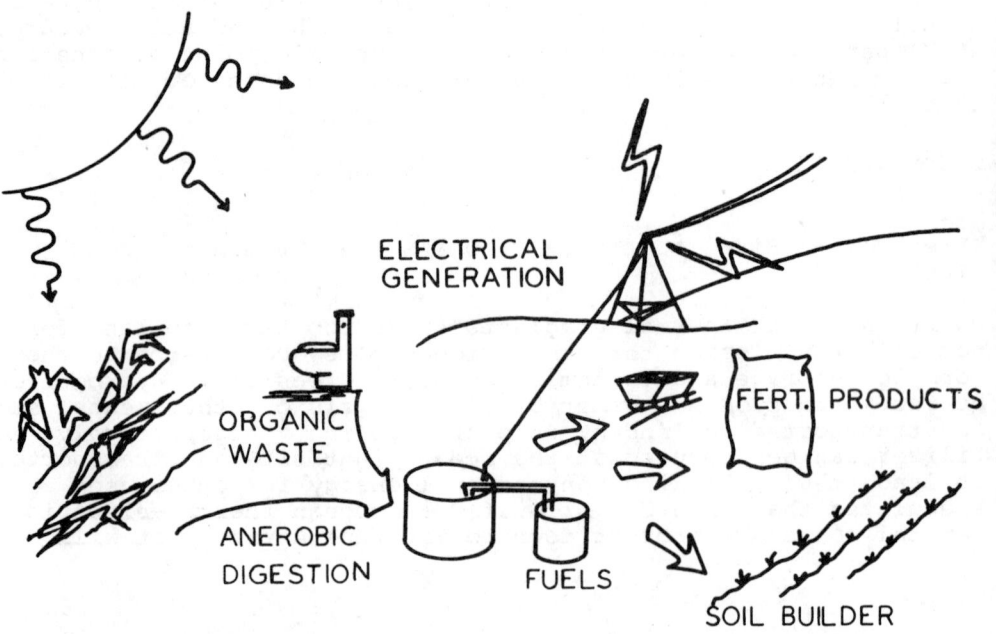

Results of the recent Stanford Research Institute (SRI) study for the Bonneville Power Administration (an agency of the U.S.A. Department of the Interior) indicate what may be expected from the solar-waste-electric conversion technology (Witwer, 1976, pp. 33-40, 49-59). These are indicated in Table 6. In each case, the SRI data will be adjusted to 1976 $ by adding a 7% inflation factor between 1975 and 1976, and by employing a 15% annual fixed charge ratio (Witwer used 10% and 20%). Although we are interested here in a cost comparison of key solar-electric technologies, the reader should be advised that this may not be the best use of waste resources. In a given location and time, waste resources might be most appropriately used for soil-building, fertilizing, or fuels and feedstock production.

TABLE 6   Costs of Solar-Waste-Electric Conversion

Total Generation Costs:	1985 & 1995 (1976 $/MWhe)	
Direct Combustion of Agricultural Residues	$ 32	(p. 38)
Municipal Solid Waste Coal/Refuse-Fired Generator	23	(p. 53)
PUROX System Electrical Generation		
Simple Cycle	24.0	(p. 59)
Combined Cycle	23.6	(p. 59)

All prototypes are base-load plants. (The page numbers on the right refer to the SRI study (Witwer, 1976.) The PUROX System is a proprietary process developed by the Linde Division of Union Carbide (pp. 55-59).

An obvious advantage to the use of solid waste for fuels, feedstocks, or electrical generation is the elimination (or transformation at least) of an increasingly critical disposal problem. However, soil degradation may pose a problem in the case of agricultural and forestry residues.

Fuels and feedstock production from biomass may be economically attractive, both at large-scale and at a small, neighborhood scale, but it will not be considered here, for lack of time. Similarly, the economics of energy plantations, land and sea, are beyond the scope of this review. In neither case should it be inferred that cost projections do not exist or that the economics are non-competitive with other technologies.

Hydroelectric Conversion

This is the best known and, at present, the most easily utilized solar-electric technology. It offers essentially loss-free storage, responsive throttling to match rapidly fluctuating loads, and clean, low cost electricity (typically $2-10/MWhe), and is ideal for base-loading, peaking, and anything between.* It is advantageously integrated with those solar-electric technologies which are faced with a variable energy input. (Ocean thermal gradient and biomass-electric could operate continuously.)

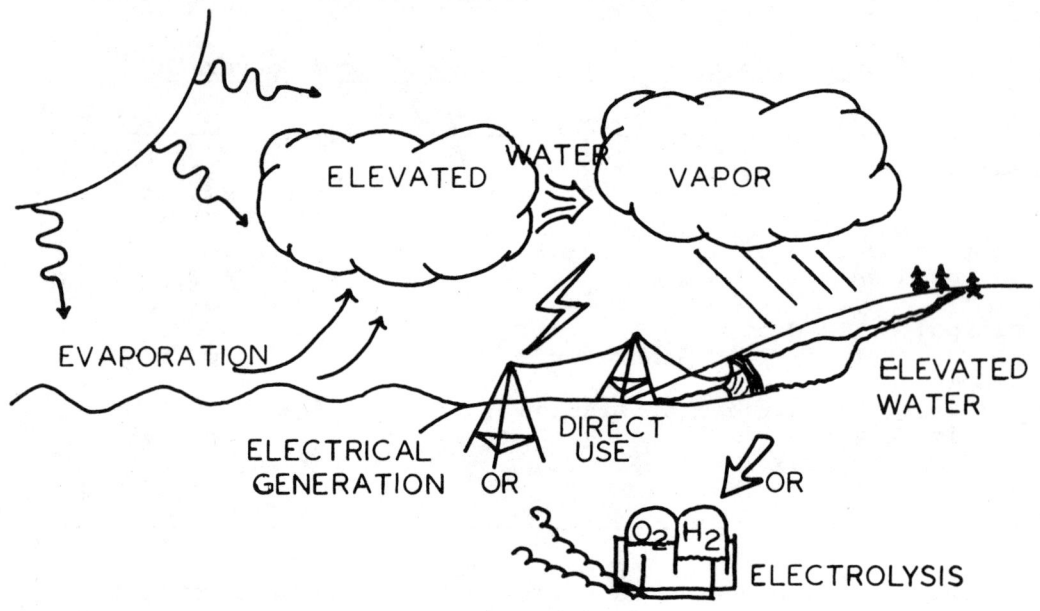

Satellite Power Systems

Sun/Earth Power Satellite: It is possible to place an earth satellite in a synchronous orbit (stationary with respect to earth) to receive sunlight and transform it into electrical energy by photoelectric arrays, transform it back to electromagnetic energy in microwave generators, and then transmit it at microwave frequencies to terrestrial receiving antenna sites where it would be

---

*The cost penalty for peaking versus base-load operation is probably the least for hydroelectric conversion than for any other technology, due to the zero-entropic nature of gravitational energy (i.e., zero entropy per unit energy: Dyson, 1971, p. 52).

transformed into electricity and distributed. Between 12 and 20 launches of heavy-lift rocket freighters would be required for each 1000 MWe inserted into the terrestrial power grid (Glaser, 1976, pp. 8 & 16). Obviously this is an ambitious undertaking, although Glaser argues that this technology can contribute significantly to meeting global energy requirements beyond 1995 (Glaser, 1976, p. 25).

We have not included this technology in our assessment for the following reasons: (1) it could upset the global heat balance, if deployed in large numbers; (2) possible human health and environmental effects of increased microwave radiation; (3) possible military implications inherent in the control of a high power density beam; (4) much of the required financial commitment would be spent on non-solar or non-terrestrial technology (e.g., launch vehicles, microwave power transmission, photocell arrays designed for space); (5) the technological risk factor is considerably higher than those of the more conventional solar technologies; it is more akin to the fusion program.

Earth/Earth Transmission Relay Satellite: Bockris (1975) has suggested a power relay satellite, for long-range energy transmission from high-solar regions, such as the Arabian and Saharan Deserts, to high-use regions, such as Europe. This not only avoids the global heat balance problem, but if it proves feasible, it offers an intriguing means of furthering inter-regional cooperation.

SOLAR WATER HEATING, SPACE HEATING AND COOLING

We now deal briefly with technologies directly converting sunlight into thermal energy for heating and cooling in structures (see Figure 1, p. 230, for the role this can play in the U.S.A. energy picture, as an example).

"Active" systems typically employ a solar energy collector external to the insulated shell of a structure, which converts sunlight to thermal energy inside the collector. This energy is then transferred to thermal storage by one or two working fluid circuits which are driven by some external energy source. Heat distribution is usually provided by a separate fluid circuit, also externally energized. If cooling is required, a Rankin sorption refrigeration cycle is employed, so that the collector fluid at temperatures of 85-100°C (185-220°F) provides the energizing input.

"Passive" systems are considerably different in philosophy and technique. Philosophically, the internal and external environments are in relationship. The building is conceived of as a solar collector: Its structure, choice of materials, texture, color, form, and orientation are all considered in relation to the natural energies of the site. Key design elements are sun control, integrated storage, movable insulation, natural convection, and natural daylighting. Although the resulting design may appear simple, the know-how required may exceed that for an active system.*

In practice, no all-satisfying distinction separates "active" and "passive" systems. Any structure acts as a passive solar collector, thus a purely "active" system cannot exist. Furthermore, in what are termed "passive" systems, a small energy subsidy may be used to control sunlight shutters and/or movable insulation. The economic optimum design will normally call for supplemental (subsidy) energy for each type of design. The point is not to eliminate all backup energy, but to make the best use of natural resources. A good supplemental system for a solar heating system may be a wood stove. Nevertheless, it is natural to separate the two design types for descriptive purposes.

Passive Systems
Although this is almost a "lost art" in the developed societies, it normally results in a more economical design. In a study of residential solar water and space heating systems presently used in northern California homes, Greene (1976, p. 9) observes:

> Most cost-effective of the systems located were the socalled passive-type systems, whether owner or contractor built. In some cases, the solar heating/cooling system was so integral to the house structure that add-on cost was zero or nominal.

In much of the world today, passive design is the rule, and some of this indigenous architecture is quite ingenious in its matching of local materials and human skills with the climate. While thousands of passive design examples are known, just two will be cited.

Since 1962, a school near Liverpool, England (52° 25' North Latitude) has relied on passive solar space heating and has performed quite satisfactorily. It initially cost about the same as similar schools in that area, requiring no backup energy for heating (Davies, 1976).

Haggard (1976) projects that the renowned Harold Hay residence in Atascadero, California (the Skytherm design) could be built a second time for slightly less than a conventional home of the same size in the same location. This design requires essentially no commercial energy for heating and cooling, and it maintains a comfortable inside temperature all year.

---

*The phrase "low-technology" has been applied to such designs. This constitutes a semantic inversion, since "technology" means knowing the best way to do a thing, not necessarily applying the most esoteric techniques.

Self-cycling solar hot water heaters ("thermosyphons") are commonplace in many parts of the world. Thousands were installed routinely in Florida, U.S.A. after World War II until natural gas became available and cheap. The economics are favorable today in any area of the world where freezing is not common.

Active Systems
The Mitre Corporation recently completed an evaluation for the U.S.A. ERDA of the relative economics of solar water and space heating in the U.S.A. (Mitre Corporation, 1976). They concluded that at today's installed system costs ($20/ft^2) an active solar design which utilizes commercially available components and minimizes the total life cost over an assumed 20 year lifetime is competitive today against electric resistance heating throughout most of the U.S.A. (p. iii). The only exception is the Seattle, Washington area, where electricity prices are still very cheap: $8.60/MWhe (p. A-3). A 25% reduction in installed costs (to $15/ft^2) would become competitive with oil-fired water and space heating and electric heat pumps. A 50% reduction (to 10/ft^2) by 1980, through technological innovation and incentives, would be competitive with natural gas and all other fuels (p. iii). (If natural gas prices are de-regulated, and that appears likely, the curves may cross much sooner.)

The economics look very good. However, non-economic impediments may still be formidable. To deal with these obstacles, the State of California has targeted 1980 as the year in which at least half the housing starts in California will utilize solar water and space heating. This is an example of imaginative and determined governmental action of the type required to catalyze the transition to residential solar heating.

The economics of solar space heating "retrofitting" (installation into existing buildings) are not as favorable as for new buildings, although each case must be examined individually. Besides, the likelihood of fuel shortages may outweigh economics in such decisions, as the American winter of 1976-77 demonstrated. Solar water heating units can be readily installed in existing buildings, and are cost-competitive in most areas already, if installed by the owner. Commercial installation will probably become competitive within very few years; the adaption rate being more a function of the number of experienced installers in a given locale than of inherent economics.

Solar space cooling (active) can be accomplished in several ways through: Sorption refrigeration cycle, Rankine cycle, night sky radiation, rock bed regenerators, vapor jet air conditioning, solar-boosted annual cycle energy systems (ACES), evaporation, solar-induced natural ventilation, and combinations of the above. Estimates of ultimate cost-effectiveness are too dependent on building type and location, and on current experimental work to form a consensus. In general, active solar cooling technology is not as far advanced as active solar heating, which is consistent with common sense. (Note that passive solar cooling is already economical in specific locations, as mentioned above.) Ultimately, solar cooling may be the more economical, since the available energy is greatest when the cooling loads are a maximum (summer, daytime). The key may lie in the development of high performance collectors (collector fluid temperatures ranging between 85°C and 120°C), at a reasonable installed cost. However, solar cooling cost estimates are still rare in the solar technical literature.

This concludes the Solar Technology section.*

THE NEW ROLE OF GOVERNMENT

As has been suggested above, the solar energy family of technologies fulfills the basic requirements for humankind's ideal permanent power source. The best strategies for promoting solar energy will vary, depending upon the particular solar technology, location and energy use pattern. But lead times are long, and further delays in making the commitment will exact a serious toll in environmental damage and global security. In this respect, government agencies can play a leading role.

Solar technologies for the heating and cooling of buildings are already cost-effective in many parts of the world and can be pioneered and developed by individuals and small business as well as large corporations. Such technologies are best promoted by vigorous legislative action, such as by changing building codes and resale requirements. Also, government-sponsored educational programs are needed to upgrade the skills of planners, engineers, architects, and installers, relevant to solar designs. Finally, in free market economies lending institutions should implement life-costing, rather than first-costing, so that utility bills are integrated with rent or mortgage payments; this would promote the design of energy self-sufficient building structures.

---

*Several important matters have been omitted from this brief review. One such omission is full consideration of the different type and mix of solar technologies appropriate in different stages of economic development.

Another omission is careful, detailed examination of the important, related question of de-centralization, energy self-reliance, and integrated system design which thermodynamically matches energy sources and uses (See Lovins, 1976a; Schumacher, 1973; Clark, 1975; and Stanford Research Institute, 1977.)

Further, details of the use of interim, non-renewable energy technologies deserve treatment in an innovative, disaggregated, locally-relevant manner.

There is not space or time for the assessment of important uses of solar energy, such as natural lighting, improved urban food production, and crop and timber drying.

With the above measures solar heating and cooling technologies could develop on their own accord due to the demand stimulated by the rapidly escalating price of conventional energy sources. Even here, the commercialization of solar technologies could be substantially accelerated in free market economies if government would take on a new role, that of market catalyst. For example, by requiring all new public buildings to be designed for energy self-sufficiency, and by requiring existing public structures to be adapted for water heating and for solar space heating and cooling where appropriate, a substantial boost would be given to the solar and energy conservation industries. As a result of volume production, the overall cost of these technologies would decline, and the effect would become self-reinforcing.

On the other hand, when considering methods of stimulating the commercialization of solar-electric generating plants, particularly photoelectric designs, market catalytic intervention becomes not only desirable, but necessary. Unlike the heating and cooling technologies, the sheer magnitude of such undertakings coupled with their novel nature rules out the possibility of their development by private business. Even though the cost projections look favorable, large manufacturing and business corporations and privately owned energy utilities tend to shy away since these engineering concepts have not yet been commercially proven. Moreover, the availability of the well-promoted nuclear alternative reduces the urgency to go solar as felt by today's utility planners.

Thus, to accelerate the development of these solar-electric technologies, the governments of some countries have begun to take the lead and have financed not only research and development, but pilot demonstration projects as well (e.g., U.S.A. ERDA). The pilot plant approach in which government serves as both funder and ultimate customer of newly developed technology is a step in the right direction; however, many of the presently available solar-electric technologies demand a bolder approach. Such is the case with the solar photoelectric (photovoltaic) technologies which, by the use of photocells, allow the direct conversion of sunlight into electricity. Adequate basic research on these technologies has been completed and they are essentially waiting to be commercialized. All that is needed is high volume production to make them economical. The barriers to their implementation are primarily political and economic, not technical.

Consequently, to promote many of the solar-electric technologies, government must be cast in a new role, one that varies significantly from the role of research sponsor. Governments, as legitimate custodians of the long-term public interest, must, where appropriate, take on the responsibility of market catalyst. In countries where utilities are owned by the state, appropriate action would begin with an administrative decision by the state power authority to commit public funds to the construction of one or two solar-electric power stations, for example, of the photoelectric variety. An undertaking of this magnitude would provide the solar photoelectric industry with sufficient stimulation to launch it into full-scale production, lowering costs to the point where industry growth would be self-catalyzing.

These "pilot" projects would be full scale power plants, <u>not</u> scaled down experimental versions* because, as will be demonstrated, the principle of market catalysis necessitates a bold approach, solar-electric power development being one example where too much caution only leads to disaster. The launching of a new power source into competitive commercialization is like the launching of a rocket: If the rocket is to small for its payload, its fuel may prematurely run out before orbital velocity is achieved, and hence, it will fall back to earth. It will have attempted to journey in vain. In designing a successful launching, therefore, size is of prime importance. The same is true of solar-electric power development.

Provided that a substantial commitment is made, <u>electricity from the first solar photoelectric power plant (constructed in a favorable geographical location) would be cheaper than that produced from nuclear power plant of comparable generating capacity</u>, where both come on-line in 1986. Although photoelectric power is presently more expensive than nuclear, a one-time market catalytic action of this sort would reverse the comparative economics within 5-10 years, making solar-electric power the more affordable alternative in many parts of the world.

In countries where utilities are privately owned (as in North America), market catalysis might take a modified form. Private utilities will not voluntarily bear any (perceived) risks. Hence, an appropriate mode of catalytic action in situations such as this would be for government agencies to cooperate with electric utilities by underwriting the (shrinking) solar-nuclear cost differential for the required solar-electric power generating capacity. Government would not necessarily need to finance the project, just underwrite it in case its costs exceeded that of the nuclear alternative. A political commitment such as this would be similar to, but less involved than, the method by which the USA government has created, nourished, and protected the American nuclear power industry, a primary difference being that substantial on-going financial outlays would not be required.

The role of government as market catalyst will be illustrated in the next section by detailed reference to a prototypical example: the solar photoelectric receiver industry. Furthermore, although particulars change, the same principle may be usefully employed to stimulate other solar-electric technologies, and other ancillary manufacturing technologies (e.g., storage devices, or the key components of a hydrogen economy).

---

*While it might be useful to construct small scale pilot plants for engineering purposes, i.e. to test production feasibility, such units should <u>not</u> be built for the purpose of testing <u>economic</u> feasibility.

THE SILICON SOLAR PHOTOELECTRIC RECEIVER INDUSTRY: AN EXAMPLE

The silicon photocell industry, as it stands today, is characterized by high prices and a small sales volume. In 1975 the market was in the neighborhood of 100 peak kilowatts. Assuming a 1975 selling price of $17,000/KWe peak (Morris, 1976, p. 3), this would be about $1.7 million. Because the market is so small, mass production is not economically feasible, hence cells are made by hand in an inefficient manner, about 70-80% of their total cost going to labor (Morris, 1976, p. 4). This self-reinforcing set of circumstances, as depicted in Figure 4: Mode 1, has stabilized the industry at a high price level.

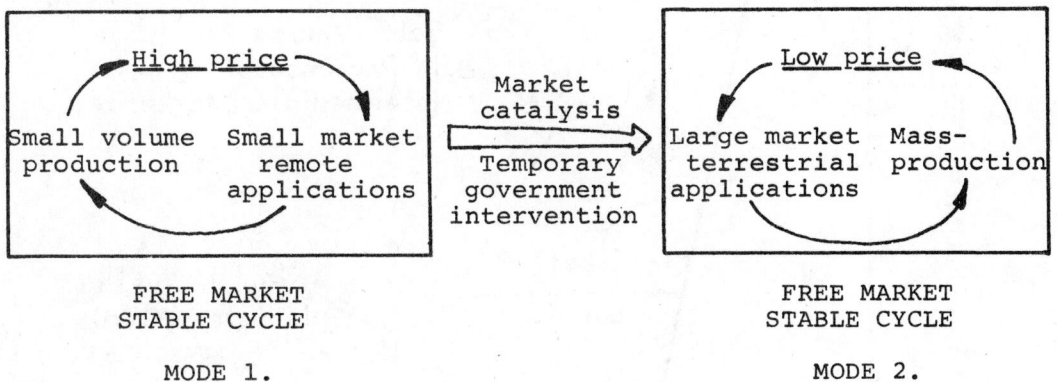

Fig. 4. Self-stabilizing modes in the solar photocell industry and the role of market catalysis.

However, with mass production and a sufficiently rapid market growth, the cost of the 1976 state-of-the-art technology could be brought down to at most $500/KWe peak (Magid, 1976, p. 2) by 1986 for production of 500,000 KWe/year peak, or annual sales volumes of $250 million. Considering that the most recent cost figure for solar cells was $13,000/KWe peak (for 1976) (Morris, 1976, p. 3), this is about a 26:1 reduction. This magnitude of price reduction might be compared to that of the transistor whose price dropped from $20 in the early '50's down to 25-30 cents within 10 years (Morris, 1976, p. 12).

Nevertheless, the photocell market has been growing rather slowly. At their present high price, the use of silicon photocells has been limited to satellite power generation, other remote applications, and novelty items. While a large market potentially

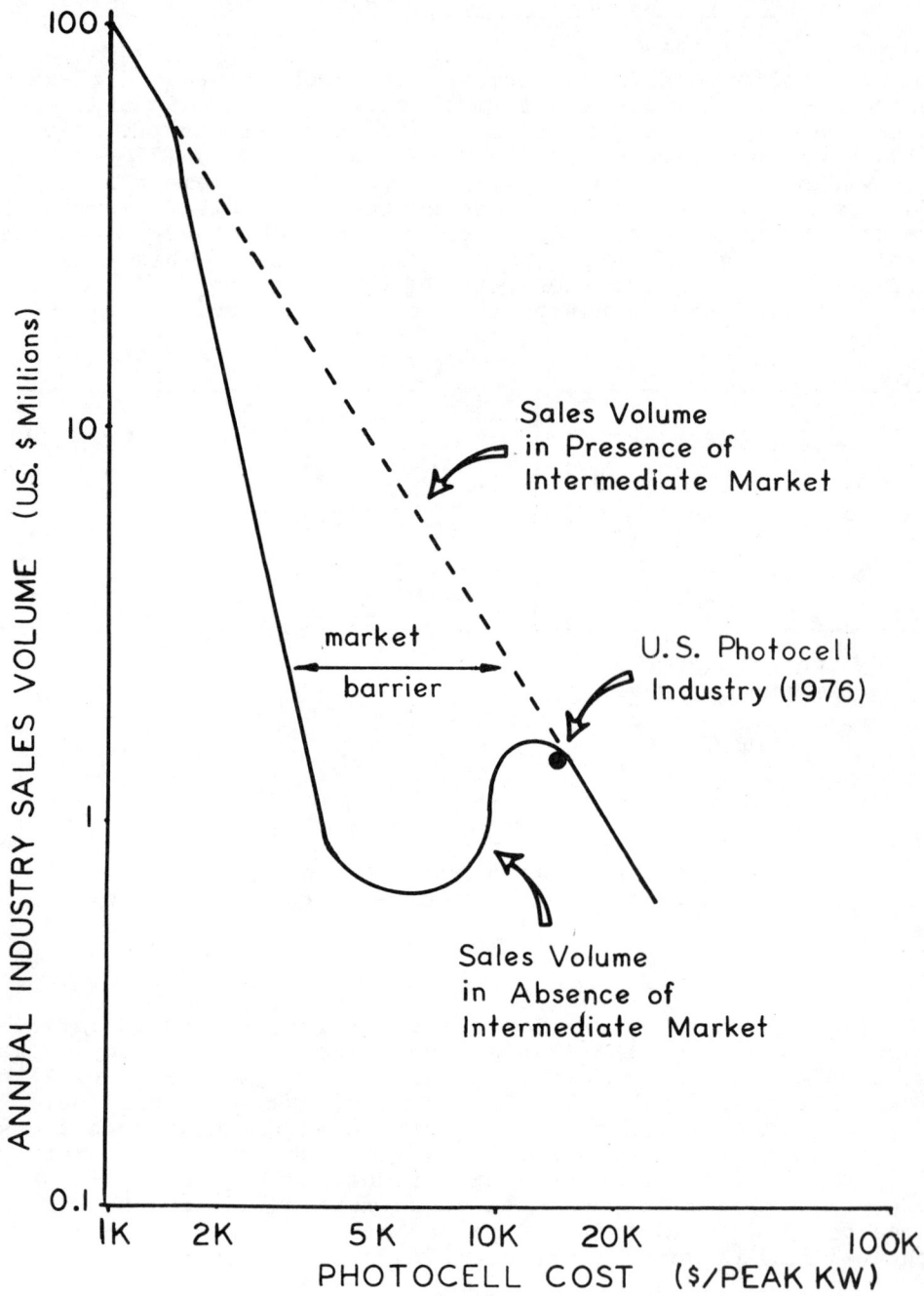

Fig. 5. Relationship between market and production in silicon solar cell industry.

exists for low priced cells for use in terrestrial power generation (both for residential and for central power generation) serving this market necessitates making a significant jump both in production volume and in production methods. Such changes in mode of production require the commitment of a significant amount of capital investment over an extended period of time. However, the solar cell industry through its own efforts is powerless to expand the present size of its market. Efforts to cut price would only shrink sales volume in monetary terms, due to insufficient stimulated demand, see Figure 5 (solid line); hence, the industry remains trapped in a region of inelastic demand.

This hurdle dictates a cautious stance on the part of solar cell manufacturers who must wait for a real growth in terms of purchase orders before making the move to cut price. If an intermediate sized market were present in which cells could be sold at medium volumes and at medium prices (i.e., $5000/KWe peak at 2000 KWe/year peak, or $10 million/yr.), then this could serve as a stepping stone of reasonable proximity. Manufacturers could acquire venture capital to expand production and cut price sufficiently to settle into this new market. However, such a market does not exist. <u>The new, creative role for government will be to create such an intermediate market.</u>*

The fresnel lens industry finds itself in a similar predicament. Fresnel lenses constitute an important component in photoelectric conversion systems; used as light concentrators they reduce the area requirement of the photocell component, making possible reduced overall system costs. Presently the cost of large aperture fresnel lenses is high on the order of $6/$ft^2$ (such as for the circular geometry lenses used in overhead projectors) (Burgess and Edenburn, p. 4). As in the case of solar cells, this high cost is mainly due to the low production volume (measured in ft^2/yr.). At larger production volumes it is estimated that mass production techniques could bring this cost down to $1-1½/$ft^2$ for cast acrylic fresnel lens.** At sufficiently large production volumes, on the order of millions of ft^2/year, (tens of hectares/year) this cost could be further reduced to less than $0.50/$ft^2$, where it would become feasible to extrude cylindrical fresnel lenses as continuous strips of plastic for essentially the cost of the material (Szulmayer, 1973). However, there is no intermediate market which would prompt such mass production developments.

---

*On the other hand, there was always an intermediate volume market for transistors, so no external stimulus, or catalysis, was required.

**Conversations with Donald G. Schueler, Project Manager, Photovoltaic Systems Definition Project, Sandia Laboratories, Albuquerque, N.M. 87115.

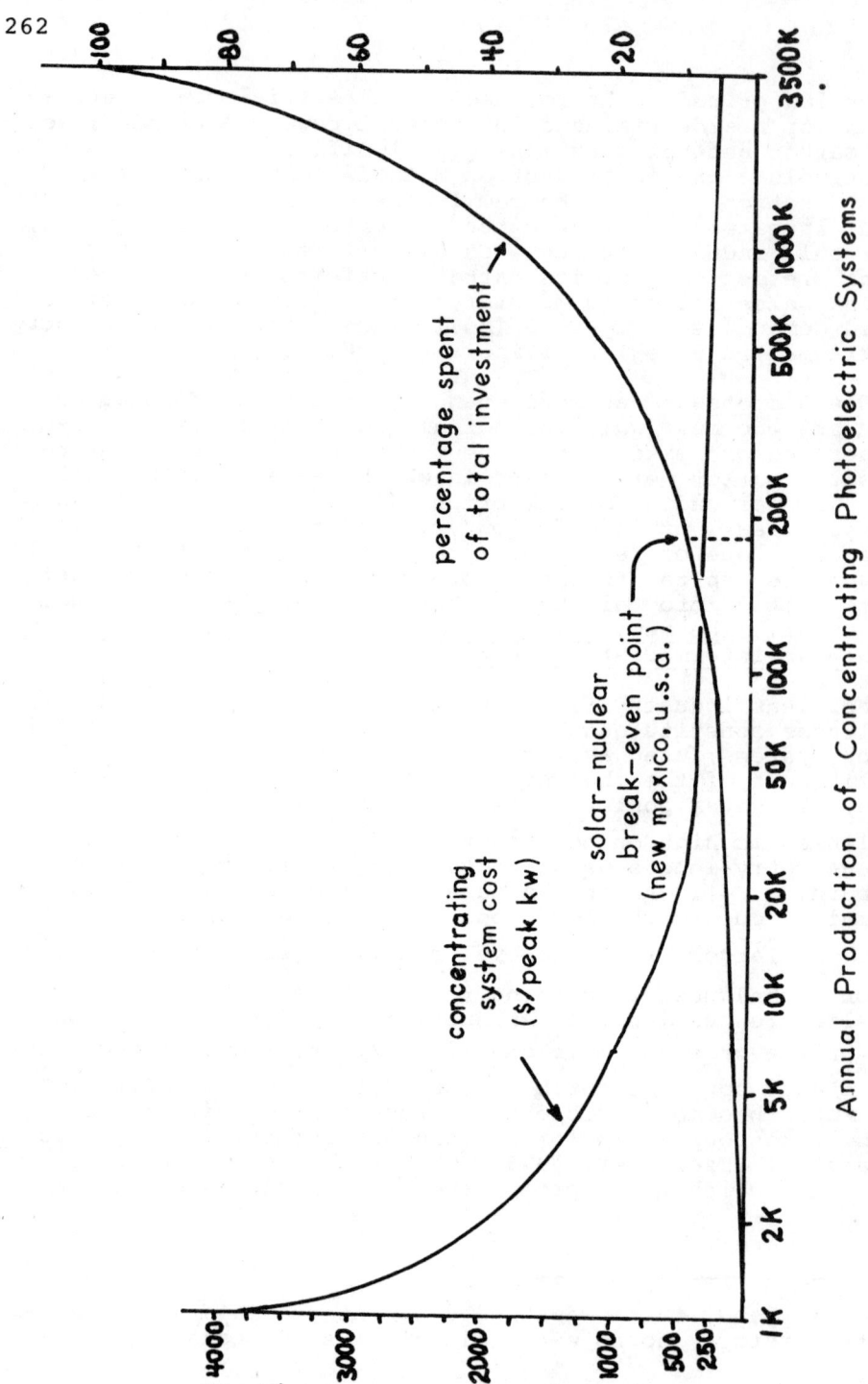

Fig. 6. Solar electric system cost compared to percentage of total investment.

Despite the presence of a market barrier hindering the development of low priced solarcells and fresnel lenses, the thickness of this barrier is not excessive in cumulative monetary terms. It appears that the cumulative production volume needed to bring the solar cell market up to the point where economies of scale begin to operate is quite tractable. For example, the cost and production volume data, shown in Table 7,* indicate that <u>the construction of a single solar electric power generating plant having a 4900 peak megawatt capacity (generating about 9600 million kilowatt-hours per year in an Albuquerque, New Mexico type location),** would be all that would be required to bring the cost of solar electric technologies down to a competitive level</u>. The cumulative cost of such an undertaking is estimated at $1340 million ($274/KWe peak) and would take 9 years (1977-1986). By comparison, to build a nuclear generating plant of equivalent annual generating capacity it would cost approximately $1850 million*** (38% more), and would take about the same time for siting and construction.

For simplicity, operating and maintenance costs have been excluded from the above comparison; if such costs were included, as was done for the photoelectric data plotted in Figure 3 (p. 234), the solar option would look even better. Also, not taken into account is the fact that the solar plant, being assembled in a modular fashion, would be producing useful electricity during its construction period whereas the nuclear plant would remain unoperated until construction was completed. Another advantage of modular construction is that differences in individual designs of the modules would not affect overall plant performance. This would allow a high degree of flexibility with regards to manufacturer participation and design change through the course of the project.

One may wonder how it is possible, with solar photoelectric power initially 8 times the cost of nuclear power, that the overall cost of the solar electric plant ends up cheaper than a nuclear plant of equal generating capacity. This may be understood by reference to Figure 6 where it is seen that the most expensive initial outlays for the solar electric plant, i.e., those for photoelectric systems costing over $380/KWe peak, comprise only 10% of the total investment.

---

*Based on U.S. Energy Research and Development Administration projections, production goals for silicon solar cells and concentrator systems for the years 1976-1986 (Magid, 1976, p. 6). For a similar estimate based on solar arrays without concentration, see Morris, 1976, p. 13.

**4,885,400 KWe/peak x 22.5% (capacity factor) x 8760 hrs./yr. = 9629 million KW-Hr./yr.

***$\dfrac{9629 \text{ million KW-Hrs./Yr.}}{8760 \text{ hrs./yr.} \times 59.3\% \text{ (capacity factor)}} \times \$1000/KW = \$1853.6 \text{ million}$

TABLE 7 Production Volume and Cost Projections for the Construction of a Large Scale Photoelectric Power Plant Utilizing Solar Concentration

Year	(Annual Production) Power Generating Capacity KWe Peak 1(A) Solar Cells	1(B) Concen. Systems	$/KWe Peak 2(A) Cell Cost	2(B) System Cost	(Millions of Dollars) 1(B) x 2(B) Annual Cost to Purchase Power Generating Cap.	Cumulative % of Total Investment
1977	150	1.0 K	13 K	3485(a)	3.5	—
1978	270	1.9 K		2000	3.8	—
1979	500	3.5 K		1500(b)	5.3	0.9
1980	1000	7.0 K		1000	7.0	1.5
1981	2000	14 K		740(b)	10.5	2.2
1982	3000	21 K	2 K	500	10.5	3.0
1983	11 K(c)	77 K		420(c)	32.3	5.4
1984	40 K(c)	280 K	1 K	350(c)	98.0	12.8
1985	140 K(c)	980 K		300(c)	294.0	34.7
1986	500 K	3500 K		250	875.0	100%
	4885.4 K KWe PEAK Cumulative Capacity				$1339.9 million Cumulative Cost	

Data for columns 1(A), 2(A), & 2(B) taken from Magid, L., op. cit., p. 6, Figure 2 (10-Year Planning Milestones for the U.S. Solar Photovoltaic Conversion Program).

Data entered in column 1(B) is the corresponding data from column 1(A) multiplied by 7, that is, if a 10:1 concentration ratio is assumed, peak generating capacity of a concentrating photoelectric system will be about 7 times the peak generating capacity of the cell component alone. Assumes a 30% loss of generating capacity due to reduced system conversion efficiency.

NOTES: (a) Value for $/KWe peak for 1977 taken from Burgess, E.L., "One Kilowatt Photovoltaic Subsystems Using Fresnel Lens Concentrators," op. cit., p. 4. -- (b) Interpolated as mean of values of preceding and following years. -- (c) Interpolation based on an assumed 3.6 fold increase in sales per year, accompanied by an assumed 16% drop in production cost per year (interpolated between 1982 and 1986 from Magid's data).

This figure of $380/KWe peak (achievable by 1984, according to Table 7), is considered the point at which the construction cost of solar breaks even with that of nuclear for a New Mexico, U.S.A. type location (i.e., $1690/KWe avg.).* Consequently 90% of the construction cost of the solar plant would be put toward photoelectric systems whose $/KW avg. rating is at or below that for nuclear. On the other hand, if total operating costs are considered, then the breakeven for solar vs. nuclear would occur in 1982 when solar electric systems cost $500/KWe peak ($2500/KWe avg. for a New Mexico type location) (see Figure 3, p. 234). If these considerations are taken into account, then only 2% of the total investment would be put toward "excessively priced" arrays.

This astounding conclusion, <u>that based on present technology a solar electric plant may be constructed for 3/4 the cost of a nuclear plant</u>, runs contrary to popular belief. However, it is just in the last few years that government and industry cost projections have become available throwing a new light on photoelectric power generation. This evidence implies that, in some geographical regions, utilities which continue to purchase nuclear facilities may in fact be making long range commitments that are unwarrantably costly for their customers. But, for utilities favoring "road-tested" technologies there appears to be no other choice.

Nuclear energy remains in use because it is better known (hence its use appears to be less risky from a financial point of view), because it now has an influential array of political supporters, and because the social, institutional, and industrial infrastructure built up around this industry has created conditions facilitating its perpetuation. On the other hand, solar photoelectric power remains uncommercialized not because it is uneconomical (in the long run) but because it is unused, it remains financially uncertain (investors being reluctant to risk start-up costs); and because it continues to stand high on the "learning curve," i.e. its manufacturing costs will remain high for a period of time due to the lack of large-scale manufacturing experience. These latter circumstances are shared by most novel technologies and constitute an unfortunate paradox. As long as photoelectric power remains unused and the photoelectric industry trapped in its small volume market niche, expensive photoelectric power will remain a self-fulfilling prophecy.

Nevertheless, a state or national government would be in an ideal position to break this vicious circle by promoting a project to construct a 4900 peak megawatt solar power plant. <u>A government backed utility project would act as a catalyst providing the required intermediate market which would allow the photocell and</u>

---

* $\dfrac{\$1000/KW \text{ (nuclear)}}{59.3\% \text{ capacity factor}} = \dfrac{\$380/KW \text{ peak (solar)}}{22.5\% \text{ capacity factor}} = \$1690/KW \text{ avg.}$

fresnel lens industries to overcome their local sales barriers and expand production. This industrial expansion could be fostered within the regional boundaries of the host state or nation allowing for a minimal capital drain for the region and providing the base for a potentially lucrative export trade. The photoelectric manufacturing industry would then become stabilized in a new self-reinforcing cycle characterized by low prices and high volume. As seen in Figure 4, p. 259, this would constitute a transition from Mode 1 to Mode 2.

How this kind of government action might influence the solar-nuclear cost differential is better understood by reference to Figure 7. Presently, there is a wide gap between the cost of solar photoelectric and nuclear power, with photoelectric power costing on the order of $15,800/KW avg. for a New Mexico, U.S.A. type location ($3485/KW peak), and with the presently developed and widely used nuclear fission technology costing on the order of $2000/KW avg.* This initial pricing state (State 1) is marginally stable, thus with "business as usual" the solar-nuclear gap would close only slowly with time.** For example, the price of solar is stable to minor fluctuations in photoelectric system sales volume. Small purchase orders by the government or private sectors tending to temporarily increase solar-electric sales volume, do not justify investment in mass production facilities; hence, the industrial infrastructure remains unchanged and manufacturing remains in the custom-made mode. These temporary increases in throughput serve only to temporarily decrease price, for when surplus purchases cease, self-reinforcing causal loops (see Figure 4: Mode 1, p. 259) drive the price of photoelectric systems back to their market equilibrium level. Hence, the pricing system remains in State 1 (high priced solar power relative to low priced nuclear power) and nuclear energy (in the short run) appears as the only rational choice from an economic standpoint.

However, it should be recognized that at the present time (1977) the relative pricing pattern characteristic of State 1 is only

---

*All costs here include operating costs, being based on data shown in Figure 3, p. 234.

**The initial portion of the solar cost curve (Figure 7: State 1) does not represent the actual cost history of solar system arrays whose price dropped from $444,000/KW avg. ($100,000/KW peak) in 1972 without the use of concentrators (Morris, p. 3), to the 1976 cost of $15,800/KW avg., a 28:1 cost reduction. Reductions during this period occurred because moderately higher volume sales permitted lower pricing with existing custom-made manufacturing techniques and because the technique of using solar concentrating devices permited overall system cost reductions. Rather, the hypothetical solar cost curve plotted here depicts the behavior of the solar array industry around its present market equilibrium, i.e. how solar array price would respond to small changes in purchase order volume given the present state-of-the-art which is non massproduction oriented.

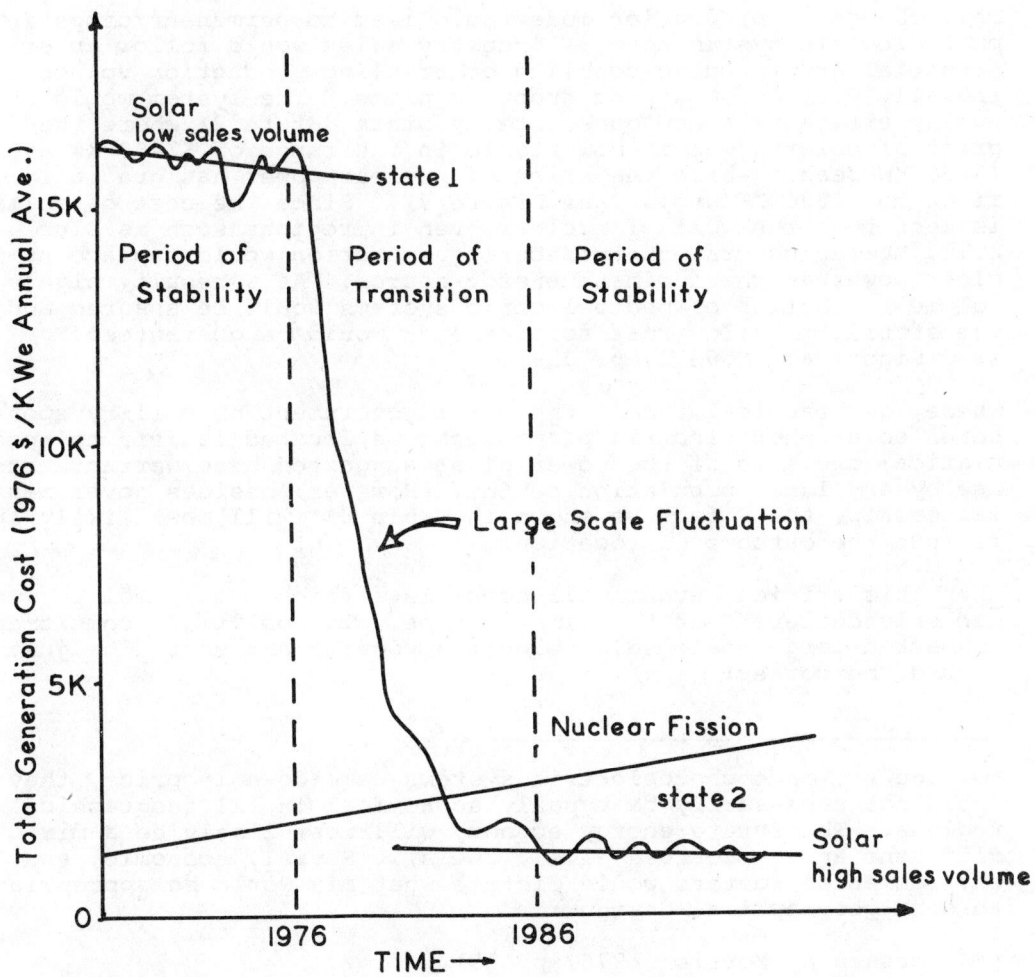

Fig. 7. Effect of a simple solar power plant purchase on solar and nuclear power prices, New Mexico, U.S.A.

marginally stable; the social system is in the vicinity of a critical threshold ready for transition. That is, a fluctuation in photoelectric industry purchase orders of sufficient magnitude and duration (i.e., $1340 million over 9 years) would be sufficient to alter the infrastructure of that industry. Contractual assurances on the part of the government or utilities that an increasing quantity of photoelectric arrays would be bought each year at progressively lower prices would allow manufacturers to raise the required investment capital to gear up for mass production.

This change in production mode would lead to permanent drops in photoelectric system costs. Industry sales would follow an exponential growth curve doubling or tripling production volume annually with accompanying drops in price. The system would eventually arrive at a new quasi steady state (State 2) where the price of solar power is now stable in the range of $1400/KW avg. ($250/KW peak), while the price of nuclear power has gradually risen to $2800/KW avg., (see Figure 7). Since the cost of solar is less than the cost of nuclear even in regions such as Blue Hill, Massachusetts, photoelectric generation would replace nuclear power as the dominant energy source. As a result, high volume production of photoelectric systems would be assured and the stability of low cost solar energy would be guaranteed,* (see Figure 4: Mode 2, p. 259).

Where, geographical terms, the first government or utility sponsored solar photoelectric plant might be located is left to speculation; the size of the power plant suggested here warrants its use by any large population center. However, besides government leadership, the 7 factors shown in Table 8** will most likely influence the outcome of location.

When this critical event will occur is difficult to predict. One can only declare that the time is ripe. The political commitment to back a large scale solar electric power plant should be just around the corner.

---

*Of course, once photoelectric systems came down in price, they would not necessarily be equally economical in all geographical regions. The future energy economy will most likely be a mix of different energy sources (i.e., fuels). Social, economic, and environmental factors would dictate what mix would be appropriate to each geographical design.

**Discussed by Morris (1976, p. 15).

TABLE 8 Factors Which Will Influence the Probable
Location of the First Commercial Solar Plant

---

1) A region which has large tracts of undeveloped land with close proximity to a large urban center.*

2) A region having a large residential sector which could make use of rooftop solar arrays to reduce utility dependence and which could serve as a decentralized secondary market.**

3) A dry climate having a great deal of sunlight and few cloudy days, preferably a low latitude location.

4) A region where the peak power load comes during daylight hours, i.e., a locality where air conditionaing makes up a significant portion of the electrical load.

5) A region having hydroelectric pump-storage facilities capable of storing extra power generated during the day for night time use.

6) An area which is far removed from fossil fuel reserves, i.e., has a heavy dependence on foreign oil; or a region where there is some controversy over nuclear reactor siting, such that an alternative power source would offer a welcome situation.

7) An area willing to develop an industry in the manufacture of solar photoelectric arrays which would have the potential of generating sizeable revenues for the host region through export trade.

Table Notes

*A "solar farm" capable of generating 4,885.4 MWe Peak would have an area of about 26,000 acres (11,000 hectares, or 42 miles^2). This calculation assumes a concentration efficiency of 75%, a cell conversion efficiency of 12%, and an array land utilization factor of 50%. It might therefore, be desirable to break this total area up into, say, 488 small generating stations having a plant size of 10 MWe Peak each. These would be in the 4-10 MWe optimal size range (Morris, 1976, p. 9), and would be capable of serving about 2000 homes in a decentralized fashion. Each 10 MWe Peak plant would then require an area of only 55 acres (22 hectares). Land cost would be a small fraction of the total plant cost; for example, at $400/acre land cost would comprise less than 1% of the total construction cost.

**One of the attractive features of photoelectric power generation is that solar-electric arrays could be mounted on building rooftops allowing homeowners to become energy self-sufficient. The average sized family house, even in northern latitudes such as in

CONCLUSION

We hold that humankind is presently in a critical period when long-range perspectives must take precedence over incremental thinking in carefully guiding the choice of the desired global energy future. We have articulated the basic criteria for making such a choice and have concluded that solar energy, through its many technologies, constitutes the best and only rational choice. The feasibility of several solar transition pathways has been discussed and the necessity of an active government role has been emphasized.

In our inquiry and analysis, we found solid reasons to believe that the solar transition <u>will</u> occur; that it <u>can</u> occur is, in our view, certain. <u>An assessment of the solar transition is not a question of engineering and economics: It is a question of the hopes, vision and determination of people.</u>

Table Notes (continued)

**the northern U.S., could supply about 3 times the average household electricity consumption (Morris, 1976, p. 9). Once the initial government-utility project served its purpose of getting the photoelectric industry off the ground, supplementary power development could continue through free market sales to local residents. With the proliferation of rooftop power generation capacity, residential utility grids might take on the additional function of power collection, rather than just power distribution.

APPENDIX A -- INTERNATIONAL ASPECTS OF SOLAR TECHNOLOGY

Solar energy research, development and utilization is presently underway on an international scale. Although little coordination is yet apparent, technical information is being actively exchanged. The following briefly summarizes some of the current activities going on in different parts of the world.

The French experimental center, at Odeillo in the Pyrenees, achieved a "world first" when its solar-electric generating plant began feeding its output into the national electricity grid in October, 1976 (Dixon, ed., 1977). The famous Odeillo solar furnace facility is acknowledged as the world's leading research center for the production of very high temperatures from sunlight (mean temperature of 3825°C on a 2 cm. diameter target, and 2950°C on a diameter of 40 cm.; Trombe & Royere, 1974, p. 167).

Brazil, as mentioned earlier, may soon lead in fuels production from biomass. India has a considerable capability in several solar technologies, expecially passive space heating and cooling. Greece is the leader in solar distillation; Israel, Australia, and Japan in solar water heating, Iran in rural area sterilization of medical instruments, Israel in solar ponds. The U.K. leads in natural lighting and wave energy research and is strong in components for appropriate technology. Canada's Brace Research Institute and the U.S.A.'s New Alchemy Institute are quite advanced in integrated, appropriate technology. Denmark and Germany seem to be in the lead in wind energy technology.

The U.S.A. has the lead in photoelectric and ocean thermal conversion and has made some contribution to (almost) every solar technology. It has the potential for a very well-funded and comprehensive solar R & D program, but, until now, the primary federal energy agency, the Energy Research and Development Administration (ERDA), has favored nuclear programs, especially the breeder reactor, almost to the exclusion of everything else. If this position is changed, then the U.S.A. could become an important contributor to the full spectrum of solar technologies and applications. However, in no case will one country dominate this diverse field.

REFERENCES

Abelson, Philip H. and Tinker, Irene, 1977. Technology transfer. *Science*, 195 (28 January): 351.

The Aerospace Corporation, 1974. *Solar Thermal Mission Analysis*; Volumes I-IV.

_____, 1975. Solar Thermal Conversion Mission Analysis -- Southwestern United States; Volume I: Summary Report. Prepared for the National Science Foundation/ Research Applied to National Needs. January, 1975 El Segundo, California. 227 pp.

American Institute of Physics, 1975. *Efficient Use of Energy*. (The American Physical Society Studies on the Technical Aspects of the More Efficient Use of Energy). AIP Conference Proceedings No. 25. American Institute of Physics, New York. 304 pp.

Anderson, D. E., 1976. Solar thermal system requirements. In: Joint Conference of the American Section, ISES, and the Solar Energy Society of Canada. Volume 5: Solar Thermal and Ocean Thermal. Winnipeg, Manitoba, Canada. (15-20 August) pp. 1-8.

Beers, Roger and Lash, Terry R., 1977. *Choosing an Electrical Energy Future for the Pacific Northwest: An Alternative Scenario*. (Final Draft). (With Robert H. Murray) Natural Resources Defense Council, Inc. Palo Alto, California, U.S.A. (January 31) 177 pp.

Berg, Charles A., 1974. Conservation in industry. *Science*, 184 (April 19): 264-270.

Bockris, J. O'M., 1975. *Energy: The Solar-Hydrogen Alternative*. Halstead Press (John Wiley & Sons), New York. 365 pp.

Bupp, Irvin C.; Derian, Jean-Claude; Donsimon, Marie-Paule; and Treitel, Robert, 1975. Economics of nuclear power. Technology Review (February): 16-25.

Burgess, E. L., 1976. Photovoltaic energy conversion using concentrated sunlight. Presented at the 20th Anniv. Tech. Symp. Soc. of Photo Optical Instrum. Engineers, San Diego, California, (23-27 August).

_____ with Edenburn, M.W., 1976. One kilowatt photovoltaic subsystem using Fresnel lens concentrators. Presented at the 12th IEEE Photovoltaic Specialists Conference.

Clark, Wilson, 1974. *Energy for Survival: The Alternative to Extinction*. Anchor Press (Doubleday), Garden City, New York.

Colorado State University, 1974. Solar thermal electric power systems. Final report, November, 1974. Ft. Collins, Colorado.

Commoner, Barry, 1976. Poverty of Power. Knopf (Random House), New York.

Coty, Ugo, and Dubey, Michael, 1976. The high potential of wind as as energy source. Presented at the 2nd Annual Energy Symposium $Q = E^3$, Los Angeles Council of Engineers & Scientists, 19 May.

Davies, Morris, 1976. Performance data from buildings: St. George's School, Wallasey. Presented at: Conference and Workshop on Passive Solar Heating and Cooling. Energy Research and Development Administration. Albuquerque, New Mexico. 18-19 May, 1976.

Dixon, Bernard (ed.), 1977. France scores an energy "first." New Scientist, 73 (3 February): 254.

Duff, William S. and Shaner, Willis W., 1976. Solar thermal electric power systems: comparison of line focus collectors. In: Joint Conference of the American Section, ISES, and the Solar Energy Society of Canada. Volume 5: Solar Thermal and Ocean Thermal. Winniped, Manitoba, Canada. (15-20 August), pp. 244-271.

Dugger, G. L. and Francis, E. J., 1976. Maritime aspects of producing products at OTEC plants at sea and delivering them to the United States. In: Conference Proceedings Workshop on Energy from the Oceans. Raleigh, North Carolina, (27-28 January). pp. 53-73.

Dyson, Freeman J., 1971. Energy in the universe. Scientific American, 224 (September): 50-59.

Elmer, Donald B., 1976. Energy conservation policies and strategies. (Unpublished). Prepared as Task 3.2 of the Portland Energy Conservation Demonstration Project; City of Portland, Oregon, U.S.A.; sponsored by the U.S.A. Department of Housing and Urban Development. Portland, Oregon, U.S.A. (7 July). 294 pp.

Energy Policy Project of the Ford Foundation, 1974. A Time to Choose: America's Energy Future. Ballinger Publishing Co., Cambridge, Massachusetts. 511 pp.

Ezra, Arthur A., 1975. Technology utilization: Incentives and solar energy. Science, 187 (28 February): 707-713.

Federal Energy Administration, 1974. Project Independence Report: Solar Energy Task Force.

Gabel, Medard, 1975. Energy Earth & Everyone: A Global Energy Strategy for Spaceship Earth. (With the World Game Workshop). Straight Arrow Books, San Francisco. 160 pp.

Gelinier, O., 1972. L'Enterprise Créatrice, Paris. p. 23.

Gérardin, Lucien A., 1973. Study of alternative futures: A scenario writing method. In: A Guide to Practical Technological Forecasting (James R. Bright & Milton E. F. Schoeman, eds.). Prentice-Hall, Inc., Englewood Cliffs, New Jersey. pp. 276-288.

_____, 1973. Topological structural systems analysis: An Aid for selecting policy and actions for complex socio-technological systems. Look-Out Studies, Thomson/CSF (France). (21 June).

Glaser, Peter E., 1976. The status of satellite solar power development. In: Joint Conference of the American Section, ISES, and the Solar Energy Society of Canada. Volume 1: Government and Solar Aux., Winnipeg, Manitoba, Canada. (15-20 August), pp. 1-29.

Golding, E. W., 1976. The Generation of Electricity by Wind Power (reprinted). (Additional chapter by R. I. Harris). E. & F. N. Spon Ltd., London. Distributed in U.S.A. by Halstead Press (John Wiley & Sons), New York. 332 pp.

Greene, B.A., 1976. Residential solar hot water heating and space conditioning systems in Northern California: A brief survey. LBL-5229. Prepared for the U.S. Energy Research & Development Administration. Lawrence Berkeley Laboratory, University of California, Berkeley. August, 1976.

Griffith, William, 1976. Natural daylighting. Presented at the Conference and Workshop on Passive Solar Heating and Cooling. USA Energy Research and Development Administration, Albuquerque, New Mexico, (18-19 May).

Ha, Joseph M., 1977. Can international nuclear energy be controlled? Great Decisions '77 Series, The Sunday Oregonian, (February 6): p. E1.

Haggard, Kenneth, 1976. Economics: The Atascadero residence. Presented at: Conference & Workshop on Passive Solar Heating & Cooling. USA Energy Research & Development Administration. Albuquerque, New Mexico. (18-19 May).

Hammond, Allen L., 1977a. Nuclear moratorium: Study claims that effects would be modest, foresees low growth rate for total energy demand. Science, 195 (14 January): 156-157.

_____, 1977b. Alcohol: a Brazillian answer to the energy crises. Science, 195 (11 February): 564-566.

_____, 1977c. Energy: Brazil seeks a strategy among many options. Science, 195 (11 February): 566-567.

Hinrichsen, Don and Cawood, Patrick, 1976. Fresh Breeze for Denmark's Windmills. New Scientist, 10 June. pp. 567-569.

Hornburg, C. D.; Lendal, B.; and El-Ramly, N., 1976. Preliminary research on ocean energy industrial complexes. In: Joint Conference of the American Section, ISES, and the Solar Energy Society of Canada. Volume 5: Solar Thermal and Ocean Thermal. Winnipeg, Manitoba, Canada. (15-20 August). pp. 412-435.

International Energy Agency, 1976. Implementing agreement for a programme to develop and test solar heating and cooling systems. Paris. 39 pp.

Jacobs, M. L., 1974. Testimony at Wind Energy Hearing before the Subcommittee on Energy of the Committee on Science and Astronautics, U.S. House of Representatives, Ninety-Third Congress, Second Session. 21 May, 1974. pp. 206-208.

Jet Propulsion Laboratory, 1975. Comparative assessment of orbital and terrestrial central power stations.

Justus, C. G., 1976. Wind energy statistics for large arrays of wind turbines (New England and central U.S. regions). In: Joint Conference of the American Section, ISES, and the Solar Energy Society of Canada. Volume 7: Agriculture, Biomass, New Developments. Winnipeg, Manitoba, Canada. (15-20 August). pp. 268-288.

Komanoff, Charles, 1976. _Power Plant Performance: Nuclear and Coal Capacity Factors and Economics_. Council on Economic Priorities, New York. 214 pp.

Lockheed California Co., 1975. Wind Energy Mission Analysis Major Task Element: No. 8 - Evaluation of Possible Wind Energy Applications. Draft prepared for ERDA; Contract AT (04-3) - 1075. Report No. LR 27368-8. Burbank, California. 33 pp.

Lovins, Amory B., 1975. _World Energy Strategies: Facts, Issues, and Options_. Friends of the Earth International (Ballinger Publishing Co.), San Francisco, California 131 pp.

_____, 1976a. Energy strategy: The road not taken? _Foreign Affairs_, October, 1976: 65-96.

_____, 1976b. Scale, centralization, and electrification in energy systems. Presented at: Future Strategies for Energy Development, a symposium at Oak Ridge, Tennessee, U.S.A. (20-21 October).

Magid, Leonard M., 1976. The current status of the U.S. photovoltaic conversion program. Division of Solar Energy, U.S. Energy Research & Development Administration, Washington, D.C.

Metz, William D., 1976a. Solar politics: Lame-duck officials initiate a major new study. _Science_, 194 (17 December): 1256, 1258-1260.

_____, 1976b. An illuminating new use for solar energy. Science, 194 (24 December): 1404.

_____, 1977. Paris and Bonn alter nuclear stand. Science, 195 (7 January): 32.

The Mitre Corporation, 1976. An economic analysis of solar water and space heating M76-79. Prepared for the U.S. Energy Research & Development Administration (November).

Morris, David, 1976. The dawning of solar cells. Institution for Self-Reliance, Washington, D.C. 16 pp.

Naef, Frederick E., 1976. Economic aspects of ocean thermal energy conversion. In: Joint Conference of the American Section, ISES, and the Solar Energy Society of Canada. Volume 5: Solar Thermal and Ocean Thermal. Winnipeg, Manitoba, Canada. (15-20 August). pp. 392-411.

Olds, F. C., 1974. Power plant capital costs going out of sight. Power Engineering (August): 36-43.

_____, 1975. Environmental cleanup 1975-1985: Huge new costs, little benefit. Power Engineering (September): 38-45.

Platt, J., 1970. Hierarchical restructuring. General Systems Handbook, XV: 49-54.

Prigogine, Ilya; Nicolis, G.; and Babloyance, A., 1972. Thermodynamics of evolution. Physics Today, 25.

_____ with Allen, Peter M.; and Herman, Robert, 1977. The evolution of complexity and the law of nature. (This volume).

Reistad, Gordon M., 1975. Potential for non-electrical applications of geothermal energy and their place in the national economy. In: Lawrence Livermore Laboratory Report UCRL 51747. University of California, Berkley, California, USA. pp. 2155-2164.

Rosenfeld, Arthur H. and Selkowitz, Stephen E., 1976. Beam daylighting: Direct use of solar energy for interior lighting. In: Joint Conference of the American Section, ISES, and the Solar Energy Society of Canada. Volume 7: Agriculture, Biomass, Wind, New Developments. Winnipeg, Manitoba, Canada. (15-20 August). pp. 375-391.

Schipper, Lee and Lichtenberg, Allan J., 1976. Efficient energy use and well-being: The Swedish example. Science, 194 (3 December 1976): 1001-1013.

Schumacher, E. F., 1973. Small is Beautiful, Harper & Row, New York.

Scott, Robert E., 1975. Projections of the cost of generating electricity in nuclear and coal-fired power plants. Energy Task Force of the Center for the Biology of Natural Systems, Washington University, St. Louis, Missouri (December).

Skidmore, Owings & Merrill, Inc., 1976. Electric Energy Conservation Study. Prepared for the Bonneville Power Administration, U.S. Department of the Interior, Portland, Oregon. (July).

Smith, Otto J. M., 1976. Smith multimodule solar-electric plant. In: Joint Conference of the American Section, ISES, and the Solar Energy Society of Canada. Volume 5: Solar Thermal and Ocean Thermal. Winnipeg, Manitoba, Canada. (15-20 August). pp. 98-116.

Solar Energy Intelligence Report, 1976a. 1 March 1976.

Solar Energy Intelligence Report, 1976b. Wind power seen promising, already competitive, in Lockheed California study. 24 May 1976.

Sorensen, Bert, 1975. Energy and resources. Science, 189 (25 July): 255-260.

Sorensen, Bert, 1976. Dependability of Wind Energy Generators with Short-Term Energy Storage. Science 26 November: pp. 935-937.

Stanford Research Institute, 1977. Solar energy in America's future: A preliminary assessment. Prepared for the Environmental and Resource Studies Branch, Division of Solar Energy, U.S.A. Energy Research and Development Administration, Menlo Park, California, (February).

_____, 1972. Patterns of Energy Consumption in the United States. Prepared for the Office of Science and Technology, Executive Office of the President, Supt. of Documents, U.S.A. Printing Office, Washington, D.C. (January).

State of Oregon, 1975. Transition. Office of Energy Research and Planning. Salem, Oregon. (January).

Szulmayer, W., 1973. A solar strip concentrator. Solar Energy 14: 326-335.

TRW, 1975. Ocean thermal energy conversion. Final Report, 5 Volumes; to U.S. Energy Research & Development Administration. (Robert Douglas, Principal Investigator). (June).

Thorndike, Edward H., 1976. Energy & Environment: A Primer for Scientists & Engineers. Addison-Wesley Publishing Co., Reading, Massachusetts. 286 pp.

Trombe, F. and Royere, C., 1974. The French CNRS 1000 kw solar furnace description, performance characteristics, present utilization, and perspectives. In: Proceedings of the International Seminar on Large Scale Energy Test Facilities, Las Cruces, New Mexico, U.S.A. (18-19 November). pp. 137-186.

U.S.A. Atomic Energy Commission, 1974. The Nuclear Industry - 1974. WASH 1174-74 (UC-2) Sup't Doc., U.S. Print. Ofc., Washington, D.C. 113 pp.

U.S.A. Energy Research & Development Administration, 1975. Definition Report: National Solar Energy Research, Development & Demonstration Program. ERDA-49. Division of Solar Energy, Supt. Doc., U.S. Govt. Print Ofc., Washington, D.C. (June).

_____, 1975. A National Plan for Energy Research, Development & Demonstration: Creating Energy Choices for the Future. (1975). Volume 1: The Plan. ERDA-48, Vol. 1. Supt. Doc., U.S. Govt. Print. Ofc., Washington, D.C. (28 June 1975).

_____, 1975. A National Plan for Energy Research, Development & Demonstration: Creating Energy Choices for the Future, 1976. Volume 1: The Plan. ERDA 76-1. Supt. Doc., U.S. Govt Print. Ofc., Washington, D.C. (15 April 1976). 122 pp.

United Press International, 1977. Solons form alliance to save energy. The Oregon Journal, (February 11): 25.

Witwer, Jeffrey G., 1976. Costs of alternative sources of electricity. Final report prepared for Bonneville Power Administration. Stanford Research Institute, Palo Alto, California. July 1960. 60 pp.

Zener, Clarence, 1976. A comparison of the economics of nuclear and solar power. In: Joint Conference of the American Section, ISES, and the Solar Energy Society of Canada. Volume 5: Solar Thermal and Ocean Thermal. Winnipeg, Manitoba, Canada. (15-20 August). pp. 535-548.

WHITHER THE CLUB OF ROME?

The following articles came out of a doctoral seminar on the work of the Club of Rome given at Portland State University in the fall of 1976 by Ervin Laszlo. Although discussions at the seminar provided a joint motivation and a shared pool of information for these contributions, they were written independently and reflect their authors' personal viewpoints.

THE CLUB OF ROME OF THE FUTURE VS. THE FUTURE OF THE CLUB OF ROME

Ervin Laszlo

The Club of Rome is a non-organization that aims at its own demise. It was called into being by Peccei and King as an informal braintrust dedicated to generate more awareness of dangers and opportunities ahead -- an awareness which did not seem to materialize fast enough to avert the worst of the dangers and seize the best of the possibilities. Should mankind evolve a more global consciousness and the humanism that goes with it, the Club of Rome would have no further raison d'être. Its position is similar to that of medical researchers whose work is obviated by their own success -- if there are no longer diseases, there need not any longer be medical researchers. But it is a moot question which will come sooner: the conquest of disease or an adequate range of vision for humanity. Like medical researchers, the Club of Rome is as yet here to stay -- despite its own best efforts.

The question is what the Club should do to live up to its self-appointed self-destructive mandate. The first report under its auspices, by Meadows, et alia, operated in the doomsday mode and uprooted complacency and belief in business as usual being usual -- although it drew criticism from just about every quarter. The second report by Mesarovic and Pestel, spreading gloom rather than heralding doom, called attention to the need for harmonious, organic growth and the grave gaps which stand in its way. On a positive tack, the Tinbergen report on the new international order requested specific steps to transfer resources and reduce the rich-poor gap. And the report headed by this writer was designed to prompt nations and organizations to review their goals and compare them against desirable long-range objectives, questioning, if need be, their own ethics and beliefs. These reports did, and are still doing, much to raise world consciousness on global problems and strategies. But they are waystations, not terminals. Together with other work carried out under Club of Rome auspices (world models in Japan and Argentina, population and resource studies in Holland, and science, energy and resource research in England) they make a good beginning -- and call for an even better continuation.

The work of the Club has been influential and its thrust has been clear -- perhaps too clear at first to allow for flexibility. "Do all you can now, to avoid even greater problems later" is a basic theme underlying all reports. What is to be done now was said to be to achieve an equilibrium world system by Meadows, an organically growing multiregional system by Mesarovic and Pestel, a more equitable international economic order by Tinbergen, and a cooperative and collectively self-reliant world of harmonized goals and objectives by Laszlo. The prescriptions have varied, but the diagnosis of the world's ills has not been very different: as King put it in his State of the Planet Report, the patient is sick but there is hope for recovery.

Thanks largely to the efforts of the Club of Rome, international awareness of the world problématique has rapidly grown. The Club pioneered the way (to continue the medical analogy) from diagnosis (Meadows, Mesarovic and Pestel), to prescription (Tinbergen, Laszlo and the other reports). But notwithstanding heroic efforts on the part of Aurelio Peccei, relatively little has been achieved in the area of therapy.

To use another metaphor, the Club helped point the way, but did little to generate the will to take it. If it is true that where there is a will there is a way, then the cart has been put before the horse. Of course, it is easier for a group of concerned world citizens to point the way than it is to generate the great upsurge of will needed to set out on it. Nevertheless there is a real danger that the work so far done will achieve the fine patina that only comes with prolonged disuse. It would be better -- and in this the present writer believes that he is joined by the other Club of Rome authors -- for the reports to go down in the heat of constructive controversy than to gather dust as the respected but unfollowed documents of an era.

Constructive controversy in the area of the world problématique must be more than controversy on the pages of learned journals and academic discussions in economic, social and political forums. Controversy must involve designs for action; the confrontation of alternatives to be essayed. How to move from the level of the word to the level of action -- that is the great issue facing the Club, as it did all other revolutionary groups before it.

Being a non-organization (a body without a formal constitution, budget and authority) the Club cannot formulate policies and make decisions, but can only advise and proselytize. Its tool must remain the word, and its problem how to use it to catalyze action. Not all words constitute mere rhetoric -- some gain the force of overpowering social movements, vide the French Revolution, the movements in 19th century Europe, the Russian Revolution and that in China. Words addressed to the informed often call forth informed responses -- and little else. But words addressed to challenge the beliefs, ethics and imagination of the masses can call forth vast new movements, first germinating in many minds and later coming to expression in some unpredictable yet logical social transformation.

The Club of Rome has long addressed itself to the informed. It preached to the converted and to those whose minds are already made up. It moved in the rarified atmosphere of international decision-making, where it was welcomed as an eccentric who need not be taken seriously, yet may have something of interest to say.

Success with the broad public (to date of writing) was reserved for the Meadows report, and there it was due to the magic of a computer spewing forth doomsday scenarios. The time has now come to reach the broad public in other ways than through finished reports, neatly bound in attractive covers. The time is ripe for two-way interactions, raising questions and getting answers, and then raising further questions.

Even if the world has become a "global village" through the technologies of telecommunication, it has turned out to be a poorly informed village. There are many areas where the medium itself is not the message -- where the message, pace MacLuhan, fails to measure up to the potentials of the medium. Knowledge of world issues and opportunities is one of them. Despite television, telephone and telex, few people know what lies ahead, and what feasible alternatives exist. And even what knowledge there is stops short of penetrating all layers of society. Two kinds of gaps atomize the meager flow of relevant information: gaps between nations and regions, and gaps between different strata within nations. One is as noxious as the other, and both together reduce our interconnected global community into a series of encapsulated backwaters.

Failure to inform the majority of the people (in the literal sense of in-forming attitudes, values and actions) makes many segments of our provincial global village almost equally impotent. Decision-makers cannot act because they would not be supported by their people and would only succeed in manipulating themselves out of popular favor -- and eventually out of office. Large masses do not act because they are not organized, and do not sufficiently know the options and alternatives. A few informed scientists and intellectuals do not make much difference because when it comes to setting policies, few take their word as authority. Informed and adaptive people feel themselves alone -- a feeling that is curiously comforting when the loneliness is due to belonging to the avant garde. They doubt that anybody else is as forward looking, adaptive and advanced as they are themselves. As a result many of the brightest people share pessimistic views concerning everybody else, and resign themselves contentedly to their impotence.

These self-reinforcing feedback loops have to be broken. Policy-makers need to be shown that many people are more open to new approaches, new values and new institutions than they suspect. Informed people need to be shown that their policy-makers are not as slow and bureaucratic as they, in turn, suspect. And people and decision-makers in each country need to be shown that other countries also respond to changing needs and ideas. Thereby a major hindrance to progressive international action could be removed: the belief that in this predatory environment if 'our' nation and government would act as it should, it would merely dig its own grave.

The Club of Rome could play a vital catalytic function in breaking these viciously self-reinforcing cycles. With its prestige in national and international circles, it could initiate new inquiries into popular attitudes concerning needed changes in policies, lifestyles and institutions. It could bring the results of such surveys to the attention of decision-makers, and inform the international community of significant new trends.

The effects of such an informational cross-pollination could be epochal. Most people are more open to new ideas and alternatives than they are given credit for. Even politicians tend to underestimate the adaptability of the public's attitude. Moreover the world is not neatly divided between good guys and bad guys, with the good ones on 'our' side and the bad ones on the other. Countries large and small, democratic and communist, developed and developing, are struggling with the problems of rising demands, falling growth-curves, growing populations, and mounting resource costs. Solutions that work would be willingly tried in many nations even if some traditional objectives would need to be revised and a few sacred cows sacrificed. Few nations, other than those in the chronic trouble-spots, would risk continued socioeconomic crises just to spite an adversary. Few would want to pour billions into humanly useless armaments merely to exploit the weakness of a potential enemy -- who may feel very much the same way. But people and governments do not know enough of such new currents, and they continue to operate on the outmoded premises of zero-sum adversary games.

New flows of information must be created to in-form world opinion with respect to mankind's changing mood. These flows must focus on the world <u>problématique</u>, and on alternative strategies for ultimately transcending it. They must operate in two directions (with feedback), and be oriented vertically within nations and horizontally among international policy-makers.

The Club of Rome could and should help create such information flows. It could work with local research institutes to poll public opinion and bring the results to local policy-makers. It could and should exchange the results internationally. Numerous individuals and institutes would willingly collaborate. What they need is a joint umbrella with good visibility -- a transnational framework that assures cooperation and respect. Though grudgingly, most governments and public opinion leaders pay respect to the Club, and the great majority show themselves willing to cooperate. The task of creating a bi-directional and a bi-dimensional information flow is not impossible, even if its beginning would be relatively modest. The longest journey starts with taking the first step, and if that step is successful the succeeding ones could come quicker and measure a longer stride.

The Club of Rome of the past has proclaimed doom and spread gloom; the Club of Rome of today offers numerous prescriptions.

The Club of Rome of the future could and should become an active informational catalyst. That would be the surest way of contributing to the future of mankind -- and assuring that the Club of Rome of the future has no future of its own.

PUBLIC FEEDBACK FOR THE CLUB OF ROME

Michelle Carlson

In recent years the public has been exposed to a number of published documents associated with various Club of Rome projects on the world future. Perhaps now is a good time to consider whether more reports in this style will add very much to the achievement of the present aims of the Club of Rome. These aims fall into two categories:

<u>Intrinsic Goals</u>. The Club of Rome desires to <u>refine its own world futures perspective.</u>, its concern with the development of human experience as a whole, as well as to find new ways to increase public feedback and public debate. A significant increase in political sophistication within the Club may already be noted. At first political considerations were added as an enrichment of the reports, then, in more explicit language, they became a central concern. Increased complexity may also be seen in the new emphasis on socio-economic limits in addition to physical limits to resources.

<u>Extrinsic Goals</u>. The Club of Rome clearly desires to become more knowledgeable about <u>getting the word out</u>. This not only will require that it continue to send its members as ambassadors to august international gatherings (from the sedate Modern Language Association to the not-so-sedate gatherings of Third World socialists) and continue to publish one report after another, but it will also require that it begin to explore other avenues of communication designed to reach large audiences.

In a sense all of the Club of Rome documents following the initial <u>Limits to Growth</u> have tended to answer with greater and greater refinement the criticisms which Marie Jahoda and others made of the Forrester-Meadows world model, namely, that it took no account of "politics, social structure and human needs and wants." It is a measure of the integrity of the Club of Rome membership that they would attempt to answer such an imposing challenge.

Mesarovic and Pestel's <u>Mankind at the Turning Point</u> sets a different course from the <u>pessimistic one mapped out by</u> Forrester, Meadows et al. From the optimistic note of its opening dedication ("To Future Generations") there flows a solemn <u>will</u> to have things done differently. What this means, however, <u>is</u> as muddy and romantic as their analogy of organic growth. Two types of organic growth are presented but not distinguished from each other. The key idea of the one is specialized and functional interdependence; of the other, a gradual over-all growth slow-down. Statements such as the following characterize, to me, the development of this theme. "Each part -- whether a region or a group of nations -- has its own contribution to make to the organic development of mankind: resources, technology, economic potential, culture, etc. In such a system the growth of any one part depends on the growth or non-growth of others (Meadows, et al., 1972: p. 5). Such a vision may reveal the unhappiest of scenarios-viz-we send our culture, Macburgers and all, to South America in return for their hardwood, copper, etc. The variable which remains unaccounted for through the chapters on development, food, and energy which follow is <u>exactly that of power</u>. Why would a rich man give to a poor man? Why indeed? Only if the rich man (or country) saw that it was in his own self-interest would such an exchange be made.

The Tinbergen report, RIO, which followed <u>Mankind at the Turning Point</u> some two years later, expands the rich vs. poor issue -- "Changes in the International order designed to redress existing inequalities and imbalances call ... for changes in the forces which define the power structure." This statement, which seems forceful at first reading begins to dissolve as one looks for the meaning of "forces which define the power structure." Perhaps the forces which define are people's needs and wants, that last class of overlooked cultural variables which Jahoda urged the Club of Rome to consider. Goals, myths, values, forces, beliefs, it doesn't much matter: with the publication of the Goals Project report we have gotten to the great class of cultural insubstantials and the challenge will be (substantially) answered. A picture of the human future, more or less complete, will have been painted according to the Club of Rome's vision. A picture with a broad brush and a light wash.

The next task, I propose, is the filling in of detail. It requires constructing a highly defined program out of this slightly Eastern view of our place in the scheme of things; this slightly Marxist economics; this liberal democratic political bias. The criticisms offered here are no more than those which seemed necessary to make. The suggestions, I hope, are specific and adaptable.

The Club of Rome has made no attempt to hide its proselytizing fervor. Indeed there is some attempt to produce reports which are conceptually accessible to the broadest sector of the public, speedily translated into the largest useful number of languages, and then widely and deeply dispersed. This policy is in keeping with the goal of getting the word out. It is, however, not the best way to meet this goal if one is to believe communication theorists.

It is one of the tenets of communication theory that words in themselves are highly ambiguous and that even within a single culture, the images, and therefore the reactions which specific words evoke, are bound to differ from individual to individual.

Translations across cultures are likely to run into even more severe problems: semantic problems, problems of meaning. If, as I take it, the object of the Club of Rome is to disseminate what is essentially the same message to a wide variety of cultures, this problem will have to be addressed.

However, writing a single report for world-wide consumption may not be the best way to accomplish the aims of the Club of Rome, since the effort to make the report acceptable to a world-wide audience appears to require a great deal of indirection verging on misinformation. It has been suggested that a first step in converting the average person into a "student of the future" is to increase his or her knowledge of the realities of the present. There is some question, in the first place, whether reports can do this. It seems quite likely that highly generalized reports cannot do it to the extent needed. They serve rather to place the immediate local reality within a world system made up of such realities. They define from the outside in. We also need definition from the inside out.

Instead of producing a single massive report which attempts to cover all the bases why not try individualized reports? The advantages are that short range interests of the specific area could be taken into account when discussing adoption of one or another of the alternative long range goals. The impact of long range proposals on immediate interests could then be specified.

Students of attitude change have found that when a message is matched more precisely to an audience's self-image, a much higher degree of motivation is likely to be achieved. If a new idea and its complementary opposite are debated in the same forum and with reference to real tasks, action will be taken on that idea. Why not put these findings to use?

A revealing comparison may be made between the discussion of transnational corporations which appears as Chapter 15 in the RIO report and that which appeared in the first two December issues of the 1974 New Yorker magazine. The magazine, because it is designed for U.S. consumption and in particular for middle class liberal Americans, devoted equal coverage to the long range, contribution of transnational corporations to the world problématique (issue 1) and to the effect of transnationals on local and short range self-interest of labor in this country; specifically the adverse effect on jobs, on capital, on worker morale (issue 2). This then is a two stage process in which the world system perspective is not lost. Instead the international long view is supplemented by a national close focus.

It is difficult to produce a report which stresses the cultural insubstantials and yet does not look farfetched and complex to some sectors of the public, naive to others. Rapid social and technological change makes the alternative of stressing facts and figures just as hazardous: the material may be out of date before it is printed.

Whichever emphasis they choose, therefore, the documentarians are exposed to either criticisms of naiveté or of being behind the times. If they chose to emphasize both, as RIO does for example, they are exposed to both -- as RIO was in our seminar room.

Why not mini-reports, working papers and loosely bound periodcials?

Projects could be on-going and include not only the mandates for assessment and goal setting but advocacy and intervention as well. Newsletters and updated briefs from project director and staff could be collected in a central office and a source list provided to all interested groups and individuals. Copies of particular reports and supplementary materials could be provided as requested and at the level of specificity required.

There comes a point of diminishing returns for book length reports in the public alarm genre. There comes a point when the public response is "Alright, so I'm awake already -- what do you want me to do?" The familiar fable of the boy who cried wolf may be instructive. Although the sense of alarm has diminished from one report to the next, there is still very much the sense that someone else should pick up on this and act to give precise instructions to decision makers and the public at large. It will not do to simply state that a responsible world coordinator should be found. All existing potential world coordinators should be mobilized. The Club of Rome is one such body and it should try out an active leadership role while encouraging other internationalist organizations to do likewise. Obviously a second section of active futurists engaged full time in intercultural communication research will need to be employed. University departments of Systems Science, Communications and Future Studies in various nations could provide the skilled personnel. If such openings were established, a number of existing research awards, internships and so forth could generate the necessary funds.

Responsibilities of an Idea Vendor. "The 'power of the idea,' the particular weapon of scientists, moralists and concerned citizens, must prove of decisive importance in constructing a fairer and more peaceful world and the search for relevant new ideas must be organized and intensified so as to support it" (Tinbergen, 1976: p. 107).

One of the early criticisms of the Club of Rome membership was that it was made up exclusively of intellectual technologists. Parenthetically it might be added that it was made up of such to a man. The intellectual and male orientation continues. To many of its readership the "Club" appears to be just that, and this vision, which the Club of Rome has not dispelled (second-class air flights notwithstanding), cuts deeply into its credibility. The political understanding of members of lower socioeconomic groups is rapidly evolving, particularly in industrialized countries. Many attribute this development to the communications explosion. Whatever the cause there are enough indicators of the phenomenon that characterization of the masses as concerned only with the most immediate survival goals seems grossly oversimplified. The push for increased political consciousness among ordinary people in Third World countries has begun and is found to have a large effect on policy with these countries.

In the U.S. the phenomenon may be seen in the emergence of a new type of labor leadership concerned with the development of truly international labor unionism, as well as in the populism of many of the recent political campaigns.

If the Club of Rome is acting as an idea vendor the question of importance is who would likely sample their supply. Quite obviously the Club supports the notion of a two-step flow of ideas from idea specialists to opinion leaders. Having once convinced opinion leaders and decision makers around the world that its view of the future is correct, the Club of Rome expects to have an impact -- through education, creation of new jobs, new defense policy, new energy technology -- on those whose daily tasks and habits make each society run.

But alternatives to the Club of Rome vision will continue to raise a challenge. Already it is clear that V. Leontief has come up with an economic scenario much more pleasing to the industrial and political community in the United States. The daily press has given this version of the future significant coverage. As a matter of fact, the mass media has a version of the future of its own which may be refined and rigidified into a system as the international press becomes a more coherent community.

This is perhaps over-extended discussion of a simple point -- just getting the word out does not assure its acceptance. Although acceptance of an idea depends on the climate of the times, it may be promoted by good advance work.

Ideas _do_ change history. So do dramatic events. Ideas which remain with the intellectuals, however, change nothing. Ideas which bloom among the masses, whatever the source of these ideas, produce the dramatic events which from time to time have changed our human course.

If the work of the Club of Rome is to have an effect it must get beyond pencil wagging and involve the people of the world. Involvement does not result automatically from getting information to the public. In fact, as the quality and volume of information rises, there is the classic divergence: the information rich, in this case, get richer and the information poor get poorer (Katzman, 1974).

The attempt by the Club of Rome to feed forward to the public (through opinion leaders and decision makers) a condensed version of those issues or attitudes which they believe to be the important ones, can only be one half of the process. Only when the people assimilate the information and promote their own insights, suggestions and pressures will the process be complete.

Some questions are likely to arise regarding public feedback:

1. How do people make their views known to the 'power structure' at this time? How effective are these means in terms of actual policy changes or other signs of action on recommendations from the people?

2. How can we get involvement feedback rather than service feedback? (Service feedback includes inquiries, requests and complaints; involvement feedback includes opinions, suggestions and participation.)

3. How much of the population needs to be participating in a dialogue with public officials and at what level?

4. What innovations in communication technology can be used to increase public participation?

Each of these questions may be taken in turn. The answers are partial and depend on U.S. data.

<u>Channels in present use</u>. There are any number of means presently available for the people (in their role as voters, consumers, etc.) to register their confidence or lack of it in public officials or public issues. Those which easily come to mind are polls, ballots, boycotts, petitions and so forth. It is to these that the old rhetoric of "the people's choice" or "the people have spoken" referred. However, all these means have one strategic limitation in common -- they are in the digital mode. That is to say, in using them a person's range of expression is filtered down to a yes or a no, a + or a -, on some preconstructed measure. An extreme example of this kind of feedback is a 1969 Paris experiment in which T.V. viewers were invited to express their opinions by switching off lights or other electrical devices. Their reactions were recorded by sensitive meters connected to the power grid. Push button telephones have been used in a similar manner in a recent California T.V. poll.

A serious limitation of this type of procedure is that one's individual vote seems to get swallowed up. In the Paris experiment voters got no indication that turning the lights off had any impact whatsoever. The likely result, according to the principles of operant conditioning, is that the next time they were asked to perform this maneuver, they themselves would turn off.

In building forums for citizens to express their views on the future, care must be taken not to increase the sense of impotence which shows up, for example, in metaphors for the future found by Kaufman (1976).

Bogus questionnaires designed to inform rather than elicit information are another way the public has been misused by decision makers. A recent survey shows that over 75% of Congressional offices regularly send out surveys and questionnaires to constituents although only 10% of such offices perceive these surveys to be 'very important.' The conclusion is that "the main purposes served are to get the name of the Congressman before constituents and to give constituents something to respond to (Wood, 1974).

In light of this it is interesting to note that direct action on issues, whether by those on the right or on the left, has had far more visible and immediate impact on policy in the last fifteen years than talking to decision makers has.

To reverse the trend toward public cynicism (often mistaken for apathy by self-serving leaders) several steps need to be taken. Wood suggests that "analog and involvement only" channels need to be opened for the informed and innovative ideas of concerned citizens. A means of speedy and visible response to these ideas needs to be developed. People at all social levels need to be involved in the same effort.

The development of alternative visions of the world future and programs of response to these visions may most properly involve the general public. However, an increase of cynicism at this level could be somewhat dangerous to us all.

Access to response channels does not guarantee use. But how does one motivate a population which is not one homogeneous mob but rather a number of sub-populations with different socio-economic statuses, tastes and interests? One must decide in advance not only how many of the people need to be involved in a dialogue on a particular issue, but exactly what groups need to be represented. If a decision maker hears only from a certain group on an issue, this may be a function of the issue, or of the group, or of the type of message projected.

In the 1968 elections in the U.S., for example, when one looks at data on eligible voters in each income category who actually participated, one finds that of those who had incomes under $3,000, less than 54% participated; 58% from the $3,000 to $5,000 group; 72% from the $5,000 to $15,000 group; and 84% of those having incomes over $15,000 participated.

It is not lack of response but differential response which should be of concern.

<u>Increasing participation through innovative technology</u>. In several articles Stuart Umpleby has promoted the use of the teaching computer as a means to involve the public in policy planning. By means of a graphic display unit, the computer presents pre-stored information to an individual at a rate which he or she controls. The user may type in his or her own ideas. These may include: 1) suggesting additional alternatives; 2) noting inadequacies in background material, and 3) speculating about consequences.

Approval or disapproval of specific proposals is less important but is implied in the user's suggestions and comments.

Umpleby cites two advantages of the teaching computer:

> There are two principle advantages to having computer-based citizens sampling simulations . . . Each communication system lends itself to the transmission of a particular type of information. With a teaching computer the student or citizen controls the rate at which information is presented to him. He need never be either bored or lost. If he is familiar with the information being presented, he can jump ahead. If he does not understand a particular point, he can ask for additional information. Thus the teaching computer is very well suited for presenting logically complex material to people at different stages of familiarity with the issues.
>
> Second, a citizen sampling simulation requires a model of the social processes involved in the situation being discussed in order to be able to predict the consequences of alternative actions. The need for an operating model requires experts to state explicitly their notions about how the world works. The ideas held by different people about the probable consequences of actions can then be compared (Umpleby, 1970).

Since 1970 a number of "anticipatory democracy" programs have attempted to educate citizens in the U.S. about problems at the state level and to solicit from the citzens some alternatives for the future, each of which has had specific goals for legislative action associated with it. The best known of these programs are the Alternatives for Washington, HAWAII 2000, Iowa 2000 and Minnesota Horizons. Alternatives for Washington was typical of this movement:

> A 150-person task force initially generated new information about alternatives for the state. 1,500 persons participated in regional conferences reviewing the findings of the task force. 2,400 people participated in a Delphi poll . . . With the information collected, the task force identified 11 alternative futures for the state . . . Through an effective media campaign and a unique call-in program, over 60,000 people participated in the program, with 100,000 to 200,000 persons watching programs on public television.

Was all the hard work and good will of all these people turned into legislation as they had supposed it would be? It was not. The probable result of this more or less well-intentioned effort was an overall increase in frustration and alienation. Let the futures surveyist beware, get guarantees of support, in terms of action, before requesting ideas from the people.

The area of interest discussed here is communications. The two general aims of Club of Rome members, first, that of increasing their own future consciousness, and second, that of informing the people of all nations of the importance of concerted action at the present moment to insure viable futures may not be adequately served by a continued reliance on lengthy and generalized reports. I suggest that the Club disaggregate the reports, act more assertively in its role as an idea vendor, and consider various ways to establish a survey process which will get people at all levels of each society involved.

SCIENCE AND MYTH: TWO PROPOSALS TO THE CLUB OF ROME

Ann Corrigan

INTRODUCTION

Two proposals to the Club of Rome are offered below. Each proposal describes a project which is believed to be in consonance with the Club of Rome's goals and which would follow naturally from the previous reports. The proposals represent two approaches to the question of the world's future. The first, "Conference on Stability and Value in the World System," is intended to resolve some theoretical questions, which yet have practical implications, about how the new world order can and should be organized. The second, "Myths for a Global Society," is designed to bring the artistic and spiritual elements into the efforts to construct a new world order.

PROPOSAL 1. CONFERENCE ON STABILITY AND VALUE IN THE WORLD SYSTEM

A conflict exists today between two conceptions of humanity's future possibilities. One conception argues that human civilization has reached the natural limits imposed upon it from resource scarcity, space limitations, and industrial pollution. Humanity must halt its growth processes and move toward an equilibrium condition. The concerns of global stability must override all other considerations, and drastic measures will need to be taken to avert an impending doom. Some of the proponents of this conception also believe that the necessary measures will have to be imposed from without on individuals who will be unable to curb their natural material desires.

An alternative conception has more recently been presented. This conception is based on two premises. Fist, individual human needs and desires must be valued, protected, and satisfied. Individuals must not be sacrificed for the whole, just as the whole must not be sacrificed for the individual. Second, humanity has vast reserves of creativity and capacity for change. Mankind is quite able to perceive a need for change and can expand or revise its value systems to adapt to changing conditions or even to direct changes in internal and external conditions.

It is proposed that the Club of Rome continue its sponsored research into the future of humanity through a series of conferences in which the proponents of stability and the proponents of individual human values will meet and discuss their respective views. The purpose of this project would be to promote a much needed confrontation and dialogue between the attitudes of stability and human values with the hope that such a meeting will encourage the design of futures in which the human world system will be both stable and supportive of individual human values.

Background and Rationale
Spurred by the many difficulties and potential catastrophes now confronting the world, researchers in many fields have turned to the questions of stability and survival. Ecologists such as C. S. Holling (1976) and R. Margalef (1969) and systems theorists such as M. R. Gardener and W. Ross Ashby (1970) have investigated the concept of stability from both a theoretical and an empirical viewpoint. New definitions such as "metastability," "persistence," and "resilience" have resulted from these studies. Other theoretical studies dealing with multiple domains of stability, or "attractors," have added to the growing understanding of stability, survival, and evolution. R. Thom's "catastrophe theory" (1975), Prigogine's "thermodynamics of open systems" (1976), and J. Bronowski's "stratified stability (1970) are among the concepts and theories now being developed.

Futurists, systems theorists, and social scientists have attempted to apply these concepts and theories of stability to the design of human systems, often with the intent of finding a path to a more desirable future for humanity than now appears likely. The work of authors such as E. Jantsch, M. Maruyama, A. Taylor, and O. W. Markley can be included in this category.

Other efforts to stimulate the formation of a new social order include the two most recent reports to the Club of Rome, Reshaping the International Order (abbreviated RIO) and Goals for Mankind. Major emphasis in these reports is placed on the importance of satisfying the needs and desires of all individuals, with special emphasis on the satisfaction of basic needs. The concept of global goals and values is used as a "guiding image" for new world development.

Standing in dark contrast to the more positive and hopeful forecasts are works such as Heilbroner's An Inquiry into the Human Prospect (1974). The best known "forecasts of doom," however, are the Limits to Growth studies based on Jay Forrester's World III System Dynamics model. These studies argue that a total cessation of growth is necessary in order to avert the forecasted catastrophes, whereas reports such as Rio and Goals for Mankind hold that such a policy is contrary to the needs of many humans and violates basic human values. The forecasts made with another world model developed by M. Mesarovic and E. Pestel (1974), while not quite so bleak as the World III forecasts, still question the probability of man's survival and insist upon a very high probability being placed on the occurrence of major catastrophes within the next fifty years.

A conflict seems to exist between the requirements for world stability and the demands of human needs and desires. A stable or equilibrium world system seems to demand an enormous amount of individual suffering and still may not, if lessons from ecology are valid, survive large disturbances from the environment. A fluctuating world system may qualify as "resilient" according to ecological theory, but may require fluctuations in population or other variables that will also cause undue suffering. A system designed to support and enhance human values, on the other hand, is criticized by J. Forrester as being in the long run detrimental to human values, because such a system will not survive (Meadows and Meadows, 1973).

In a recent letter to the Society for General Systems Research (SGSR), Sir Geoffrey Vickers recognizes the existence of this conflict and proposes that an effort should be made to "emphasize the basic conflict between the criteria of stability/instability on the one hand, and success/failure on the other."*

---

*... as I see it there is a marked difference between human systems and other systems....Natural systems do not fail or succeed ....human systems have to be mindful of the laws of stability and instability since these constitute at least constraints within which human cultures and cultured human individuals pursue success and failure.

"But the problems of our day, political, economic, ecological, legal, cultural, and social, seem to me to be capable of being stated only in terms which include both the value criteria of human cultures and the stability criteria of all cultures. Indeed the present economic, ecological, and probably other problems of the West derive largely in my view, from a conflict between the two.

"Now the question is what kind of people are interested in this kind of thinking. They comprise in my view two radically distinct populations. On the one hand is the scientifically oriented type which is anxious to play down the significance of human culture or to resolve it into its biological constituents so as to extend scientific generalities more widely to human affairs. On the other hand there are the humanistically inclined who want to learn what they can about systems generally, in order more clearly to understand the limitations under which human beings exercise their initiative both personally and generally.

"These two populations do not correspond with sets of disciplines, but rather with attitudes of mind. Historians and students of policy making will be found in both camps, so will those who are by training, natural scientists and mathematicians.

"If this is a valid analysis, what can the Society usefully do? It seems to me (though I am powerfully biased by the nature of my own interests) that its most important current function to-day, should be to emphasize, rather than mute, the basic conflict between the criteria of stability/instability on the one hand, and success/failure on the other."

Sir Geoffrey suggests that SGSR undertake the task of sharpening the conflict between stability and human values. There is another organization, however, which is perhaps uniquely suited to this task. The Club of Rome's sponsored reports have already been referenced. Each of these reports is concerned with the possible future of mankind; each deals to some extent with the question of the stability of the world system and how this may be upheld; and each report either emphasizes the importance of goals and human needs, desires and values, or totally ignores the issue.

Thus the themes of stability and human values run through the Club of Rome reports. Each report, however, tends to focus on one or the other theme, and each report either ignores or does not fully answer the problems presented in those reports that emphasize the contrary theme. The <u>Limits to Growth</u> study is purely oriented toward the question of stability. Mesarovic and Pestel's report does consider human values to some extent in their emphasis on a regional view and on balanced growth; nevertheless, this report is mainly oriented toward stability and often shows that policies designed from the value or success/failure point of view fail from the stability point of view. The <u>RIO</u> and <u>Goals</u> reports emphasize the concept of human values. Both of these latter reports contradict many of the "stability propositions" of the previous reports; e.g. the amount of natural resource reserves. Still, these reports leave one somewhat uncertain as to the accuracy of their claims that the stability question can be resolved adequately.

Both sides of the conflict have been well represented in the literature. The proponents of the two sides, however, have never discussed for any length of time their differences of view nor have they consciously tried to organize a world system that will satisfy both the need for stability and the desire to fulfill human needs and values. A Hegelian synthesis is required; without such a synthesis the world system is more likely to be, at the best, doomed to major catastrophes, and, at the worst, doomed to failure.

I propose that the Club of Rome sponsor a series of conferences with the intent of:

    a.   provoking a confrontation between the concepts of stability and human values,

    b.   establishing a synthesis between the two views in order to design principles for constructing a stable and successful world system.

These conferences may take a variety of forms. Each conference would have an objective that supports the overall goal stated above. A preliminary description of the proposed conferences is given below.

Planning the Conferences

The first step in the project would be to convene a group of persons knowledgeable in the controversy described above. The task of this group would be to identify prospective participants in the conferences and to design and implement the conferences.

Participants could be chosen from the following groups: world modelers and other modelers, systems theorists and practitioners, futurists, ecologists, economists, politicians, historians, anthropologists, philosophers, psychologists, and religious/spiritual leaders. Many, if not all, of the authors referenced above would be candidates for inclusion in the conferences. The team selecting the participants should strive for a balance both among the proponents of the two sides (and those who hold with neither side) and among the various professions and disciplines.

The design of the conferences should have the following two characteristics: the conferences should as much as possible form a system, relating to and supporting each other, and the conferences should unfold in time. The conferences should not be static; designers should not set forth prior to beginning the conferences a complete description of the conferences to be held. Rather, an initial set of conferences should be designed, and the set should be revised and expanded as the results of the conferences indicate or as members of the conferences desire.

Some possible conferences that could be included are as follows (the types are not meant to be mutually exclusive):

a. Debates between proponents of stability/instability and the proponents of success/failure or human values. These conferences should aim at emphasizing and clarifying the differences between the two views. Proponents who feel very strongly about their views should be selected for these sessions.

b. Conferences in which the attendees consciously attempt to synthesize the two views and to begin to design principles by which stable and successful world systems can result.

c. Presentations and discussions of the ecological and systems theoretical concepts of stability. In these conferences it should be questioned to what extent these theories are applicable to human societies.

d. Conferences in which humanists attempt to define criteria for success and failure of human systems. The results of these conferences should be compared with the RIO, Goals, and other normative studies. The results of these conferences should also be studied to determine to what extent these criteria are in concert with theoretical and empirical concepts of stability.

e. Conferences in which historians and anthropologists review the nature of stability in human societies. Past and current societies could be used as examples of how humans have designed their societies to be stable. The results of these conferences should be compared with the concepts of stability from the physical sciences and from recent developments in ecology and systems theory.

f. Conferences in which the world models of Forrester/Meadows and Mesarovic/Pestel are reviewed by modeling theorists and systems theorists to determine to what degree these models are valid and comprehensive descriptions of the world system.

The structures of the various conferences will differ. Some conferences will be classical conferences spanning a few days. Others will be workshops lasting over a longer period of time. Still other conferences might be on-going, relatively unstructured discussions that could be carried out over long distances, possibly using techniques such as the Delphi method and computerized conferencing (Linstone and Turoff, 1975).

The results of the conferences could be gathered into one volume which could be used as reference material for researchers in the future. In fact, a useful first step in the project would be to prepare a preliminary volume containing work available at the present time on the subject of human values and world stability.

The above description is admittedly broad and could result in a mammoth project. The Club of Rome may wish to hold a few select conferences from the types described above. It may then be desirable to issue an invitation for proposals for further work dealing with the conflict between stability/instability and success/failure. Many permutations of these ideas exist that could help to resolve the question of whether or not the world must choose between stability and human values.

An attempt to stimulate a confrontation between the opposing ideals of world stability and individual human values is an appropriate and potentially fruitful project for the Club of Rome. It would complement and extend the previous reports to the Club of Rome. I believe that the proposed effort would contribute substantially to the knowledge needed to move the world onto a path toward a more desirable world order.

PROPOSAL 2. MYTHS FOR A GLOBAL SOCIETY

Two basic approaches exist to forecasting the future: exploratory and normative. The exploratory approach extrapolates from the present situation and from current trends in an attempt to "predict" the future. The normative approach attempts to create a vision of a more desirable future and to design a path or paths that will lead from the present situation to the more desired future state.

The two most recent reports to the Club of Rome, Reshaping the International Order (RIO) and Goals for Mankind are explicitly normative. Both reports portray a future world order that is considered a more desirable state than the current state of affairs, both for those living today in material plenty and for those who lack basic requirements for life. Both reports also attempt to outline a path from the current world order to the "new international order" through a series of goals or issues.

A system of goals that prescribes a world order that will satisfy the basic needs of all humanity and humanity's less material desires, and that is accepted by the people of the world, is clearly desired. The goals presented by the RIO and Goals reports are thus an important contribution to the design of viable world futures. Both reports, however, present their goals in abstract, skeletal forms. The prose of both reports tends to be dry, often technical, and at times tedious to read. It is the thesis of this paper that global goals presented in such a format will not be successful in reaching a large portion of the world, and, even more importantly, in becoming a part of the common person's accepted world views.

The classical means by which a shift in commonly held world views is accomplished, consists of one of the many forms of myths. Whatever form they take, myths reach down to all levels of the human mind. They engage the entire soul and stimulate the mind and body to action. It is proposed, therefore, that the Club of Rome seek to embody the goals presented in its latest reports, but more especially in the Goals study, through the creation of myths and the dissemination of these myths to the peoples of the world.

Guiding Images of Mankind

The utility of myths as guiding and unifying principles for humanity has recently received renewed attention from planners and futurists. Donald Michael (1975) has discussed the use of myths in planning in order to align the process of planning with the reality of a turbulent, unpredictable universe. O. W. Markley has described myths as "guiding images," "images of man," and "images of man-in-the-universe," where these terms refer to "the set of assumptions and fundamental premises held about the human being's origin, nature, abilities, characteristics, relationships with others, and place in the universe" (1976). E. Jantsch has argued that "for the first time, we have now the opportunity to use conscious learning to further their (images of man) emergence" (1976).

Fred Polak also discusses the use of myths as "guiding images" in his book, The Image of the Future (1973). In this book, Polak states that when the dominant images of culture are anticipatory, they lead social development and direct social change. As the culture moves toward fulfillment of the goals expressed in its myths, the culture and its myths become complementary and mirror each other clearly. A culture, however, may "outstrip"

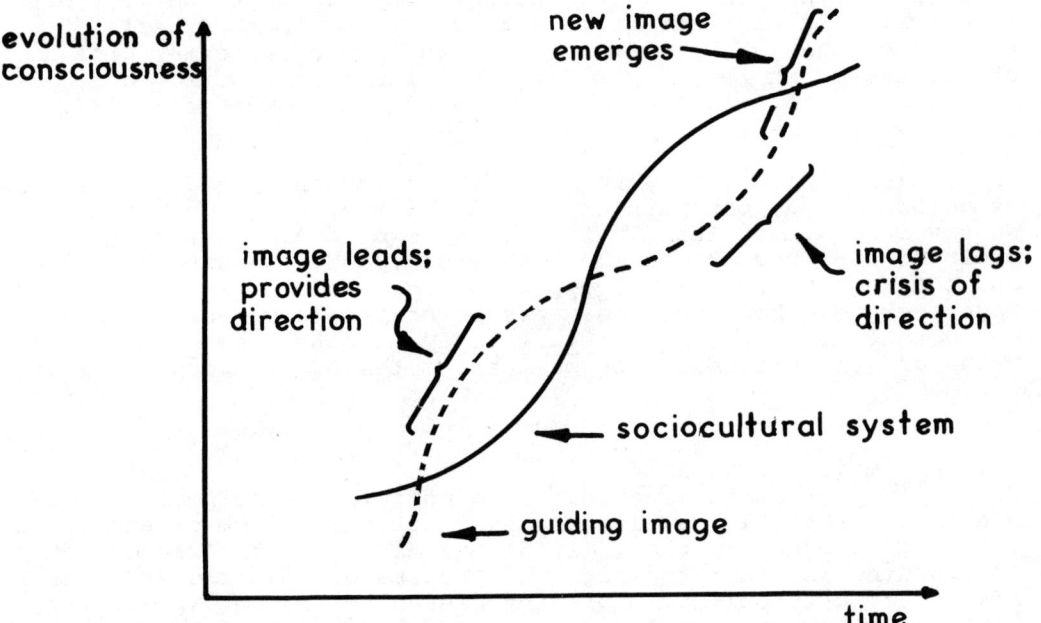

Fig. 1. The cyclic relationship between a culture and the guiding images.

its dominant images, resulting in "frustration, cultural disruption or social crisis" (Markley, 1976). These crises then lead to the formation of a new guiding image, and the cycle begins anew. Figure 1 diagrams this cycle of the relationships between a culture and its myths. It has been argued that the world society of today is one in which the dominant images are lagging behind the social realities. New images or myths are needed that will be able to act as guiding images of social change.

Forms of Myth
Myths over the millenia have taken a myriad of forms and have been transmitted in many different ways. The early myths were transmitted in the form of stories told in prose, poetry, or song, orally or, in later times, written. Many of the myths were embodied in rituals that actively involved the members of the cultures.

Later, especially in the classical and medieval periods, art forms and dramas supplemented the telling of myths through story and ritual. Myths from many cultures were combined and extended to form complex myth cycles such as the Grail legends in France and Britain. Myths also evolved around key political and social events and around the person or persons who were associated with these events or who were among the driving forces of these events.

The modern age has, to a great extent, seen an ebbing of the forces of myths, or so it has been argued. Nevertheless, myths have been created and transmitted, although they have perhaps been unrecognized as myths. Some of the means by which modern myths have been transmitted are: fantasies and science fiction novels, essays such as A. Toffler's Future Shock (1970), movies, folk songs, rock operas, and television. Myths surrounding individuals have been fairly numerous and include persons such as Mahatma Gandhi and Mao Tse-tung.

The RIO and Goals reports have outlined a new set of images of man that can be used to direct needed changes in the world society. Before these changes can be accepted as part of the common person's world view, however, they must be presented in a fuller, more completely embodied form. The goal statements of these two reports should be translated into myths of a form that will be readily accepted by the peoples of the world. It is proposed, therefore, that the Club of Rome sponsor a project in which myths embodying the global goal statements are created and disseminated to the various cultures and societies.

Project Design and Implementation
In implementing the project proposed here, the Club of Rome would have tremendous scope of possibility. As seen above, a variety of forms of myth could be chosen and the myths could be directed to many areas of the world and many different social and cultural strata. The first step in the project, therefore, would be to determine what forms of myth would be used and which peoples would receive the myths.

The forms of the myths will depend on the cultures of the people receiving the myths. It is not possible to design a myth or myths that would be understood and accepted by all peoples of the world. It would also be impractical to create myths of a global society for every nation and culture. Thus it should first be decided what cultures or societies would be the best candidates for receiving myths relating to the formation of a global society. Some criteria that could be used in selecting the candidate areas or cultures are:

1. How many people would be reached?

2. How important is it for this group of people to receive and accept the global goals? In other words, how great an impact will this culture's acceptance of myths embodying global goals have on the rest of the world and on the formation of a world society congruent with the global goals?

3. How likely is it that the myths will be accepted?

4. If the common people of this culture do accept the myths, what effect will this have on the government of their country or on other powerful bodies (e.g. multinational corporations)?

Members of the candidate cultures should be consulted in answering these questions and in deciding who will embody the myths and what form the myths should take. Of course, the person(s) who embody the myths should be members of the target culture.

It is difficult to say much at this time (and by this author) about the types of myths that would be useful and the forms they should take. It must be emphasized that the design of the myth creation and transmission processes should be done by members of the cultures that will receive the myths. A few comments about the design of myths for the Western, "developed" countries, particularly the U.S., however, are included.

It is this author's belief that the Western, developed countries are among the best initial candidates for the mythmaking project. The audience is quite large and relatively easily reached. The countries of this area will be required to make some significant, and sometimes drastic, shifts of perception in order for the "new international order" to be fulfilled. Thus it is very important for these societies to make a change in their value systems. In addition, a shift in values in these societies should have a great impact on the rest of the world. Finally, the common people of these countries can have a much larger influence on their governments than the majority of the peoples in the rest of the world. The Western countries, therefore, appear to be very good candidates for the reception of myths about a global society. (This part of the world has to some extent already been exposed to "world society" myths and utopias. Nevertheless, it is believed that myths pertaining to the goals presented in the Goals report could have a significant effect on the attitudes of the people in these countries.)

It must be admitted that the above argument is by a Westerner who found it very difficult to know how myths could best be transmitted in societies very different from her own. Consulting with members of the major cultures of the world is thus an extremely important first step in the project.

The mythmaking project in the U.S. could employ a science fiction writer such as Ursula LeGuin, a popular essayist such as A. Toffler, and/or a television/film writer or producer. Use of a popularly based medium could be very successful in terms of the number of persons reached and the impact that would be made on individuals.

Myths have been used as "guiding images" throughout mankind's existence. "Guiding images" in fully embodied form are now needed to spur the world to the formation of a new order that will meet all of humanity's basic needs and encourage the development of mankind's less material desires. I believe that a project, sponsored by the Club of Rome, to create and disseminate myths embodying the goals presented in the Club's two most recent reports will be beneficial to the movement toward a new global order.

VALUE ORIENTATION IN SOCIAL ANALYSIS

Larry McCord

The values people hold must be a fundamental part of any analysis of society. This paper challenges the Club of Rome to mobilize resources and direct its energies toward a new course of action: the explicit identification and measurement of values. To this time, the Club of Rome has offered reports concerning the predicaments facing mankind, but their impacts upon societies have been slight. A concentration on resources has prevented adequate definition and consideration of human needs and desires. But explicit definition of a culture's values is essential in formulating possible solutions for mankind's predicaments. The timing seems to be appropriate for the phasing of explicit value considerations into the calculus of society. The Club of Rome is in a unique position to assemble people and provide direction toward making a breakthrough in the quantification of human values.

The need for such a value measurement is in fact tied to limitations imposed by the ecosystem. The earlier works sponsored by the Club of Rome addressed material and energy limitations (Meadows, et al., 1972; Mesarovic and Pestel, 1974; Tinbergen, 1976). A later dimension includes society's abilities to control and adjust to the increasing complexity imposed by technological growth. If demand for these resources is to continue to increase, society may reach the limits of the ecosystem. Demand for material resources reflects the economic value system. While the elimination of poverty is basic to human survival, many developing nations now view a high material standard of living as a desirable goal; but the realization of this goal will place increasing pressure on the ecosystem limits.

The threatening inbalance between man's economic values and nature's limits can result in three possible outcomes. Either man will find the means to extend the limits of the ecosystem through science and technology (an assumption implicit in the action of most industrialized nations), or man's values will be reorganized to fit the ecosystem limits, or human society will disappear. Human survival and fulfillment have the greatest probability of realization through a consistent definition of human value satisfaction within the constraints of the ecosystem. My purpose here is to suggest one way consistent value definition can be achieved so that the balancing of material needs and humane values will be understood with greater clarity.

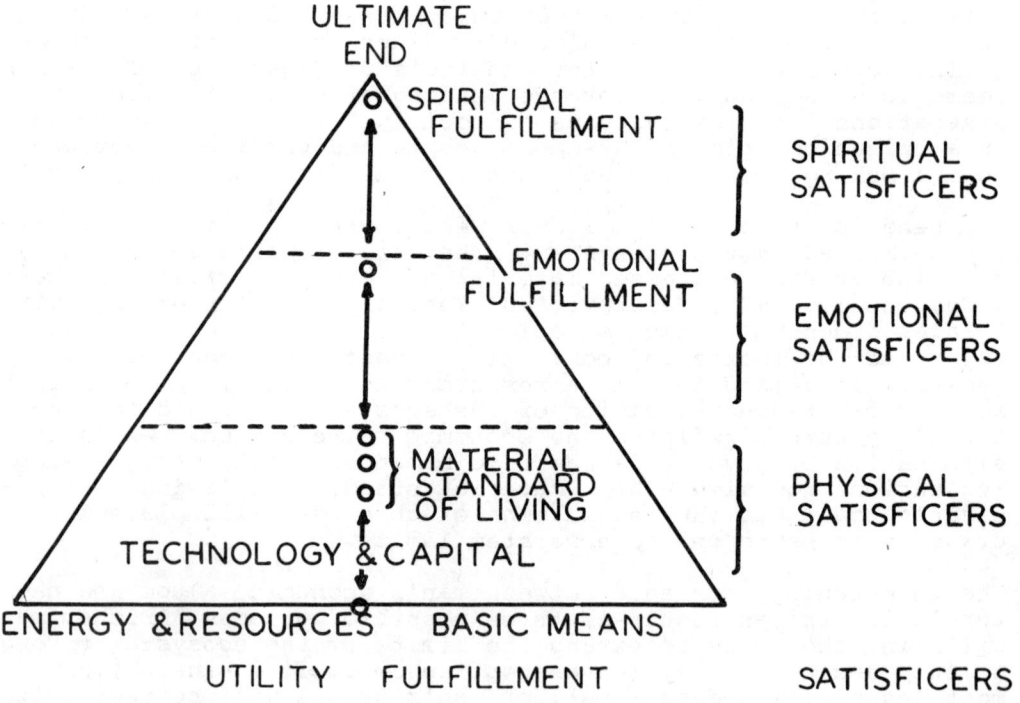

Fig. 2. Framework for utility fulfillment.

Human values throughout this paper are discussed in terms of utility fulfillment; the capacity to satisfy the needs and wants of humanity. Human needs and wants are not fulfilled exclusively by the material goods consumed. Much more basic to society and the individual are those values included in the hierarchy suggested by Abraham Maslow (1970). Five basic needs were identified, progressing from physiological needs at the lowest level through safety, belongingness and love, esteem, and the need for self actualization at the highest level. Further, Maslow noted that once a lower level need is satisfied, the motivation for the fulfillment of that level of value diminishes and the next higher level need takes its place.

A distinction between higher and lower levels of values is also made by Gunnar Myrdal (1969). Economic, social and sexual desires are lower level values which predominate in daily life. Higher level values consist of humane desires, such as happiness, contentment, freedom, curiosity and hope. People tend to conceal and suppress these higher level values in day-to-day life, with the results that the lower values become established as dominant goals in our social analysis.

Conceptualizing utility requires distinguishing satisfaction of values from the values themselves. The term satisficer is chosen to describe the counterpart of value fulfillment. Herbert A. Simon developed the concept of satisficing economic behavior as an alternative to maximizing behavior (1959). Satisficing implies fulfillment at a certain level rather than maximizing all possible returns. An example of this would be a private firm establishing a profit level which will satisfice return on investment rather than the maximization of profit.

A conceptual framework of utility fulfillment is developed (Fig. 2) which proceeds from the basic means to the ultimate end. It is not necessary for a complete fulfillment of a particular level of values before seeking higher level fulfillment. As a result, for a particular society or sub-group, some combination of physical and emotional satisficers will be active simultaneously, as will combinations of emotional and spiritual satisficers.

The basic means of culture are energy and resources available to sustain life in the ecosystem. Applying technology and capital to the basic means will produce levels of material standards of living. These levels will vary from society to society and will depend upon the level of material fulfillment required by the physical and psychological characteristics of that society. Physical satisficers are primarily members of the economic value system.

The higher levels of values, addressing other human desires, require the use of emotional and spiritual satisficers. Emotional and spiritual fulfillments are the levels attained after achieving basic human needs. On an individual basis these could be of a relatively long duration, such as happiness and love found with one's spouse, or they can be of an almost instantaneous nature, such as a sudden flash of enlightenment or awareness as achieved through meditation.

When considering only a material definition of utility, the satisfaction received has relevance only over the time period of the material reward's usefulness. As the physical object deteriorates or becomes obsolete, continued utility can be received only by its replacement. A time period of usefulness is not considered when utility is defined in terms of emotional and spiritual fulfillment. Higher level satisficers, not possessing a physical time span, do not require replacement for continued value fulfillment.

In value-oriented social analysis, the values become the starting point. We can hypothesize that values determine the goals of society, which in turn establish the behavior of the society. An important feedback loop exists between behaviors and values which allows for the updating and modification of values resulting from changes in behavior.

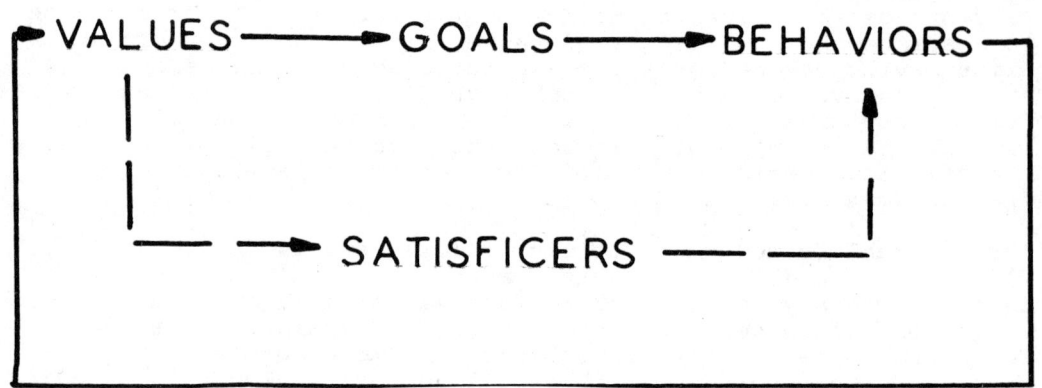

Fig. 3. Behavior to values feedback loop.

It can be thought of as an interactive process composed of costs and rewards. The reward component is the process by which values are fulfilled. The cost component is analogous to the process of expending resources in the achievement of value fulfillment. Satisficers can then be analyzed using the framework of social cost-benefit analysis.

Social cost-benefit analysis is a methodology developed by economists as a decision criterion to evaluate projects. As such, it struggles to internalize relevant indirect costs and unintended rewards attributed to undertaking a project. These indirect effects will tend to be higher level satisficers. Physical satisficers lend themselves quite readily to economic measures and as such will be included as direct costs yielding benefits by the nature of their contribution to the economic value system.

The difficulty arises in the attempt to assign a solely monetary cost and benefit to satisficers on the emotional or spiritual levels. For example, the increased employment of women in the labor market has resulted in an improvement in the conditions of women's rights in society. A measurement of this benefit solely in monetary terms is inadequate and misleading. It assigns a lower level value indicator to a higher level of utility fulfillment resulting in an inconsistency in the analysis. Further, the extreme difficulty in adequately assessing indirect benefits often leads to discounting their worth.

An analogy can be drawn from cost-benefit analysis which contributes to consistent identification of satisficers to value fulfillment, as diagramed in Figure 4. Given a set of values (V_i), a set of associated satisficers (S_i) can be described. A satisficer can be thought of as analogous to the "cost" of fulfilling the associated value. The curve connecting the individual satisficers is described as the "total cost" or total satisficer curve.

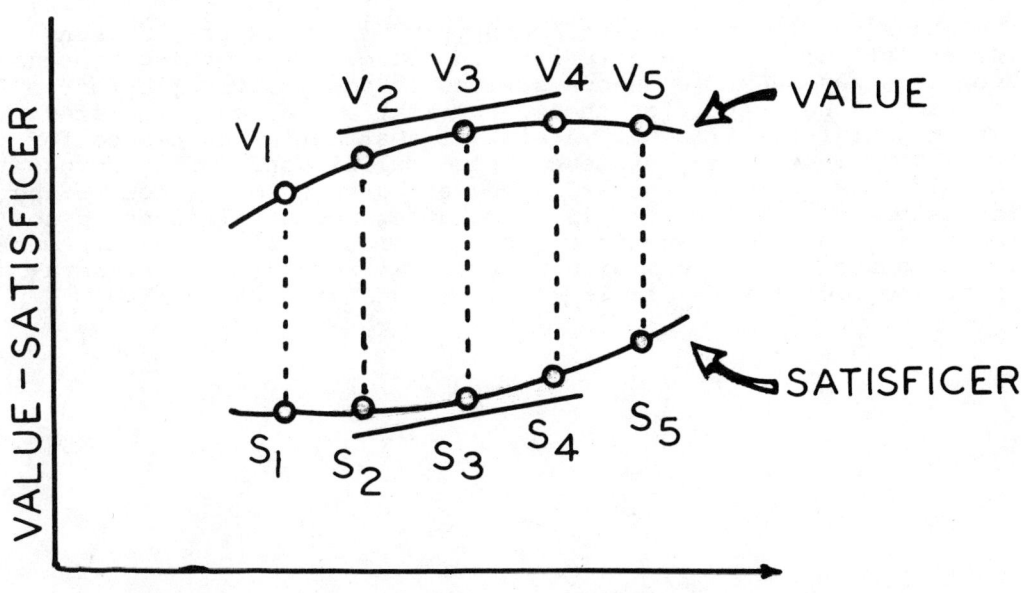

Fig. 4. Values and satisficers.

A similar concept can be applied to the set of distinct value fulfillments. In this case the curve connecting the points is the total value curve and is analogous to the "total benefit" curve.

With each added unit of value fulfillment, the added unit of satisficer is contributing to an increasing total cost which is reflected in a rising total satisficers (total cost) curve. However, if the value is a normal good, the marginal benefit from each added unit of value fulfillment will decrease; i.e., the more you get of a particular item, the less satisfaction you gain from each additional unit of that item. The shape of the total value curve reflects this concept.

In this system the maximum net value fulfillment (value fulfillment less satisficer) will be achieved when the tangent line to the total value curve (for any pair of value-satisficers) is parallel to the tangent line of the total satisficers curve. For any activity to the left of this combination, an improvement can be achieved in net value fulfillment. However, any activity to the right of this combination will result in imposing additional and unwarranted costs upon the ecosystem. A maximum net value fulfillment should be determined for each level of values; e.g., material standard of living, emotional fulfillment and spiritual fulfillment. When this occurs, satisficers contributing to the next higher level of value fulfillment would then be employed until this level's maximum net value fulfillment is achieved.

The major hurdle to be overcome in value analysis is the means for analytically including values in our decision making processes. Economics has made tremendous strides in the construction of an abstract value system for the measurement of values associated with material fulfillment. A similar abstraction is needed for the measurement of higher level value fulfillment. The approach to value considerations briefly suggested here points toward the inclusion of humane values in calculating man's relationship to the ecosystem. Such explicit consideration of humane values must be recognized as systems significant. Without value considerations, no social analysis is likely to bear future meaning.

TOWARD A GLOBAL SPIRIT

Selected Ideas Relative to the Continued Efforts of
the Club of Rome

Daniel Schwartz

> If we could fully realize for only a single moment just
> how lucky we are to be here, we would not stop weeping
> for the rest of our lives.
>
> Hindu maxim

Whither the Club of Rome? At least in part, the aim of the next project should be to stimulate an inquiry into the meaning and purpose of human existence.

Some of contemporary man's attitudes and wants must now change. The wealthy must assist the poor; developing nations must become self-reliant; people's life styles must come into alignment with mutually beneficial global goals. Every effort should be made to close the existing "goals gap," and all nations should strive to transform the "world solidarity revolution" from a utopian ideal into a concrete reality. This much has been explained by <u>RIO</u> (Tinbergen, 1976) and <u>Goals for Mankind</u>.

But in order for these changes to take place, not only leaders of states, but all people -- the grass roots of society -- must awaken to a new realization of their participation in a world community. Each man, woman, and child must acquire a new understanding of his universal brotherhood and sisterhood. Each individual must become aware of his interconnectedness with all other inhabitants of the planet, and he must become motivated to reach out of himself to take a concerned and active interest in global affairs.

Necessarily, therefore, a global understanding must be generated that goes beyond the meager level of emotionalism or polite sentimentality. Everyone must fully realize that he shares in the responsibility of establishing and maintaining the well-being of all, not only for the sake of others, but also for his own sake. Hence, the idea of a world community must become comprehensible to each world citizen as an idea that encompasses immediate practical benefits. That is to say, this new understanding must be personally relevant and realis<u>ti</u>cally achievable.

Furthermore, it must spurn cynicism and decry pessimism. With there now being only 150 nation states accounting for over four billion world inhabitants, the final push toward global unity is evidently near. Concerned references to a nihilist "realism," allusions to man's ineptness and his past failings, cannot bear fruit. The achievement of world solidarity will not come about through intimidation or counter-persuasion.

Mankind's potential to achieve ever higher perspectives and to cooperate on a grander scale is inborn, and his actualization of that potential is an ongoing process. The task is to promote this process; and, for this, what mankind needs is inspiration.

Man needs to discover the advantages that are implicit in higher levels of cooperative action. He needs to be shown how, through striving consciously for global harmony, each individual can gain a fuller experience of life. The task is therefore to shift humanity's sights onto a higher plane. In a few words, it is to inspire among mankind a conscious global spirit.

<u>Limits to Growth</u> (Meadows, et al., 1972) and <u>Mankind at the Turning Point</u> (Mesarovic and Pestel, 1974) provided arguments in favor of world solidarity from the standpoint of material limits and impending crises. <u>RIO</u> (Tinbergen, 1976), explored the possibility of international controls, and, in that context, it defined the "new order" as being equivalent to a "global awareness." The latest report, <u>Goals for Mankind</u>, has taken the discussion of the "problematique humaine" out of the language of material and organizational constraints, and has restated it in a language of goals, aspirations, and values. The thesis of this essay is that the most natural follow-on to the goals study would be a project that explores mankind's psychic dimensions.

In order that man achieve a true global spirit, he must first of all achieve a more enlightened self-image. And, in order to achieve a new self-image, he must reflect upon his own nature and his existential needs, his truer inner wants. Such perennial values as happiness, freedom, justice, love, and truth should be allowed to assume a fresh significance, and the ways in which man strives to realize those values in his own life should be critically examined. Man should take new cognizance of his existence, and he should become more fully aware of his motivations.

This means that man must be inspired to a higher level of self-apprehension. He should be awakened to his intrinsic beauty. He should learn how Reason fools Intuition. Man should become aware of his tendency to always look outward in an effort to fill himself with something that is within. He should understand his suffering, and how he projects that suffereing onto others. To alleviate suffering, he should learn to realize his birthright to a lifetime of happiness and joy. It is therefore time to evaluate mankind's position in light of its inner dimension. It is time for mankind to take new stock of its heart's true desires.

"The Great Religious and World Solidarity," a chapter in <u>Goals for Mankind</u>, asserts the relevance of mankind's spiritual heritage to the existing world dilemmas. In principle, it asserts the need for a rejuvenation of the ancient lessons in humane understanding. The wisdom expressed by humanity's philosophers and spiritual teachers can be shown to provide insight into all of contemporary man's problems, and a new concept of universal brotherhood can be propagated through appeal to mankind's finer, spiritual aspirations.

The following sections expand a few selected ideas related to this theme. First, we draw on psychology by encapsulating two perspectives on human nature, one from classical psychoanalysis, and one which incorporates some ideas from eastern philosophy. Second, we consider human nature from the unique perspective of various scriptures and spiritual teachers. Third, we discuss the implications of these views on the topic of service to one's fellow man. A fourth section relates the idea of service to the idea of self-reliance. The final section is a summary.

Ego, Self and Self-concept -- Two Psychological Perspectives

The psychoanalytic approach has provided the backbone of western psychology for several decades, and its survival as a theory of personality among a scientific populace is an indication of the clarity with which it describes the human condition. In recent years, however, this approach has exhibited deficiencies. It has been found to explain how human suffering occurs, without providing a good methodology for remedy. The success of psychoanalysis can be attributed, rather, to the ability of practicing psychiatrists to go beyond this particular theory in the clinic.

Many approaches toward an expanded theory of personality have therefore been advanced. Two noteworthy ones are Gestalt Psychology, which is now fairly well-known, and Transpersonal Psychology, a more recent development. These contemporary innovations have displayed a more positive approach to the problem of human suffering and, together with psychoanalysis, can lend insight into how a more enlightened self-image might be inspired globally. This section attempts to explain this by an encapsulation of some of the basic ideas.

The psychoanalytic perspective on human natures comes out of the writings of Sigmund Freud. Freud believed that all psychic activity is empowered by a subliminal force, "libido," which simultaneously provides the motivation to love, and is the life force. The role of libido in the emergence of "ego" was depicted as follows.

Before a person is born, libido expresses itself freely through the "id," where the id is a kind of undifferentiated, unaware consciousness. Immediately after birth, however, the child comes into contact with the external world; it sees lights, hears sounds, feels the air coming into its lungs, and, as a result of these experiences, it makes a distinction between itself and its surroundings. It then forms a concept of this distinction and, in so doing, the distinction becomes internalized.

Ego is then this internalized distinction. It is visualized as forming a covering over the id, so as to bring libido under conscious control; and it is taken as the primary determiner of the individual's personality. Ego is that by which a person demarcates a conceptual boundary for his system of self-concepts and, as the person matures, this boundary and system go through stages of transformation.

The idea of ego has provided the foundations for Erickson's discussion of the "identity crisis." It sometimes happens that a person's "ego-identity" becomes no longer operable. A contradiction arises which causes the ego-identity to collapse; this collapse is followed by a process of reconstruction; out of this process a new ego-identity will emerge. Depending on the severity of the collapse, undergoing the process of reconstruction is more or less difficult. In extremely severe cases, the person never recovers. In less severe cases, reconstruction might result in changing careers, adopting a new life style, or moving to a new community. Overall, it is usually marked by a change in values and a heightened self-awareness.

From this perspective, we can see that almost any significant change in a person's conscious awareness is mirrored as a change in his system of self-concepts. Personal growth is a process of shedding old self-concepts and adopting new ones. Crises are those phenomena of growth that are most noticeable, those instances of shedding and reconstructing which affect the person most profoundly, those which cause anxiety or other kinds of psychic pain.

However accurate a description of human development this might be, it is not very inspiring. For, the conclusion it leads us to is that, if people are to achieve a new self-image, then they will have to undergo some personal psychological discomfort. This difficulty can be amended by appeal to the more recent movements. Many of these new theories incorporate ideas from the East, and an eastern idea that is particularly relevant here is the idea of "personal freedom through non-attachment." The perspective based on this notion might be delineated as follows.

Instead of focussing on the problem of ego disintegration and reformation, and so on the experiences of anxiety and pain, this view focusses on the fact that throughout this process there is something that remains constant. There is, in addition to ego, an "inner self" which survives ego loss and hence exists independently of all self-concepts. This intransient inner self may be taken as a person's truer identity, and it may be regarded in much the same way as the Freudian notion of libido, i.e., not as a static entity, but as a dynamic force.

Here the psychoanalytic image of ego as something which brings the inner self under its control still applies, but now the negative aspects of this control become emphasized by the idea of non-attachment. Identity crises become instances of the inner self's successfully breaking through one or more of the ego's self-imposed barriers, and the severity of crisis, counted in terms of anxiety or personal suffering, becomes a measure of the attachment that the individual has to those particular self-concepts. When the attachment is strong, the suffering is great; when the attachment is weak, suffering is slight. When there is absolutely no attachment, the ego completely disappears, and the inner self becomes totally free.

That there is an inner self constantly seeking to break free of all egoistic confines is a standard theme from eastern philosophy, and its implications are diverse. It describes the individual as constantly going forward, evolving, on the impetus of a desire to be "reborn" into a freer state of self-realization.

Complete self-realization is complete happiness, and responsibility for getting onto a path of self-realization rests on the individual. It is up to each individual to loosen his hold on self-images that lead his thoughts and actions into pathways that conflict with his desire for freedom. Thus, people need to become more aware of their inner nature and their various forms of attachment. On this note of understanding one's inner self, psychology might or might not become spiritual.

The Spiritual View of Human Nature

Many philosophers and all the great spiritual teachers have spoken to the subject of human nature, and there is suprisingly widespread agreement. Plato, after Socrates, said that we are all "made in the image and likeness" of a divine form. Christ said that "the kingdom of God is within you." The Buddha said that "the greatest of all miracles is that within each living human being, the entire universe resides."

The word "Yahweh," if pronounced by saying "Yah" on an inhalation, and "Weh" on an exhalation, constitutes a double play-on-words which captures an idea identical with the Hindu idea of prāna, or "the breath behind the breath." This, in turn, is equivalent with such concepts as "The Word," "Satnam" (True Name), and "Brahmanam" (Cosmic Vibration), which are all concepts of something that is all-pervading, sublime, and which brings all existence into being.

A specific Christian reference to a "word" appears in the works of John the Apostle: "In the beginning was the word, and the word was with God, and the word was God." The Chinese concept of "Tao" as "the way of the universe" and as the "eternal name" also bears this interpretation. In Islamic tradition, the word is "Allah's Will."

Further references may be found in the teachings of the Sufi poet, Rumi, the words of Kabir, Guru Nanak, Sri Ramakrisna, and countless others. The fundamental import of such teachings is always the same: The true nature of man is the nature of God.

The greatest secret for mankind is the secret of happiness; but it is a secret only to the extent that God is secret, and is hidden within the hearts of every living human being. The teachers themselves demonstrated the meaning of this conclusion by their own joyousness, and by showing how that joyousness could be achieved by others.

This characteristic, the consciousness of joyousness, explains the origin of the scriptures and religious institutions. Disciples who had "been saved," had "found nirvana," had "entered samadhi," had "experienced satori," and so on, took care to record their experiences and the teachings of their masters. The religious institutions preserve these teachings; and in so doing they have naturally become the great servants of humanity that they are. The lessons in charity, the compassion, the understanding of humanity's sufferings and joys, the concern for human dignity, and the desire to serve righteously but not self-righteously, are stabilizers in the process of social evolution. Increased participation by the churches in the promotion of global harmony should therefore be encouraged.

In addition to the established churches, however, there are today many other spiritual groups and teachers. In the West, these number well into the hundreds; in India alone, they number in the thousands. The Transcendental Meditation movement headed by Maharishi Mahesh Yogi, although not exactly a religion, professes a philosophy of inner awareness through practice of a meditative discipline. The B'hai Faith and the Unification Church were mentioned in <u>Goals for Mankind</u>. Other groups worth mentioning are the Campus Crusade for Christ and the Self-realization Fellowship. My own favorite is the Divine Light Mission, currently headed up by Guru Maharaj Ji, which propagates a lifestyle of satsang (discourse), service, and meditation. Members of these and other such groups could also be instrumental in the next Club of Rome project.

<u>The Joy of Service</u>
"Service" means "actions performed in love." Most established religions and many contemporary smaller groups teach the importance of service to one's fellow man. In order to experience the joy of service, it is only necessary to have faith, specifically, to have faith in own's own capacity to experience love.

The psychological and spiritual perspectives can be combined to expand on this idea as follows. Since the most joyous states are those in which the inner self is least inhibited by ego, surrendering ego on behalf of one's fellow man is a means for these attainments. Acknowledging the intrinsic beauty of others inspires us; we extend our trust; the inner self comes forth freely in thoughts, words and actions; and the mind and body come into one's control as instruments for the just performance of egoless activity. In this way, one begins to experience non-attachment, not only from his self-image, but also from the desire for fame and fear of failure. He begins to experience a new freedom, and wants. In order for people to change their wants, they must acquire a new self-image.

The new self-image must be an enlightened self-image. It must encompass the concept of a global community, and show how this concept has practical foundations along humanity's inner dimensions. It must constitute a deeper understanding of mankind's nature and its desires. It must bring the reality of humanity's inner connection up to the level of a conscious identity.

Contemporary psychology, the established religions, and many past and present philosophers and spiritual teachers have insight into the human condition, and the next project could incorporate them, or at least encourage their assistance. With their help, mankind could be brought to reconsider its current answers to its timeless questions: Who are we? What is our origin? What is our destiny? What is the reason for our being here? Are we reaping life's full benefits? Are there better ways to achieve happiness than those we are now pursuing? Why, indeed, do we want the things we want? Where is joy? Where is truth? Where is nobility and strength of character?

By asking such questions, and by promoting a new understanding of service and self-reliance, we could put a new edge on Aurellio Peccei's call for a "quantum leap" in the quality of human beings, and bring forth Ervin Laszlo's idea of a "world solidarity revolution" with new credibility. When people find inner harmony, then global harmony will be achieved.

In conclusion, the possibility of creating a world-wide identity crisis should not be treated with any more disdain than was the possibility of producing a global panic with the publication of Limits to Growth. Whereas the limits alarm perhaps made people fear for their material well-being, an identity crisis could do no worse than create a population of new seekers.

Where the truth hurts, let it hurt. Given that we have the faith to trust our own inner selves to ultimately break through into a superior state of awareness, we can extend that trust to the selves residing in others, and allow new senses of identity to manifest as they will. It is only comforting to know that in times of psychic insecurity it is usually a person's religion that he turns to for support. But even supposing that not everyone has such resources, or is not able to utilize them, it is still possible to take faith. For, as it says in the Baghavad Gita, "When the student is ready, the teacher appears."

Mankind's capacity to right itself, and to learn the lessons it needs, is absolute, and needs only be appealed to. Sincere people will adopt a concern for humanity's future and will become active in the pursuit of world order.

With regard to the time factor, and the sense of urgency projected by those who fear that the world community will not act fast enough to forestall the impending crises, we can take counsel from the Chinese book of Confucian wisdom, the I Ching:

> ...the way to success lies in apprehending and giving actuality to the way of the universe (Tao), which, as a law running through end and beginning, brings about all phenomena in time.
>
> Thus each step attained forthwith becomes a preparation for the next.
>
> Time is no longer a hindrance but the means of making actual what is potential.

Hence we can do no better than to take the next most natural step.

Mankind's capacity to make actual its own potential to achieve the highest states of being still lies dormant, but perhaps in the long term we shall succeed. Perhaps one day we shall truly awaken to our own inner beauty and experience the reality of joy in service to others. Perhaps, amid the hustle and bustle of our mundane day to day existence, we shall each momentarily stop and, indeed, fully realize just how lucky we are, simply to be alive.

"WHITHER THE CLUB OF ROME" or THE READINESS IS ALL

Judah Bierman

I do not wish to seem overdramatic but I can only conclude from the information that is available to me as Secretary-General, that the Members of the United Nations have perhaps ten years left in which to subordinate their ancient quarrels and launch a global partnership to curb the arms race, to improve the human environment, to defuse the population explosion, and to supply the required momentum to development efforts. If such a global partnership is not forged within the next decade, then I very much fear that the problems I have mentioned will have reached such staggering proportions that they will be beyond our capacity to control.

U Thant (1969)

...for nothing destroys description so much as words, and yet there is nothing more necessary than to place before the eyes of men certain things the existence of which is neither provable nor probable, but which, for this very reason, pious and scholarly men treat to a certain extent as existent in order that they may be led a step further towards their being and their becoming.

Albertus Secundus: tract. de cristall. spirit. ed. Clangor et Collof. lib. 1, cap. 28.

"Whither the Club of Rome?" contains, in the very best sense of the term, a utopian proposal. It suggests a critical analysis of the failure of present endeavor to meet societal needs. It strikes powerfully at a dominating ideology that threatens to still the birth of a new order. It suggests a radically different topos, an image of possibility based on an alternative historical hypothesis. All that is needed to make it a utopian fiction is a story that would capture the people's imagination by showing a "cooperative and collectively self-reliant world of harmonized goals and objectives" in successful action. The plot of that fiction would organize human and social actions to exhibit energy release and problem solutions beyond our present beliefs. The theme would be a society in which humanity finally came to its maturity as a symbolizing animal. But this is not the place for the scenario. Perhaps, however, a brief note on the activities of the Club of Rome as a utopian venture might be helpful.

Let me begin by emphasizing again that I regard utopian fictions, utopian questions, utopian ventures not as foolish if harmless, and not simply as positive and desirable human actions but as absolutely necessary to the survival of the future. Utopias are best understood as ways of relating knowledge to power, ways of proclaiming that with this new knowledge we now know how to meliorate the human condition, if only we could persuade ourselves to try, and those who run things to let us. The knowledge spoken of here emerges in utopia as a new science or technology, like Plato's educational system or our own behavioral engineering, or the various systems in ecologically-organized small societies that manage both trees and men. And the power referred to is not simply the good or bad guy tyrant, capitalist or communist, but also human weakness, pride, and for us the baffling complexity of things. It is in this extended sense of utopian I would consider the Club of Rome and the question of whither.

Professor Laszlo's recommendations for whither describe the program of the Club of Rome first in a medical analogy -- from diagnosis through prescription to therapy. That is the first of three basic images: the medical analogy is followed by the cart and horse figure and then by the terminal image of the Club as information catalyst, the role that would enable the words as acts: "challenging the beliefs, ethics and imaginations of the masses [in images that may] call forth vast new movements [leading to] social transformation." The medical analogy grows out of a description of the Club of Rome as a non-organization with a self-destruct mandate -- like medical researchers who work themselves out of their task by finding a cure. But, of course, though medical research can find cures, it can never obliterate human disease.

The image serves, however, to get us through doom and gloom to the proverb-based cart and horse -- the realization that the most shining truth may not of itself command assent, or if it does, such assent may not be followed by suitable action. It is the recognition that the Club may have put the cart carrying the solutions before the horse, human and social motive power. But consider the relationship implied. Knowledge is conceived as expertise about the structure of the environment -- resources and institutions -- and power as the commitment of decision makers, the new title for kings. Thomas More made clear why such an advice relationship would not work. Fortunately, the new knowledge role goes beyond advice and philosopher kings. Information itself carries with it or itself generates power to act. But how?

At this point, the Club of Rome becomes a utopian venture, for it begins to define the knowledge that power must have to solve the problem of survival in new terms: values, goals, objectives. What is needed is a goal great enough for men and governments to live for, an image of a valued future, collectively reached, cooperatively designed and realized -- shared global community. And so we move from the cart and horse toward the third image through a statement of mixed hope and despair: better that all the Club of Rome reports should be rejected than ignored, so long as they are lost as smoke in the fire of constructive controversy whose flames will yield guiding light. Thus prepared, we come to the Club's new image, what is in fact the emerging form of the dominant utopian image of our time.

The Club of Rome represents new utopists everywhere, a-political, non-partisan intellectuals united by their deep concern for humanity's future. They share also a proper fear of the destructive power of political idealism, especially in the shadow of the mushroom cloud. They have no mandate and so no power, but their self-image rejects the label of technicians for hire. They are intellectuals who will make a contribution to the future of mankind. And so they have come to what is perhaps the ultimate form of the belief that knowledge is power, to be not simply an advisor to the king but to be an active information catalyst for the peoples of a global community.

Information flow and the informing of peoples seems to be the key to its new philosophy. But in the limited framework of these notes, the catalyst role seems more important. The Club is seen as a substance, or a force, whose presence initiates or makes possible reactions between other substances -- new relationships. But it will remain unchanged. Moreover, this role is not seen as a permanent activity. Once bi-directional and bi-dimensional information flows are started and established, the peoples of the world will not need a knowledge master to guide them, even as catalyst. They will have learned to speak to each other. It is the ultimate sufficient condition for building the tower on the plains.

This quite proper reading of mankind's moment is exciting. It speaks to the needs and hungers of peoples and offers a new way of hope without discarding the real achievements of the Club and all concerned intellectuals. Goals, values, objectives will of necessity now be formulated to some degree in light of the knowledge of possibilities and constraints already described. Most important of all, and perhaps not fully recognized, this whither can release new energy from the ever renewable human source. It is man's fate to hope. This whither can give voice to hopes that otherwise would remain mute, and so impotent. It offers not another static image but a process for image making and thus future making, the essence of utopian thinking.

The greatest social speculation and the most significant social actions are utopian in the sense I call this proposed venture utopian. It seeks ways to make the best that is known available to those who must act and to make those who must act open to those who know. Implicit in it is the recognition that all people have dreams and all humans are symbolizing animals who can create an image and call it a goal. It recognizes futurity not simply as an existential condition of symbolizing mankind but as the hard fact at the very center of the world's power negotiations.

It asserts that the new necessary politics begins where all utopian thinking begins, beyond the zero sum game. To that condition the Club can speak and its speech will be its action.

Goal making is a risk taking venture, but the future is always dangerous. It would be reckless only to hesitate. We have lived so long in the shadow of Yeats' question

> And what rough best, its hour came round at last,
> slouches toward Bethlehem to be born?

we have forgotten "the readiness is all."

BIBLIOGRAPHY

Bronowski, J., "New Developments in the Evolution of Complexity: Structural Stability and Unbounded Plans," *Zygon*, 5, 1, March 1970.

Daly, H., et al., *Toward a Steady State Economy*. San Francisco: W. H. Freeman and Co., 1973.

Erickson, G. M., "Maslow's Basic Needs Theory and Decision Theory," *Behavioral Science*, 18, 3, May 1973.

Forrester, J. "Churches at the Transition Between Growth and World Equilibrium," *Toward a Global Equilibrium*, D. Meadows and D. Meadows, (eds), Wright-Allen Press, Cambridge, Mass., 1973.

Galbraith, John Kenneth, "Economics and the Quality of Life," *Science*, 145, 3628, 10 July 1964.

Gardener, M. R. and W. Ross Ashby, "Connectance of Large Dynamic (Cybernetic) Systems: Critical Values for Stability," *Nature*, 228, 1970.

Heilbroner, Robert, *An Inquiry into the Human Prospect*. New York: W. W. Norton, 1974.

Holling, C. S., "Resilience and Stability in Ecosystems," *Evolution and Consciousness*, E. Jantsch and C. Waddington (eds), Reading, Mass.: Addison-Wesley Publishing Co., 1976.

Horn, Joyce, "Anticipatory Democracy and Citizen Involvement," presented at Western Speech Communication Association Convention, San Francisco, November, 1976.

Hughes, B. B., "An Approach to the Simulation of Value-System and Value-Changes," *Multilevel Computer Model of World Development System*, VI, M. Mesarovic and E. Pestel (eds), International Institute for Applied Systems Analysis, Laxenburg, Austria. April-May, 1974.

Jantsch, E., "Evolving Images of Man; Dynamic Guidance for the Mankind Process," *Evolution and Consciousness*, E. Jantsch and C. Waddington (eds), Reading, Mass.: Addison-Wesley Publishing Co., 1976.

Katzman, Natan, "The Impact of Communication Technology--Some theoretical premises and their implications," *Ekistics*, August, 1974.

Kaufman, O., *Teaching the Future: A Guide to Future Oriented Education*, Palm Springs: *ETC*, 1976.

Linstone, H. and Murray Turoff, *The Delphi Method: Techniques and Applications*, Reading, Mass: Addison-Wesley, 1975.

Laszlo, E., *Goals for Mankind*, New York: Dutton, 1977.

Margalef, R., "Diversity and Stability: A Practical Proposal and a Model of Interdependence," *Diversity and Stability in Ecological Systems*, Brookhaven Symposia in Biology, 1969.

Markley, O. W., "Human Consciousness in Transition, *Evolution and Consciousness*, E. Jantsch and C. Waddington (eds), Reading, Mass.: Addison-Wesley Publishing Co., 1976.

Markley, O. W., et al., *Changing Images of Man*. Report CSSP-RR-4, Stanford Research Institute, 1974.

Maslow, Abraham, *Motivation and Personality*, New York: Harper and Row, 1970.

Meadows, D. L., and D. H. Meadows (eds), *Toward Global Equilibrium: Collected Papers*, Cambridge: Wright-Allen Press, 1973.

Meadows et al, *Limits to Growth*, Universe Books for Potomac Association, New York, 1972.

Mesarovic, M. and E. Pestel, *Mankind at the Turning Point*, New York, Signet Edition, 1974.

Michael, Donald, "Planning's Challenge to the Systems Approach," presented at the S & H conference, Portland State University, February, 1975.

Mishan, E. J., *Cost-Benefit Analysis*, (revised edition), New York, Praeger, 1976.

Myrdal, Gunnar, *Objectivity in Social Research*, The 1967 Vimmer Lecture at St. Vincent College, Latrobe, Pennsylvania: New York, Pantheon Books 1969.

Polak, F., *Images of the Future*, San Francisco, Jossey-Bass, 1973.

Prigogine, I., "Order Through Fluctuation: Self-organization and Social Systems." *Evolution and Consciousness*, E. Jantsch and C. Waddington (eds), Reading, Mass., Addison-Wesley Publishing Co., 1976.

Simon, Herbert A., "Theories of Decision Making in Economics and Behavioral Science," *The American Economic Review*, 99, 3, June 1959.

Thom, R., *Structural Stability and Morphogenesis*, Reading, Mass, Benjamin Advanced Book Program, 1975.

Tinbergen, J., coordinator, *Reshaping the International Order (RIO)*, New York, E. P. Dutton and Co., 1976.

Toffler, A., *Future Shock*, New York Random House, 1970.

Umpleby, Stuart, "Citizen Sampling Simulations: A Method for Involving the Public in Social Planning," Policy Sciences, 1, 361-375, 1970.

Vickers, Sir Geoffrey, Letter to the Society for General Systems Research, SGSR Bulletin, Fall, 1976.

Wood, Fred, Monograph No. 20, George Washington Policy Studies, 1974.

INDEX

331

agriculture(al), 3, 67, 77-83, 84, 137
alienation theory, 207-213
ants, 35, 36, 56
appropriate technology, 125
Argentina, 281
attitudes, 207

belief(s), 68, 102, 108, 127, 128-129, 183, 184, 281, 282, 288
bioconversion (biomass), 159, 250-251
biology, 7, 8, 32
biosphere, 102, 111, 123
brain, 2, 191, 192
Brazil, 271
breeder reactors, 164-166
business, 118, 198

Canada, 166
capital, 127, 145, 289
capitalism, 93, 100, 101
change, 4, 5, 87, 94, 97, 110, 181, 194, 196-198, 305
chemistry, 2, 32, 40
China, 120, 202, 282
circular economies, 132, 134, 137-147
civilization, 77-83, 104
closed system, 9, 52
clothing, 136, 137
Club of Rome, 202, 280-328
coal, 102, 103, 118, 119-120, 148-152
collectivity, 71, 106
combustion, 1, 122
commerce, 105
communications, 105, 132, 135, 292
community, 71, 77, 84, 106, 317, 327
complexity, 1, 5, 7, 58, 105, 106, 207, 209, 214, 217, 218
conference, 297-301
conservation, 126, 132, 136, 137, 142, 143
constraints, 67, 109, 117, 127-130, 171, 173, 309
consumption, 118, 119, 126, 138, 171
control(s), 103-104, 109, 111, 129, 131, 146, 318
crystal, 2, 16, 17
cultivation, 73, 74, 77-82

culture(s), 59, 92, 94, 224, 288, 305, 306, 311

Darwinian, 3, 53, 100, 108, 110
decision-making, 77, 109, 213, 215, 283
Denmark, 202
development, 102, 106, 127, 137, 171
disorder, 14, 20, 80
dissipative structures, 2, 19-36, 38, 41
distribution, 118
diversification, 6, 78
dynamics, 1, 6, 7, 18, 19

earth, 9, 67, 79, 107, 109, 110, 121, 138, 252
ecologic(al), 102, 109, 117
ecology, 71
economic(s), 93, 96, 100, 102, 108, 109, 110, 117, 118, 125, 127, 128, 129, 134, 155, 198, 219, 223, 233, 257
economy, 119, 132, 134, 138, 139, 146, 167, 169, 216, 225 (see also linear economy and circular economy)
ecosystem, 3, 46-71, 111, 309
education, 148, 137, 195, 220
electronic(s), 111, 135-136, 148, 172
empire, 83-86, 90, 107
employment, 136, 137
emulsification, 149-152
energy, 1, 2, 8-11, 14, 36, 38, 59, 66, 95, 102, 103, 110, 118-120, 121, 122, 125, 126, 133, 134, 136, 140-147, 147-171, 172, 221-271, 309, 311
alternative sources 152-150
(see also: coal, fossil fuels, geothermal, hydroelectric, natural gas, nuclear, oceans, oil, petroleum, solar, wind)
entropy, 1, 11-18
environment(al), 1, 52, 58, 59, 67, 71, 103, 104, 108, 111, 117, 122-126, 130, 132, 133, 136, 138, 142, 145-147, 181, 208, 211, 212, 215, 217, 218, 223
equilibrium, 2, 7, 17, 20, 32, 36, 38, 99, 107, 282
ethics, 81, 98, 281

Europe, 86-102, 110, 120
evolution, 1-4, 5, 8, 12, 13, 14,
    39, 46-60, 65-70, 72, 75, 70,
    83, 90, 93, 94, 97, 101, 105,
    106, 110, 111, 298
exponential growth, 46, 66
exponential increase, 96

family, 70, 76, 106, 137
feedback, 2, 139, 214, 215, 283,
    286, 292, 312
fertilizers, 104, 249
feudal, 86, 110
fluctuation(s), 2, 3, 4, 7, 21,
    27, 36-46, 53, 56, 118
food(s), 69, 111, 137, 216
food-gathering, 69-73, 74, 76,
    82, 103, 104, 106
food-producing, 69, 73-77, 82,
    105, 107, 172, 187
fossil fuels, 103, 118-120, 122,
    123, 125, 148-152, 170
France, 271
    French Revolution, 101, 282
    Paris, 292
fuel, 117, 126
future, 4, 6, 65, 102, 120, 122,
    133, 141, 144, 169, 194, 217,
    221, 224, 225, 226, 285, 288,
    293, 297, 305, 326, 328

global goal, 117, 129, 132, 317,
global planner, 207-220
global society, 68, 197, 198,
    202, 302
goal(s), 4, 68, 73, 80, 96, 108,
    117, 127, 128-129, 181, 183,
    194, 195, 197, 198, 202, 215,
    216, 286, 288, 298, 300, 303,
    306, 327, 328
government, 84, 96, 107, 172,
    227, 256-261, 265, 270, 283,
    306
Greeks, 84, 85, 88-90
growth, 50-66, 106, 108, 109,
    110, 111, 117-174, 189, 194,
    198 (see also: sustainable
    growth)

health, 96, 137
heating, 103, 154-155
history, 57, 65, 119, 291
Holland, 281
housing, 136, 137
hunters, hunting, 70-73, 76,
    103, 106, 107

hydroelectric, 253

income, 118, 128, 136
India, 166, 199
Industrial Revolution, 87, 102,
    103, 104, 105
inflation, 118, 130
information, 58, 105, 111, 132,
    134, 135-136, 148, 172, 188,
    208, 327
inner dimension, 65, 68, 70, 76,
    78, 79-83, 87-93, 97-101, 106-
    108, 110
innovation, 3, 53, 94, 102
institutions, 127, 172, 173,
    215, 283
invisible hand, 100, 109
irreversible process, 8, 12

Japan, 66, 120, 281

knowledge, 73, 93, 105, 106,
    111, 183, 326

labor, 105, 118, 134, 136, 313
"Lamarckian", 3, 53
land(s), 71, 76-82, 111
laws, 8, 10, 11, 19, 59, 99
limit(s), 47, 58, 66, 109, 111,
    117-130, 140, 211
linear economies, 132, 138

macroscopic, 2, 13, 57
mankind, 65, 66, 73, 95, 96,
    197, 223, 288, 303, 317, 327
matter, 8, 9, 10, 36, 38
media, 132, 135, 202, 283
medieval, 86-87, 91-94, 99, 110
metallic ore(s), 118, 121, 122
metal(s), 103, 117, 118, 119,
    121, 126
microscopic, 2, 13
Middle East, 119
minerals, 103
Model(s), 181, 184, 281, 294
    cognitive, 184, 188-189, 191,
        195, 196
    combined, 190, 194
    homeostatic, 184-185, 191,
        194, 196
    humanistic, 184, 189-190, 191
    incentive, 184, 185-188, 191,
        194, 196
    psychological, 181
motivation, 171-173, 181-202,
    310

motives, 191-192, 196-198, 199
multi-national, 106
mutation, 48-53
myth, 72, 80, 288, 297, 302-307
mythic, 73, 76, 88
mythology, 58

nation(s), 68, 106, 109, 110, 122, 128, 134, 283, 288, 306
nation-state, 68, 93, 94-108
nationalism, 96
natural gas, 102, 103, 148-152
Neolithic, 73-77, 82
Newtonian, 1, 100, 110
nomadic, 70, 76
nonequilibrium, 2, 7, 17, 41, 57, 60
nonlinear, 4, 19-32, 60
nonlinearity, 7, 36
nonrenewable, 111, 117, 118, 128
nuclear energy, 152-171, 236-239, 265
   fission, 159-171
   fusion, 152-154
nuclear weapons, 163, 165-166, 223

objective(s), 99, 117, 132-133, 171, 173, 284, 327
oceans, 111, 122, 159, 248-250
oil, 102, 103, 118, 119, 148-152 (see also: petroleum)
open system(s), 2, 10, 20, 129, 298
order, 17, 18, 21, 36-46, 80, 89, 97, 106
order principle, 17
outer dimension, 65, 68, 69-70, 73-76, 77-79, 83-87, 94-97, 102-106, 110, 111

paleolithic, 70-73, 74, 82
perturbation, 29, 37-46
petroleum, 119, 120, 148-152 (see also: oil)
philosophy, 81
photocell, 240, 259-264
photoelectric conversion, 228, 239-243
physics, 5, 7, 8, 19, 32, 40, 99
planet(s), 67, 104, 111
planning, 210
plastics, 121
plutonium, 124, 163, 164-166
policy(ies), 127, 132, 141, 168, 169, 225, 283, 288

political, 96, 99, 100, 109, 127, 128, 129, 131, 132, 169, 223, 257, 267
pollution, 104, 109, 111, 117, 122-125, 127, 128, 132, 134, 138, 141, 145-147, 172, 223
poverty, 130, 136
power, 73, 80, 96, 99, 100, 108, 326, 327
population, 33, 47-60, 66, 67, 77, 96, 104, 109, 111, 137, 281, 292
predator, 3, 46-52
pre-modern, 69, 83-102
prey, 3, 46-52
price(s), 122, 128, 150, 170
probability, 14-16, 19, 33, 40, 41, 65
problem(s), 117, 121, 129, 167, 209, 210, 281
production, 111, 117, 118, 119, 138, 141
productivity, 118

quality of life, 4, 59, 133
quantum leap, 102, 212, 323
quantum mechanics, 1, 7

R & D, 127, 171, 226 (see also: research, development)
radioactive, 153, 154, 162 (see also: nuclear energy, nuclear weapons)
raw materials, 84, 102, 105, 111 (see also: resources)
reactor, 124, 152-154, 159-171 (see also: nuclear energy)
reality, 72, 80, 110
recycling, 111, 119, 122, 133, 140-147
Renaissance, 87, 92, 97, 107
research, 102, 127, 148, 155, 171
reserves, 2, 119, 121, 122, 172
resources, 84, 96, 97, 109, 118, 119, 121, 122, 128, 132, 133, 136, 140-147, 172, 309
revolution, 76, 101, 282, 323
Romans, 84, 85, 90-91

satisficer, 311-314
school, 82, 91, 134
science, 98-102, 108, 110, 128, 281, 297
self-organization, 2, 36
service, 132-136, 320

slave(s), 82, 90, 105
social insects, 34-36
social sciences, 99, 129
social services, 75
social system, 2, 3, 33
socialist, 101, 219
society(ies), 65, 69-111, 129, 172, 295, 309, 317
sociocultural, 105, 106, 117, 118, 173
sociology, 7
solar energy, 154-157, 221-271
  economics, 233-239
  satellite power systems, 252-253
  solar chemical, 228
  solar electric, 155-157, 228, 233, 239-243, 243-246
  solar farms, 155, 242
  solar food and fiber, 229
  solar heating and cooling, 154-155, 253-256
  solar mechanical, 228
  solar thermal and lighting, 228, 229, 233, 253-256
  solar transition, 221-271
solid waste, 122
Soviet Union, 66
space, 95, 96
spiral, 106, 118, 217
stability, 38, 43-46, 59, 110, 299, 302
standard of living, 118
state, 68, 80, 81, 94-108
structure(s), 3, 14, 19-36, 38, 41, 59, 80, 106, 183, 256
substitution, 111, 143
sun, 76, 97, 138, 245, 252
sustainable growth, 126, 132-140
synthetic, 121, 146, 150
system(s), 1-4, 9, 10, 11, 12, 24-36, 48-60, 70, 78, 99, 100, 105, 109, 111, 118, 134, 137, 138, 167, 169, 200, 207, 211, 214, 216, 222, 225, 282, 289, 298, 320, 326 (see also: socialsystem, sociocultural, economic, nonequilibrium, open, closed)
systematology, 192

tax(es), 128, 133
technology(ies), 3, 67, 71, 75, 84, 85, 96, 97, 108, 110, 111, 117, 118, 121, 122, 127, 128, 132, 133, 135, 136, 142, 146, 148, 169, 172, 225, 227, 293
technology assessment, 129, 134
thermodynamic(s), 1, 7, 8, 10, 11, 19, 59, 229, 298
town(s), 2, 10, 103
transformation, 79, 97, 102, 282, 320, 326
transport, 103, 104
transportation, 126, 148, 242

United Kingdom (England), 164, 254, 281
United States, 119, 124, 160, 164, 199, 225, 236-239, 247, 254-255, 271, 306
uranium, 160-171
USSR, 120, 153 (see also: Soviet Union)
utopia, 306, 325-328

value(s), 68, 73, 99, 100, 101, 102, 108, 127, 128-129, 171, 181, 183, 184, 200, 201, 208, 283, 288, 298-302, 309-314, 320, 327

war, 93, 97, 109, 118, 169, 198, 226
water, 122, 123, 149-152
watershed, 251
Western Civilization, 93
wind, 158-159, 246-248
world, 103, 106, 118, 197, 211, 223, 283, 303, 306
World Bank, 136
world order, 80, 303
world system, 289, 293, 297, 298, 300
world view, 73, 98, 101, 102, 107

CB
430   Goals in a global
G63
v.1

DATE DUE

UPS AUG 29'81			
UPS AUG 21 '87			

COLLINS LIBRARY
UNIVERSITY OF PUGET SOUND
Tacoma, Washington